36th Congress, 2d Session. } HOUSE OF REPRESENTATIVES. { Report No. 78.

ABSTRACTED INDIAN TRUST BONDS.

February 12, 1861.—Laid upon the table, and ordered to be printed.

Mr. Isaac N. Morris, from the select committee, submitted the following

REPORT.

The select committee, to whom was referred the resolution of the House, adopted on the 24th day of December last, directing them to inquire into and report the facts in relation to the fraudulent abstraction of certain bonds, held by the government in trust for the Indian tribes, from the Department of the Interior; and to whom were also referred the communication of Hon. John B. Floyd, late Secretary of War, and the letter of Hon. Robert McClelland, late Secretary of the Interior, beg leave, respectfully, to report:

That, upon the day of their appointment, they repaired to the Interior Department and held an interview with Hon. Jacob Thompson, then Secretary of said department, and expressed to him their desire to enter upon the duty assigned them, at as early a period as would comport with his convenience, and be consistent with the public interest. Three days thereafter, and as soon as they were authorized to employ a stenographer, your committee organized, and have labored to bring their investigation to an early termination, with a diligence that has been quickened by an appreciation of the grave character of the subject committed to them, and of the interest felt by the House and the country in its remarkable details.

It soon became evident that the mere abstraction of certain bonds from the Interior Department—a fact easily ascertained, and, indeed, admitted by the person who took them—was an incident of minor importance in comparison with the transactions preceding and connected with that act, and your committee therefore considered it incumbent upon them to trace as accurately and thoroughly as possible, through the tortuous windings of vast and complicated interests, and extensive, though concealed, ramifications, the motives and purposes and deeds of those who have been the parties to a daring and unprecedented fraud upon one of the departments of the government. In view of the magnitude of the offence and the great loss involved, they have regarded themselves fully justified in pushing the investigation to the furthest limit of the authority vested in them. The want of time, rather than the lack of zeal, has prevented them from obtaining all the information they desired; yet enough has been ascertained to satisfy, in their opinion, the material inquiries with which they were charged by the House, as they think will appear from a succinct account of the evidence that has been adduced before them.

THE INDIAN TRUST BONDS.

By reference to the abstract marked "A," herewith transmitted, it will be seen that the government still holds State bonds and certificates and United States stocks for certain Indian tribes, to the amount of $2,525,241 82. These bonds, as well as the eight hundred and seventy abstracted, and one Indian bond handed to Hon. G. N. Fitch, and not returned by him to the department, for reasons assigned in his correspondence with Godard Bailey, were purchased from time to time by authority of law with the money of the Indians arising from treaty stipulations. Originally, they were in charge of the Indian bureau, while that bureau was connected with the Department of War, and remained in its custody after it became one of the bureaus of the Interior Department in 1849, and from that time up to 1857. In that year the custody of the securities was transferred to the Secretary of the Interior. The government, having the bonds in its possession, was the trustee for the Indians, who were the actual owners of them; and presuming that its agents have exercised ordinary diligence and care as their custodians, the question arises as to the extent of its liability for their loss.

Your committee do not, however, propose to pursue that inquiry, as they cannot doubt that a great and magnanimous government will not permit those who have committed themselves to its protection to be robbed by its officers or employés, without making prompt and ample compensation. Yet the disregard of these fiduciary obligations would seem to aggravate the turpitude of the offender whose felonious hand could rifle so sacred a trust. Such an act furnishes most melancholy evidence of the decay of public virtue, and will remain a blot upon our history, and an indication of our downward career. In this respect it matters but little who was the transgressor. The fact of the commission of the act, at a moment when we thought we had reason to boast of our good faith and integrity, will remain fixed in the public mind, and be remembered as a dark offence when its guilty perpetrators have been long forgotten.

THE MANNER OF KEEPING THE BONDS.

Under previous administrations the bonds were placed in the immediate charge of some clerk, selected for his integrity and capacity, who kept them in a safe in the Indian office. No stamp or other mark of designation was placed upon any of them, with the exception of a small portion, and the only safeguard the government had was the faithfulness and honesty of the person intrusted with their keeping. So careless a mode of transacting the public business and administering a trust so delicate and important astounds us by the magnitude of its folly. Neither the Commissioner of Indian Affairs nor the Secretary of the Interior ever counted the bonds in person, and the only information that either of them could have possessed touching their safety was the payment of the coupons every six months, and such examinations as they occasionally chose to order to be made by others. Fortunately for the government, however, no loss was sustained during previous administrations; nor is there the slightest ground to believe that Hon. Robert McClelland, of Michigan, former Secretary of the Interior, whose supervision of the trust while it remained in the Indian office has been called in question, and whose letter was referred to your committee, acted at any time or in any way unfaithful to it. On the contrary, the evidence of Mr. Henry Beard entirely exonerates him from any blame, further than the expression already made by the committee of their opinion of the mode in which the business was generally managed.

Your committee will not pause to inquire which Secretary exercised the greatest watchfulness and care; for it is not within their province to institute such an investigation. Those desirous of further information upon that point can obtain it from the records of the Interior Department. Still, they deem it but justice to add that they have discovered nothing to involve the late Secretary, Hon. Jacob Thompson, in the slightest degree in the fraud, and nothing to indicate that he had any complicity in the abstraction, or that he had any knowledge of it until the time of the disclosure by Godard Bailey. Soon after he entered upon the duties of his office, at the commencement of the present administration, he appointed two additional disbursing clerks for his department, one of whom was Mr. Bailey, who was placed in charge of the Indian trust bonds. His letter of appointment, signed by J. Thompson, Secretary, bears date July 1, 1857, and, among other things, says: "Under this appointment I desire particularly that you should take charge of the stocks held in trust by the head of the department for the benefit of the Indians, collect the interest thereon as it may become due, and see that the same is properly paid into the public treasury." A bond was required of him, which he subsequently executed, in the penal sum of $5,000, with Benjamin McCollough, of Texas, and William C. Corrier, of Charleston, South Carolina, as securities. This bond was acknowledged before Moses Kelly, justice of the peace, and its sufficiency certified to by Philip Barton Key, United States district attorney. It was then approved by J. Thompson. Copies of the appointment and bond will be found among the accompanying documents. The evidence shows that Mr. Bailey came to Washington a bankrupt in fortune, and a political adventurer seeking office. He brought with him, however, the highest testimonials of confidence and respect from various distinguished men in Alabama, where he lived, and in South Carolina, where he was born, and had previously resided. Being a man of acknowledged talents, with these evidences of capacity and respectability, we are not surprised that the Secretary of the Interior reposed confidence in him. While he should, perhaps, have exercised a more watchful guardianship over the stocks, and the movements of his subordinate, it cannot be inferred that he was intentionally negligent of his duty. Any other public functionary might have been deceived in the same way.

THE ABSTRACTED BONDS.

All the stocks, including those that were abstracted, were kept in a room in the Interior Department occupied by Mr. Bailey, in a safe, the key of which was in his sole possession. The accompanying extract, marked "B," will show the character and respective amounts of the abstracted bonds, as well as the States by which they were issued, except in this—that the whole amount, as shown by said abstract, is eight hundred and seventy-two, of $1,000 each, when, in fact, Mr. Bailey delivered to Mr. William H. Russell eight hundred and seventy only. One of the other two is accounted for by the correspondence between Mr. Fitch and Mr. Bailey, already referred to. The reason why the remaining one is embraced in the abstract, and was included in the published list, is explained by the evidence of Mr. Henry Beard, the faithful custodian of the bonds under Secretary McClelland.

Mr. Beard says, "in the advertisement, eight hundred and seventy-one bonds were embraced. The Indian bond handed to Mr. Fitch, as stated, was not embraced. It occurred in this way: It needed only one hundred and forty-three Tennessee bonds to complete the eight hundred and seventy missing; but our office book, or list of bonds, as prepared by Bailey, indicated one hundred and forty-four as missing. The Secretary directed us to include all the one hundred and forty-four, as at that time some uncertainty was felt whether there might not be more than eight hundred and seventy missing. The advertisement was prepared in haste, and before the full investigation by Mr. Lammond, Mr. Williamson, and myself was completed."

To avoid the inconvenience of referring to abstract "B," your committee will state that ninety-nine of these bonds were issued by the State of Missouri for the St. Louis and Iron Mountain railroad; ninety by the same State for the Hannibal and St. Joseph road; one hundred and thirty for the North Missouri road; fifty-one for the Missouri Pacific road; seventy-two by the State of North Carolina, dated January, 1856; one hundred and four by the same State, dated July, 1857; one hundred and nineteen by the same State, dated January, 1857; forty-five by the same State, dated October, 1856; two by the same State, dated April, 1857; fifteen by the same State, dated October, 1857; fourteen by the State of Tennessee, dated January, 1852; five by the same State, dated January, 1854; ten by the same State, dated January, 1855; forty by the same State, dated January, 1856; and seventy-five by the same State, dated January, 1857.

Some difficulty occurred in the identification of the North Carolina bonds. Several witnesses stated that they held bonds whose numbers corresponded with those given in a printed list, and as they had been held by themselves, or those from whom they obtained them, long before those in the Interior Department were abstracted, they inferred that the list was incorrect. The solution of the difficulty or misunderstanding may be found in this: the State of North Carolina issued

bonds to aid in various enterprises, and these were divided into classes, each class bearing a different date, yet having a precisely similar series of numbers. A party might, therefore, hold a bond whose number corresponded with a number on the printed list, but the bonds would not be identical, because belonging to separate classes, designated by different dates. There seems to have been no cause for similar mistakes in reference to the bonds issued by other States.

NEGOTIATIONS BETWEEN MR. RUSSELL AND MR. BAILEY.

William H. Russell is the head of the house of Russell, Majors & Waddell, a firm widely known as contractors with the War Department for transporting army provisions over the western and southwestern plains. Mr. Russell stated to the committee that he had heard in New York of such a man as Mr. Bailey, although he did not exactly remember his name, who had been in that city to sell Chiriqui securities and Florida bonds, the latter for Mr. Yulee, a senator from that State. When asked from whom he received his information, he gave the answer usually resorted to in such cases, namely: he could not remember. The next heard of Mr. Russell is, that he is on his way from New York to Washington, in company with Luke Lea, esq., a banker in the latter city. Mr. Lea was formerly Commissioner of Indian Affairs, and is a partner of Mr. Russell in the banking business at Leavenworth, Kansas.

In a conversation that ensued between them, Mr. Russell made known to Mr. Lea his embarrassed circumstances, and asked if he (Mr. Lea) did not know of some one that could assist him, (Mr. Russell.) Mr. Lea answered in the negative. He states in his testimony that Mr. Russell suggested that he had heard of a man in Washington, by the name of Bailor or Bartey, who was a relation of Governor Floyd, and an agent for the negotiation or sale of stocks, and asked his friend if he knew him. Mr. Lea was again compelled to give a negative reply, but stated that he knew a man there by the name of Bailey; and Mr. Russell said that he supposed he was the man of whom he was in search.

It is very evident, from Mr. Lea's examination, that he was both an artful and unwilling witness. He had to be pressed with great pertinacity to induce him to disclose what he knew, and even then his answers were so interspersed with irrelevant and equivocal remarks, designed to relieve him from suspicion of complicity, that your committee are compelled reluctantly to notice the absence of the candor and frankness that they might reasonably expect to find in his responses. He was compelled, however, to say that he informed Mr. Russell that Mr. Bailey was in no condition to assist him; that he had no stocks or money, "and was as poor as anybody." Before separating, Mr. Russell, seeming still to believe that aid might be obtained in the quarter indicated, requested Mr. Lea to see Mr. Bailey in regard to the matter. Mr. Lea complied with this request, and stated to Mr. Bailey that Mr. Russell had said, unless assistance was rendered, the acceptances of Governor Floyd would be protested, and he would be compelled to retire from the cabinet. Mr. Lea is, however, careful to state in his evidence that he gave no intimation to Mr. Bailey that he might use the stocks he had in his charge belonging to the Indian trust fund. Mr. C. G. Wagner, who is nearly related to Mr. Bailey, and in whose hands was first placed his confession, states, in his evidence, given, your committee are pleased to say, with full and honorable frankness, that he learned from Mr. Bailey that Mr. Lea *did* mention the stocks in the conversation between them. And, indeed, this would naturally be inferred, from the fact that Mr. Lea was perfectly familiar with the business of the department, and knew that Mr. Bailey had the stocks in charge, and had no large command of private means. Mr. Lea admits that after the delivery of the first instalment of bonds to Mr. Russell, he knew that Mr. Russell and Mr. Bailey were engaged in rifling the Indian trust safe; that they so confessed to him; that he had conversations with them on the subject, and that he endeavored to dissuade them from further commissions of the crime.

He also states that he refrained from informing the Secretary of the Interior of the transactions referred to, and that he exacted the most solemn pledges from his two friends that his name should never be publicly known in connexion with the business. But his precautions have not availed to afford him entire exemption from responsibility in connexion with the transactions your committee have inquired into. Mr. Lea did not introduce Mr. Bailey to Mr. Russell, nor does he state that he appointed for them a place of meeting; yet it happened that these two persons did meet *at the War Department* on the same day that the interview between Mr. Lea and Mr. Bailey occurred. Mr. Russell says this was between the 12th and 15th days of last July. It was probably on the 13th day of that month. The chief clerk of the War Department, Secretary Floyd's most intimate friend, Colonel W. R. Drinkard, was the medium through whom the introduction took place. On that day they had their first interview at the War Department. Colonel Drinkard, as shown by his own evidence, impressed Mr. Bailey with the belief that Mr. Russell was a gentleman of great respectability and pecuniary resources, and that if the acceptances of the Secretary of War were allowed to go to protest, he (the Secretary) would be greatly annoyed and disturbed. Messrs. Russell and Bailey held a private interview in the third story of the department, and within a few hours thereafter Mr. Bailey delivered to Mr. Russell $150,000 of bonds, at the room of the latter person, in Washington city, and on the same evening the recipient returned with them to New York. Mr. Russell states that he left with Mr. Bailey the note of Russell, Majors & Waddell in their stead as security. Ninety of these one hundred and fifty bonds were Missouris, and the rest Tennessees. Mr. Russell does not recollect, at first, whether or not the January coupons were on the bonds, but states that subsequently the most of the bonds were retired by him, in order to obtain those coupons to return to Mr. Bailey, as he (Bailey) was positive in his request to have them returned. These coupons having been taken off, the bonds were afterwards disposed of. The object was, of course, to conceal the fraud; for if the coupons were on hand, it was not probable that the bonds would be demanded or inquired for.

According to the statement of Mr. Russell, there was no further correspondence or communication between Mr. Bailey and himself until the September following. At that time he returned to Washington for the purpose of obtaining others. An interview was held with Mr. Bailey, the result of which was that three hundred and eighty-seven bonds, in addition to those first taken, were transferred to Mr. Russell on the following day. The protection of the honor of Secretary Floyd, the necessity of providing for the other acceptances and the bonds previously delivered, and which were alleged to have been hypothecated, were assigned as the reasons for requiring further assistance. In this, as in the first instance, the paper of Russell, Majors & Waddell was left as security. Mr. Russell states that at this conference Mr. Bailey first informed him that the bonds in his possession belonged to the Indian trust fund. It was the agreement that the bonds first taken should be returned within ninety days, but at the second interview the time was extended to the 4th of March, 1861.

In October Mr. Russell returned South Carolina and Florida bonds, which he had previously received, one hundred and forty or fifty in number, having ascertained that he could not negotiate them, and North Carolina bonds were substituted in their stead. Mr. Russell again appeared in Washington in December following, and on the grounds so successfully relied upon before, namely: the protection of the War Department from disgrace, and the bonds previously taken from sacrifice, he was enabled to obtain from Mr. Bailey three hundred and thirty-three bonds, as an additional advance, making the entire number abstracted eight hundred and seventy. From the bonds obtained on the second and third occasions, already referred to, it is evident the January coupons were cut off, as a precaution against detection. Nine Tennessee coupons, belonging to other bonds than those abstracted, were returned by Mr. Russell, doubtless because the abstracted bonds had passed beyond his reach. The transaction last referred to appears to have closed the business relations of these two persons, so far, at least, as they related to the abstraction of bonds.

MR. BAILEY'S MOTIVES FOR TAKING THE BONDS.

Why Mr. Bailey abstracted the bonds is a question to which your committee can present no satisfactory answer. As he and Mr. Russell were entire strangers previous to their meeting at the War Department, neither the obligations of friendship nor the suggestions of kindly feeling seem to have prompted the act. Mr. Russell insists that no money or other valuable consideration ever passed to Mr. Bailey, or, indeed, was ever mentioned in their interviews. Mr. Bailey confirms this statement in various communications which have reached your committee. It is not ascertained, either, that Mr. Bailey came suddenly into the possession of any large amounts of money. His bank account was kept with Messrs. Riggs & Co., of Washington city, and Mr. Riggs testifies that between July and the 13th of December, his deposits increased largely over former ones; but amounted in the aggregate to not more than five or six thousand dollars. It is true that this sum is a large one, to be in the possession of a person whose salary was but $2,000 per annum, and who was supporting a family; yet it would not, of itself, constitute a ground for grave suspicion, or afford a clue to the discovery of the purposes of the abstractor.

Mr. Bailey, in his conversations with various witnesses, stated that his design was to protect the character of Governor Floyd, and to save him from the dishonor and retirement from the cabinet that would be necessarily incident to the protest and discovery of the acceptances which had been illegally issued to the firm of Russell, Majors & Waddell. Whether this consideration was the sole motive of his conduct, it is left to the House to determine. Your committee are, however, constrained to express the conviction that behind the events that have been made conspicuous, and beneath the exterior of the transactions that have been described, is a purpose which, although successfully hidden, was none the less powerful and efficient, and has given unity and vitality to the schemes now partially exposed.

MR. BAILEY'S CONFESSION.

A part of the evidence adduced is a communication from Mr. Bailey, dated December 1, 1860, and addressed to Hon. Jacob Thompson, Secretary of the Interior, containing a statement that a portion of the bonds constituting the Indian trust fund, amounting to $870,000, were no longer in his possession. This confession was, on the 13th of December, placed in the hands of Mr. Wagner, with the request that it should be delivered to the Secretary of the Interior five days before the expiration of his term of office; or, as Mr. Wagner understood it, five days before the 4th of March. On the 20th of the same month Mr. Bailey addressed a note to Mr. Wagner, requesting that the note previously committed to him (Mr. Wagner) should be given to the Secretary of the Interior immediately upon his return from North Carolina. Mr. Thompson arrived on the afternoon of the 22d of December.

On the evening of that day the acceptances issued by the War Department, and the receipt given for the bonds by Mr. Russell, were handed to Mr. Thompson, at the office of the President, in the Executive mansion, by Hon. H. M. Rice, United States senator from Minnesota. No earlier intimation of the abstraction had reached Mr. Thompson. Your committee not designing to examine Mr. Bailey as a witness, the chairman addressed to Mr. Rice a note, and politely requested his attendance. To this he replied that he would answer any question that might be propounded to him in writing. Seeing that he stood so pertinaciously on his privilege as a senator, it was not thought consistent with the duty of the committee or dignity of the House to press any further inquiries, unless the House shall so order.

Had the original intention of withholding from the Secretary all knowledge of the fraud until within a few days of the 4th of March been carried out, the confusion incident to a change of administrative officers would have prevented prompt investigation, and deprived Mr. Thompson of the means of immediate defence.

Mr. Bailey, in the exercise of forethought prudent to avoid detection, made up his stock account for the current year, showing on its face that all the bonds were safely in his custody, and had caused its presentation to the Second Auditor, Mr. Fuller. That officer refused to approve it for the reason that the coupon account, designed to be a check upon it, did not accompany it. It is, perhaps, to this refusal that may in part be attributed the early disclosure of the fraud.

It will be observed that, while Mr. Bailey's statement is dated December 1, 1860, and embraces the entire number of bonds, and fixes the month of July as the time at which he intrusted them to other parties, the testimony of Mr. Russell shows that they were not all delivered at one time, but that three hundred and thirty-three were transferred to him on the 13th of December—nearly two weeks subsequent to the date of Mr. Bailey's confession. The only satisfactory explanation that can be given of this noticeable discrepancy is the supposition that the statement was actually prepared on the day it was given to Mr. Wagner, and the day the last bonds were delivered to Mr. Russell, and dated wrongfully "December 1," to allay any suspicion that might be excited if it were seen that the date of the abstraction was identical with the date of the last acceptance which was issued by the War Department, for the purpose, as your committee think, of making up a definite amount of securities.

THE DISPOSITION OF THE BONDS.

As soon as the abstraction of the bonds was made known to the Secretary of the Interior, he applied himself diligently to discover with whom they were lodged, that proceedings might be instituted for their recovery. Moses Kelly, esq., his chief clerk, was despatched to New York, and he there caused writs of injunction to be served upon a few parties, in whose possession he had reason to believe some of the bonds to be. But ascertaining this mode of obtaining the desired information to be both slow and unsatisfactory, Mr. Thompson advised that your committee should hold some of its sessions in the city of New York. Being desirous of expediting the investigation, and of avoiding the heavy expense that would be incident to the summoning of a large number of witnesses from that city, your committee concurred in the propriety of this suggestion; and having asked for and obtained leave to sit in such places as they believed the public interest required, proceeded, at considerable inconvenience, to New York.

From the testimony there procured, it was apparent that the bonds had been disposed of by Mr. Russell and his agent, and that Mr. Russell did not have it in his power to restore any of them. A limited number were traced into the possession of certain individuals and corporations, as follows:

Merchants' Benevolent Association, New York city, (witness, Hector Morrison,) Missouris	$1,000
Meigs & Greenleaf, for account of C. W. Purrel & Co., Richmond, Va., (witness, C. A. Meigs,) Missouris	10,000
Mitchell, Schenectady, N. Y., from one to three, State not mentioned, (Meigs witness)	2,000
Sanders, Haydensville, Mass., one to three, State not given, (Meigs witness)	2,000
James G. King & Sons, New York city, (J. G. King witness,) Missouris	10,000
Clark, Dodge & Co., New York city, (witness, L. C. Clark)	2,000
Captain Porter, New York city, (Matthew Morgan witness)	2,000
Jerome Fitzhugh & Co., New York city, purchased with knowledge of their character, (J. H. Garland witness)	10,000
W. T. Coleman & Co., New York city, (Coleman witness)	50,000
George Smith, Chicago, (A. Campbell witness)	21,000
Thomas Swann, Baltimore, (William McKim witness)	10,000
R. D. Gaither, Baltimore, (W. Fisher witness)	3,000
B. Atkinson, Baltimore, (W. Fisher witness)	1,000
Townshend Scott, Baltimore, (W. Fisher witness)	5,000
Lowndes, Thompson & Co., Baltimore, (Martin Lewis witness)	5,000
	134,000

A few other bonds were ascertained to have been purchased by Riggs & Co., bankers of Washington, for other parties, and by other individuals, which are not included in the above statement.

At an early stage of our proceedings, and before the examination of any witnesses, your committee designated two of their number, the chairman and Hon. Mr. Thomas, to consult with Robert Ould, esq., United States district attorney for the District of Columbia, in reference to the abstraction of the bonds, and the legal questions connected therewith. That officer advised that the testimony of both Mr. Bailey and Mr. Russell should be taken.

An important witness, Jerome B. Simpson, who would be found in New York, it was expected, could not be obtained. He had acted in that city as the confidential business agent of Russell, Majors & Waddell, and knew, it was believed, all the details of their business transactions with the government, and of the abstraction of the bonds. The most active and diligent search for him proved unavailing. As none of his acquaintances remember to have seen him since about the day following Mr. Russell's arrest, and as no trace of him has yet been discovered, it is evident that he absconded or concealed himself to avoid the responsibility of his acts, and an appearance before the committee or the courts.

In view of this circumstance, and of the advice given by the district attorney, and under the belief that, unless a full statement could be obtained from some one immediately connected with the transaction, no satisfactory report could be made of "the facts in relation to the said fraud," as was required by the resolution of the House, it was determined to afford Mr. Russell an opportunity of appearing before the committee. Previous to his appearance, it had been decided to leave it optional with himself to answer or not as he might elect. This purpose will plainly appear from the following extract from the record of the proceedings.

"MONDAY, *January* 14, 1861.

"William H. Russell appeared.

"The CHAIRMAN. Mr. Russell, your counsel have doubtless apprised you of your rights. You are under a criminal prosecution, and I deem it my duty to state to you that the committee do not propose to require of you to answer any questions. If you choose voluntarily to do so, you can; but if you do not prefer to do it, as indicated to you, you can withhold your answer.

"Mr. RUSSELL. I am anxious to make a full statement in regard to the bonds. I claim to be an honest man, and would prefer to make out a statement of the whole transaction in writing, and have you spread it at length on your record. I ask that as a favor from the committee. I am under a criminal prosecution, and think it due to me that I should be permitted to make a full statement, although I do not fear the result of the criminal prosecution. If the committee prefers the statement made verbally, I will make it in that way; but I should like to make it in writing."

Mr. Russell was then sworn, but after a few questions had been proposed, he again expressed a desire to submit a written statement, and leave was accordingly granted. On the 18th of January he was again before the committee, and presented a statement (which will be found among the accompanying papers herewith submitted) prepared, as he stated before the committee, by his attorneys, "the night after he asked permission" of the committee.

Various interrogatories were proposed, which were promptly and freely answered. But when asked, "Did you ever, directly or indirectly, give to any person any consideration, or make to any person any present for services rendered to you connected with your business with the War Department?" Mr. Russell declined to respond before consulting with his counsel.

Upon this suggestion the examination was at once suspended.

On the 23d of January he again appeared, and was reminded of what had been said to him on a previous occasion, and more fully admonished that he was not required to answer any questions. He was also advised that his examination would be waived, if he desired it, in whole or in part, and that, if he so elected, his evidence already given would be expunged. The act of Congress, approved January 24, 1857, entitled "An act more effectually to enforce the attendance of witnesses on the summons of either house of Congress, and to compel them to discover testimony," was shown to Mr. Russell; and after reading it, he requested further time to advise with his counsel. Before leaving the committee-room, however, he stated, in reply to a question, that he understood the statute, and that it had been explained to him previously to his appearing before the committee.

On the 25th Mr. Russell presented to the committee a paper, prepared, he states, as an answer to the question that had been previously proposed to him, and requested that it should be placed upon the record. He left it with the committee, and no further questions were proposed. This instrument, though not properly belonging to the record of our proceedings, is transmitted to the House for its inspection as one of the accompanying papers. On examination, it will be found to be not an answer to the question that had been asked as introductory to more important ones, but an elaborate effort made by Mr. Russell, with technical adroitness and legal acumen, to avail himself of the act of Congress before referred to, and to interpose it as a shield between himself and the consequences of his deeds. Nearly all the material statements therein contained are wholly incorrect. It is not true, as he alleges, "that he was not permitted by law to refuse to testify to any fact" within the scope of our inquiries. Neither is it true "that he was required to testify." He testified of his own free will, and was not "compelled," as declared by the title of the act, "to discover testimony," nor was he "required," as expressed in the body of the law, to give his evidence. Your committee, therefore, while they are constrained to consider the course adopted by Mr. Russell as a confession of his moral guilt, do not deem it within their province to anticipate or prejudge a question of law which may arise in legal prosecutions.

THE ACCEPTANCES ISSUED BY THE SECRETARY OF WAR.

When the iniquitous act perpetrated by one of the subordinate officers of the Interior Department in the abstraction of bonds was made known, it was discovered at the same time that acceptances, unauthorized by law, and deceptive and fraudulent in their character, had been issued by the Secretary of War in favor of Messrs. Russell, Majors & Waddell. As a portion of these are inseparably connected with the history of the bond embezzlement, it is proposed first to inquire into the circumstances attending their issue.

It is stated by Mr. Russell that, on the day he made his last application for securities, Mr. Bailey agreed to furnish them on the condition that there should be deposited with him, in their place, the acceptances of Governor Floyd, as Secretary of War. Mr. Russell, it would appear, had then on hand $735,000 of acceptances, $72,000 of which were unconditional, and the balance conditional, and payable out of the earnings of Russell, Majors & Waddell for 1861. [Copies of the acceptances will be found embraced in the testimony of Hon. Jacob Thompson.] The amount of the bonds he received on that and previous occasions was eight hundred and seventy, or $870,000. There was therefore wanting, to make up the requisite sum of securities, $135,000; and we accordingly find that there is an acceptance, bearing date December 13, for that precise amount. When it is remembered that that is the date of the last delivery of bonds, and of the receipt therefor, the inference seems unavoidable that the acceptance was issued to make up an ascertained deficiency, and that it was anticipated that it would go into the possession of Bailey.

There are other facts that should be stated in this connexion. Mr. Russell fixes the probable earnings of his firm, for the year 1861, at from $500,000 to $600,000, while Captain Van Vliet estimated them at $488,000 for 1860; and General Johnson says, in his testimony, that, for the present year, they will be about what they were in 1860, which was $540,000, including a payment made in Washington, by Captain Miller, of a little more than $69,000. The conditional acceptances given to Mr. Bailey amount to $798,000, or $248,000 more than the maximum sum that could have been earned by Messrs. Russell, Majors & Waddell during that year, according to the estimates of the department, based upon the earnings of the previous year. The acceptances for the $798,000 were the only conditional ones issued, and these, together with those for $72,000, issued unconditionally, must be regarded as a loss, as the government will, doubtless, acknowledge the obligation to replace the bonds belonging to the Indian trust fund; and there is little reason to expect that Russell, Majors & Waddell will make a return of what they have received.

If your committee could rest here, and could feel justified in expressing the belief that there are no other outstanding liabilities, and that no further demands would be made upon this or any future Congress, in connexion with these extraordinary proceedings, they would deem this an occasion for congratulation to the House. But, unfortunately, there are transactions of a similar character, but of a still greater magnitude, that claim your attention.

In 1858 the Secretary of War commenced the issue of acceptances, and, at the same time, wrote to various banks and individuals urging their purchase or discount. One of his letters, and one from Colonel Drinkard, chief clerk of the War Department, to James T. Soutter, esq., president of the Bank of the Republic, will be found included in the testimony taken in New York. Copies of various other letters relating to the same subject, obtained from the War Department, accompany this report. Mr. F. P. James, of New York city, testified before the committee that Mr. Soutter, to whom reference has been already made, said to him upon one occasion that he had a draft for $15,000, and with it a letter from the Secretary of War, stating that he had issued, or was about to issue, acceptances in favor of Russell, Majors & Waddell, but that at no time should he issue those acceptances to exceed one-half of the amount which he knew, of his own knowledge, was actually due to the parties for services already performed. Mr. Soutter, on being called on to produce this communication, says that "he had an impression, and he supposed it was derived from a letter of Mr. Floyd, that the War Department issued acceptances to the extent only of one-half of the amount that would become due to Russell, Majors & Waddell on work in process of execution." Although an examination of the letters received by the bank, and his own private letters, failed to bring to light such a communication as he had expected to find, Mr. Soutter does not change his opinion, but concludes that it was derived from the statement of some person whose name he cannot now recall. These letters and representations are important as showing the means adopted by the Secretary of War to get the paper he issued into circulation.

NEARLY $7,000,000 OF ACCEPTANCES ISSUED.

In relation to the acceptances issued unconditionally by the late Secretary of War, your committee deem it their duty to state all the facts they have been able to discover, as fully as possible. They amount, in the aggregate, to the enormous sum of $6,179,395. Add thereto the conditional acceptances which have already been thrown back upon the government through the agency of Mr. Bailey, and the sum total is $6,977,395. This estimate is based upon data furnished by the War Department. It appears therefrom that acceptances to the amount of $840,000 were returned to the department for cancellation. Mr. Russell, however, claims to have returned only $200,000 or $250,000. He further states that the acceptances which he did return were those which had matured in his own pocket, and could not therefore be negotiated. But this assertion is positively contradicted by the indorsements on the returned acceptances, and by the testimony of Mr. Irwin, a clerk in the War Department.

From the careless and irresponsible manner in which business was transacted by Mr. Russell and the late Secretary of War, and from the fact that it was the habit of Governor Floyd to issue acceptances at the department or at his house, or at whatever place he happened to be, it is a matter of great uncertainty whether or not the $840,000 should be deducted from the sum heretofore stated. The probability is, that when the acceptances were returned to Governor Floyd by Mr. Russell, he accepted others at the same time for the same amount, of which there was no registry made. It is deemed safest to proceed, however, upon the supposition that the acceptances made in the place of those returned were registered. Upon this hypothesis, the $840,000 must be deducted from the $6,179,395 of unconditional acceptances made and registered in the War Department. This would leave of them, so far as is shown by the records of that department, $5,339,395 still in circulation; add to this amount the $798,000 of conditional acceptances received by Mr. Bailey in lieu of the bonds, and the aggregate is $6,137,395. Here, then, confining the statement to the records of the War Department, is a deficit of $6,137,395 to fall upon the holders of these acceptances, or to be assumed in some way by the government.

WHAT WAS DONE WITH THE ACCEPTANCES?

The evidence shows that the acceptances have been sold in various parts of the United States, wherever a bank or private individual could be induced to purchase. Inasmuch, however, as the amount of those that have been traced directly into the hands of present holders constitute but a small fraction of the sum still unaccounted for, and as owners are daily filing additional claims at the War Department, it is deemed unnecessary to give a detailed statement of the discovered acceptances, or to make other mention of them than to refer to the papers relating thereto presented by the War Department, and to the general evidence.

It is proper, however, to remark in this connexion, that while your committee do not deem it necessary to give said details, the data in the War Department fix the *minimum* amount of outstanding acceptances known to that department at $1,445,000.

FURTHER LIGHT ON GOVERNOR FLOYD'S PROCEEDINGS.

Mr. Richard B. Irwin, the faithful and intelligent clerk to whom reference has been made elsewhere in this report, says, in his evidence: "There may, of course, be other outstanding acceptances, of the whereabouts of which the department has no knowledge." There will also be found embraced in his evidence, given upon being recalled before the committee on the 6th instant, a letter addressed by R. A. Barnes, esq., president of the Bank of the State of Missouri, under date of January 24, 1861, to Hon. Joseph Holt, Secretary of War, which is of interest, and will throw light upon the conduct of Governor Floyd's proceedings and assurances in regard to the acceptances. Mr. Irwin still further testified to the receipt of other letters by the War Department since the papers furnished to the committee by that department were transmitted, of a character similar to Mr. Barnes's. This branch of the inquiry is evidently prolific, and could be pursued to a great length if necessity required or time would permit.

MR. RUSSELL'S ESTIMATE.

To avoid all appearance of unfairness, your committee consider it proper to give Mr. Russell's estimate of the amount of acceptances issued and taken up, as set forth in the following extract from his testimony:

Question. State as nearly as you can, of your own knowledge and recollection, the amount of acceptances of Governor Floyd shown by that (his) account to you.

Answer. I have got but an idea about it. It was very large. I cannot tell how large. I believe it exceeds $3,000,000.

Question. Does it not exceed $4,000,000?

Answer. I do not recollect.

Question. Does it not exceed $5,000,000?

Answer. I judge not; it is all impression on my part.

Question. Can you state that you have not received his acceptances to an amount exceeding $6,000,000?

Answer. I do not think I have.

Question. How much less than $6,000,000 can you say was the amount?

Answer. I will not fix the amount. I know it was very large. I know it was millions.

Question. Will you fix any amount short of $6,000,000 which you can say covers it?

Answer. I do not think it exceeds $4,000,000.

Question. Can you state to the committee within a half million dollars the amount of the acceptances of Governor Floyd which you have paid?

Answer. No, sir, I cannot. We have certainly paid upwards of $3,000,000, and probably $3,500,000, and cancelled them or retired them.

Question. Does $3,500,000 cover the amount?

Answer. I cannot say positively.

Question. Can you name a sum which you can be positive does cover the amount?

Answer. I am sure we have paid $2,000,000.

Question. Are you sure you have paid and cancelled $3,000,000?

Answer. Well, I am pretty confident in my mind that we have.

Question. Can you state any amount larger than that which you are confident in your own mind was paid and cancelled?

Answer. No, sir.

Question. Did you not pay and cancel Governor Floyd's acceptances to an amount larger, at the outside, than $3,500,000?

Answer. I think $3,500,000 will cover the sum. I am very confident in my own mind that it will.

Mr. Russell then stated that, besides the acceptances he has used and those still remaining in his possession, (the latter somewhat less than $200,000 in amount,) Governor Floyd gave him others, which he returned unused to the War Department. If credence should be given to these explanations, the amount of acceptances still outstanding is very large. But Mr. Russell's statements are so rambling, vague, and unsatisfactory, and he shows such utter ignorance of the details of his business, and such incapacity, or unwillingness, to make an exhibit of his affairs, that your committee have considered it much safer to base their conclusions upon the records furnished by the War Department. These records are of a character too peculiar to be passed without comment.

PECULIAR RECORDS IN THE WAR DEPARTMENT.

By reference to the testimony of Mr. Irwin, clerk in the War Department, it will be seen that he kept a registry of the acceptances on loose pieces of paper only, as they were reported to him from time to time, and no other was made. He states, too, that there was no registration of the $798,000 of conditional acceptances which fell into Mr. Bailey's hands; and that immediately after the discovery of the abstraction of the bonds, Governor Floyd went to his office and directed him (Mr. Irwin) to enter an order of cancellation of those acceptances, which he did upon a slip of paper, as he had entered the dates and amounts of others that had been issued. The acceptances being in the hands of Hon. Jacob Thompson, having been placed there by Mr. Bailey in lieu of the abstracted bonds, an order of cancellation at such a time was simply an order against the government. Had the acceptances been held by other parties, the order would have been equally futile; for, if legally issued, it could not invalidate them.

PAYMENTS TO RUSSELL, MAJORS & WADDELL.

It also appears from the records of the War Department that while these acceptances were being issued to the amount of millions of dollars, Russell, Majors & Waddell were regularly receiving their pay for the services performed under their contract, in money, from the government. The aggregate amount of the payments made to them, in cash, during the years 1858, 1859, and 1860, is $4,842,964 41, and a large portion of this sum was paid by the proper officer at Leavenworth City, Kansas. Governor Floyd admitted in his evidence that every acceptance which he made "ran against unearned money," and was designed to give them (the contractors) "the credit of their contract." Yet there has not been discovered the slightest indication that he made any inquiry about the payments, or concerned himself to see that they were, when made, applied to the acceptances.

By reference to the testimony of General Johnston, of the army, and of Hon. Mr. Atkinson, the Third Auditor of the Treasury, and to a detailed statement of the payments presented to the committee the amounts of the earnings and payments, will more fully appear. It would, perhaps, be sufficient to say, upon this point, that Mr. Russell acknowledges that there is now but a small sum due his firm for current earnings. But it was considered desirable to remove all uncertainty from this question, and to ascertain positively whether Russell, Majors & Waddell had ever presented any claim to the War Department for extra services, and whether any claim for such services had ever been paid by that department, and correspondence was accordingly had with the present Secretary of War, Hon. Joseph Holt, who referred the letter of the committee to General J. E. Johnston, quartermaster general, and Colonel J. P. Taylor, acting commissary general of subsistence.

It will be seen from their replies that no such claim has ever been made or allowed. General Johnston, however, states that there is an account amounting to $27,390 49 still suspended, which the late Secretary of War directed to be reduced by a "disallowance" of $9,125 62. He also states the sum due them on the 4th of January last, upon current earnings, to be $27,750 49, from which must be deducted $15,000 for a duplicate payment. This amount was ascertained by telegraphing to Leavenworth, (at which place the accounts of Russell, Majors & Waddell are kept,) and, although it may not include other earnings in New Mexico, it cannot be largely increased. The facts, therefore, are, that Russell, Majors & Waddell not only absorbed all the sums earned by them under their contracts, and sold all the bonds they received from Mr. Bailey, but also raised very large sums of money upon the acceptances issued by the Secretary of War.

COMMENTS ON GOVERNOR FLOYD'S LETTER.

The information thus plainly presented seems to demand that some mention should be made of the communication of the late Secretary of War, Hon. John B. Floyd, addressed to the House, and by the House referred to your committee. In his letter occurs this passage: "Within the four years since I have presided over this department, not a dollar, I believe, has been lost to the government by embezzlement or theft, and within that time $60,000,000 have been disbursed. No system of administration, no line of policy, I think, could reach better results. No system of accountability could be more perfect." If by the best "results" are understood to be the depletion of the public treasury and the debasement of public virtue, the approval of the vicious and the reprobation of the good; if by "the most perfect system of accountability" is meant a method of transacting business that promises rewards to negligence, and affords the most valuable facilities and incentives to fraud, then, indeed, may the late Secretary have reason to speak with confident self-praises of his "system of administration" and "line of policy."

Whether or not his assertion that there has been no "embezzlement" or "theft" in his department is true will soon be decided in the courts. The recklessness of his official conduct, his inattention, and the ignorance of the details of his affairs, have been already shown, and will stand out in still greater distinctness on examination of the contradictions and obscurities of his testimony. Your committe will, therefore, leave judgment to be pronounced by the House, and by the country; but will present, as a valuable aid in coming to a correct conclusion, a brief abstract of the testimony of Hon. J. P. Benjamin, United States senator from Louisiana.

IMPORTANT TESTIMONY OF SENATOR BENJAMIN—THE PRESIDENT NOTIFIED OF GOVERNOR FLOYD'S SYSTEM OF ISSUING ACCEPTANCES.

Mr. Benjamin, who promptly appeared at the request of the committee, and testified with commendable and courteous frankness, states that during the first session of the present Congress, some twelve or eighteen months ago, he was written to by the attorney of Duncan, Sherman & Co., of New York, and his opinion requested as to the legality of acceptances issued by Governor Floyd to Russell, Majors & Waddell. It was mentioned in that letter that these "drafts," as they were then called, were offered for negotiation with the assurance that they were issued with the approbation of the President and Attorney General. Mr. Benjamin visited the President, and submitted the inquiry to him. The President replied that he knew nothing about the matter; that they had been issued without any knowledge of his; that he did not know by virtue of what law they were issued; but that he [Mr. Benjamin] might rely, if Governor Floyd had issued them, he had issued them properly, and that he had better apply to him [Governor Floyd] to ascertain by virtue of what law he was acting.

INTERVIEW WITH GOVERNOR FLOYD.

In pursuance of this suggestion, Mr. Benjamin called on Governor Floyd, and was informed by him that the matter had not been submitted to the Attorney General, as was stated; that the drafts were issued in pursuance of a long-established custom of the office; that he was not aware of any law actually authorizing their issue; that he would inquire into it; that the acceptances were issued to Russell, Majors & Waddell only after he had ascertained that the trains for transportation, which they had contracted to send from St. Louis to Utah, had actually started on their way; that the payments were to be made, under the contract, in instalments as the trains arrived at different points; and that, having received intelligence of the actual departure of the trains, he had accepted, in advance of their arrival at the intermediate point, having a certainty that they would arrive.

"I suggested to him," says Mr. Benjamin, "that I thought he was acting imprudently; that if any accident should happen to these trains by attacks by Indians, or any other cause, and they should fail to arrive, it would be impossible for him to pay the acceptances upon intelligence of that fact, and that that would give good reasons for complaints and investigations which would be injurious to him, and I urged him to discontinue the practice. Two days afterwards I received a note from him, informing me that he was obliged for the frank statement I had made to him, and that, upon reflection, he had determined he would accept no more."

GOVERNOR FLOYD CONTINUES TO ACCEPT.

It has been shown that, contrary to the assertion of Governor Floyd, no practice of issuing acceptances had ever prevailed in the War Department previous to its introduction by himself; that he issued these acceptances indiscriminately, and without reference to instalments, or the arrival or departure of trains, and without regard to money which was due. One would naturally expect to find that Governor Floyd, having been admonished by one whose position and legal learning gave authority to his advice, having confessed the illegality of his proceedings, and expressed a determination to make no further acceptances, would have proceeded thereafter with great caution and circumspection, even if he did not entirely discontinue his previous policy. It appears, however, that, supposing the note to Mr. Benjamin, before referred to, to have been written a year ago, there have been issued by Governor Floyd, since that time, acceptances to the amount of $2,163,000, namely: In April, $40,000; in May, $250,000; in June, $350,000; in July, $95,000; in August, $235,000; in September, $125,000; in October, $270,000. To this amount must be added the $798,000 of unconditional acceptances, of which there is no registry, and the sum total is as above stated. Only $60,000 of these acceptances have been returned to the War Department, and cancelled.

Having had his error and its consequences distinctly pointed out, having expressed his intention to refrain in future from the commission of similar acts, he still persists in his former course, and actually issued an acceptance for $135,000, at a date so late as the 13th of December, 1860. Whether this manifest contempt of counsel, disobedience of law, and violation of a solemn promise, can be reconciled with purity of private motives, and faithfulness to public trusts, is for the House to determine. It is the opinion of your committee that they cannot.

RECOMMENDATIONS FOR NEW LEGISLATION.

Your committee have now reported, so far as ascertained, all the material facts connected with the abstraction of bonds from the Interior Department, and with a series of transactions unprecedented in their character, and remarkable for alternate exhibitions of fraud and folly.

As one of the results of the examination they have made, they submit a bill to provide for the more certain and effectual punishment of crimes, such as those that have been brought to their notice, and also amendatory of the second section of the act of Congress, approved January 24, 1857, entitled "An act more effectually to enforce the attendance of witnesses on the summons of either house of Congress, and to compel them to disclose testimony."

They also beg leave to suggest that the fluctuations of the stock market, and the delay and uncertainty in the collection of the interest on the bonds, seem to demand some further legislation in regard to the Indian trust fund, as a measure of obvious justice and humanity to the Indians.

All of which is respectfully submitted, on behalf of the committee.

I. N. MORRIS, *Chairman.*

Journal of select committee, appointed under resolution of the House of the 24th of December, 1860, *to investigate alleged frauds in the Department of the Interior.*

COMMITTEE.

ISAAC N. MORRIS............................of Illinois.
ROSCOE CONKLING..........................of New York.
JAMES H. THOMAS..........................of Tennessee.
J. MORRISON HARRIS.......................of Maryland.
CHARLES CASE................................of Indiana.

WASHINGTON, *December* 27, 1860.

The committee met upon the call of the chairman.

Present: Messrs. Morris, Conkling, Thomas, Harris, and Case.

The following communication from the Clerk of the House of Representatives was laid before the committee.

"THIRTY-SIXTH CONGRESS, SECOND SESSION.

"CONGRESS OF THE UNITED STATES.

"IN THE HOUSE OF REPRESENTATIVES,
"*December* 24, 1860.

"Mr. Sherman moved the following, which was adopted:

"Whereas the Secretary of the Interior has this day addressed a communication to this House, stating that an extensive fraud had been committed upon his department, in the abstraction therefrom, by one of its officers, and the conversion to private use of a number of State bonds held in trust by the government for the benefit of certain Indian tribes, and asked that a committee be appointed to investigate and report upon the subject:

"*Be it resolved*, That a select committee be appointed, consisting of five members of the House, who shall proceed to inquire into and report to the House the facts in relation to said fraud; and that said committee have full power to send for persons and papers.

"The Speaker appointed the following members to act as said committee:

"Mr. ISAAC N. MORRIS.......................of Illinois.
"Mr. ROSCOE CONKLING.......................of New York.
"Mr. THOMAS S. BOCOCK.....................of Virginia.
"Mr. J. MORRISON HARRIS...................of Maryland.
"Mr. CHARLES CASE............................of Indiana.

"Attest: JOHN W. FORNEY, *Clerk.*
"By DANIEL BUCK, *Assistant Clerk.*"

Mr. Harris moved that the chairman be instructed to present the following resolution to the House:

Resolved, That the select committee, appointed under the resolution of the House of the 24th instant, to investigate the alleged frauds in the Department of the Interior, have leave to sit during the sessions of the House, and at such places in this city or elsewhere as they may deem advisable; also, that said committee be authorized to employ a stenographer, at a rate of compensation not exceeding that paid to the reporters of the House for the Congressional Globe."

The motion was agreed to.

On motion of Mr. Case, it was

Ordered, That the chairman be directed to request the attendance of Jacob Thompson, the Secretary of the Interior, before the committee, at 2 o'clock this day, with such papers and documents pertaining to those alleged frauds in the Department of the Interior as he may have in his possession.

On motion of the chairman,

Ordered, That a subpœna issue for the attendance of Luther R. Smoot.

The committee then took an informal recess until 2 o'clock p. m.

At two o'clock the committee re-assembled; all the members present.

On motion of Mr. Harris

Resolved, That Francis H. Smith be appointed stenographer and clerk of this committee.

On motion of Mr. Case,

Resolved, That the testimony taken and proceedings had before this committee be kept inviolably secret until its labors are concluded, except so far as it may be necessary to make disclosures, by order of the committee, on the floor of the House, for the purpose of furthering business.

Resolved, That the stenographer be sworn to keep secret all the doings of this committee.

The oath of secrecy was administered to the stenographer.

The chairman laid before the committee a communication from the Hon. Isaac I. Stevens, of Washington Territory, which was placed on file.

The Hon. Jacob Thompson, Secretary of the Interior, was then examined as a witness.

The committee adjourned to meet on the call of the chairman.

SATURDAY, *December* 29, 1860.

The committee met at 11 o'clock, a. m. upon the call of the chairman.

Present: Messrs. Morris, Conkling, Thomas, Harris, and Case.

Luke Lea was examined as a witness.

Committee adjourned until Monday morning at 10 o'clock.

MONDAY, *December* 31, 1860.

The committee met pursuant to adjournment.

Present, all the members.

On motion of Mr. Harris, it was

Resolved, That the chairman be authorized to have the testimony taken before the committee from day to day printed by such person as he may select, under such circumstances of guarantee that it will be kept inviolably secret, as will be satisfactory to the chairman.

Hon. John B. Floyd appeared and was examined as a witness; without concluding his examination,

The committee adjourned until to-morrow, at half-past ten, a. m.

TUESDAY, *January* 1, 1861.

The committee met at half-past ten o'clock.

Present, all the members.

Hon. John B. Floyd was examined; without concluding his examination,

The committee adjourned until to-morrow morning at 10 o'clock.

WEDNESDAY, *January* 2, 1861.

The committee met at 10 o'clock a. m.

Present: The chairman and Messrs. Thomas, Harris, and Case.

Luther R. Smoot and John B. Floyd were examined as witnesses.

Adjourned until Friday next at 10 o'clock a m.

JANUARY 4, 1861.

The committee met at 10 o'clock a. m.

Present: Messrs. Thomas, Harris, Case, and the chairman.

Mr. William R. Drinkard, Mr. George W. Riggs, and Mr. Richard B. Irwin were examined as witnesses.

The committee adjourned until to-morrow at half-past ten o'clock.

SATURDAY, *January* 5, 1861.

The committee met at half-past ten o'clock.

Present: Messrs. Thomas, Harris, Case, and the chairman.

Mr. George W. Riggs, Mr. Thomas J. D. Fuller, Mr. Lammond, and Mr. Irwin were examined as witnesses.

The committee adjourned to meet upon the call of the chairman of the committee.

MONDAY, *January* 7, 1861.

The committee assembled at the St. Nicholas Hotel, New York.

Present, all the members.

John Thompson was called and examined as a witness.

The committee adjourned until to-morrow.

TUESDAY, *January* 8, 1861.

The committee met at 10 o'clock a. m.

Messrs. G. B. Lamar, Luther C. Clark, Richard Schell, Matthew Morgan, John R. Garland, William T. Coleman, Alexander Campbell, and Robert H. Lowry were called and examined as witnesses.

The committee adjourned until to-morrow at 10 o'clock.

WEDNESDAY, *January* 9, 1861.

The committee met at the usual hour.

Hector Morrison, H. L. Williams, A. E. Silliman, C. A. Meigs, R. Bayles, and J. G. King were examined as witnesses.

The committee adjourned until to-morrow.

THURSDAY, *January* 10, 1861.

The committee met at the usual hour.

Frederick F. Thompson, Stephen L. Miles, and C. A. Macy were examined as witnesses.

The Sergeant-at-arms having reported that Robert W. Latham was unable to attend the committee at their room on account of indisposition, on motion, the chairman was deputed to examine the witness at his residence, in Brooklyn. The chairman thereupon proceeded to the residence of Mr. Latham, and examined him as a witness.

The committee adjourned to meet on the call of the chairman, at their room in the Capitol, at Washington.

MONDAY, *January* 14, 1861.

The committee met pursuant to the call of the chairman.

Present: Messrs. Thomas, Case, and the chairman.

William H. Russell, J. A. Williamson, and R. J. Atkinson were examined as witnesses.

The committee adjourned until to-morrow at half-past ten o'clock.

TUESDAY, *January* 15, 1861.

The committee met at half-past ten o'clock.

Present, all the members.

James T. Soutter, General J. E. Johnston, Henry Beard, John J. Bogue, and James Chestney were examined as witnesses.

The committee adjourned until Thursday next at half-past ten o'clock.

THURSDAY, *January* 17, 1861.

The committee met at half-past ten o'clock.

Present: Messrs. Harris and Case.

William McKim, William Fisher, Martin Lewis, Ceorge W. Riggs, and C. G. Wagner were sworn as witnesses.

The committee adjourned until to-morrow at half-past ten o'clock.

FRIDAY, *January* 18, 1861.

The committee met at half-past ten o'clock.

Present, all the members.

General J. E. Johnston and William H. Russell were examined as witnesses.

The committee adjourned until Monday next at half-past ten o'clock.

MONDAY, *January* 21, 1861.

The committee met at half-past ten o'clock.

Present: Messrs. Conkling, Thomas, Case, and the chairman.

The committee adjourned until to-morrow morning at 11 o'clock.

TUESDAY, *January* 22, 1861.

The committee met at 11 o'clock a. m.

Present: Messrs. Thomas, Harris, Case, and Mr. Chairman.

The committee adjourned until to-morrow at half-past ten o'clock.

WEDNESDAY, *January* 23, 1861.

The committee met at half-past ten o'clock.
Present: Messrs. Conkling, Thomas, Harris, Case, and the chairman.
Frederick P. James, William H. Russell, and Ashton S. H. White were examined as witnesses.
The committee adjourned until to-morrow morning at half-past ten o'clock.

THURSDAY, *January* 24, 1861.

The committee met at half-past ten a. m.
Present: Messrs. Harris, Thomas, Case, and the chairman.
The committee adjourned to meet upon the call of the chairman.

FRIDAY, *January* 25, 1861.

The committee met at 11 o'clock upon the call of the chairman.
Present: Messrs. Thomas, Harris, and the chairman.
Messrs. George W. Riggs and William H. Russell appeared before the committee as witnesses.
The committee adjourned to meet on Monday next at 11 o'clock.

MONDAY, *January* 28, 1861.

The committee met at half-past ten o'clock.
Present: Messrs. Thomas, Case, and the chairman.
The committee adjourned until to-morrow at half-past ten o'clock.

TUESDAY, *January* 29, 1861.

The committee met at half-past ten o'clock.
Present: Messrs. Case, Thomas, and the chairman.
The committee adjourned to meet upon the call of the chairman.

WEDNESDAY, *January* 30, 1861.

The committee met at half-past seven o'clock p. m. upon the call of the chairman.
Present: Messrs. Case, Thomas, Harris, and the chairman.
Henry Beard was recalled and examined.
The committee then adjourned to meet upon the call of the chairman.

MONDAY, *February* 4, 1861.

The committee met at half-past ten o'clock upon the call of the chairman.
Present: Messrs. Conkling, Case, Thomas, and the chairman.
Hon. J. P. Benjamin was examined as a witness.
The committee adjourned to meet on the call of the chairman.

WEDNESDAY, *February* 6, 1861.

The committee met at half-past ten o'clock upon the call of the chairman.

William R. Drinkard and R. B. Irwin were recalled and examined as witnesses.

The committee adjourned to meet upon the call of the chairman.

FRIDAY, *February* 8, 1861.

The committee met, on call of the chairman, at 1 o'clock p. m.

Present, all the members.

On motion of Mr. Harris, the chairman was unanimously directed to report to the House.

On motion of Mr. Conkling, Mr. Case was directed to prepare a bill amendatory of the second section of the act more effectually to enforce the attendance of witnesses on the summons of either house of Congress, and to compel them to discover testimony, approved January 24, 1857.

On motion of Mr. Harris, Mr. Conkling was directed to report back to the House the joint resolution making provision for the recovery of certain bonds belonging to the Indian trust fund, with the recommendation that it do not pass.

The committee adjourned *sine die*.

Evidence taken before the select committee appointed under the resolution of the House of Representatives of the 24th of December, 1860.

WASHINGTON, *December* 27, 1860.

Hon. JACOB THOMPSON, Secretary of the Interior, was called as a witness, sworn and examined.

Examination by the chairman:

Question. Are you Secretary of the Interior?

Answer. I am.

Question. As Secretary of the Interior, have certain bonds purchased for the benefit of the Indian tribes been in your charge?

Answer. They have.

Question. Please state to the committee the number and character of those bonds, and whether any of them have been abstracted from your office; and if so, the facts in regard to said abstraction.

Answer. I have two statements of those bonds: one made out by the clerk of my office, setting forth each of the bonds; the other made out by the Indian office. They are checks to each other. The former is a long statement. Here is the one made out by the Indian office:

A.

	Securities.
Arkansas 5's	$3,000 00
Florida 7's	132,000 00
Georgia 6's	3,500 00
Indiana 5's	70,000 00
Kentucky 5's	183,000 00
Louisiana 6's	10,000 00
Louisiana 6's	27,000 00
Maryland 6's	131,611 82
Missouri 5½'s	63,000 00
Missouri 6's	484,000 00
North Carolina 6's	322,000 00
North Carolina 6's	240,000 00
Ohio 6's	150,000 00
Pennsylvania 5's	50,000 00
Pennsylvania 5's	46,000 00
South Carolina 6's	125,000 00
Tennessee 5's	125,000 00
Tennessee 5's	40,000 00
Tennessee 6's	143,000 00
United States, 1842, coupons, 6's	63,000 00
United States, 1842, certificates, 6's	130,280 00
United States, 1847, certificates, 6's	58,050 00
Virginia 6's	581,800 00
Chesapeake and Ohio Canal Company 6's	43,500 00
City of Wheeling 6's	168,000 00
Richmond and Danville railroad 6's	3,500 00
Stock at this posting, balanced June 30, 1860	3,396,241 82

The amount is $3,396,241 82. I think both statements agree.

On Saturday evening, the 22d of December, at half-past three o'clock, I returned to the city from a visit to North Carolina. In the evening, at half-past eight o'clock, I called to see the President; I found at the office of the President Senator Rice. Immediately after my arrival Mr. Rice informed me, in the presence of the President, that he had certain papers which had been placed in his hands, with a request that he would deliver them to me, but which he declined to keep until my return—not knowing when that would be—and which he had just shown to the President. Those papers showed that bonds to the amount of $870,000 had been abstracted from the safe of the Interior Department, in which the Indian trust fund was kept. A few minutes thereafter a letter of Godard Bailey was handed to me; upon the envelope of that letter was this indorsement:

"WASHINGTON CITY, D. C., *December* 13, 1860.

"This communication was received this day from Mr. Bailey, with a request that I should deliver it to the Hon. Jacob Thompson, Secretary of the Interior, five days before the expiration of his term of office.

"CHARLES G. WAGNER."

At the same time with the delivery of that letter, was another letter directed to Charles G. Wagner, Census bureau, which letter was indorsed—

"This letter was received from Godard Bailey this 21st of December, 1860."

That letter is in the words following:

"LAFAYETTE HOUSE, *December* 20, 1860.

"MY DEAR SIR: I will be much obliged if you will deliver to Mr. Thompson, immediately on his return from North Carolina, the letter addressed to him which I placed in your hands some time ago. It concerns my honor that Mr. Thompson should receive that letter at the earliest possible moment, and I rely upon your friendship to see that he does get it.

"Yours, truly,

"GODARD BAILEY.

"C. G. WAGNER, Esq."

The first letter referred to was in the following words:

"WASHINGTON, *December* 1, 1860.

"SIR: I feel that, in justice to yourself, I ought not to permit you to quit office without informing you of the fact that a portion of the bonds constituting the Indian trust fund are no longer in my custody. Those bonds I intrusted, in July last, to third parties, for purposes which it is not necessary to discuss here. The bonds so surrendered are the following, to wit:

Missouri 6's	$370,000
North Carolina 6's, January and July	296,000
North Carolina 6's, April and October	61,000
Tennessee 6's	143,000
Making a total of	870,000

"I desire to be permitted to place on record, simultaneously with the preceding avowal, the following declaration: *First.* I have not converted any of these bonds to my individual use; I have not used them for private speculation, nor made them a source of profit to myself in any way. *Second.* When I parted with the bonds, assurances, which I deemed satisfactory, were given me that they would be returned in ninety days, and that no loss could accrue to the United States. *Third.* The United States are at this moment perfectly secured against loss. *Fourth.* I protest that the motives which prompted me to part with the bonds were wholly unselfish, and that I never had at any time the least idea of embezzling any part of the trust fund, although I could have done so with entire impunity. *Fifth.* No officer of the government advised me to part with the bonds, or even knew that I contemplated doing so. I alone am responsible for their surrender.

"I make this statement now not because further concealment is impossible or even difficult, but to afford you an opportunity of vindicating yourself from any suspicion of complicity, by instituting, before leaving office, such proceedings against me as you may deem advisable in the premises.

"Very respectfully, your obedient servant,

"GODARD BAILEY.

"Hon. JACOB THOMPSON,
"*Secretary of the Interior.*

"P. S.—I shall place this letter in the hands of a friend, without informing him of its contents, and request him to deliver it to you five days before the expiration of your term of office. In case you resign, it will be delivered to you five days before the time at which your resignation takes effect. G. B."

From Mr. Rice I received the following paper:

"WASHINGTON, D. C., *December* 13, 1860.

"We acknowledge to have received from Godard Bailey on the 13th of July last, and at various times subsequently, the following bonds, viz:

Missouri 6's	$370,000
North Carolina 6's, January and July	296,000
North Carolina 6's, April and October	61,000
Tennessee 6's	143,000
Making a total of	870,000

which we agree to return to the said Godard Bailey, or to his assigns, on demand.

"As collateral security for the return of the above described bonds, we have deposited with the said Godard Bailey acceptances of the Hon. John B. Floyd, Secretary of War, to the amount of eight hundred and seventy thousand dollars.

"RUSSELL, MAJORS & WADDELL."

Below the signature is the following: "Deliver the above described bonds to the Secretary of the Interior.

"GODARD BAILEY."

With the exception of the signature of Russell, Majors & Waddell, that whole paper is in the handwriting of Godard Bailey. With the receipt there were delivered the following acceptances, referred to in the receipt, drawn by Russell, Majors & Waddell on the Secretary of War, John B. Floyd, and accepted, as they appear at the times and in the manner in the respective drafts which I present to the committee as follows:

$15,000. WASHINGTON CITY, *September* 13, 1860.

Eight months after date pay to our own order, at the "Bank of the Republic," New York city, fifteen thousand dollars, for value received, and charge to account of our transportation contract of the 12th day of April, 1860.

RUSSELL, MAJORS & WADDELL.

Hon. J. B. FLOYD,
Secretary of War.

No. 78.] WAR DEPARTMENT, *September* 18, 1860.

Accepted.

JOHN B. FLOYD,
Secretary of War.

$10,000. WASHINGTON CITY, *September* 19, 1860.

Twelve months after date pay to our own order, at the "Bank of the Republic," New York city, ten thousand dollars, for value received, and charge to account of our transportation contract of the 12th day of April, 1860.

RUSSELL, MAJORS & WADDELL.

Hon. J. B. FLOYD,
Secretary of War.

No. 85.] WAR DEPARTMENT, *September* 19, 1860.

Accepted.

JOHN B. FLOYD.
Secretary of War.

$10,000. WASHINGTON CITY, *October*, 1, 1860.

Ten months after date pay to our own order, at the "Bank of the Republic," New York city, ten thousand dollars, for value received, and charge to account of our transportation contract of the 12th day of April, 1860.

RUSSELL, MAJORS & WADDELL.

Hon. J. B. FLOYD,
Secretary of War.

No. 90.] WAR DEPARTMENT, *October* 10, 1860.

Accepted.

JOHN B. FLOYD,
Secretary of War.

$10,000. WASHINGTON CITY, *October* 8, 1860.

Ten months after date pay to our own order, at the "Bank of the Republic," New York city, ten thousand dollars, for value received, and charge to account of our transportation contract of the 12th day of April, 1860.

RUSSELL, MAJORS & WADDELL.

Hon. J. B. FLOYD,
Secretary of War.

No. 99.] WAR DEPARTMENT, *October* 10, 1860.

Accepted.

JOHN B. FLOYD,
Secretary of War.

$7,000. WASHINGTON CITY, *October* 11, 1860.

Ten months after date pay to our own order, at the "Bank of the Republic," New York city, seven thousand dollars, for value received, and charge to our transportation contract of the 12th day of April, 1860.

RUSSELL, MAJORS & WADDELL.

Hon. J. B. FLOYD,
Secretary of War.

No. 110.] WAR DEPARTMENT, *October* 13, 1860.

Accepted.

JOHN B. FLOYD,
Secretary of War.

$10,000. WASHINGTON CITY, *October* 12, 1860.

Ten months after date pay to our own order, at the "Bank of the Republic," New York city, ten thousand dollars, for value received, and charge to our transportation contract of the 12th day of April, 1860.

RUSSELL, MAJORS & WADDELL.

Hon. J. B. FLOYD,
Secretary of War.

No. 116.] WAR DEPARTMENT, *October* 13, 1860.

Accepted.

JOHN B. FLOYD,
Secretary of War.

$10,000. WASHINGTON CITY, *October* 13, 1860.

Ten months after date pay to our own order, at the "Bank of the Republic," New York city, ten thousand dollars, for value received, and charge to our transportation contract of the 12th day of April, 1860.

RUSSELL, MAJORS & WADDELL.

Hon. J. B. FLOYD,
Secretary of War.

No. 120.] WAR DEPARTMENT, *October* 13, 1860.

Accepted.

JOHN B. FLOYD,
Secretary of War.

$110,000. WASHINGTON CITY, *October* 22, 1860.

Out of any moneys becoming due to us for army transportation in the year 1861, under our transportation contract of the 12th day of April last, pay to our own order one hundred and ten thousand dollars, for value received, and charge to our transportation account for moneys earned in 1861.

RUSSELL, MAJORS & WADDELL.

Hon. J. B. FLOYD,
Secretary of War.

WAR DEPARTMENT, *October* 26, 1860.

Accepted, payable according to its tenor.

JOHN B. FLOYD,
Secretary.

$125,000. WASHINGTON CITY, *October* 22, 1860.

Out of any moneys becoming due to us for army transportation in the year 1861, under our contract for transportation of the 12th day of April last, pay to our own order one hundred and twenty-five thousand dollars, for value received, and charge to our transportation account for moneys earned in 1861.

RUSSELL, MAJORS & WADDELL.

Hon. J. B. FLOYD,
Secretary of War.

WAR DEPARTMENT, *October* 26, 1860.

Accepted, payable according to its tenor.

JOHN B. FLOYD, *Secretary.*

$143,000. WASHINGTON CITY, *October* 23, 1860.

Out of any moneys becoming due to us for army transportation in the year 1861, under our contract for transportation of the 12th day of April last, pay to our own order one hundred and forty-three thousand dollars, for value received, and charge to our transportation account for moneys earned in 1861.

RUSSELL, MAJORS & WADDELL.

Hon. J. B. FLOYD,
Secretary of War.

WAR DEPARTMENT, *October* 26, 1860.

Accepted, payable according to its tenor.

JOHN B. FLOYD, *Secretary.*

$115,000. WASHINGTON CITY, *October* 23, 1860.

Out of any moneys becoming due to us for army transportation in the year 1861, under our transportation contract of the 12th day of April last, pay to our own order one hundred and fifteen thousand dollars, for value received, and charge to our transportation account for moneys earned in 1861.

RUSSELL, MAJORS & WADDELL.

Hon. J. B. FLOYD,
Secretary of War.

WAR DEPARTMENT, *October* 26, 1860.

Accepted, payable according to its tenor.

JOHN B. FLOYD, *Secretary.*

$170,000. WASHINGTON CITY, *October* 23, 1860.

Out of any moneys becoming due to us for army transportation in the year 1861, under our contract for transportation of the 12th day of April last, pay to our own order one hundred and seventy thousand dollars, for value received, and charge to our transportation account for moneys earned in the year 1861.

RUSSELL, MAJORS & WADDELL.

Hon. J. B. FLOYD,
Secretary of War.

WAR DEPARTMENT, *October* 26, 1860.

Accepted, payable according to its tenor.

JOHN B. FLOYD, *Secretary.*

$135,000. WASHINGTON CITY, *December* 13, 1860.

Out of any moneys becoming due to us for army transportation in the year 1861, under our contract for transportation of the 12th day of April last, pay to our own order one hundred and thirty-five thousand dollars, for value received, and charge to our transportation account for moneys earned in 1861.

RUSSELL, MAJORS & WADDELL.

Hon. J. B. FLOYD,
Secretary of War.

WAR DEPARTMENT, *December* 13, 1860.

Accepted, payable according to its tenor.

JOHN B. FLOYD, *Secretary.*

Upon the receipt of this information, at my urgent request Mr. Rice consented to apply to Mr. Bailey for the keys of the safe. Mr. Rice was absent from the Executive Mansion but a few minutes before he returned with the keys. I then requested Mr. Rice to accompany me to the Interior Department, which he consented to do. I sent for my chief clerk, Moses Kelly, and called on Mr. Bailey to go with me; and there finding Mr. Wagner, the chief clerk in the Census bureau, I took him along with me. We opened the safe, and counted the bonds which were then remaining, and found all with which he was charged to be there with the exception of $870,000, which he had confessed had been abstracted, and one Indian bond, the interest upon which had not been paid for years, and which had been delivered to Mr. Fitch for the purpose of ascertaining whether payment could not be had from the State, which bond has been mislaid. All the contents of the safe, as far as I could ascertain during the night, were safe, secure, and regular. On the next day I caused legal proceedings to be instituted against the parties who are implicated—Godard Bailey and William H. Russell.

Question (by the Chairman.) You have furnished an abstract showing the amount and character of the bonds you had in your safe: can you give the committee a particular description of each bond abstracted?

Answer. I can; and according to the best evidence within my reach, they are as follows, each bond being for the sum of one thousand dollars, viz:

Six per cent Missouri coupon bonds, issued in June and August, 1857.

State of Missouri, St. Louis, and Iron Mountain railroad State bonds.

No. of bond.	No. of bond.	No. of bond.	No. of bond.
2037	1879	1827	1831
1876	1880	1822	1832
1996	1881	1821	1868
1997	1882	1820	1869
1998	1883	1819	1870
2008	1884	1818	1871
2007	1885	1809	1872
1993	1886	1817	1873
1994	1887	1816	1874
1995	1888	1815	1875
1891	1889	1814	2030
1990	1890	1813	2029
1892	2045	1812	2018
1991	2048	1810	2017
2003	2046	1811	2016
2002	2047	1808	2015
1992	2044	2031	2014
2006	2043	2033	2013
2005	2040	2034	2012
2004	2041	2035	2010
2001	2042	2036	2111
1999	2039	2032	
2000	2038	1826	99
2009	1825	1828	
1877	1824	1829	
1878	1823	1830	

NOTE.—Bonds No. 2000 and below, of this series, issued June, 1857, and bonds No. 2001 and above that, dated August, 1857, payable at the Phœnix Bank, New York city, in 1887.

State of Missouri six per cent. coupon bonds, viz: Hannibal and St. Joseph railroad State bonds.

No. of bond.	No. of bond.	No. of bond.	No. of bond.
1853	1614	1626	1831
1852	1615	1627	1641
1851	1616	1628	1642
1850	1617	1629	1643
1849	1618	1859	1644
1848	1619	1865	1645
1847	1620	1863	1646
1846	1621	1862	1647
1845	1611	1860	1648
1844	1864	1861	1637
1832	1634	1856	1638
1835	1631	1858	1840
1833	1632	1855	1842
1834	1633	1854	1843
1836	1622	1822	1650
1837	1857	1823	1816
1838	1636	1824	1817
1839	1630	1825	1818
1649	1639	1826	1819
1640	1841	1827	1820
1635	1623	1828	1821
1612	1624	1829	
1613	1625	1830	90

NOTE.—These bonds are dated January, 1857, payable at Bank of Commerce, New York, in November, 1886. Interest payable in January and July of each year.

State of Missouri six per cent. coupon North Missouri railroad State bonds.

No. of bond.	No. of bond.	No. of bond.	No. of bond.
2952	2468	1638	1707
2940	2512	1641	2452
2939	2513	1642	2453
2941	2514	1643	2454
2942	2515	1644	2455
2946	2516	1645	2456
2945	2911	1646	2457
2944	2910	1647	2458
2943	2912	1648	2459
2947	2913	1649	2460
2948	2914	1640	2461
2949	2916	1650	2462
2950	2915	2922	2463
2937	2917	2923	2464
2938	2918	2924	2465
1653	2919	2936	2466
1654	2920	2951	2467
1655	2954	2953	
1652	2955	1657	80
1656	1651	1705	
2921	1639	1706	

Note.—The bonds numbered 2516 and below, issued in January, 1857; No. 2910, and above that, issued in August, 1857, payable at Phœnix Bank, New York city.

Missouri six per cent. coupon bonds, viz: North Missouri railroad State bonds.

No. of bond.	No. of bond.	No. of bond.	No. of bond.
2773	2765	2763	2731
2784	2768	2787	2766
2786	2769	2730	2729
2781	2770	2717	2718
2782	2771	2734	2715
2779	2785	2721	2714
2783	2778	2719	2764
2711	2772	2733	2728
2712	2775	2722	2726
2710	2774	2720	2723
2725	2780	2716	2713
2777	2732	2727	
2776	2767	2724	50

Note.—These bonds are dated July, 1857, payable July, 1887, at the Phœnix Bank, New York city. Interest payable in January and July.

Missouri six per cent. Pacific railroad State coupon bonds.

No. of bond.	No. of bond.	No. of bond.	No. of bond.
5246	5232	5261	5000
5259	5231	5258	4999
5245	5200	5256	4997
5244	5199	5255	4890
5243	5198	5254	4998
5242	5197	5253	4889
5241	5310	5252	4888
5240	5236	5251	4876
5239	5307	5250	5257
5238	5308	5249	
5237	5309	5247	51
5235	5262	5248	
5234	5306	5195	
5233	5260	5196	

NOTE.—These bonds are dated March, 1857, payable March, 1887, at Phœnix Bank, New York. Interest payable in January and July of each year.

Bonds of North Carolina—coupon six per cent. North Carolina six per cents.

No. of bond.	No. of bond.	No. of bond.	No. of bond.
35	328	301	100
33	329	300	99
32	330	297	103
23	331	235	6
9	332	234	28
7	333	203	22
349	334	166	16
348	327	104	21
347	326	20	98
346	317	19	97
343	318	18	96
342	316	17	95
341	296	15	94
340	239	13	62
339	238	8	60
338	237	11	
337	236	10	72
336	303	102	
335	302	101	

NOTE.—These bonds are dated January, 1856; payable January, 1886, at Bank of Republic, New York. Interest payable in January and July.

North Carolina six per cent. coupon bonds.

No. of bond.	No. of bond.	No. of bond.	No. of bond.
833	852	736	811
832	853	758	812
831	854	759	813
830	855	760	814
829	856	761	815
834	857	762	816
835	858	763	817
836	860	764	818
837	861	790	819
838	862	791	820
871	863	792	821
872	864	793	822
873	865	794	823
874	866	795	824
875	867	796	825
876	868	797	826
877	869	798	827
878	870	799	828
879	883	800	839
880	882	801	840
881	884	802	843
846	885	803	844
847	731	804	845
848	732	805	
849	733	806	104
850	734	808	
851	735	807	

These bonds are dated July, 1857; payable July, 1887, at Bank of Republic, New York. Interest payable in January and July.

North Carolina 6 per cent. coupon bonds.

No. of bond.	No. of bond.	No. of bond.	No. of bond.
599	650	494	537
600	651	495	518
603	652	496	529
604	616	497	516
605	617	621	515
606	618	498	517
607	619	510	514
608	455	511	422
610	457	481	545
611	458	482	546
612	470	483	547
613	602	484	548
609	439	485	560
614	440	486	562
622	442	487	471
623	430	488	472
624	431	489	473
625	433	490	474
626	436	538	475
627	437	539	476
628	427	540	477
641	429	541	478
642	425	542	479
643	426	543	480
615	423	530	512
644	421	531	513
646	601	532	
647	544	533	119
648	491	534	
645	492	535	
649	493	536	

NOTE.—These bonds are dated January, 1857; payable January, 1887, at Bank of Republic, New York. Interest payable in January and July.

North Carolina 6 per cent. coupon bonds—coupons payable in April and October, viz:

Forty-five bonds for $1,000 each, issued by authority of an act to incorporate the Western North Carolina Railroad Company, chapter 228, dated October, 1856, payable in 1886 at Bank of Republic, viz:

No. of bond.	No. of bond.	No. of bond.	No. of bond.
51	124	151	192
52	125	152	193
53	126	153	194
54	127	154	195
95	128	155	196
96	179	156	197
97	180	162	198
98	129	163	199
99	130	164	200
106	137	165	
122	144	178	45
123	146	191	

Two bonds for $1,000 each, dated April, 1857:

No. of bond.
9
10

Fifteen bonds for $1,000 each, dated October, 1857, viz: Payable at Bank of Republic, October, 1887, viz:

No. of bond.	No. of bond.	No of bond.	No. of bond.
1183	1187	1191	1195
1184	1188	1192	1196
1185	1189	1193	1197
1186	1190	1194	
			15

Tennessee 6 per cent. coupon bonds, of $1,000 each, of loan of 1852, payable 1892 in New York city, of the following numbers, and dated January, 1852.

No. of bond.	No. of bond.	No. of bond.	No. of bond.
413	419	477	498
414	476	491	723
415			

And of the following numbers issued January, 1854:

No. of bond.	No. of bond.	No. of bond.	No. of bond.
828	830	1278	1358
829			

And of the following numbers issued January, 1855:

No. of bond.	No. of bond.	No. of bond.	No. of bond.
1744	2581	2891	3066
2110	2605	2892	3121
2133	2655		

And of the following numbers issued January, 1856:

No. of bond.	No. of bond.	No. of bond.	No. of bond.
3464	3941	4208	4550
3465	3942	4209	4556
3466	3943	4210	4566
3467	3944	4211	4569
3469	3945	4212	4570
3470	3946	4213	4571
3471	3985	4214	4749
3472	4199	4431	4751
3758	4200	4527	4881
3894	4207	4529	

And of the following numbers issued January, 1857:

No. of bond.	No. of bond.	No. of bond.	No. of bond.
5056	5374	5417	5452
5195	5375	5418	5518
5326	5376	5419	5519
5359	5377	5421	5520
5360	5378	5426	5521
5361	5379	5427	5522
5362	5380	5430	5703
5363	5381	5434	5704
5364	5385	5436	5705
5365	5386	5437	5706
5366	5387	5438	5707
5367	5388	5439	5708
5368	5389	5440	5709
5369	5390	5441	5710
5370	5391	5442	5712
5371	5392	5443	5713
5372	5393	5444	5839
5373	5416	5445	

The published list varies from this statement to the extent of ten numbers in the advertisement of Tennessee bonds. The coupons do not agree in these cases with our register, but I have no doubt the coupons indicate the bonds delivered to Russell. We have coupons of January 1, 1861, for the following numbered bonds, but these numbers are not found on the official register, viz: Nos. 352, 2938, 974, 362, 210, 1001, 356, 3018, 5154, nine bonds.

There are 871 bonds advertised, but my present list makes but 870, agreeing with the amount in the receipt before mentioned.

Question. In what capacity was Godard Bailey acting in your office?

Answer. He held a position in the Interior Department as the appeal clerk of the Indian bureau, or, as we call him, he was the Indian appeal clerk. I have four appeal clerks: one of them takes charge of appeals to me from the Land Office; one from the Pension office; one from the Indian office; and one on the judiciary expenses. Mr. Bailey was the appeal clerk from the Indian office, and to him I assigned also the appeals and business from the Patent Office.

He was also one of the disbursing clerks, appointed under the act of 3d March, 1853, and had given bond, as required by that act, before he was placed in charge of the chest; and the duties of his position indicated him as the proper officer to have the custody of the keys of the iron safe, or chest, containing the trust fund bonds and certificates.

Question. Was he necessarily, by virtue of the position you say he held, placed in charge of the keeping of those bonds, or were the bonds placed in his keeping?

Answer. They were not placed in his keeping by law, but simply by regulation of the department, as there is no custodian by law for those trust funds.

Question. Who collected the interest on those bonds from time to time as it fell due?

Answer. It was collected by letters addressed, and coupons sent by the Secretary of the Interior, to the officers of the government at the various points where they were payable, and the proceeds covered into the treasury by regular warrants.

Question. Had Mr. Bailey, by virtue of his position, any more authority than any other clerk over the collection of interest upon the bonds?

Answer. It was his especial duty to prepare the letters and cut off the coupons, and keep the accounts. The check upon him was, that the financial division of the Indian bureau keeps the account of the amount of bonds held for the use of each tribe, and the amount of the annual income. From time to time it is the duty of that officer to report to me what will fall due to the respective tribes. The books of the financial branch of this department show through covering warrants what is collected and paid into the treasury. Thus it would become apparent should any collections not be made, and the reason could be easily ascertained should any collection not be made as the interest falls due.

Question. Were, then, the bonds entirely under your control as Secretary of the Interior, and in your possession?

Answer. While they were not in my manual custody, they were, in contemplation of law, in my possession as Secretary, and under my control.

Question (by Mr. Conkling.) I desire to know what was the first intimation or notice of any sort you had that these bonds were gone or missing?

Answer. The first notice, or intimation, or suspicion that these bonds were missing, was upon the evening that I visited the President, on the 22d of December, where I was informed of the fact by Mr Rice, in the presence of the President, and a few minutes thereafter I received from Mr. Bailey the letter, at that place, from Mr. Rice, who said he had just received it from Mr. Wagner.

Question (by Mr. Case.) Please state, in general terms, how these trust funds originated, and how they came under the control of the Interior Department.

Answer. By the fourth section of the act of June 14, 1836, vol. 5, page 47, of the Statutes at Large, entitled "An act making appropriations for the current expenses of the Indian department, for Indian annuities," and other similar acts for the year 1836, it is provided "that the Secretary of War be, and hereby is, authorized and directed to invest, in a manner which shall be, in his judgment, most safe and beneficial for the fund, the sum of $33,912 40, being money in the treasury of the proceeds of lands purchased from the Seneca Indians of Sandusky, by treaty concluded on the 28th of February, 1831; from the Seneca and Shawnees, by the treaty concluded on July 20, 1831; from the Shawnees, by the treaty concluded on August 8, 1831; and upon which sum the United States are, by stipulation in the said treaties, bound to pay to said Indians an annual interest at the rate of 5 per cent. per annum."

Then you find that the fourth section of an act, vol. 5, page 135, Statutes at Large, provides "that the provisions of the fourth section of the act of June 14, 1836, entitled 'An act making appropriations for the Indian department,' &c., be, and are hereby, extended in such a manner as to apply to the disposition of all moneys that may hereafter be received under the treaties therein named, or under any others containing stipulations for the payment to the Indians, annually, of interest upon the proceeds of the lands ceded by them."

By section fifth, of an act approved the 3d of March, 1849, vol. 9, page 395, Statutes at Large, all the powers of the Secretary of War over Indian business was transferred to the Department of the Interior.

Question (by Mr. Harris.) Are you able to state the whole amount of bonds under the control and in the keeping of your department specifically? I mean the bonds in detail.

Answer. Yes, sir.

Question. Is there any register in your department of the particular number, and the amount of each bond?

Answer. Yes, sir; I can give a description of each bond, the number, the amount of each, and the date of each certificate.

Question. Has there been an investigation made since this transaction, by which you have verified the fact that all the remaining bonds are in the possession of your department now, by an examination of the numbers, &c.?

Answer. That has not been done. It is a tedious work, and will take two or three clerks some days to do it. As to the identity of the bonds, we can determine those we have; as to those gone, we have to depend upon our previous registry of those bonds and the coupons still on hand. Then we have a check in the fact that in our settlements at the treasury we report to them, as I believe, each bond purchased, its number, date, and amount.

Question (by Mr. Case.) Do you know who had the manual possession of those bonds immediately preceding their passing into the custody of Bailey?

Answer. They were in the possession of Mr. Beard.

Question. When was that transfer made?

Answer. It was made late in the summer or early in the fall of 1857, Mr. Beard having been disconnected with the Indian service and put upon the land service. That was the cause of the transfer.

Question. Does Mr. Bailey fill the office Beard did?

Answer. No, sir. Beard was at the head of the financial division in the Indian office.

Question (by the Chairman.) When was Mr. Bailey first appointed to office?

Answer. A few months after I came into office. After Mr. Beard was changed from a clerkship in the Indian office and transferred to the appeal clerkship in the land service, the transfer of the chest was made, and they counted the bonds and passed receipts.

Question (by Mr. Harris.) Under the arrangement existing as to the custody of those bonds, was it or not in the power of the clerk who had the possession of the bonds to use them in any way he might think proper, without there existing any opportunity, or any reason for the discovery of such uses by the Secretary or head of department, provided the interest was regularly collected or provided for?

Answer. Since I have looked into the matter, I find that he could use some of those bonds if the interest every six months was paid. But what I have now ordered to be done, which is to stamp each bond as "Indian trust fund," will entirely prevent that for the future. Up to this time my attention had never been called to the subject; as it had gone on heretofore, so it has been conducted during my time of service.

SATURDAY, *December* 29, 1860.

LUKE LEA sworn.

Examination by Mr. Harris.

Question. I believe your business is that of a banker in Washington city?

Answer. Yes, sir; that is my principal business.

Question. Have you ever had any connexion with the Indian department of the government?

Answer. Yes, sir; I was once Commissioner of Indian Affairs.

Question. During what years?

Answer. I was appointed during General Taylor's administration. I entered upon the duties of the office, I think, on the 1st of July, 1850.

Question. Were the bonds in which investments were made for the benefit of certain tribes of Indians in your charge at that time?

Answer. Well, sir, they could not be considered as strictly under my charge, because they were under the charge directly of the Secretary of the Interior.

Question. How were they in your charge or custody?

Answer. There may be some doubt whether they were properly in my custody or not.

Question. How were they kept, and where?

Answer. They were kept, I believe, when I entered into office, in an iron safe in the office of the Commissioner of Indian Affairs, and during the whole time I was in office I believe they were kept there, but the clerk who had them in charge was an immediate appointee and confidential friend of the Secretary of the Interior, who considered this clerk as in custody of these bonds for him. They were, at any rate, in a safe in the office of the Commissioner of Indian Affairs; that is, I have always understood that such was the fact. I do not know that I ever saw one of them during the whole time I was Commissioner. My impression is that I never did.

Question. Did you keep in your office a memorandum or registration of these bonds?

Answer. I am not positive whether there was a register of them kept in the Indian office or not. It was a peculiar sort of affair—so directly in connexion with the Secretary of the Interior that I did not consider myself as having them in custody. He was the trustee of the fund, but, as I said, they were kept in a safe in one of the rooms in the Indian office. When I first came into the office they were in the custody of a man by the name of Devereaux. After the death of Mr. Devereaux, Mr. Stuart, then Secretary of the Interior, put them into the hands or custody of a confidential friend of his by the name of Miller, who was considered, I believe, as a confidential clerk. His name was James J. Miller. I recollect, after Devereaux died, saying to the Secretary that he was the clerk who had charge of these funds, and as the Secretary was responsible for them, as they were held in trust by him, it was very important for him to select some man as the successor of Devereaux who he personally knew to be a man of strict integrity and worthy of trust. I therefore declined to recommend any man to Mr. Stuart for that place, although he had allowed me to nominate to him all the other clerks in the office. He thereupon appointed this man Miller, and put the bonds under his charge, although they were really in the office of the Commissioner of Indian Affairs.

Question. I understand you, then, to state that there was no account of these bonds kept in your office?

Answer. I cannot now state with certainty; Mr. Mix, the chief clerk, would be able to give you full information upon that subject. I never had anything to do with the management of the bonds, and I am not able to speak positively as to whether there was a record in the office of them or not. Mr. Mix is doubtless familiar with all these things, and can give you any information upon the subject. I do not recollect that I ever signed any paper in reference to the funds.

Question. How long did you continue in office?

Answer. I went into office in July, 1850, I think, and remained there until the incoming of Pierce's administration—continuing about a month under that administration, when I was succeeded by Colonel Manypenny, of Ohio.

Question. While you held that office were these bonds removed from the office in any way or at any time with your knowledge?

Answer. No, sir; I will state, however, in this connexion, that when Miller was appointed in the way I mentioned, he represented to the Secretary that the safe in which they were kept was insecure; I think he got the Secretary to direct him to procure a larger and a stronger safe; I am pretty confident that he got a new safe at considerable expense—a costly one. The old safe was taken away, and the bonds were transferred to the new one, at least I have no doubt that such was the fact, though I do not remember to have seen the thing done, nor do I remember to have laid my eyes upon the bonds during the whole time I was there. It was a matter of some delicacy; for although they related to Indian affairs, and were properly in the Indian office, yet the Secretary was directly concerned in the fund as trustee; and, as he had appointed this man as their custodian, I rather kept myself aloof from the matter, and did not interfere with it in any way whatever.

Question. Do I understand you to say that you had a personal knowledge of the character of the bonds in your office?

Answer. I had a personal knowledge of the fact that there was a large number of State bonds held in the Indian office by the Secretary of the Interior for the benefit of Indian tribes.

Question. But you had no personal knowledge of the description of these bonds, of their registration, or of the amount of bonds which were held in the office?

Answer. None in the world. I do not recollect to have seen any registration of them while I was there, although I will not undertake to say there was no such register kept there. There was an account kept between the Secretary of the Interior and the Secretary of the Treasury, in reference to the collection of the coupons, and placing the amount collected in the treasury, but the business was transacted directly between the Secretary of the Interior and the Secretary of the Treasury—all the papers being drawn, I believe, by this confidential clerk. I do not recollect, as I said, that I had to sign any papers in connexion with it; it was a transaction between the two departments, through this confidential clerk.

Question. Do you know Mr. Godard Bailey, late clerk in the Interior Department?

Answer. Yes, sir; very well.

Question. Have you known him for any length of time?

Answer. I have known him for, I should say, perhaps, three years.

Question. Are you competent to tell the committee what his habits of life were, so far as relates to his expenditures, mode of living, &c., during that time?

Answer. I do not know, personally, anything about it. My relations and intercourse with him were not such as to enable me to know what his habits of life were; I have heard some casual remarks about them.

Question. Have you seen him recently?

Answer. Yes, sir; very frequently.

Question. Have you had any conversation with him in connexion with the bonds I have spoken of, which were in his charge in the Interior Department?

Answer. Yes, sir.

Question. Will you be kind enough to tell the committee about what time you had such conversations, and what was the character of them, beginning from the first?

Answer. I suppose it will be better for me to begin at the beginning, and make a connected statement of all I know in reference to this matter. I am not able to specify the exact time, but in July last—I think, perhaps, the last of the month, or possibly as early as the middle—Mr. Bailey went from Washington to Minnesota, where he had been sent by the Secretary, to negotiate a treaty with some Indian tribes away upon the Red river of the North. My impression is, though I am not certain, that I did not have any conversation with him before he went away. I have talked with him about it, and tried to fix the time when I first had a conversation with him about these bonds, but I cannot fix the time, and I will not be positive whether this matter was mentioned before he went away or after.

Question. He went away in July last?

Answer. Yes, sir; I think so.

Question. When did you see him after his return?

Answer. Almost immediately.

Question. When was that?

Answer. I think he was gone about six weeks or two months.

Question. Then he returned in the early part of September?

Answer. I think so, though I do not remember precisely.

Question. Can you tell the committee what was the character of the conversation which you then had with him?

Answer. Yes, sir; the character of the conversation itself was this—I cannot state positively everything which was said.

Question. What was the character of the conversation?

Answer. My impression is that it was at my office. I will not be positive, but I think it was. He was in the habit of coming in frequently; it may have been in his own office; we had a good many business transactions of one kind or another.

Question. Do you recollect whether he sought the interview in order to have a conversation upon this subject, or whether you sought the interview?

Answer. If it was held at his office, I presume I sought it; if it was held at mine, then he came to see me. I cannot state at which place it was held.

Question. State the conversation as distinctly as you can recollect it.

Answer. I can state the substance of it; as to the language that was used, or the precise terms of the conversation, it is impossible for me to state. In that conversation the object of the interview was to talk about his letting William H. Russell have a portion of these bonds. What was said about it I cannot now bring to mind, except that we talked about the fact of his having let Mr. Russell have the bonds under circumstances which were mentioned, and which, perhaps, it will be better to explain.

Question. Try to recollect whether that was the first conversation between Mr. Bailey and yourself in connexion with these bonds?

Answer. I have tried to do it, and I am not able to fix it in my mind. I am not able to say; with your permission I will go on and state how I came to have any knowledge of this matter. William H. Russell has been connected or associated with me in business for several years; it was an accidental connexion in the first instance; he became a partner in a firm out west of Smoot, Russell & Co., in which I was made a partner without my previous knowledge or consent; Mr. Smoot was my partner in the banking-house of Suter, Lea & Co.; Mr. Russell had been here on some business matters in some of the departments, in which he had got Mr. Smoot to assist him; I was absent from the city at the time, and had been absent for several months; this was in the spring; and I had been absent pretty much all winter; growing out of the business matter of Mr. Russell here, in which Mr. Smoot had served him, it was agreed that Mr. Smoot should go out west with Mr. Russell; when they went out there Leavenworth was about springing up as a place of importance; it was known that there was going to be a large amount of money disbursed there in connexion with the expedition to Utah and the army operations being carried on in that quarter; the city of Leavenworth was likely to be a place of large growth, as it turned out, and it seemed to be a favorable location for temporarily establishing a banking office; in order to anticipate the establishment of such an office by other parties who might be tempted by the inducements which were held out, to get the start of others Mr. Smoot proposed to Mr. Russell that they should forthwith start a banking-house there, and Mr. Russell, thinking it might be a good thing, impulsively acquiesced in it, and thereupon they took it upon themselves to advertise a banking firm under the name of Smoot, Russell & Co., using our names—Thomas R. Suter and Luke Lea—as members of that firm, thus making it appear as in connexion with our banking business here; my partner, who was left here in charge during my absence and Mr. Smoot's absence, heard of this a day or two before my return from a long absence at the west, and took no action in reference to it until my return, when he, very much to my surprise, communicated to me the information; I was displeased with it very decidedly, and determined at first with him that we would repudiate the whole thing, and disavow our connexion with it; it was a liberty they had taken with our names which was anything but acceptable to us.

[The witness was here reminded that the matter he was stating was entirely irrelevant to the subject of investigation.]

Witness. The reason why I wished to make the statement was to show how it was that I came to have this conversation with Mr. Bailey.

Question. Had Mr. Bailey any connexion with that partnership?

Answer. None in the world.

Question. Did this conversation with Bailey grow out of any matter connected with this banking-house?

Answer. No, sir; I first saw Mr. Bailey, in connexion with this matter, at the instance of Mr. Russell.

Question. Was the conversation to which you have alluded as

taking place in September or October the first you had with him on the subject?

Answer. No, sir; it was before Bailey went to Minnesota that I first saw him.

Question. Beginning, then, with this conversation, what was the substance of it; what induced you to see Mr. Bailey in reference to it?

Answer. I was proceeding to state that I had a great many matters of business with Mr. Russell in consequence of this accidental—so to speak—connexion with him as members of the partnership I have mentioned in Leavenworth. Some time in July last I was in New York; Mr. Russell was also there, and we had occasion to go on the cars from there together. Travelling along in the cars, and having nothing else to do, we had a long conversation about our business affairs, and in the course of that conversation he had given me a very full exposition of his business affairs, more full than he had ever done previously. In the course of the conversation he mentioned to me the fact that some of Governor Floyd's official acceptances, which he had received and passed, were about to be protested. He expressed great uneasiness about it. He spoke of that in connexion with the government being in his debt, and of its having withheld from him money which was justly due; that the means of the company of which he was the head were very large, but that, in consequence of the government refusing to pay the money they owed, and in consequence of their failure to receive money from other sources upon which they confidently relied, they were unable to take up the acceptances which Governor Floyd had given, and found themselves in this unpleasant predicament. It seemed to disturb him very much that these acceptances were likely to be protested in spite of anything he could do to prevent it. He manifested a great desire to raise money, and by some means or other prevent this result, which he deprecated very deeply. It seemed to make him feel very uneasy and unhappy. He said that unless he could devise some way by which these acceptances could be prevented from going to protest, Governor Floyd would be compelled to retire and break up the cabinet.

Question. Before you go further in your statement, be kind enough to inform us what acceptances of Governor Floyd he referred to, which, if allowed to go to protest, would break up the cabinet?

Answer. I do not know.

Question. Then you are not aware of the character of those acceptances?

Answer. I know nothing about them more than the public generally has been informed of. I knew that Governor Floyd, at the time of these expeditions to Utah, had been facilitating the operations of these large contractors—Russell, Majors & Waddell—by giving his acceptances from time to time, on which they raised money for carrying on the immense business of the transportation of supplies to the Utah expedition.

Question. Did Mr. Russell say about what amount of these acceptances had been given upon which Governor Floyd was likely to be dishonored about that time?

Answer. It is very likely he did, but I do not recollect now.

Question. Were they for services already rendered, or for services to be rendered?

Answer. I do not know.

Question. And you do not remember whether he named the amount?

Answer. He may have done so; I cannot state positively.

Question. Do you recollect what amount was named to you, if any?

Answer. I cannot positively; my recollection is not very good.

Question. Do you remember the amount of money he said it was necessary to raise to save them from protest?

Answer. I think, if I mistake not, it was a little over or a little less than $100,000. It may have been $120,000, though I am not able to state with certainty that it was not less.

Question. That was in July last?

Answer. Yes, sir.

Question. Did he ever tell you, and if so, tell the committee, what amount of money was raised upon these acceptances?

Answer. I never knew about that. I do not know where they were, or who held them.

Question. Did he say nothing about what amount of money had been raised upon them, or from whom he had raised it?

Answer. No, sir.

Question. In fact, did he give the impression that he had parted with the acceptances for the purpose of raising money?

Answer. Oh, yes, certainly; and I think, if I am not mistaken, he had done it in various other instances.

Question. Do you know how he had done it in the other instances?

Answer. I think he put them into market and negotiated them.

Question. How? I do not understand.

Answer. He would draw on the Secretary of War for such an amount under contract coming to them for army transportation to Utah. Governor Floyd would accept the drafts and, then Mr. Russell would go into the market and get the acceptances discounted, just as any other negotiable paper is discounted.

Question. Did Mr. Russell, in the conversation in which he complained of his pecuniary trouble, tell you that he had raised money upon those acceptances?

Answer. That was my understanding. I understood that they were in the hands of parties who held them expecting them to be paid.

Question. Did he, in no single instance, indicate to you from whom he had raised money upon those acceptances?

Answer. I do not know that I ever heard of whom he raised money upon any one of those acceptances.

Question. Do you know how he obtained money upon any one of them?

Answer. Not personally.

Question. What information have you upon that subject?

Answer. I only know that he put that paper into the market and raised money on it. I suppose he got the money wherever he could; that he used the acceptances as he would use any other negotiable paper.

Question. He did not indicate to you, nor do you know, the way in which he raised money upon any one of them; from whom, and at what place or places?

Answer. I do not know that he negotiated any one of them at any time; I know that they were upon the New York market, and that they have depreciated.

Question. Did you suggest any mode in which he could relieve himself?

Answer. No, sir.

Question. Did he suggest any mode?

Answer. Yes, sir; he urged me and said, "is there any plan by which I can raise the money and extricate myself from this dilemma?"

Question. Were you able to suggest none?

Answer. I told him I could not; that if I had the money he knew I would let him have it. He asked me if I knew any mode; if I knew anybody who had any bonds, or stocks, or securities; any one who had any capital lying idle which he could borrow temporarily on security. I told him Washington was a poor place; that I did not know anybody who had money or any considerable amount invested in bonds; that I could not think of any way in which he could raise the money or make any arrangement.

Question. In that conversation was any reference whatever made to the government securities involved in this transaction?

Answer. No, sir.

Question. None by Mr. Russell or yourself?

Answer. Possibly there might have been, but Russell thinks there was not.

Question. Do you recollect nothing in your conversation with Russell which led to the suggestion on his part whether or not bonds of some sort could not be obtained in Washington upon which he could raise money?

Answer. He suggested the idea himself. He wanted to know whether I could tell him where he could find anybody from whom he could borrow bonds. The suggestion was made entirely by him. It came into his mind under the pressure of the exigency in which he was placed.

Question. Try to recollect, on reflection, whether in that conversation there was no suggestion made by you to him, or by him to you, of the chances of his raising money on government securities, and especially on such securities as are involved in this transaction.?

Answer. None on earth. He talked a good deal in reference to the matter, and as to whether some plan could not be suggested by which he could be extricated from this dilemma, and Governor Floyd protected. That seemed to be his great point of anxiety, as he felt under great obligation to Governor Floyd who had done him a favor by giving these acceptances, and he wanted to prevent the injury which would result to Governor Floyd from having these acceptances dishonored, and which would cause Floyd to leave the cabinet. It seemed to distress him exceedingly. He was casting about, as any man would do under such circumstances, and was trying to strike out some plan, and was urging me very earnestly to see whether I could not suggest something or other to extricate him from this dilemma. I told him I could not. Then he went on and said, "I have heard of a man, I understand, in Washington, by the name of Bartey or Bailor, who is an agent for the negotiation of stocks and securities." Says he "do you know him?" I paused and said I did not know any man of that name. Russell seemed rather surprised that I should not know a man of that name who was an operator in stocks, as he understood. "Well" said he, "this man is a friend or connexion of the governor," meaning Secretary Floyd. When he suggested the idea that he was a connexion of Governor Floyd, I recollected that Bailey sustained that connexion to the governor, and supposed that perhaps that was the man he was thinking of, and whom he called Bailor. I told him I knew a man by the name of Bailey who was a connexion of the governor. Said he "I think that is the name." I said I knew him very well, but said "he has not a dollar of stocks; he is as poor as anybody; I have had frequent transactions with him, and have loaned him money from time to time when he was hard up, but he has no stocks that will answer your purpose." It is possible that in that connexion I may have incidentally mentioned the fact that Bailey was a clerk in one of the departments, and was custodian of some trust funds.

Question. Do not you think, upon reflection, that you made such a statement?

Answer. I think it is very likely, but Mr. Russell tells me he does not think I did. If I did, it was merely in that incidental way.

Question. What did Russell say?

Answer. He said he understood that Bailey was a man engaged in the negotiation of stocks; that he had heard of him in that way negotiating in New York a large amount of Florida railroad bonds. Then I recollected that Bailey had before that time consulted with me about a large amount of railroad bonds, in reference to which he had been employed by Senator Yulee on behalf of the State or railroad. He consulted me about the negotiation of them. He told me he had a good thing of it, and wanted to know if I could make any suggestion about them.

Question. When you told him about Bailey being in possession of a large amount of securities, what did he say?

Answer. I said to Russell that I had no idea that Bailey could be of any service to him in putting him in the way of getting any securities for him; but, said I, "he may be of service to you in expediting the payment of the money which the government is owing to you, and which they are delaying the payment of."

Question. How did you expect him to expedite that payment?

Answer. By using his influence with Governor Floyd, or with anybody who might have any connexion with him. Bailey had served me as to money matters in his own department, and I thought he was more efficient than anybody else.

Question. You thought he could get Floyd to pay the money?

Answer. I thought he might expedite the payment of the money which the government was withholding.

Question. Was there in that conversation any reference to the securities of the government in the control and custody of Bailey?

Answer. None on earth.

Question. When did you have your next conversation with Russell?

Answer. Russell seemed impressed with the belief that Bailey had a large amount of stocks and was a dealer in stocks, and he evidently thought that somehow or other Bailey was in a position to put him in the way of getting hold of some securities of some kind which he could borrow for the purpose of extricating him from his dilemma. He asked me to see Bailey, and said that perhaps I could be of some service to him. I told him I did not believe Bailey had control of any securities which he could avail himself of. He still wanted me to see Bailey, because I had suggested to him that he might be of service in getting this money paid at the department, the payment of which Russell said was unreasonably delayed. In that way I supposed Bailey might serve him.

Question. Did you bring the two parties together?

Answer. No, sir; not directly.

Question. Did you do so indirectly, and how?

Answer. Russell requested me to see Bailey, as he thought he might be of service to him. It was a desperate and forlorn idea of his. He asked me if I would see him on my return to Washington. I told him I would. When I reached Washington and went to my office I found that several matters of business had accumulated, and getting engrossed in those matters, this promise to see Bailey got out of my mind. About the time the bank closed Russell came in and said that he had been up to the department and had failed to get them to pay the money. He expected $75,000 or $100,000. He said he had not been able to get them to pay the money in time for his purposes. He asked if I had seen Bailey. I told him I had not. He asked me if I could see him that day. I said that I might perhaps see him the next day. He asked me if I would I said I would.

Question. Did you see him the next day?

Answer. I did.

Question. For what purpose?

Answer. For the purpose of communicating to him the information that Russell desired.

Question. What was that?

Answer. The fact of the predicament in which he was placed, and his great desire to find out some means of getting money to protect the acceptances of Secretary Floyd.

Question. You stated to Bailey that the great desire of Russell was that he might put him in the way of getting some means of protecting those acceptances?

Answer. I did not express any desire to see him myself.

Question. You told Bailey that you saw him at the instance of Russell, who was distressed about those acceptances, and that he had the idea that Bailey could help him in some way.

Answer. I suppose we had an interview of four or five minutes, in which I stated those facts which Russell had communicated to me.

Question. What did Bailey say?

Answer. He said "can it be possible?" He seemed fired up with the idea of Floyd's predicament, and said "can it be possible that Floyd is in this predicament?" or some such expression. I told him I knew nothing except what Russell had told me. He said he would look into it; he seemed to be much exercised about; he said "I am busy now, but will look into it."

Question. Did you tell him that the condition of things would make Floyd's resignation necessary?

Answer. No, sir. I said that Russell had said so.

Question. You did not, in conversation with Bailey, suggest any particular mode in which he could raise the money to save Floyd, but told him that that was Russell's anxiety on the matter, and that he desired to be put into communication with Bailey?

Answer. In conversation with Bailey I never alluded to the trust fund.

Question. Did Bailey make any remark to you indicating his ability or intention?

Answer. None.

Question. Did he ask to see Russell?

Answer. He did not.

Question. Did you make any arrangement by which they came into contact?

Answer. I did not.

Question. Did they come together?

Answer. I heard they did.

Question. Did Mr. Bailey in that conversation indicate his ability in any way to serve Russell?

Answer. He did not make the slightest suggestion about it. He said he would look into it, or inquire into it, to see whether those facts were so; not that he doubted me, but because I had stated those matters to him as information.

Question. What is Bailey's connexion with Secretary Floyd?

Answer. I think their wives are cousins.

Question. Did you see Russell immediately after this, and indicate to him this conversation?

Answer. No, sir. My impression is that I did not see him for some considerable time. He went off that evening to New York, as he had to be there the next day in order to protect the acceptances.

Question. Was this conversation with Bailey the same day Russell got the bonds and went to New York?

Answer. So I understand.

Question. Had you other interviews with Russell and Bailey upon this subject?

Answer. Numerous ones afterwards.

Question. What time in the day did you see Bailey?

Answer. In the middle of the forenoon I should think; before 3 o'clock.

Question. I understand you to say distinctly that in your conversation with Bailey there was no reference to these particular securities, or to any securities, in his custody and under his control in the department?

Answer. There was none whatever; not the slightest intimation about them. It was a thing I did not contemplate as possible. The idea did not come into my mind.

Question. You say you have had subsequent conversations with Bailey upon this subject, but that you did not communicate to Russell this particular conversation?

Answer. I did not see Russell after that conversation for some time; I am not positive.

Question. Are you positive you did not see Russell and communicate that conversation to him?

Answer. I do not think I did. If I did, it has escaped my recollection.

Question. Was he at your office the day you had the interview with Bailey?

Answer. My impression is that he was not. He was there the day before.

Question. His object in coming to see you the day before was to ascertain whether you had seen Bailey?

Answer. That was his object.

Question. Did you say you would see Bailey?

Answer. I told him I would. He did not come back to find out whether I had seen Bailey, because he had communicated with Bailey at the War Department.

Question. Have you had subsequent conversations with Bailey, in which the matter of these bonds was spoken of?

Answer. Yes, sir; repeatedly.

Question. What was the substance of those conversations?

Answer. The conversations have been frequent, and it is impossible for me to state the precise time or what took place in any one of them. Some time after Mr. Russell obtained these bonds I learned the fact. I forget now whether I learned that from Bailey or Russell, and I cannot be positive as to the time, or whether I learned it from Bailey before he went to Minnesota, or whether I spoke to him upon the subject previous to his leaving or after his return. My impression is that I first learned it from Russell; and when Russell told me he had got certain bonds from Bailey, my impression is I told Russell I was apprehensive he had got Bailey into a scrape, or that they had got themselves into a scrape.

Question. Are you utterly unable to fix the time of that knowledge? Bailey went to Minnesota about the middle of July, and returned in October.

Answer. It may be I talked with Bailey before he went away, or it may have been afterwards. I think I learned the fact from one or the other of them before Bailey's return. Whether Bailey communicated to me what he had done before he went to Minnesota I do not know; I think it probable he did.

Question. What did he communicate to you?

Answer. He or Russell communicated to me the fact that Bailey had let Russell have the bonds.

Question. What bonds?

Answer. I think there were $150,000 of North Carolina and Missouri, and perhaps Tennessee bonds—one or the other of those three classes.

Question. Did he state how he had come to do that—with what impulses, and under what idea?

Answer. Yes, sir. He stated that upon the information I gave him he went up to the War Department to see Mr. Floyd; that Mr. Floyd was closeted with General Scott; that he was in a hurry, and, failing to see Mr. Floyd, he had spoken to Colonel Drinkard, and stated to Colonel Drinkard the information which had been communicated to him—that is, the facts that Russell, Majors & Waddell had these acceptances, that they matured soon, and that there was a temporary embarrassment about allowing them to go to protest. Drinkard told him it was true. He said, "It is true that if they are protested they may compromise Mr. Floyd, and he may be obliged to leave the cabinet?" Mr. Drinkard told him it was so. It seems that just at that time Mr. Russell happened to make his appearance at the department, and Drinkard introduced them, as I understand. Bailey took Russell aside and had some conversation, in which this thing was arranged, Russell giving assurances that if Bailey placed any securities in his hands upon which he could raise the money to meet those acceptances, he would certainly return them within the time specified between them—perhaps sixty or ninety days. Russell gave Bailey those assurances, and thereupon, for the purpose of extricating Floyd from his dilemma, he made up his mind himself, without instigation from anybody, to place those trust fund securities in the hands of Russell.

Question. You have stated that before Bailey went to Minnesota—you are pretty confident it was—you learned these facts from him?

Answer. I think Bailey must have mentioned it to me before he went away.

Question. When did you see Russell after that?

Answer. Russell went to New York, and returned in a few days; afterwards he received a considerable amount of money from the government.

Question. When was the conversation, and with whom was it, in which you stated that one or both of them had got themselves into trouble?

Answer. I made the remark when I was informed of the fact by one of them, whichever it was, that those State stocks had been used.

Question. Then you saw Bailey before you did Russell?

Answer. I do not know as I did.

Question. To which one of them did you give this information?

Answer. I cannot state positively which one it was I first saw and learned this thing from.

Question. When you saw Russell after his return from New York, where he had taken this first instalment of bonds, had you any conversation with him about the bonds he had received?

Answer. Yes, sir. He told me had got those bonds from Bailey.

Question. Did he tell you that that process had enabled him to relieve himself?

Answer. That was what he said. He had taken up the acceptances.

Question. Did he tell you in what way he had used the bonds to take up the acceptances?

Answer. He had hypothecated them.

Question. With whom?

Answer. He did not tell me.

Question. Where?

Answer. In New York.

Question. Are you cognizant of the transactions which led to the delivery of the balance of the bonds to Russell?

Answer. Only partially. There were frequent conversations between Russell and Bailey and all the parties. Sometimes I talked separately with them, and sometimes altogether.

Question. After you advised either Russell or Bailey that by this operation they had gotten themselves into a bad business or scrape, did it seem to produce any impression upon them? Did not the operation still go on?

Answer. Yes, sir; it went on, and I account for it in this way: the bonds which Russell got hypothecated in the first instance were so far from meeting his necessities, that when the time came round to return the bonds, his embarrassments were increased instead of being removed.

Question. Did he know precisely where these bonds came from?

Answer. I do not think he did; he tells me that he did not at that time, though he afterwards learned; I do not know at what time Mr. Russell learned the true character of the bonds.

Question. As far as he informed you, was it before or subsequent to this first transaction?

Answer. It was subsequent to the first transaction that he learned they were taken from the Indian fund; at least, if he knew it before I have not been informed of it. I think the reason why he took the course that he did was this: Mr. Russell is a sanguine man, and was disappointed about the means that he expected to have at his command.

Question. That is not testimony; it is rather a plea put in as excuse for Russell. I understand you to say that Russell never informed you, and that you do not know into whose hands these bonds went in the city of New York?

Answer. I do not; I never knew what he did with one of them. I understood, however, that he hypothecated them with various parties.

Question. Have you never learned from Bailey what use was made of them?

Answer. No, sir; I do not think Bailey knew.

Question. Do you know from any source whose hands these bonds went into?

Answer. I do not know what Russell did with any of them.

Question. Have you any knowledge of where they are now?

Answer. I have not; not one of them.

Question. Nor any information?

Answer. No information upon the subject; I never asked Russell what he had done with them, and never received any information from him except that he had taken them to New York and hypothecated them for the purpose of raising money.

Question. Did Mr. Russell in this conversation, when speaking of the peculiarly embarrassing position in which Governor Floyd would find himself if these acceptances were not taken up, state why Governor Floyd would be compelled to resign?

Answer. No, sir; the impression made upon my mind, however, was that Governor Floyd had improperly, and perhaps illegally, made these acceptances.

Question. Did Mr. Russell make that statement to you?

Answer. No, sir; it was rather an inference of mine that Governor Floyd had been at least guilty of an indiscretion in giving out these acceptances; that he had gone beyond his strict authority; and that it would be a very delicate matter for him if the acceptances were not taken up.

Examination by the chairman.

Question. If I understood you correctly, you stated that the first conversation you had with Russell was on the cars coming from New York to Washington?

Answer. Yes, sir; that was the conversation which led me to see Mr. Bailey.

Question. That was before Bailey went to Minnesota?

Answer. Yes, sir; it was early in July. Mr. Bailey went to Minnesota, I think, in the latter part of July; I do not recollect the precise time, but it was after my conversation with him.

Question. Was it on the next day after the conversation referred to between you and Russell on the cars that Russell called at your office to know whether you had seen Bailey?

Answer. It must have been, because Russell expected me to see Bailey the next day.

Question. And it was the next day after that that you had an interview with Bailey?

Answer. Yes, sir; it was the next day after Russell called at my office.

Question. Was it that day that the $150,000 bonds were delivered to Russell?

Answer. That is what I understand.

Question. How long afterwards was it that you saw Bailey or Russell, and stated to them that they had got themselves into a scrape by delivering these bonds?

Answer. I cannot recollect precisely; it was soon after—several days after, I suppose. I think before Bailey went to Minnesota he saw me in regard to some business matters, and in some of these interviews he may have mentioned this fact.

Question. Fix the time as nearly as you can?

Answer. I am sorry I cannot do it precisely.

Question. How did that communication take place to you and Russell?

Answer. I do not think I saw them together. I do not know that

I saw them together at any time until after Bailey's return from Minnesota.

Question. Did you see them together soon afterwards?

Answer. It is quite likely that I did, though I cannot be positive whether I saw them together or separately.

Question. Did you state to them separately or together, soon after Bailey's return, that these bonds had been improperly removed?

Answer. That was the whole of my conversation with them ever afterwards.

Question. At that time had any others than the $150,000 of bonds been delivered to Russell?

Answer. I think not.

Question. But you learned from the parties separately that other bonds were from time to time delivered from Bailey to Russell?

Answer. Yes, sir.

Question. I will ask you whether you are acquainted with the Secretary of the Interior?

Answer. Very well.

Question. Did you at any time after the knowledge of the use of these bonds by Bailey call upon the Secretary and inform him that Bailey was using them in the manner he did?

Answer. I did not. It is perhaps necessary for me to state here my view of the matter.

The CHAIRMAN said the committee desired the witness only to state facts.

The WITNESS remarked that the position he occupied in reference to this matter was a very peculiar one; that by simply stating facts, without being permitted to accompany them with explanation, he might render himself liable to a criminal prosecution; when if permitted to explain, it would appear that he was innocent.

Question. You state that you have had recently conversations with Bailey and Russell with reference to these transactions?

Answer. Yes, sir.

Question. Where did these conversations take place?

Answer. Some of them have taken place at my bank, and some at Russell's room here. Mr. Bailey has been at my house, and I have been at his boarding-house. We have had repeated conversations at different times.

Question. Was there ever any person present at these conversations but yourselves?

Answer. Never.

Question. When was the last conversation you had with Bailey and with Russell?

Answer. At the jail, day before yesterday, I think.

Question. Did they send to you, and request you to come, or did you go voluntarily?

Answer. I went there voluntarily.

Question. When you got to the jail you conversed with them freely in regard to these transactions?

Answer. Yes, sir; just as anybody else would.

Question. Have you ever had more than one conversation with them at the jail?

Answer. I have been there twice, and seen Mr. Russell. I have seen Bailey there but once. When I first went Russell only was there, Bailey having been released on bail. Afterwards Bailey was remanded to jail, and the last time I was there I saw both.

Question. I understand you to say that you had no connexion with these parties in these transactions?

Answer. Only as a friend.

Question. And your friendship for the parties was so great as to induce you voluntarily to go and see them about this matter?

Answer. Yes, sir.

Question. And to hold frequent conversations at various times with both parties?

Answer. Yes, sir.

Question. You say you have known Bailey some three years?

Answer. I do not know how long. I suppose about that time.

Question. You have, if I understand you correctly, been very intimate with Mr. Bailey since he has been in the city?

Answer. No, sir; I cannot say that I have been very intimate with him.

Question. Has he been frequently at your house?

Answer. Not very often.

Question. Has he frequently been at your office?

Answer. He has not been there very often.

Question. Have you been frequently at his office or room?

Answer. Not very often.

Question. How often?

Answer. Not more than half a dozen times, I suppose, in my life.

Question. Your acquaintance was not very intimate, then?

Answer. It was not.

Question. Not such as to make you intimate personal friends?

Answer. I could not say that we were such. Our acquaintance related more to business matters than personal matters.

Question. What were your business matters to which you refer?

Answer. I must say that they had nothing to do with these transactions. I do not know that I ought to expose my business transactions.

The CHAIRMAN. I understand you say that you had frequent business transactions with Bailey. I repeat the question, what were those transactions?

WITNESS. I decline to answer. I do not think I am called upon to disclose private business.

Question. Were they of a monetary character?

WITNESS. I am willing to say that they were, but I will not be drawn into what I believe to be a wrong; that is, to expose the confidential business transactions of those who confide in me.

The witness was here directed to retire.

After consultation, the committee deternined not at present to press the question which the witness had declined to answer.

The witness was again recalled.

Question. I want to ask you if you know who compose the firm known as Russell, Majors & Waddell?

Answer. Wm. H. Russell is one. I do not recollect the christian names of Mr. Majors and Mr. Waddell. There are others, I believe, who are silent partners, but I do not know their names.

Examination by Mr. Harris.

Question. You stated before that you had frequent conversations both with Mr. Russell and Mr. Bailey after this first $150,000 transaction?

Answer. Yes, sir.

Question. And that the character of these bonds was frequently spoken of?

Answer. Yes, sir.

Question. Now I want you to recollect, if you can, whether you had any such conversation with Mr. Russell prior to this $150,000 transaction?

Answer. None in the world.

Question. I want you to state as clearly as you can whether he was not aware of the character of these bonds even before this $150,000 transaction was communicated to you?

Answer. My own best information and judgment is, that he was not. I don ot think that Mr. Russell knew the character of these bonds when he received the first $150,000 of them.

Question. You say that afterwards you had frequent conversations with these parties, both of them, in which you stated to them that the transaction was a dangerous one, and that they would get into trouble?

Answer. Yes, sir.

Question. How many conversations do you think you had with these parties after this statement was made by you?

Answer. I cannot say how many. They were frequent.

Question. All the time, however, after this disclosure of the character of the transactions was made, and the transactions still went on, these parties communicated freely to you their operations?

Answer. Partly they did. I cannot say they did fully. I did not know the precise times at which further advances were made, nor did I know the amounts. I learned afterwards, rather incidentally, that other advances had been made; not that I was consulted about them in advance at all. I was not advised what bonds they had, or the precise negotiations that took place between them, but I was advised from time to time that further advances had been made.

Question. Were you not informed of the fact that the same character of negotiations were going on that took place in reference to this first advance of $150,000?

Answer. O yes, I am free to admit that.

Examination by Mr. Conkling.

Question. I wish you would state to me at what time you had the first conversation with Mr. Russell after you learned that these bonds had been handed to him?

Answer. I am not able to state precisely when it was.

Question. I am asking you to fix the time as nearly as possble. How long after you first learned that these funds to the amount of $150,000 had been handed to him?

Answer. I am not able to state.

Question. As nearly as you can.

Answer. My impression is, that he went to New York. How long he was there, and how long before I saw him, I am not able now to state.

Question. Still I repeat the question, as nearly as you can?

Answer. It may have been a week, and it may have been two or three weeks.

Question. Is that as near as you can fix it?

Answer. It is.

Question. Was it in that conversation that Mr. Russell first spoke to you or you to him in reference to his having received the bonds?

Answer. It was.

Question. And was it in the same conversation that you first made to him the remark you did in reference to its being a hazardous and unwarrantable transaction, that "they had got themselves into a scrape?"

Answer. I do not recollect that in that conversation I stated to Russell why it was that they had got into a scrape.

Question. My question is simply whether you made that remark in that conversation, and that admits of an answer "yes" or "no."

Answer. I will use the language I then used as nearly as I can. I said: "I am afraid you have got into a scrape," or "a bad predicament about it."

Question. Did Mr. Russell reply to that remark?

Answer. Yes, sir.

Question. What was the reply?

Answer. He expressed some astonishment, and said: "Do you not believe I will return them?"

Question. What did you say to that?

Answer. I said: "I have no doubt of it."

Question. And what did he say?

Answer. "Of course I shall return them."

Question. What further conversation then, if any, was there upon that point?

Answer. I do not recollect.

Question. Subsequently between you and Mr. Russell was this same point of danger recurred to?

Answer. All the time throughout; and I urged upon them always the speediest restoration of the bonds.

Question. Did Mr. Russell, at any time subsequent to this first conversation, put any question to you for information as to the character of those bonds?

Answer. I do not think he did; I do not think Russell cared what the character of them was.

Question. Have you received any written communication from Mr. Russell at any time in reference to those bonds?

Answer. Mr. Russell has written to me letters, in which he has referred to those bonds, and to these transactions, repeatedly.

Question. When first?

Answer. I cannot say when.

Question. As near as you can tell?

Answer. It may be early after he received them, and from that time up to the present day.

Question. Was it soon after he received those bonds that he wrote you in reference to them?

Answer. I do not think it was.

Question. How soon after, according to your recollection?

Answer. I am really not able to fix any time. It may have been a month, and it may not have been until two months.

Question. How long ago, according to your best recollection, did you first receive a letter from Russell touching these bonds?

Answer. Well, perhaps it may have been two months ago; I would not be positive.

Question. And how many letters in all have you received from him touching those bonds or alluding to them?

Answer. Perhaps five or six.

Question. Where are those letters?

Answer. I destroyed them.

Question. When?

Answer. When I got them; I do not preserve private, confidential letters.

Question. When did you destroy those letters? I do not want to know what your customs are.

Answer. As I received them, as is my rule in all such cases.

Question. Is that the nearest answer you can give?

Answer. Yes, sir, because it is the fact.

Question. And that is the nearest statement as to the time of the destruction of those letters?

Answer. I have stated the time exactly. If you want to know as to the time of the receipt of those letters, I cannot tell.

Question. How recently have you destroyed any letter from Russell?

Answer. I think I destroyed one last week.

Question. What day?

Answer. Perhaps it was Friday; it may have been Saturday.

Question. When was that letter received?

Answer. Five minutes before I destroyed it.

Question. It came by post?

Answer. Yes, sir, from New York.

Question. Have you received any letter since from Russell?

Answer. No, sir.

Question. Have you received from Russell any other written communication about those bonds?

Answer. None at all, except in business correspondence, and in answer to letters I wrote to him upon the subject.

Question. Did you reply to those letters?

Answer. Yes, sir; there were letter and answer, letter and answer.

Question. Can you state how many of those letters you have referred to were in answer to letters previously written by you?

Answer. I cannot state precisely; there may have been five or six, or more; we never had much correspondence upon the subject, because our communications were generally conversational.

Question. How many in all were there of letters alluding to these bonds?

Answer. I have stated I do not know; there may have been four, five, or six, and there may have been as many as ten, in which allusion of some kind was made to them.

Question. And you cannot state how many of these letters were in reply to yours, and how many you replied to?

Answer. They were all one in answer to another.

Question. I am asking you if you can state how many, on the one hand, were replies to yours, and how many you replied to?

Answer. I think all of Russell's letters were in reply to letters I wrote him; I do not know as I got any letters in which the bonds were alluded to, except in reply to something I had said.

Question. Did you keep copies of your letters?

Answer. No, sir.

Question. Is it your general practice not to keep copies?

Answer. The bank keeps copies of business letters which we write upon the ordinary business of the bank; but my rule is not to keep copies of private correspondence. These letters were of a private and strictly confidential character—of the most sacred and confidential nature.

Question. And was it owing to their sacredness that you did not keep copies?

Answer. It was; it was for that reason that I destroyed the letters upon this subject. I betray no private confidence myself, and keep no letters which will betray it.

Question. Will you state to the committee the contents of the first letter you received from Russell alluding to those bonds, as nearly as you can?

Answer. I think the first letter was giving me some assurance that he would speedily be able to return the bonds. I had written him, as I had urged him in conversation, to do so; and I think the first letter he ever wrote upon the subject was giving me assurance that he was exerting himself to get the control of them, and that he would speedily bring them back and restore them.

Question. In what month was that letter written?

Answer. I think it was some two or three, perhaps three months ago. I think it was in October last.

Question. Give the day of the month.

Answer. I cannot.

Question. Is that all you can state of the contents of that letter?

Answer. I cannot state positively that I have given all, but that is my impression.

Question. How long after that did you receive the next letter?

Answer. It is impossible to say, but it may have been two or three weeks.

Question. Give the contents of that next letter.

Answer. They were all pretty much of the same character.

Question. Give the contents as nearly as you can.

Answer. It is impossible for me to do it. Mr. Russell never wrote me much about them; his allusions to them were brief.

Question. Can you give any part of the contents of that next letter?

Answer. Nothing, except in a general way.

Question. Can you give, in substance, any part of it?

Answer. No, sir.

Question. Why can you not?

Answer. Because I do not recollect; it was something about the bonds, and in answer to my plying him to return them; and I think all he wrote me was to quiet me about his returning them.

Question. Is that all you can state about the contents of the letter?

Answer. Yes, sir.

Question. The first letter was in October?

Answer. Yes, sir.

Question. The second one in two or three weeks after?

Answer. Yes, sir.

Question. And the third one, how soon after that?

Answer. It may have been two or three weeks; I cannot tell.

Question. Can you give the contents of the third letter?

Answer. No, sir.

Question. And for the same reason, that you do not recollect?

Answer. Yes, sir.

Question. How soon again came a letter?

Answer. It is impossible for me to tell; it may have been 5, or 10, or 15, or 20 days; I cannot fix the time.

Question. Can you give the contents of that letter, or any part of it?

Answer. No, sir; and for the same reason, that I have forgotten.

Question. The next letter, as near as you can tell.

Answer. I do not know as there was a next.

Question. Then I come to the letter which you destroyed within a week. How long a letter was that?

Answer. I suppose it was about a page.

Question. Letter paper?

Answer. Yes, sir.

Question. Can you state the contents of that letter?

Answer. Yes, sir; perhaps I can.

Question. Give it in order, and all you can of it, beginning with the date.

Answer. I cannot say what the date was; it may have been Thursday or Friday; it seems to me that I got it on Saturday morning.

Question. Dated in New York?

Answer. Yes, sir.

Question. Any place in New York?

Answer. I cannot say.

Question. Was there any stamp upon the letter indicating the particular place from which it came?

Answer. I cannot say whether it was written in his office or at the office of the Pony Express, where he generally writes his letters. The letter was in answer to one I wrote him. The substance of the letter was excusing himself for not coming over here immediately, with all the bonds he could possibly control, as I had urged him to do. That was the sum and substance of the letter, with the exception to some brief allusion to some other business.

Question. Can you give any of the language of the letter?

Answer. Perhaps I might, but it would be rather a vague thing. "Yours of such a date is received. It will be impossible for me to come to Washington, as you request. I have business that will compel me to remain here until Sunday, and I will be over on Monday morning; you may expect me on Monday morning." I forget whether he was any more specific. He had an appointment and engagements which prevented him coming over, as I had requested and urged him to do, until Sunday night. He would try to come on Sunday morning, but that his business arrangements were such there that he could not, he believed, make his arrangements to leave and come before Sunday night.

Question. What further?

Answer. Nothing.

Question. He did not mention the bonds in the letter?

Answer. I do not think he spoke of the bonds in this last letter.

Question. At whose instance had you written the letter which this letter of a week ago was a reply to?

Answer. At my own instance.

Question. And the letter urged him to get all the bonds he could?

Answer. Yes, sir; all the bonds he could control, and to get up the bonds and restore them as fast as he could.

Question. Have you any memoranda relating to this?

Answer. None in the world; I never saw one of the bonds in my life.

Question. Did you state that you had recently made a communication to the Secretary of the Interior about this matter?

Answer. No, sir.

Question. Have you stated the matter to the Secretary of the Interior?

Answer. I have stated the whole case to him.

Question. When was it?

Answer. Sunday night last.

Question. What time?

Answer. In the evening, about tea time; about dark I went up there with a certain gentleman.

Question. Who?

Answer. Senator Rice.

Question. And what you stated to the Secretary you stated in his presence?

Answer. Mostly; I think he left before I got entirely through the statement. Judge Black also was present.

Question. Did you go to the Secretary in consequence of a conversation you had previously had with any one?

Answer. In consequence of a conversation with Bailey and Rice.

Question. Was Mr. Rice present at the whole interview between you and Bailey which led you to go to the Secretary?

Answer. He was not present.

Question. Then the interviews with Rice and with Bailey were separate?

Answer. Yes, sir.

Question. Where was the interview with Bailey?

Answer. At my house, Sunday morning.

Question. And was it that interview which led you to go and make the statement to the Secretary?

Answer. Bailey had stated to me things which had taken place before the cabinet.

Question. You say Bailey came to your house Sunday morning last?

Answer. Yes, sir.

Question. Detail that interview as near as you can.

Answer. Bailey came to my house Sunday morning, some time in the forenoon—perhaps 11 o'clock—in a state of great excitement. He told me had been up all night before the cabinet; that they had investigated this matter; had examined the safe, and all about it; had interrogated him about all he knew, and that he had told everything he knew about it; that they had counted the bonds, and found it all true that he had stated to them about the bonds and coupons, and all that; that he had made, as he thought, a very favorable impression on the cabinet, and that they were disposed to sympathize with him deeply, but that he had refused, as he promised he would do, to mention my name as the party which had given him the information originally which had led him to do this thing; that they had insisted on knowing who it was who had given him these facts which had led him to put himself in the way to find out whether the facts were true or not, and which resulted in his giving the bonds to Russell. Bailey represented to me that whereas he had promised me, as he knew me to be an innocent party in the matter, he never would mention my name—and Russell had made the same pledge—he was determined to abide by the pledge, and keep it to the last, and, if I insisted upon it, he never would disclose it, yet that the favorable effect which his statement had made upon the members of the cabinet was prejudicial, in his estimation, by his refusal to give the name of the party who had given him the information which I communicated to him as to the predicament in which Governor Floyd was placed; that the members of the cabinet plied him in every way to get him to disclose the name of the party who gave the information to him; that he refused, and told them that he would suffer the tortures of the Inquisition before he would give the information. He said, "Lee, you can judge for yourself whether you will allow this fact to be made known or not; you can see how it places me." He told me, moreover, that they were suspecting various parties, and named some who had been suspected as the parties who had imparted this information from Russell. "Well," said I, "I had hoped that it never would be necessary for my name to be mentioned in connexion with this transaction; you know how much I have deprecated it; you know that I had no interest in it; that I was an innocent party in regard to it; and you can very well understand how, in my situation, the disclosure of the fact that I had in any way a connexion with it would subject me to suspicion." Said I, "I believe it will ruin me to have it known; but if what you have said is true—you are under excitement now, and it may be you may not judge correctly about it—if it is necessary for you to have the benefit of a full disclosure in regard to it, and if other parties whom we know are innocent are subjected to suspicion in regard to it, I will go and communicate the information myself that I was the party who imparted the information to you."

"Now," said I, "you may be mistaken about this. There may not be a necessity for it. You say that Senator Rice was present during your examination before the cabinet; do you suppose that he would have any objection to seeing me, and talking with me about it?" He said he thought not. I asked him if he thought Senator Rice would be willing to come to my house during the day. He said he thought he would. I then said, "present my respects to Senator Rice, and tell him he will do me a favor if he will call at my house at 3 o'clock." He came, and, in answer to my inquiry, said that the refusal to disclose my name had created a prejudice in the minds of the members of the cabinet; that it had created a suspicion that there were other parties connected with the transaction. "Well," said I, "Senator Rice, although I know that the fact of my name being publicly mentioned in connexion with this thing will be to me the greatest calamity that ever befel me in the course of my life, yet it is not in my heart to refuse to disclose it. Will you go with me to see Secretary Thompson?" He said he would. I asked him to do me the favour to take a seat in my carriage. He did, and went there with me. I went voluntarily before him, and stated all I knew in reference to the matter.

Question. Will you state, as nearly as you can, Bailey's language when he told you that he was suffering for his refusal to withhold your name?

Answer. I wish I could, but I could not do his language justice. He is an eloquent fellow sometimes—a man of fine sense.

Question. Please state just that one remark which informed you that he was suffering in the estimation of the cabinet in consequence of withholding your name.

Answer. The idea was, that—

Question. I do not want the idea—you have given that—I ask you simply to give your verbal impression of his remark.

Answer. I would be glad if I knew how to do it.

Question. Give it as nearly as possible.

Answer. I do not recollect precisely what were his words. It was the ideas and not the language that impressed me.

Question. If you cannot give the language, will you be good enough to repeat what were the ideas.

Answer. The idea was, that in the estimation of the cabinet he was greatly prejudiced in consequence of his suppressing the name of his informant. With regard to the rest of his statement, they believed him to be stating the truth; they believed that he had made a fair and honest disclosure. He said Secretary Thompson told him he had as much confidence in him as he ever had had.

Question. Suppressing the name of his informant of what?

Answer. The man who gave him the information that Governor Floyd was about to be compromised, and which information led him to do this thing.

Question. Do you mean the committee to understand that you thought it was a cause of ruin to any man that he should have informed another of the fact that Governor Floyd's acceptances were out?

Answer. No, sir, by no means; but what I mean to say is this: that these bonds having been abstracted, if the fact were to become publicly known that I furnished the information which led to the abstraction of the bonds, it would, in the estimation of the public, so connect me with the transaction as to blast my reputation and destroy me. I have felt it most keenly.

Question. Is there any other explanation you desire to make in connexion with this point?

Answer. No, sir.

Question. Did you understand that the mere fact of conveying to Bailey a knowledge of the predicament of Governor Floyd was the thing of which other parties were suspected, and whose reputations were to suffer by it?

Answer. No, sir. The suspicion in the minds of the members of the cabinet was, that the man who had communicated these facts was one of a band of conspirators who were concerned in concocting a scheme for the plunder of this fund. Mr. Bailey said, "I know you are innocent."

Question. Then I understand you that the point was as suggested by Mr. Bailey, who had suggested the doing of this thing, that what the cabinet desired was the name of the man who had suggested the doing of this thing—who had conceived the idea?

Answer. No; the idea upon the mind of the cabinet was, that the man who had given the information upon which Bailey had acted was connected with a conspiracy or a combination, entered into, as they believed, in New York and elsewhere, for the abstraction of these bonds.

Question. And it was the name of the man who had given such information that they wanted?

Answer. It was the name of the man who had communicated the facts which led him to do this thing, because they thought the possession of the name of the man who had communicated the facts which brought about an interview between Bailey and Russell leading to this transaction, would give them a clue by which they could learn the names of other parties concerned in the abstraction of the bonds. They believed they could find out through this man the names of all the parties concerned.

Question. Will you account for the fact that during the whole progress of this matter, in your efforts to obtain the restitution of these bonds, you never inquired of Mr. Russell where they were, or who had them?

Answer. I simply account for it in the fact that it did not concern me one way or the other to know.

Question. Have you never inquired of Mr. Russell what he knew of the whereabouts of these bonds?

Answer. Never.

Question. Or the possibility of regaining them?

Answer. I never have.

Question. And the only explanation you can give of that is, that it did not concern you to know?

Answer. That was all. I only knew that they had been abstracted, and that was sufficient for me.

Question. How did it concern you to have them returned?

Answer. You may have your suspicions. I have my knowledge, and I am glad of the opportunity of stating what my motives were. I am glad you have called for such a response.

Question. The simple question was, how it concerned you to have those bonds returned?

Witness. That is precisely what I wish to have an opportunity to answer, and I hope I shall not be interrupted this time. The fact was just this: having been innocently instrumental in leading Mr. Bailey to do this thing, I in my heart felt great anxiety to have the bonds restored as speedily as possible. And that is not all: these gentlemen were my friends—Mr. Russell more particularly—and I would have considered myself a dishonored man if I had disclosed the facts of the case, having come to my knowledge in the way that they did. A third reason was, that I believed the best way to prevent loss to the public, and to have the bonds restored, was not to have the thing made public until Russell should have had an opportunity of making the restoration. These were the considerations which influenced me. Both Russell and Bailey will bear witness, if they tell the truth, that, from the first, my main desire and object was, that they should shape their course so as to bring back the bonds as speedily as possible.

Question. Have you no suspicion where any of these bonds are?

Answer. I have not the slightest.

Question. Have you no suspicion where any of them have been since they left Bailey's possession?

Answer. I have not. The truth is, I did not want to know. I simply knew that these bonds had been taken, and I wanted them to bring them back. I thought the best way to accomplish that object was to keep the matter a secret, and let them have the opportunity of bringing them back. Coming to me in the way in which this information came, I would have died—I would have suffered martyrdom before I would have made it public.

Question. When did the obligation upon the part of Bailey arise?

Answer. Some time ago. I cannot recollect precisely the date. I think it was when I saw Bailey and Russell together on some occasion. I was manifesting great anxiety and uneasiness—for I tell you it gave me great anxiety and distress—in reference to the matter; that they told me I need not be uneasy about it; that I had not been connected with it in any manner, and that, whatever occurred, my name should not be mentioned in connexion with it.

Question. When was that?

Answer. I think perhaps three months ago.

Question. How soon after the bonds had been delivered?

Answer. It was some considerable time, but I cannot say how long.

Question. Cannot you state more definitely how long?

Answer. I cannot. I know that I manifested considerable uneasiness in reference to it from the beginning. I urged that the bonds should be brought back.

Question. Was there, on the first interview between you and Bailey, any injunction of secrecy?

Answer. None in the world.

Question. Then, so far as that first interview was concerned, in what you communicated to Bailey, there never was any injunction of secrecy about it at any time?

Answer. There was an injunction of secrecy, so far as mentioning my name was concerned. They gave me their assurance that I need not be uneasy, for my name never should be mentioned. I said to them, "I trust that, whatever occurs, my name never will be mentioned in connexion with the affair;" and they both promised it never should; and if I had not voluntarily disclosed it, I do not believe it ever would have been. I do not believe either of them would have betrayed my confidence.

Question. Did you ever, at any time, promise not to disclose this transaction?

Answer. I do not recollect that I ever promised not to disclose it. I certainly never intended to disclose it.

Question. Why did you not disclose this first transaction?

Answer. I have already stated that I was innocently the cause of Bailey's having been led to do this thing, and I considered it a matter of sacred honor that I should not involve him in trouble or difficulty about it.

Question. Then, if I comprehend your position, you having told Bailey that Governor Floyd had issued acceptances which were likely to be dishonored, which information led him to other things, you thought there arose from that transaction an obligation of secrecy paramount to your general obligation to disclose a dishonest transaction?

Answer. That was one reason. Although what I did was innocently intended, yet it led him into the predicament in which he was afterwards placed.

Question. Was there any other reason?

Answer. I have already stated that I believed the only way to have the government protected was not to disclose the transaction. I had full confidence up to a very late period, as I have every reason to believe was his intention, that Mr. Russell would bring back the bonds.

Question. Did you continue in that belief after the abstraction of the bonds went on?

Answer. Up to a very late period.

Question. How soon did you know that $800,000 worth of bonds had gone?

Answer. I did not know it until they were gone.

Question. As these deliveries were made, you knew of it soon after?

Answer. I did not know what amount of deliveries were made from time to time. I think, at the very last, a large amount was delivered of which I had no knowledge.

Examination by Mr. Harris.

Question. You say you have known Bailey about three years?

Answer. Yes, sir.

Question. And you assumed and considered him to be an honest, upright man?

Answer. I knew nothing to the contrary.

Question. Upon what theory do you explain his going to this particular fund for the relief of Russell?

Answer. I have no knowledge of his motives; my opinion is that his object was to extricate his friend Governor Floyd.

Question. My question is, whether there was anything at all that you can recollect, or in your knowledge, that explains his recourse to this particular fund for the purpose of raising money to extricate Russell from his difficulty?

Answer. I know of nothing, except his desire to serve Governor Floyd.

Question. Are you in possession of any particular information which explains his recourse to this particular fund?

Answer. No, sir; except the fact that he had these funds in his possession.

Examination by the chairman.

Question. Was the last letter you addressed to Russell sent before or after this transaction was disclosed?

Answer. It was before.

Question. Did you take any measures after the fraud had been detected, directly or indirectly, to inform Russell of the fact in New York?

Answer. I think, in one of the letters I wrote to him, I told him that the fact would be made known to the public.

Question. That is not answering my question. My question is, whether you, directly or indirectly, adopted any measures to inform Mr. Russell, after the disclosure of the fraud had been made, of the fact that it had been made?

Answer. Not after there was a public disclosure.

Question. Just before?

Answer. Yes, sir; I think two or three days before I wrote to him that the thing would soon be disclosed.

Question. What induced you to believe it would soon be disclosed?

Answer. Mr. Bailey told me he should disclose it before Secretary Thompson left the cabinet.

Question. And then you wrote immediately to Russell?

Answer. Yes, sir; I think I did.

Question. Was that the last letter you wrote to him?

Answer. I think it was; I think I had expressed before to him my apprehension that it would not be possible to conceal it.

Question. What was the date of that letter?

Answer. I think it was Thursday or Friday. Bailey had then told me that he might tell Governor Floyd about it.

Question. Do you know whether any other measures were adopted to inform Russell that Bailey had been arrested and the fraud disclosed, or that the fraud had been disclosed, and that Bailey would be arrested, by any other person?

Answer. I do not. I did not advise Russell that Bailey had been arrested.

Question. How long after Russell had been arrested and brought to this city before you saw him?

Answer. He was brought here on Monday morning; he was first taken to jail, I think, and then went to his house; he had rented a house in this city, on F street; I heard in the afternoon that he had again been taken to jail, and I went there to see him.

Question. Did you know of any use that Russell had for money in this city?

Answer. I know that he is in the habit of spending a good deal of money in Washington; I do not call to mind any particular case just now.

Question. Do you know whether he has purchased property in this city within the last few years?

Answer. I do not remember to have heard of his having done so. He bought some property in New York some time ago, but I think I never heard of his buying property in this city.

Question. For himself, or anybody else?

Answer. No, sir, not that I ever heard of. He has rented a house here, but I never heard of his having bought property here.

Question Have you received any letters from Mr. Bailey in reference to this transaction?

Answer. I think he has once or twice sent me notes that he wanted to see me, or wanted me to call on him.

Question. How many notes have you received?

Answer. I have received, it may be, at different times half a dozen such notes.

Question. What did you do with them?

Answer. I destroyed them; I never keep notes of this sort.

Question. Did you answer them in writing?

Answer. I think I have written notes to him sometimes when I have received them from him, and sometimes have responded verbally.

Question. Can you inform the committee of about the date of the first note you received?

Answer. I cannot; I did not attach any importance to them at the time.

Question. As near as possible.

Answer. I cannot mention any time.

Question. When did you receive the last note from him?

Answer. I am not able to say positively.

Question. Fix the time as near as you can.

Answer. Some time within the last week.

Question. Since he has been arrested?

Answer. No, sir. I think I received a note requesting me to call and see him after he had made the exposure, but they were permitting him to run at large. The note requested me to call and see him at his house.

Question. I understand you to say you cannot inform the committee of the time of the reception of any note sent you by Bailey?

Answer. I am not able to do it now; upon reflection I may be able to do so.

Question. What were the contents of the first note?

Answer. I cannot say.

Question. Can you give the substance of it?

Answer. I cannot.

Question. Can you recollect the language of either letter?

Answer. I cannot. I do not think I received any note at all which contained anything except an invitation to see him, or something of that kind.

Question. Do I understand you to say you cannot recollect the language of either of the notes you received?

Answer. I said I could not.

Question. Can you recollect the substance of either note?

Answer. I cannot.

Question. What did he want to see you about?

Answer. To talk about this affair. It was a matter of absorbing interest to him and to me.

Question. Did you understand him to state in the notes that his only object was to have a conversation with you in regard to this matter?

Answer. I think he simply requested me to come and see him.

Question. Did you go and see him?

Answer. I did, frequently.

Question. What occurred at those interviews?

Answer. We talked about this affair. Nothing material occurred, further than I have already stated; such general conversation as men would have who had knowledge of such a thing. We were in the habit of talking about it in its various bearings.

Question. Do you think it was as much as three months ago that you received the first letter from him?

Answer. It is possible, but I cannot say. My recollection of dates is bad, and always has been.

Question. To the best of your recollection, the first note must have been received as much as three months ago?

Answer. I do not think it was as long ago as that. I have told you I did not recollect, and it is impossible for me to say. I do not think his first letter contained any reference to this thing.

Question. Was it two months ago?

Answer. Possibly, but I cannot say. I really cannot say when the first communication was received from him. It may have been two, and it may have been three months ago. I do not think it was as long as three months ago.

Question. Did you keep copies of your replies to Bailey's notes?

Answer. No, sir.

Question. And you did not preserve the originals from him?

Answer. No, sir.

Question. You say you went there to talk about this matter. Was there no special object in your visit, or was the object merely a general one, to have a general conversation?

Answer. Sometimes there might have been some special feature which I wanted to talk with him about, or he wished to talk with me about.

Question. What was that special feature?

Answer. I cannot recollect.

Question. Can you recollect what he said to you or you to him?

Answer. It is impossible for me to single out any particular thing. We talked about Governor Floyd and other things.

MONDAY, *December* 31, 1860.

Hon. JOHN B. FLOYD sworn.

Examination by Mr. Conkling.

Question. Mr. Floyd, you have been for some time Secretary of War?

Answer. Yes, sir.

Question. From what time to what time?

Answer. From about the 4th of March, 1857, until day before yesterday, when I resigned.

Question. Do you know Wm. H. Russell?

Answer. I do.

Question. How long have you known him?

Answer. Some two or three years. I have known him since about the time he entered into his last contract for the transportation of army supplies, which I think was in the winter of 1857.

Question. Where was his residence when you first knew him?

Answer. I do not know; at the west somewhere.

Question. Do you know in what firm he was a partner?

Answer. I do not know. The contract was entered into in the name of Russell, Majors & Waddell.

Question. You know of none of his partners except Majors and Waddell?

Answer. I do not know them. I saw Majors once.

Question. What contracts exist now between the government and Russell's firm.

Answer. They are contracts for the transportation of supplies to New Mexico, Arizona, and the southwest.

Question. One contract, or more?

Answer. I think but one. There may be some minor contracts. The general contract may be divided into different heads. There is a general contract for transportation to New Mexico, and there may be some contracts for transportation from New Mexico to the different posts, but of that I am not certain. My answer would be that I know of but one contract.

Question. Which provides for transportation from what point to what point?

Answer. From any point the government may designate to New Mexico and the southwest. The contract itself would be the best proof of what the terms of the contract are.

Question. Have other contracts with Russell previously existed?

Answer. Yes, sir.

Question. How many?

Answer. But one I know anything about, which is the contract for the transportation of supplies to Utah.

Question. And has that contract expired?

Answer. It has.

Question. When?

Answer. Last year.

Question. Are there, or have there been, other contracts, whether in the name of Russell or not, in which Russell was interested?

Answer. No other that I know of, either now or in the past.

Question. These contracts are executed in quadruple?

Answer. I think they are in duplicate. They are in the usual form the department has adopted in the execution of contracts.

Question. Have there been at any time, to your knowledge, any transactions or business relations between Russell and any officer of the government?

Answer. None that I know of.

Question. Between any officer of the War Department and Russell's firm, or Russell himself?

Answer. None that I know of.

Question. Under these contracts you speak of, explain, if you please, where and in what manner, by the terms of the contracts, payments were to be made.

Answer. Payment was to be made, under the terms of the contract, when the work was done, and to be made by the nearest quartermaster—at the nearest point—according to my recollection of the contract. I will not undertake to say positively, because the contract is the best proof of it, and it is easy to be obtained; but I think the payment was to be made by the quartermaster that might be designated for that purpose; chiefly they have been made at Fort Leavenworth.

Question. In point of fact, from what point has this transportation taken place?

Answer. From the upper part of Missouri and from Kansas Territory.

Question. From what station?

Answer. From Fort Leavenworth chiefly, and from several places along the Missouri river.

Question. By what quartermaster at Fort Leavenworth?

Answer. Mr. Van Vleet. The transportation across the plains is a heavy business, and the number of cattle engaged in it is very large. The habit has been to designate different points along on the river at which the trains should start, for the purpose of accommodating them to the grazing. The contract, however, will show the stipulations as to the point of starting.

Question. The point is this, whether the loading was chiefly at Leavenworth and from there onward.

Answer. That is the case.

Question. And there was no transportation this way from the station you have referred to?

Answer. I think there was not under their contract. There may have been a stipulation in their contract requiring them to do any transportation which the army wanted; but if you mean to ask whether they have been employed in transporting goods this way, I answer no.

Question. Explain the mode of making payments by the department through the quartermaster at Fort Leavenworth.

Answer. The payment is generally made by requisition. The quartermaster makes a requisition upon the quartermaster general here for a particular amount of funds. He states that there will be needed for the payment of all concerned—not to contractors in particular—a certain sum of money, and calls for a requisition of $50,000, for instance. That requisition is sent over by the quartermaster general to the Secretary, and the Secretary signs a requisition upon the treasury, and then the Secretary of the Treasury directs that that money shall be placed to the credit of the quartermaster at Fort Leavenworth; the quartermaster at Fort Leavenworth pays out that money, and sends his vouchers to the treasury. The vouchers upon which the money has been paid agree precisely with the amount of money placed to the quartermaster's credit, and then his accounts are settled.

Question. And between the quartermaster and the contractor, what is the operation?

Answer. I suppose, of course, the quartermaster pays to the contractor upon being satisfied that so much money is due him upon such vouchers as may have been given to him at the treasury, and he takes up the vouchers.

Question. The quartermaster pays the money, takes the vouchers, and remits them here?

Answer. Yes, sir.

Question. In the case of these contracts with Russell, Majors & Waddell, was any direction given to the quartermaster there to depart from the ordinary usage?

Answer. None whatever.

Question. Did any departure from the usage take place in respect to making payments upon those contracts?

Answer. None whatever. If you have reference to those acceptances, then there was; if you mean in the ordinary payment of dues, there was not.

Question. I did not point my question to acceptances generally, but to what directions had been given, and to what changes had been made originally?

Answer. None whatever.

Question. Who, upon the part of these contractors, has conducted the business in reference to these contracts?

Answer. Mr. Russel himself.

Question. And no other person?

Answer. Nobody authorized by Russell that I know of. A great many persons have come to me—Mr. Green, of the Senate, Mr. Phelps, of the House, and other members of Congress—as friends of the contractors, have spoken to me, asking that certain facilities should be afforded to Russell in the ordinary transaction of his business there, but no agent of Russell—no one but himself.

Question. What facilities do you speak of?

Answer. Such as starting the trains from one point instead of another. There is a place upon the river called White Cloud, from which they were anxious that a portion of the supplies for the army should start. These gentlemen and other gentlemen from Pennsylvania spoke to me about it.

Question. They desired to have the service adapted to the convenience of the service, and not facilities in any other sense?

Answer. That is all.

Question. Who, on behalf of the War Department, conducted this business with Russell & Co.?

Answer. The quartermaster only.

Question. Who is he?

Answer. Quartermaster General, General Jesup, and after his death General Johnston, except at such periods when he was absent from the department, and then by the next in command.

Question. Do you mean that the transactions between Russell and the War Department have been confined to those gentlemen?

Answer. I do, unless there was some particular thing that Russell himself would address a letter to me about, and then it was done directly between Russell and myself.

Question. What has that business been?

Answer. The ordinary routine of business which I have attempted to describe.

Question. Do you know how much, under this contract now subsisting, has been paid by the government to the contractors?

Answer. I do not know the amount; it is a large sum.

Question. Have the accounts been made up recently?

Answer. I dare say they have; I have not looked into it.

Question. Have you any idea of the proximate amount?

Answer. Yes, sir; I should think half a million of dollars.

Question. Who has the custody of the accounts between the government and these contractors?

Answer. The quartermaster and the Treasury Department.

Question. Are you able to state whether, at any given time for the last year, the contractors have been overpaid.

Answer. They have never been overpaid a dollar at any time, either this year or at any time since I have been Secretary of War.

Question. Are you able to state at any given time the amount due them?

Answer. No, sir; because that depends upon the amount of work they have done.

Question. Has there been any time during the last year when you at the time have known yourself whether the government was in arrears, or how the balance stood?

Answer. The government is always in arrears as the work goes on; they are to be paid as the work is done. When a train starts from Fort Leavenworth to Utah or New Mexico, they get a receipt for so much freight shipped. When they get to a particular point, so much money is due upon it; and when the freight is delivered, the entire amount is due for the transportation. As the thing progresses from the start to the conclusion, of course the government becomes indebted to them to the extent of the work done; but the indebtedness is never consummated until the work is done, so the government could never be in arrears to them, except as the work progressed in that way. As soon as the work is done, and satisfactory vouchers presented of the completion of the work, then the government pays.

Question. That is, the quartermaster there pays?

Answer. Yes, sir.

Question. The particular question is, whether at any time you have known, at the time, whether, as between the contractors and the quartermaster there, anything earned has been unpaid?

Answer. I do not know. I would know from orders given for so much transportation in any particular month that there would be about so much due at another time. The prices of transportation vary according to the month they start. If in May, they receive so much a pound; in June, so much; and so on through the year. It is a sliding scale of prices.

Question. Then you never had in your hands at the time the means, either by calculation or by vouchers, of stating whether they had been fully paid up the amount they had earned or not, varying as the amount did according to the time of starting?

Answer. I could have told if I had put myself to the trouble of ascertaining the orders for transportation, and ascertaining the probable time it would take to do the transportation.

Question. Did you ever do it?

Answer. No, sir.

Question. You alluded to acceptances: what acceptances did you refer to?

Answer. Those you are investigating, and which have been in the hands of a delinquent clerk in the Interior Department.

Question. The $870,000?

Answer. Yes, sir; and others which have been given along in the progress of the business of the department.

Question. When first was any acceptance given by you to either of these contractors?

Answer. The first was given about the time the order was made for the removal of the troops from Fort Leavenworth to Utah.

Question. At what date?

Answer. It was in 1858. I do not know what period of the year it was. It was before Congress made an appropriation.

On that subject I have written a communication to the House, which will be sent in to day, and I would ask that that communication be spread upon your record as my testimony and my explanation upon that point.

Here the examination was closed for the day.

TUESDAY, *January* 1, 1861.

Hon. JOHN B. FLOYD recalled.

Examination by Mr. Conkling.

Question. About what time was the first contract made with Russell, Majors & Waddell?

Answer. I think it was in the winter of 1857—the winter after the present administration came in; the winter of 1857–'58.

Question. Designate the contract in some way.

Answer. It was a contract for the transportation of army supplies to Utah across the plains. It was for general army supplies, I think. The contract itself is the best evidence.

Question. And was there a contract made a year ago, in April?

Answer: I cannot remember when the contract was made.

Question. Was there a contract for the delivery of flour?

Answer. The contract about the delivery of flour was one I explained in a report to the Senate, I think.

Question. Was there a contract for the delivery of flour separately?

Answer. There was, and that contract was of this sort, which I will give particularly and carefully. Under the contract for the transportation of supplies to Utah there was a provision which required that notice should be given that supplies of a certain character and amount would be sent off at particular times. Upon giving that notice to the contractors for the transportation of supplies they were entitled to take the transportation, and in case the government thought proper to countermand the order, for any reason whatever, then, according to the terms of the contract, as you will see by reference to it, the government was called on to take off of their hands, at their cost, all the transportation which they had supplied. Notice had been given, in due form and at the proper time, for transportation to be gotten ready, to take out supplies of flour to the army of Utah.

Question. The question I intended to point to this contract was this: I desired to know which contract, if any, first was given to these men by your direction?

Answer. The first contract given by my direction was a contract for the transportation of supplies, which was given in the winter of 1857–'58, after due advertisement for the lowest bidder, they being the lowest bidders.

Question. Then that was not given by your direction, but by law to the lowest bidder?

Answer. No, sir, for the Secretary of War has a right to approve or disapprove contracts.

Question. When was the next contract given to these parties by your direction?

Answer. If you refer to the contract about flour, which I was going on to explain when I was stopped, then it was some time after that; I do not know when. The next one was a contract for the transportation of supplies; the last contract for the transportation of supplies.

Question. Then each contract they had was given by your direction?

Answer. Yes, sir, after advertisement, and in each instance they were the lowest bidders, except in reference to the flour contract, and that was the modification of a contract, as I was going to show you when you stopped me.

Question. When and under which contract were acceptances first given?

Answer. Under the contract for the transportation of supplies to Utah.

Question. And that was the first contract of all they had?

Answer. That was the first.

Question. And under all those contracts, by the terms of them, payments were to be made and vouchers taken at Fort Leavenworth by the quartermaster there?

Answer. That was the usual mode of business, but the contract will show that. It is a matter of detail, and I cannot say anything more about it than I have stated.

Question. Describe the paper accepted in the first place?

Answer. The paper accepted in the first place was paper purporting to be paid when the work under the contract should be done to the amount of it.

Question. In the form of drafts?

Answer. In the form of drafts by them on the Secretary, and accepted as Secretary, when the work should be done. Those were the first.

Question. And what was the amount of the first acceptances?

Answer. I do not know.

Question. As near as you can state?

Answer. I do not know; a very large amount, and they have been regularly paid up.

Question. Give the committee some idea of the amount of the first batch of acceptances.

Answer. I do not think I can unless I refer to some memoranda. The transportation under the first contract amounted to several millions of dollars.

Question. Will you give some idea of the amount of the first batch of acceptances?

Answer. I should suppose somewhere between $200,000 and $500,000. I suppose so; it is mere conjecture.

Question. And were these acceptances all made the same day?

Answer. No, sir; they were not all made the same day. They were made at different times, and made in the regular progress of the business whenever they wanted to raise money.

Question. I want to get at the date of events. State to the committee about the time when the first acceptances were made, as nearly as you can.

Answer. I cannot state, for I do not know.

Question. About how long after this first contract was made was it that the first acceptances were made?

Answer. I do not know; it could have been but a few months, as well as I remember.

Question. And in the first instance, what was the amount, as near as you can state it, of the acceptances?

Answer. I have no idea whatever now.

Question. At whose request were those acceptances given?

Answer. At the request of Russell, Majors & Waddell.

Question. Made by whom?

Answer. By Russell.

Question. To you?

Answer. To me.

Question. Was any registry of these acceptances kept in your office?

Answer. A memoranda was kept by a clerk in my department.

Question. By whom.

Answer. By Mr. Drinkard, I think. It was kept in the clerk's office, through the chief clerk.

Question. Is it there now?

Answer. I presume so.

Question. When these acceptances were paid, as far as they were paid, what became of them?

Answer. I do not know. I never heard of them afterwards. They were paid, cancelled, and destroyed, I presume.

Question. Do you know that was so?

Answer. I do not.

Question. Did you see them afterwards?

Answer. I did not. I never heard of any difficulty about them.

Question. How long after the first batch of acceptances was given was there another given?

Answer. I cannot tell, nor can I form the least idea. It was along in the progress of the business of transportation.

Question. At whose request?

Answer. At the request of Russell, Majors & Waddell.

Question. And communicated to you by whom?

Answer. By Russell always.

Question. Verbally or in writing?

Answer. Verbally generally, but sometimes by note.

Question. Did any other person apply or communicate with you upon the subject before the acceptances were made in the first instance?

Answer. Not on their behalf. Before I made the acceptances I went to Riggs & Co. to consult as to the shape of the acceptances, and the manner in which to put the acceptances in form. I had a consultation with Mr. Riggs about it.

Question. Have there ever been such acceptances given during your administration except to Russell, Majors & Waddell?

Answer. No, sir.

Question. Previous to the giving of those acceptances to Russell, had there been any transactions, or relations, or accommodations of any sort, with him, except the execution of these previous contracts?

Answer. I do not know. There had been none with me.

Question. Can you state the amount, in all, of the acceptances which you gave to Russell, Majors & Waddell?

Answer. I cannot, but I suppose they are upwards of $2,000,000.

Question. And when were the last acceptances given?

Answer. In December, this last month.

Question. On more than one occasion?

Answer. Yes, sir.

Question. On how many occasions?

Answer. I cannot tell. I do not know how many. Two or three times, and probably more, but I do not remember.

Question. Where were they given?

Answer. They were given here in this city.

Question. At the War Office?

Answer. At the War Office; at least, the transaction was consummated at the War Office. I may have signed some of the acceptances, and probably some at my office in my house.

Question. Nowhere else than at the War Office and at your house?

Answer. No, sir; never one, except at my place of business, at the War Office, and in my house.

Question. Was there any registration made of these acceptances?

Answer. Yes, sir.

Question. By whom?

Answer. By a clerk in the War Department.

Question. By this same clerk, Drinkard?

Answer. I think so; at least, the register will show. I gave him the memoranda which I kept myself, and he entered them upon the books.

Question. What is the book that contains them?

Answer. No particular book that I could name; these memoranda were merely entered in a book.

Question. Is there no way by which you can designate the particular book?

Answer. There is not.

Question. It is a bound book?

Answer. I do not know; I never saw it that I know of.

Question. Then you do not know that there was a register kept?

Answer. Only as I have stated.

Question. How is that?

Answer. From my clerk.

Question. Who?

Answer. Mr. Drinkard.

Question. Then you do not know that there was a registration?

Answer. I do know that I gave to him memoranda of these acceptances. I have already stated that I have not seen the book. I have never seen any book in the department except those containing orders for me to sign.

Question. What did Mr. Drinkard register—the acceptances themselves, or the memoranda?

Answer. The acceptances themselves.

Question. In the case of those acceptances made out at your house how were they conveyed to Mr. Drinkard for registration?

Answer. I do not know that the acceptances themselves were conveyed to Mr. Drinkard. I gave to Mr. Drinkard memoranda of the acceptances for him to register. He could not have the acceptances themselves, because at the time of making them they were handed over to Mr. Russell; he had the memoranda.

Question. Then he kept a list of the acceptances, and registered them not from the acceptances themselves, but from memoranda? It seems to me that there is a little discrepancy in your statement that the registration was made from the acceptances themselves.

Answer. I did not observe any discrepancy. When the acceptances were made at the War Office, the registration may have been made from the acceptances themselves; those that were made at my house were registered from memoranda made from the acceptances themselves.

Question. Can you give the committee any idea of the proportion of acceptances which were made out at your house?

Answer. No, I cannot.

Question. Can you state whether the amount given at your house would be a half, a quarter, or any given proportion of the whole amount?

Answer. No, I cannot; I do not know anything about it; I just signed them whenever there was any necessity for it wherever I happened to be.

Question. And upon what data did you act in signing them wherever you happened to be?

Answer. Upon a general knowledge of the amount that was coming to these people from their transportation, and in the last instance upon the data particularly that money was to be paid whenever the work was done; that it could mislead nobody, it could deceive nobody, being merely an accommodation to these people to enable them to raise the means to sustain themselves in carrying out their contract. I gave the acceptances upon that general data.

Question. At the time of the giving of the first acceptance in December, did you know the amount due Russell, Majors & Waddell?

WITNESS. What December do you mean?

Mr. CONKLING. I mean this past month, ultimo.

Answer. I had a general knowledge of the probable amount that would be due to them for the transportation covered by the acceptances.

Question. I would like, if you please, to have a more specific answer to the question. Did you, at the time of giving the first acceptance in December, know the amount due them?

Answer. I had a general idea of the amount that would be due them under these acceptances?

Question. What was that amount?

Answer. I suppose they would range from $700,000 to $1,000,000. There was no means of having accurate information.

Question. What was the amount of acceptances on the first occasion in December?

Answer. I have forgotten.

Question. Can you approximate?

Answer. No, I cannot.

Question. Can you state within $100,000?

Answer. O yes; it was more than $100,000.

Question. I say, can you state the amount within $100,000?

Answer. I could not.

Question. Where was the first batch of acceptances executed, in fact, in the War Office or at your house?

Answer. I think it was done in this way: the arrangement was made in the War Office, where the first batch was prepared under my order.

Question. By whom?

Answer. By Russell, I think.

Question. Was anybody else present when they were signed?

Answer. Nobody else was present.

Question. Did you take a memoranda of the acceptances then?

Answer. I did.

Question. In your own handwriting?

Answer. No, sir; in Russell's handwriting, because I write with difficulty; but they were put down in my presence.

Question. Put down upon what?

Answer. Upon a piece of paper.

Question. To whom did you deliver them?

Answer. To Mr. Drinkard.

Question. With the direction that he should make a registration from them?

Answer. Yes, sir.

Question. What date in December was that, as near as you can state?

Answer. I cannot tell.

Question. Cannot you give some general idea?

Answer. The giving of these acceptances began about the middle of December, and continued until towards the last of December.

Question. Then these first acceptances were given about the middle of December?

Answer. I think it was earlier than that. They were given on several different occasions, and there was not a good many days between them. They were taken immediately by Russell, and put into the hands of Bailey.

Question. I will come to that presently. I first desire to know the date of these first acceptances?

Answer. I do not know.

Question. You think they were before the middle of December?

Answer. I think so.

Question. You cannot be more definite in respect to the date?

Answer. No, sir.

Question. How soon afterwards in December were other acceptances executed?

Answer. I do not think there was more than 10 to 15 days between all of them.

Question. How many days intervened between the execution of the first acceptances in December and the next that were executed?

Answer. I cannot tell; I do not remember; they were all executed in the course of ten days.

Question. On how many different days in December?

Answer. I do not know.

Question. Were the acceptances all given out at your house in December?

Answer. I cannot tell that; it is a thing to which I paid no attention?

Question. Were they given in the presence of any one besides Russell?

Answer. They were given in the presence of no one besides Russell, that I remember.

Question. Can you state the amount of acceptances given within this period of ten days?

Answer. Yes, sir, very nearly; I think it was about $700,000.

Question. Was this $700,000 all of the same character of paper?

Answer. Yes, sir.

Question. Were there in December any other acceptances given than this $700,000 of similar paper?

Answer. I think not.

Question. Were these acceptances, any of them, numbered?

Answer. I do not remember. The acceptances themselves will show that.

Question. Were any of the acceptances given at any time numbered?

Answer. At first the practice of numbering them was pursued, then they were lettered, and latterly—these last acceptances—I do not know whether they were numbered, or lettered, or neither. The character of the paper changed, and it was not very essential.

Question. What was the object of the practice of lettering the acceptances, or numbering them?

Answer. I gave the direction, in the first place, to have them numbered as a guide to prevent the issue of more acceptances than there was likely to be money coming to these parties for transportation.

Question. And when did that practice cease?

Answer. When it was found to be more convenient to letter them. I do not know the time the first practice ceased, but the change took place from this cause: it went on until there was a very large number of acceptances in different amounts, and Russell represented to me that the number indicated that all the acceptances that had ever been given were still in existence, and that therefore he was unable to negotiate. For instance, he would get an acceptance for $50,000 that was numbered 10, 20, 30, or 40, for there had been acceptances of $10,000, and even of $5,000, and the inference would be drawn that there were acceptances in existence for an immense sum of money. For this reason, finding that he could not negotiate, he desired that the numbering should be discontinued and the lettering should be substituted, which enabled the department to understand the amount of acceptances given just as well as the numbers. With that view, and upon that representation, I consented to change the numbering to lettering, because letters represented the truth, and numbers did not.

Question. And the object was to give greater negotiability and facility to the paper?

Answer. The whole object from first to last was to give these parties greater facilities to enable them to raise money.

Question. And with that object a practice was discontinued which impeded the negotiability of the paper?

Answer. Yes, sir; because many of the numbers had been long before paid and cancelled.

Question. Did I understand you to say that you had never seen them afterwards?

Answer. I never saw them. There was never anything heard at the War Department about them, and I never doubted at all but that they were cancelled and paid.

Question. When did the habit of either lettering or numbering them cease?

Answer. I do not know. I have no idea.

Question. To put the question in a more direct form, when did you first execute acceptances that were neither numbered nor lettered?

Answer. I think never until the December acceptances.

Question. How did these come to go out without being either lettered or numbered?

Answer. In this way: it was the last transaction; I intended to give no more. There was a change in the paper, and it was understood distinctly that it was to go into the hands of bankers and firms who held acceptances issued during the past season that had not been redeemed.

Question. Please name the bankers and firms into whose hands they were to go.

Answer. Into the hands of bankers in New York, as represented to me, and in St. Louis.

Question. Were none of the New York banks named to you?

Answer. I never heard the name of but one that I remember.

Question. Which was that?

Answer. The Shoe and Leather Bank.

Question. Can you name any other?

Answer. I cannot. There was a large firm in Boston, I believe, which held a considerable amount of the paper.

Question. What was the name of that firm?

Answer. Pierce & Bacon, or Bacon & Pierce; I do not remember which. It was understood that these acceptances were to go into the hands of those people who held acceptances of a different sort, and that they were to be held as collateral security, to be paid when the work required under contracts had been performed to a sufficient extent.

Question. Can you name any bank in St. Louis?

Answer. I cannot name it.

Question. Was there more than one bank there?

Answer. I am not sure but there were two or three.

Question. What object was to be accomplished by the absence of either letters or numbers on these last acceptances?

Answer. There was never anything said about it. I never heard about it, and never thought of it, to tell the truth.

Question. Then the omission of letters and numbers on these acceptances was, in fact, accidental.

Answer. Yes, sir, purely accidental. I do not know that either letters or numbers were put upon all the others that have been issued. I do not know about that.

Question. Who put these letters or numbers upon the papers?

Answer. The man who drew them; the clerk who prepared them.

Question. Were the acceptances prepared by Russell or in the office?

Answer. The last ones were prepared by Russell under my direction.

Question. Where was that done?

Answer. I do not know. He brought them to me. I gave him the form, and he brought them to me prepared. I did not know that they had not been prepared by a clerk in the office until I saw them in Russell's handwriting.

Question. You say these were the last acceptances you were to give?

Answer. Yes, sir.

Question. Why?

Answer. Because I would not consent to give any more. I would not oonsent to give them except in large amounts, to keep them from being put into market. I would not consent to give them except with the understanding that they were to go into the hands of those who already held other acceptances. The paper simply indicated the probable amount that would be likely to accrue under their contract up to next June.

Question. Did these acceptances in December anticipate all that would be due up to next June?

Answer. They indicated the amount of work that would be likely to be required, and when the work was done the money would be due, but not otherwise.

Question. Was the fact that you intended to make these acceptances cover the earnings of Russell, Majors & Waddell up to June next the reason why you considered these the last acceptances you would give?

Answer. That was one reason. There were a multitude of other reasons which will readily suggest themselves to you.

Question. Such as what?

Answer. Such as that my term of office was nearly out; that I would not give acceptances to go into the general market; I would not give acceptances that did not indicate upon their face that they were to be paid when the work was performed, so that they could deceive no one, nor for more than in my opinion was necessary to enable these people to raise money sufficient to extricate them from their difficulties. In other words, the transaction was intended to carry them through this year and into the next year. The reason of that was that there was a general breaking up of the commercial prosperity of the country, and these people were likely to fail, as I believed, unless they obtained the additional accommodation and credit to which they were entitled under this contract. It was another form and shape of showing what would be due under their contract if the work was performed.

Question. For what purpose were the first acceptances given to Russell, no matter when they were given?

Answer. That I have stated several times.

Question. I mean what was he to do with them?

Answer. I do not know. Raise money on them, I suppose.

Question. And were acceptances given him for no other purpose than to raise money?

Answer. Never, except these last, which were given to be substituted in the place of the others as collateral security.

Question. Collateral security or renewals?

Answer. Collateral security for the redemption of the others, as it was represented to me.

Question. Am I right, then, in supposing that all the acceptances given were for the purpose of raising money, except those given in December, which were to be placed as collateral security to cover discounts that had been obtained?

Answer. The first acceptances were given for the purpose of raising money to enable them to start the trains. Then the next acceptances, and from that clear on, were given, as I have said, as a matter of necessity for a renewal of the first, and afterwards as a matter of convenience to enable these people to get along with their large business.

Question. Did you know what was to be done with these acceptances?

Answer. I did not, except that I supposed these people were to raise money on them.

Question. Is it true, then, that all the acceptances were given to raise money upon, except those in December, which were given as collateral?

Answer. As collateral, and in all probability to raise money upon. They were given with the same intention precisely, and in the same mode as all the others, except that the character was changed.

Question. Except as the character was changed; how?

Answer. As I have already designated.

Question. By leaving off letters and numbers?

Answer. And that they expressed more distinctly on the face of them that the money was to be paid only when the work was done.

Question. Was it the intention to change their character in that respect?

Answer. Yes, sir; and for a reason which I will explain, if you wish it.

Question. What was the reason of that?

Answer. It was that while I was Secretary of War I could control the payment of these acceptances if they were filed in the War Department. If an acceptance given and not paid was sent by the person holding it to the War Department, I could cause it to be filed and paid as the money was due to them; but when I ceased to be Secretary of War I could have no such command over them; therefore I intended more distinctly than formerly that the paper should express upon the face of it how it should be paid, and when it should be paid, and then I gave the acceptances in large numbers, so that they could only go into the hands of parties who had had transactions in them before.

Question. When did you first know that persons other than Russell, Majors & Waddell held these acceptances?

WITNESS. What acceptances?

Mr. CONKLING. Any that you had given?

WITNESS. Do you mean to ask when I first knew that acceptances had been negotiated and not paid?

Mr. CONKLING. Yes, sir.

Answer. In July last, or somewhere thereabouts. In June or July, I think.

Question. What amount was then outstanding unpaid?

Answer. I do not remember. A small amount.

Question. About what?

Answer. I cannot tell. I have not the least remembrance. I think my attention was called to it by some notice of a bank in St. Louis of an acceptance held by them which had not been paid.

Question. From that time on from whom did you receive other notices of that description?

Answer. I do not remember. I presume the letters on file in the War Department will show.

Question. From a number of parties?

Answer. Not a great number.

Question. What amount of acceptances had been protested up to December?

Answer. I should think about $300,000, or perhaps $350,000; I do not remember the exact sum.

Question. Was the acceptance protested in St. Louis in July ever paid?

Answer. I do not know.

Question. It was never paid, then, to your knowledge?

Answer. No, sir. The house of Russell, Majors & Co. represented to me that they were making arrangements to restore their credit and take up these acceptances—that they could arrange the matter with the parties who held these acceptances—otherwise their pay would have been stopped in the Quartermaster's department.

Mr. CONKLING. That is not in answer to my question.

WITNESS. If you will permit me to go on I will show how it is. About the time that I speak of they were a good deal embarrassed, and were attempting to arrange with their creditors to reinstate their paper, which had been temporarily under protest. The president of one of the banks in Missouri came here and had a good deal of conversation with me in regard to the matter. He inquired as to the probable amount of transportation that would be due these people. Being informed from the Quartermaster's department of what would be likely to be the proximate amount, he told me that Russell, Majors & Waddell would be able to make arrangements for going on with their business and paying up these acceptances.

Question. Then the answer is the same as that already given, that they have never been paid that you know of?

Answer. I know nothing about it since. I have heard nothing about it.

Question. Of what amount were those acceptances issued in December to be placed as collateral to other acceptances?

Answer. As far as they were out.

Question. How far was that?

Answer. I think about $450,000.

Question. Do you think now it was about that amount?

Answer. I do suppose so now, and I did suppose so then, and I gave them this amount to raise upon the balance, if they could do so. The object of giving them was to substitute them for those out, which I supposed to be about $450,000; and then, so far as they could, upon the balance, over and above that amount, raise money for their ordinary purposes to enable them to get along. It was done to give them the full credit of their contract.

Question. And did you know with whom they were to place this $450,000 as collateral to other securities?

Answer. I had an idea.

Question. Who was it?

Answer. Bacon & Pierce were to get $260,000—as I understood it—one of the banks in Missouri was to get about $80,000, and their banks in New York and other banks which held their paper were to get the balance, as I thought.

Question. Who was that president of a St. Louis bank that came to see you?

Answer. I think his name was Barnes.

Question. Of what bank?

Answer. I do not know; the oldest bank there.

Question. Allow me to understand you precisely. Bacon & Pierce, and other persons, who held $450,000 of unpaid acceptances, were to receive other acceptances to the same amount as collateral?

Answer. That was what I supposed.

Question. And the residue of this $800,000, or whatever the sum was, to be used generally for the purpose of raising money?

Answer. Yes, sir.

Question. Do you know the precise amount of acceptances put into the hands of Bailey by Russell?

Answer. Bailey gave me a memorandum of them.

Question. When?

Answer. After the exposure.

Question. I will assume, then, that they were $870,000. If you gave Russell, in December, $800,000 of acceptances, how do you account for his having the other $70,000?

Answer. He must have had $70,000 of acceptances which had been formerly given, and which he never had used.

Question. And you gave him, in December, no more than $800,000?

Answer. I think that was the sum. I certainly never gave him the $70,000, in December, which he put into Bailey's hands.

Question. Have any acceptances which you ever gave to Russell been destroyed, to your knowledge, before being used at all?

Answer. I have understood that they have been. He often told me that he had done so; and some, to my knowledge, have been destroyed.

Question. When first did Russell tell you he had destroyed acceptances?

Answer. I cannot tell, and I have no idea.

Question. Has he frequently told you so?

Answer. I do not think he has.

Question. Several times?

Answer. I cannot tell; it was a thing to which I paid no great deal of attention, and a matter about which I never expected to hear again. Occasionally there were acceptances given and destroyed without being used. Occasionally he told me they had been paid, cancelled, and destroyed.

Question. I am asking you about what he told you of the destruction of acceptances unused. I want to know whether he told you that on only one occasion, or on more than one?

Answer. I do not remember.

Question. Did he tell you the amount of unused acceptances?

Answer. No, sir.

Question. Did you ever know the amount?

Answer. No, sir; nor of the used acceptances.

Question. In giving him additional acceptances did you assume that he had destroyed the unused acceptances, as he said he had?

Answer. Whenever he told me he had destroyed them I assumed it was true.

Question. And then you deducted the amount?

Answer. The amount was always within the power of the department to pay.

Question. Do you mean by that, assuming that he had used them all?

Answer. Yes, sir; as he said he had used them.

Question. Explain your meaning.

Answer. Suppose the amount due him for transportation of last year is $500,000, and I give him in the aggregate, from one time to another, $500,000 of acceptances; the $500,000 would be paid by the work when it was done.

Question. And do you mean that you never gave him in all a greater amount of acceptances than there were earnings due?

Answer. Never, except in this last instance, and that bore upon its face that he was to earn them; that was the intention, and that was about the fact, I think.

Question. Since the giving of these $800,000 of acceptances, in December, have you given any other?

Answer. I have not, as I stated before.

Question. Shall the committee understand that the acceptances which you gave Russell would have exceeded the amount of earnings if it had not been true that he had paid or destroyed others as he said he had?

Answer. I am not prepared to say. You put a supposititious case.

Question. Well, did you, in point of fact, execute to Russell an amount of acceptances larger in the whole than the earnings upon his contract?

The WITNESS. Do you mean from the time the acceptances were first issued up to this time?

Mr. CONKLING. I do.

Answer. Then I think the acceptances have never been equal to the amount of money which, from the first to the last, he was entitled to; that is my opinion.

Question. Have you ever issued to them acceptances larger in the total than the amount due them at the time you executed them?

Answer. Oh! yes; because the object of the acceptances was to anticipate what would be due them.

Question. That was so previous to December?

Answer. Yes, sir; I stated at first that the object of the acceptances was to enable them to raise money and give them the credit of their contract.

Question. Then every acceptance ran against unearned money?

Answer. Every acceptance ran against unearned money.

Question. Was there any difference in that respect between the December acceptances and any other?

Answer. No; of course in that particular there was no difference, because all the acceptances were against unearned money.

Question. I do not yet understand whether or not these acceptances overran the amount which you intended to anticipate, and whether or not you deducted from them those which he said he had paid and destroyed?

The WITNESS. I do not comprehend the question.

Mr. CONKLING. I do not understand whether or not, in order to keep the amount of these acceptances within the bounds of what they would earn, you assumed that Russell had destroyed what he said he had, and had paid what he said he had.

Answer. From the first to last acceptances have never been, as I think, and as I have always thought, issued to an amount that was likely to accrue to him from his earnings. It was certainly necessary that he should have paid the acceptances, as he said he had paid them, in order to keep the account straight. I have answered that question in half a dozen different ways.

Question. When did you first receive from Bailey any communication about these acceptances?

Answer. I have a letter from Bailey here that discloses the whole thing, and it will answer your question.

Question. Was that the first communication?

Answer. Yes, sir.

The letter was read as follows:

["Private.]

"LAFAYETTE HOUSE,
"*December* 19, 1860.

"MY DEAR SIR: I enclose herewith the draught of a letter addressed by me, on the 1st instant, to the Secretary of the Interior. The letter itself is in the hands of a friend, and I think that I ought to direct that it be delivered to Mr. Thompson immediately on his return from North Carolina.

"I am very loth to disturb you on your sick bed, but I feel bound to show you the letter, and to inform you that the bonds were delivered to Wm. H. Russell, to enable him to raise money to protect certain acceptances of yours, which otherwise would have been protested.

"The facts are as follows: I was informed on the 12th of July last that certain official acceptances which you had *illegally* given would mature on the following day; that there were no means of meeting them, and that they would consequently be protested; and that your retirement in disgrace from the cabinet would necessarily follow. I called immediately at the War Department to ascertain from you if the facts alleged were true. You were engaged with General Scott. I then stated the case to Drinkard, and he told me that I had been correctly informed. I did not tell Drinkard, neither did I intend to tell you, what I proposed to do. I merely called at the department to get the facts. Having satisfied myself, I returned to my own office and procured 150 bonds, which I gave to Russell. Subsequently I let him have other bonds to a very large amount. When I gave him the first lot of bonds Russell assured me that the embarrassments of Russell, Majors & Waddell were only temporary, and that the bonds would certainly be returned in ninety days.

"I have no right to require you to consider this communication confidential, but I earnestly request that you will take no action upon it until you have had an interview with me; and inasmuch as I have made the statement in writing only because I could not see you, I feel justified in asking you to burn this letter, and consider the statement made to you verbally. I ought to add that I hold your official acceptances as security for the return of the bonds. I required this of Russell.

"Very respectfully, your obedient servant,

"G. BAILEY.

"Hon. JOHN B. FLOYD, *Pennsylvania avenue.*"

Question. When did you receive that letter?

Answer. I probably received it that day or the next—the 19th or 20th. I was sick in bed. I have not a distinct recollection about it, but I did not see Bailey until Saturday morning. Bailey came to see me Saturday morning, which is the first time I had an opportunity of seeing him, and in that interview with him I told him that it was a thing which must be at once revealed; that I was the last man in the world he should have made any such communication to if he wanted it kept secret; that I would wait until Thompson returned, who was absent, and expected that day; that as soon as Thompson came I would make a statement to him. Bailey said that there were two men in town—one a senator, and somebody else—who knew it, and that he had put this letter which he wrote to Thompson in the hands of somebody to give to him. Well, he left me immediately, and went off and directed that the papers should be put into the hands of the President. I think he was afraid that Thompson might be delayed a day or two. I had no idea, and he did not give me any distinct idea—and I had no idea, I am so little acquainted with the matters in the Interior Department—what funds he had in his hands. I did not know that he or anybody else had in their hands any such amount of property as that, that they could dispose of. He attempted to explain to me how it was, and I did comprehend it pretty well, and then I told him the revelation must be made. Thompson came home that night. The President told me that Thompson happened to be in his room when the revelation was made to him. He and Black came to my house the next day, and we had a full conversation about the whole affair. The letter the draught of which he had prepared for Thompson was enclosed in the envelope with the letter to me. I think there is a difference in the date between that letter and the letter to Thompson, but I do not know.

Question. Have you had any other communication with Bailey about this matter?

Answer. I received a note simply asking for an interview, but no other communication.

Question. Any statement from him?

Answer. None, except this conversation I have attempted to det between him and myself.

Question. Did he show you those acceptances?

Answer. No.

Question. Have you seen them?

Answer. I have.

Question. And examined them?

Answer. I did, and cancelled them. I made an order at the War Department to cancel them. It was a fraud perpetrated upon me, and, as it was in my power to acknowledge the validity of them or not, I cancelled the acceptances, and entered a memorandum that those acceptances were cancelled.

Question. So that the holder of those acceptances, whether it be the government or anybody else, when the acceptances mature, will not be able to collect them.

Answer. They cannot collect them, because they were a fraud perpetrated upon me, and the only remedy I had, in my judgment, was to annul the whole transaction by cancellation.

Question. Did any other officer of the government consent to these acceptances being cancelled?

Answer. No, sir; and I did not care whether they did or not.

Question. Have you any communication from Russell in relation to these acceptances, or any acceptances?

Answer. I have not.

Question. Have you ever received any written communication from Russell about them?

Answer. I have not.

Question. Any letter from Russell in relation to any acceptances whatever?

Answer. I have, often.

Question. Where are they?

Answer. They may be on file in my department.

Question. Are they on file in the War Department?

Answer. I do not know.

Question. Did you go to Mr. Thompson about this matter first, or did he come to you?

Answer. He came to me, because he only got home Saturday night, and I had not any opportunity to see him. I intended to go to him the next day and make the revelation, but it was made before I got there.

Question. Did you go to any other persons than Mr. Thompson about this matter?

Answer. I did not.

Question. Did any persons, at the time of this exposure, except Bailey, come to you about this?

Answer. No, sir.

Question. Did you go to any persons besides Mr. Thompson about this matter?

Answer. I did not.

Question. Did any persons besides Thompson and Bailey come to you about it?

Answer. No, sir.

Question. Did you communicate with any other person about it?

Answer. I did, but not fully.

Question. With whom?

Answer. I did not communicate the intelligence nor the fact; but I sent this word to Russell——

Question. I ask you with whom did you communicate?

Answer. Upon this subject I communicated with nobody beyond what I tell you, unless you call the earnest message I sent to Russell to come here a communication.

Question. Did you write to Russell?

Answer. I did not.

Question. You sent to him?

Answer. Yes, sir.

Question. By whom?

Answer. By Latham.

Question. But you did at that time communicate to Latham something?

Answer. I communicated a message by Latham to Russell.

Question. Did you communicate with any other person touching this matter other than Latham, Bailey, Thompson, and the President, for I think you mentioned him?

Answer. I communicated to the President, but not until after I saw Thompson.

Question. Then, Bailey, Thompson, Latham, and the President are the only persons with whom you communicated in any way about this matter about that time?

Answer. And Black. Black was with Thompson; they came together.

Question. Did Latham write to Russell?

Answer. I think not.

Question. Did he telegraph him?

Answer. I do not know whether he did or not.

Question. Did he go to New York?

Answer. I happened to meet him as he was going to New York.

Question. I ask you did he go to New York?

Answer. He did. I said I met him as he was going to New York, and sent the message by him to Russell. He did not go to New York for the purpose of communicating with Russell.

Question. My question is simply whether Latham went to New York?

Answer. He did.

Question. When?

Answer. I think it was Friday night.

Question. And where was your interview with him?

Answer. At my house.

Question. Did he come there by your request?

Answer. No, sir.

Question. Of his own accord?

Answer. Of his own accord.

Question. Had you previously had any communication with Latham in reference to these contracts with Russell, Majors & Waddell?

Answer. No particular communication. I do not know that I ever had any communication with him about it or about the acceptances.

Question. Did Latham ever have any of these acceptances, to your knowledge?

Answer. Not that I know of.

Question. And when did Latham return from New York?

Answer. I do not know.

Question. When did you next see him?

Answer. After Russell was arrested.

Question. Did you receive any communication from him in the meantime?

Answer. I did. I directed Drinkard, my chief clerk, to telegraph to Russell to meet Latham by all manner of means.

Question. My question is whether you received any communication from Latham?

Answer. I did.

Question. What was it?

Answer. It was a letter.

Question. Did it come by post?

Answer. Yes, sir.

Question. Where is that letter?

Answer. I do not know whether I have it or not. It was a private letter, about other things. There was an incidental remark in it, that he had seen Russell, and that Russell would be here on Sunday morning or Monday morning, or whatever morning it was.

Question. Now, before Latham went to New York did you communicate with Mr. Drinkard on the subject?

Answer. I never communicated with Mr. Drinkard on the subject at all about it. Mr. Drinkard did not understand the purport of the telegraphic despatch which I sent.

Question. Did he write it?

Answer. Yes, sir; I directed him to write it so emphatic as would insure the meeting between Latham and Russell, and that Russell's presence here might be certainly secured.

Question. Was this letter from Latham the only communication you received from him before he saw you again?

Answer. The only one.

Question. When did you see him again?

Answer. I answer again that I saw him after he returned here, and that he returned here after Russell had been arrested.

Question. Cannot you fix the time more definitely?

Answer. I do not remember.

Question. The next week, I suppose?

Answer. I think that Russell came here on Saturday; you have the proof before you, I suppose, as to the time when he came. It was a day or two after that I saw Latham.

Question. Was there any reason for communicating to Latham and requesting him to see Russell, rather than to have communicated direct to Russell that his presence was required here?

Answer. Yes, sir, there was a very good reason. I wanted him here immediately. I wanted him here before there was any development made about this thing publicly, because I did not know but if he got an inkling of it he might never come at all. I therefore desired this communication to reach him without fail.

Question. But Latham could not see Russell as soon as a telegraphic despatch sent directly to him would reach him.

Answer. That is true; but I sent a telegraphic despatch to Latham, requesting him to see Russell and press him to come on immediately upon matters of urgent importance.

Question. Perhaps you do not comprehend my question. It was whether there was any reason for telegraphing Latham to meet Russell rather than to have sent the despatch directly to Russell?

Answer. Bailey told me that he had the assurance from Russell that he would be here on Saturday morning. Russell had been telegraphed, as I understood from Bailey, and was certain to be here; but not knowing whether I could place reliance on his being here, I telegraphed Latham to see him and have him here if possible.

Question. Was there anything to be accomplished by sending the despatch to Latham rather than to Russell himself?

Answer. I have already stated that I understood Russell had already been telegraphed on the subject.

Question. Does Latham know Russell well?

Answer. I presume he does know him very well.

Question. Have Russell, Majors & Waddell ever received from the

War Department or from you anything other than those acceptances upon their contracts?

Answer. They have received the money on their contracts.

Question. Have they received their payments in money and nothing else?

Answer. Nothing else.

Question. From whom have they received the money which has been paid them?

Answer. I answer as before, that, as I understand, they have received their money from the quartermaster's department.

Question. At Leavenworth?

Answer. At Fort Leavenworth, or wherever else they were to be paid?

Question. What I wanted to know was whether they received the money which they received through the regular channel and not from any one else irregularly?

Answer. I presume they received it through the regular channel. I myself never saw a dollar of money paid to anybody in the War Department.

Question. Have Russell, Majors & Waddell, or either of them, ever furnished any means or facilities or accommodations of any kind to the government that you know of?

Answer. Yes, sir, they have.

Question. In what manner?

Answer. I cannot just at this moment describe the manner in which they have done it; but I recollect that on some occasions they did afford to the government very considerable accommodations. I think it was in the postponement of money due to them. I am not clear about that, however. It was some arrangement in reference to their contracts for transportation. I recollect it was taken and received at the time as a very great accommodation to the government.

Question. Any other?

Answer. Not that I remember.

Question. Have Russell, Majors & Waddell, or either of them, ever furnished to any officer of the government, to your knowledge, any facilities or accommodations or means?

Answer. Not that I know of.

Question. Or in indorsements?

Answer. None that I know of or ever heard of.

Question. None for you?

Answer. Certainly none for me.

Question. Do you know how Bailey came to communicate this thing to you?

Answer. I do not. I have my conjectures; and, if it is a matter of any interest to the committee, I will state them.

Question. I do not care for them. Have you known Bailey long?

Answer. Yes, sir, a good while; that is to say, it is a good while since I first knew Bailey's person.

Question. Is he a relative of yours?

Answer. His wife is the daughter of a cousin of mine.

Examination by the chairman.

Question. I understood you to speak of Russell, Majors & Waddell as gentlemen of large means.

Answer. It has always been so represented to me.

Question. I want to ask you what are your means of knowledge as to that fact?

Answer. I knew it from two or three sources. The first was generally from army intelligence—from army officers who had connexion with the quartermaster's department. Then I knew it afterwards from the representations of members of Congress from the west, generally speaking, who have taken a very earnest and active part in advancing Russell's interest; then I knew it from the representation of this Mr. Barnes, bank president in St. Louis, who came to see me in July last.

Question. Can you name those army officers and members of Congress who gave you that information?

Answer. The army officers were both of the quartermasters general—General Jesup and General Johnson; Major Van Vliet I remember particularly. As to the members of Congress, I do not now recollect specific conversations; I only remember general conversations and the impression left upon my mind by Senator Green, Mr. Phelps, Mr. Craig, and, I think, Mr. Barrett. I do not remember any specific time, but that was the general impression.

Question. The general impression at the time they made their first contract, then, was that they possessed means sufficient to carry out their contract and fulfil all their obligations, independent of those they derived from the government?

Answer. Yes; I understood at the time that they were worth between $2,000,000 and $3,000,000.

Question. Before they entered into their first contract?

Answer. At the time they entered into that contract I understood they were good for any business transaction that they might engage in; I understood this at the time I gave acceptances, and intended to give them facilities for raising ready money.

Question. Do you know whether they ever gave any bonds to any person or persons to assist them in getting or renewing any contract from the government?

Answer. Not to my knowledge, and I do not very readily see why they should do it, because they got these contracts as the lowest bidders.

Question. I ask you whether the government is in arrears for services performed by Russell, Majors & Waddell, or either of them, upon any contract existing for work already done?

Answer. No, I should think not.

Question. What amount of work did they perform during the past season, since last spring?

Answer. I think it must have amounted to something like half a million dollars, and probably more; I do not know certainly the amount.

Question. Will it be larger next year?

Answer. It will be if things go along smoothly. There is an addition to the army at the points they transport to, and it will be a good deal larger next year.

WEDNESDAY, *January* 3, 1861.

LUTHER R. SMOOT sworn.

Examination by the chairman.

Question. Be good enough to state your residence and business.

Answer. My place of residence is Leavenworth City, Kansas; my business is banking.

Question. When did you first locate in Kansas?

Answer. I first went to Kansas in 1856; I date my residence there, however, from February, 1857, at which time I embarked in business there.

Question. Have you any partners in the business of banking?

Answer. Yes, sir.

Question. Please state who they are.

Answer. I had better first state the name of the firm; it is Smoot, Russell & Co. The partners are Suter, Lea & Co., of which I am a member, and Wm. H. Russell; I am in charge of the business of the firm.

Question. You are then a partner of the firm of Suter, Lea & Co., of Washington, and also of the firm you have mentioned in Leavenworth, Kansas Territory?

Answer. Yes, sir; Russell is not a member of the firm of Suter, Lea & Co.

Question. When was that partnership formed with Russell?

Answer. In February, 1857.

Question. What amount of means did he put in, or has he put into, the firm?

Answer. I am not prepared to answer, because I have not the books of our house here, and I do not know from recollection.

Question. State as near the amount as you can.

Answer. I shall say, then, to the best of my recollection, that Russell has never put in any means as capital. What amount has been from time to time to his credit on our books has been subject to his check though our partnership arrangements, provided that he should put in such an amount of capital.

Question. Has he been in debt from time to time to your house in Leavenworth, Kansas?

Answer. His account has been over-drawn at times, I believe; I know I wrote to him once upon the subject.

Question. Does he owe anything to the firm now?

Answer. I think not.

Question. Where did you formerly reside before you went to Leavenworth?

Answer. In this city.

Question. Were you at any time, when a resident of the city of

Washington, engaged in any public department in the employ of the government?

Answer. I was.

Question. Please state what position you occupied.

Answer. I was a clerk in the Indian department from November, 1850, up to my resignation, which, I think, was on the first of December, 1853. I have not had occasion to call up these dates recently, but my recollection is pretty good on that point.

Question. What duties did you discharge while in the employ of the government?

Answer. My duties were various. Shortly after I was appointed my duties were promiscuous. Towards the latter portion of my term I was in the finance division of the Indian department. The Indian office is divided into divisions, such as the civilization division, finance division, &c.

Question. What were your duties, then?

Answer. My duties in the finance division were of a miscellaneous character. I was confined to no one particular desk.

Question. Do you mean to inform the committee that you were assigned to no particular branch or department of the public business, but that you were to perform any duty that might be required of you from time to time by the Secretary?

Answer. The duty, if I had any special duty assigned me in the finance division, to the best of my recollection, was the care and examination of miscellaneous claims and accounts, or anything of that sort which might be put into my hands by the chief clerk or head of the division. I attended to everybody's business, as it were, in that room. I was familiar with it all.

Question. Did you not perform any duties as disbursing clerk?

Answer. Never.

Question. Did the nature of your duties in the Indian office make you acquainted with the funds or bonds that were in charge of that department?

Answer. Yes, sir; as every one in the same room and office was to a greater or less extent, I suppose.

Question. Can you inform the committee what bonds were held in trust by the government for the Indian tribes at the time you were there?

Answer. I cannot with certainty, although I made out what was called the Secretary's account for Mr. Miller, who was the disbursing clerk, and who was looked upon as the one to arrange that matter for the Secretary. He could not make it out, he said, and I made it out for the Secretary, but I have not refreshed my recollection upon that point, and cannot speak with certainty. There were stocks of nearly all kinds—some United States stocks I know. Some Alabama stocks and some Virginias were either bought or other stocks exchanged for them. Some were sold and others purchased by the direction of the President, through the request of the Ottawas and the Chippewas of Lake Superior, I believe. I have not, however, as I said, refreshed my recollection on the subject, nor have I seen a bond since I left there in 1853.

Question. Do you know the aggregate amount of the bonds held in trust while you were there?

Answer. I cannot state with any certainty. It must have been in the neighborhood of $2,000,000.

Question. Mr. Miller had these bonds in charge?

Answer. Yes, sir, Mr. James J. Miller.

Question. Where is he now?

Answer. I don't know; have not seen him or heard of him for a long time.

Question. When did you first become acquainted with the fact that a portion of these bonds had been fraudulently abstracted from the department?

Answer. Last Sunday week.

Question. From whom did you learn that fact?

Answer. Mr. Lea advised me of the fact.

Question. What time in the day was it that Mr. Lea advised you of that fact?

Answer. It must have been between one and two o'clock in the afternoon.

Question. Where were you at the time you held this conversation with Mr. Lea?

Answer. It was at his house.

Question. Were you informed by anybody previous to being informed by Mr. Lea?

Answer. I was not.

Question. Have you since learned from other persons that they knew of the transaction previous to your being informed by Mr. Lea?

Answer. I have.

Question. Please state who they were and when they were so informed?

Answer. I have tried my best to recollect. As many as two or three have so informed me in casual conversation, perhaps at the hotel, but I cannot remember who. I was informed by these persons that they knew of the transaction as early as Saturday night.

Question. In your conversation with Lea, did he tell you how he learned the facts?

Answer. Yes, sir. He told me that Bailey had informed him. I think he said Bailey had just informed him that he had made known the facts.

Question. In that conversation did Lea say whether he had any previous knowledge of the use which had been made of those bonds by Bailey?

Answer. I do not recollect of his so stating.

Question. Please say what he did say to you in that conversation?

Answer. I went to his house and was in his parlor when he came in. In talking about this matter, he said, as near as I can recollect, "If Gabriel were to blow his trumpet you could not be more astonished than you will be about the communication I am about to communicate to you. Mr. Bailey has just advised me that he had advised the President, or the Secretary, or somebody, that he had abstracted those bonds from the Indian department and gave them to Russell." He also stated that he presumed that Russell and Bailey would be arrested. We then debated the question whether we should send for Mr. Suter, in order to communicate the information to him, and see what action should be necessary, or what he thought about it. I advised against it on the ground that Suter knew nothing about it; that it would be folly to worry him about it; and, furthermore, it was Sunday, and Suter was a church-going man. Our conversation was desultory, and after leaving that topic we commenced talking about our own business here and at the west.

Question. Why was it deemed necessary by Mr. Lea to send for Suter?

Answer. That I am not prepared to state. Russell was a partner of ours in our western business, and, of course, a matter so affecting his reputation was a matter of importance to us.

Question. I only asked what reason Lea assigned?

Answer. None whatever.

Question. Have you had any conversation with Russell since you have been here in reference to this matter?

Answer. I have not. I have purposely avoided seeing Russell since receiving your summons.

Question. Did you see him before that?

Answer. I did.

Question. Where, and how often?

Answer. I saw him in New York and here. I cannot say how many times.

Question. I mean since this transaction.

Answer. I have seen him several times, but I do not know how often; but I have not seen him since I received your summons.

Question. When did you first see him after the fact of the abstraction of the bonds was made public?

Answer. I saw him in New York on the morning of his arrest.

Question. Did you have any conversation with him at that time in relation to the loss of the bonds?

Answer. I did. I had not seen Mr. Russell before since my arrival from the west. After salutations were over, Mr. Russell took up his mail, which was lying upon the table in his office, and read it. I had seen the morning papers before I left my hotel. I then asked him if he had read the papers. He said he had. I said, "Mr. Russell, if the facts be as I see in the papers, you are interested in the facts recorded there." Said he, "What is it?" I took the paper and showed it to him. I think it was the New York Herald. He said he had not noticed the statement I showed him, although he had read the morning papers. That was Monday morning, the 24th day of December. He asked me if I thought he would be arrested, or if I had heard that he would be. I told him I presumed he would be. He replied, "I have done nothing criminal, and they certainly will not put me in jail," or something to that effect; to which I replied, "Mr. Russell, you know better than I whether you are mixed up in it at all."

Question. Had you any knowledge previous to that time that Bailey had abstracted these bonds?

Answer. Up to the hour, moment, and second that Lea informed me on Sunday of the fact, I had not.

Question. This conversation took place in New York on Monday?

Answer. Yes, sir.

Question. Did you go over to New York on the Sunday evening before?

Answer. I did.

Question. Did you meet with Mr. Russell before you saw him in his office on Monday morning?

Answer. I did not, nor did I expect to find Russell in New York at all.

Question. When you saw him on Monday morning did you inform him of what Lea had said, or did you merely show him the Herald?

Answer. I merely showed him the Herald. He asked me some question about business, but instead of answering it I asked him if he had read the morning papers.

Question. Was the object of your business to New York to inform Mr. Russell that this matter had been disclosed?

Answer. It was not. I had other business which called me there.

Question. Did you go at your own suggestion, or at somebody's else?

Answer. I went at my own suggestion. Lea advised me not to go, but my business was urgent and pressing.

Question. Did Russell state to you on Monday morning, at the time of the interview, where any of these bonds were?

Answer. He did not.

Question. Do you know where they are?

Answer. I do not, except from hearsay. I have no personal knowledge. I know where Russell kept his account in New York.

Question. Did you ever, at any time, see any of these bonds?

Answer. I never have.

Question. And, until the Sunday morning referred to, when you had a conversation with Lea, you had no knowledge, directly or indirectly, in reference to the abstraction of those bonds from the Interior Department, or that Russell was, in any way, connected with the matter or had received the bonds?

Answer. I have stated that my conversation with Lea was between 1 and 2 o'clock. If you call that morning, I answer, emphatically, I had not.

Question. Were you familiar with Russell's mode of transacting business at the War Department?

Answer. I was familiar with the transactions in reference to the first acceptances of the Secretary of War.

Question. When were they given, who held them, and to whom did Russell deliver them?

Answer. When the contract was entered into between the Quartermaster General and Russell, Majors & Waddell, in 1858—January 16, 1858, is my impression of the date—I was in this city. It was a contract for carrying supplies to Utah. It became necessary for those gentlemen to have means to start the work. Mr. Russell and myself conned the matter over with a view to ascertain how that money could be raised. Not at my suggestion, but at the suggestion of some one, or of Russell, this project of having the Secretary of War accept payable out of funds to be received when the work was performed, was hit upon and proposed to the Secretary of War. He addressed a letter to the President of the Bank of America, in New York, setting forth the fact of this large contract, the importance to the government of having it carried out, and stating that it would be very agreeable to him to have it done. The result was (without going into particulars) acceptances to the extent of $200,000 soon after were furnished. Additional acceptances, if I recollect aright, were made, which were discounted by Augustus Belmont, Riggs & Co., of New York, and another house. I was delegated by Mr. Russell to pay those acceptances when they became due. They were payable the 1st of July, 1858. I came here with over $100,000 worth of quartermaster's receipts for transportation by Russell, Majors & Waddell, and a letter setting forth the fact that, in consequence of the very wet spring, further receipts could not be had in time, and asking the Secretary of War to give another acceptance or other acceptances, to take the place of those then due. I received from the Secretary of War—or rather indirectly from him through his office, for I never saw the Secretary of War myself, as I recollect of—one or more acceptances, and with that, and the receipts I brought on, and others which were afterwards sent on to me here, I succeeded in paying the $200,000 of acceptances, in full, by borrowing, and by discounting at the Bank of the Republic one acceptance for $25,000. Mr. G. W. Riggs, because I would not pay that money in Washington as soon as I got it, and before the notes were due, wrote me down his enemy from that day to this. That is the last I had to do with the acceptances of the Secretary of War.

Question. What did you do with those acceptances you took up?

Answer. I cannot say, positively, but I think I returned them to the War Department.

Question. Did you say you paid off those $200,000 partly in money and partly in new acceptances?

Answer. I paid the old acceptances entirely in money, but I was compelled to negotiate one of $25,000 in order to give me full means, or rather, Mr. Suter, of the Bank of the Republic, had it done for me.

Question. And where did you get the balance of the money to pay the $200,000.

Answer. I have already stated that I brought a certain amount of quartermaster's receipts with me; that others were forwarded to me; and that with those and the new acceptance of $25,000 which I got discounted, I paid the $200,000. I have at home all the figures in reference to this transaction, which I kept at the time because I had to make an account of the matter to my firm.

Question. What was the amount of those receipts of the quartermaster you subsequently received?

Answer. My impression is that I came on with about $135,000 worth of receipts. I cannot say precisely, because it is over two years since the transaction occurred. If I am correct, I must have received by express enough, with what I had originally, to make $175,000, because I had only to borrow $25,000 to pay the $200,000.

Question. Was it a new acceptance of the Secretary of War of $25,000 that you got discounted, or was it an old acceptance?

Answer. It was a new one—one I got as I passed through here.

Question. Are you connected with Russell, Majors & Waddell in their contract?

Answer. I am not, and never have been.

Question. You informed the committee that it was necessary for them to raise means by those acceptances for the purpose of putting their contract into operation: had they, besides that, means to do it?

Answer. They had not; the previous year had exhausted their resources in money. They had an abundance of stock, but their losses the year before, and the crisis of 1857, left them, as it did everybody else in our country, without money.

Question. In your estimation, what were they worth at the time they entered into this new contract with the government, in 1858?

Answer. I regarded them as men of very large means; I cannot say of what amount.

Question. Can you tell in what those means consisted?

Answer. In lands and property of various descriptions—wagons, oxen, mules, farms, houses, and everything of that kind.

Question. You were then acquainted with their business sufficiently to know that they were possessed of a very large amount of real estate and personal property?

Answer. Yes, sir.

Question. When were those lands purchased, and where were they located?

Answer. I knew of their owning a large amount of land in Kansas and Missouri; I was not present at the buying of all of it.

Question. Do you know, of your own knowledge, that they owned a large amount of real estate? and if so, state to the committee how you knew it.

Answer. Well, sir, so far as my personal knowledge of this matter is concerned, I saw Mr. Russell, at the sales at Fort Leavenworth in 1856, buy a large amount of land for himself and his firm, and I have repeatedly seen deeds upon deeds to them, and to him individually, for real estate.

Question. When was the first partnership between Russell, Majors & Waddell formed?

Answer. I do not know.

Question. Do you know what they were engaged in previous to the formation of their partnership?

Answer. I do not know, but I think they were contractors.

Examination by Mr. Harris.

Question. Do you know where any of these bonds have gone?

Answer. I do not.

Question. Do you know R. W. Latham?

Answer. Yes, sir.

Question. Have you ever had any conversation with Mr. Latham as to the transactions between Russell and the War Department?

Answer. Never to my recollection.

Question. Have you ever had any transactions with Latham of a pecuniary character?

Answer. I think I had when he was in business here, on his private account, or with Selden, Withers & Co.

Question. Have you had any transactions with Latham in which, in any way, the government securities were concerned?

Answer. No, sir.

Question. How lately have you seen Latham?

Answer. I have seen him in the streets the last few days.

Question. Have you had any conversation with him in reference to these bonds, or any of these matters?

Answer. No more than I have had with anybody I have met in the streets. I presume the subject has been brought up between us.

Question. Has Latham imparted to you any knowledge on his part?

Answer. He has not.

Question. Do you know Drinkard, chief clerk in the War Department?

Answer. Yes, sir.

Question. Have you had any conversation with him upon this subject?

Answer. Only as I have already stated.

Question. Have you had any conversation before or since this transaction with any persons whatever, who communicated to you in such conversation a knowledge of these transactions?

Answer. The only person is Mr. Lea, when I called upon him the other day, and that conversation I have stated. Mr. Russell made no admission whatever to me.

Question. When work had been done under this contract for the transportation of supplies, did you receive at your banking-house any of the certificates of the quartermaster which authorized the payment of money earned?

Answer. No, sir.

Question. Had your house any connexion with it?

Answer. None in the world.

Question. When moneys were earned under these contracts for transportation, did I understand you to say that the usage of the government was that the quartermaster at Leavenworth, or wherever the proper point was, paid the money to the contractor, if he had it in his possession?

Answer. I think their contract provided that they should have the money where they choose, whether in Leavenworth, St. Louis, or New York.

Question. Were they paid through the quartermaster at Fort Leavenworth?

Answer. They were entitled to be paid there if they saw fit. Their contract left it at their option to say where they should be paid?

Question. I understand you to say that if the quartermaster at that point had not the money they transmitted his certificates to the department, and that Mr. Miller, the quartermaster here, paid the money on the accounts of the quartermaster at Fort Leavenworth?

Answer. Yes, sir, on the accounts which would have been paid at Fort Leavenworth if the quartermaster there had had the money.

Question. Then I understand you to say that these vouchers for work done by the contractors out there were paid by the quartermaster out there if he had the money, if not, by Mr. Miller here?

Answer. That depends very much upon the wants of the contractors, and upon various circumstances. I have known them to have sums of money due when the quartermaster there had no funds in his possession, and the vouchers were not forwarded to Washington, because the quartermaster expected every day to receive the means of paying them.

Question. But still was not the quartermaster there the proper person to pay the money upon their vouchers?

Answer. I believe so.

Question. Then I can ask you, if in cases where the Secretary of War gave acceptances covering amounts due to these contractors, which amounts were also included in vouchers in the hands of the quartermaster at Fort Leavenworth, they could not have been paid by the process you have stated?

Answer. If I understand your question to be as to whether the moneys earned were applicable to the payment of these acceptances, I answer certainly they were.

Question. How do you mean applicable to these acceptances? Do you mean that Russell's vouchers could have been paid by either of the quartermasters, notwithstanding the amounts covered by them were also covered by the acceptances of the Secretary of War? Were they assumed to be bound to take up these acceptances out of the money they received?

Answer. Yes, sir; that money was applicable to these very acceptances.

Question. Then when Russell, Majors and Waddell received such acceptances it was understood that they were to pay them out of these moneys?

Answer. That was my understanding. Let me say that, so far as my statement to the committee in reference to these acceptances is concerned, my personal knowledge extends only to one transaction; in that transaction the money which I drew could not possibly have been diverted to any other purpose than the taking up of these acceptances?

Question. Because you made the arrangement that the acceptances should be taken up?

Answer. Yes, sir.

Question. Now, why was it that money was more easily raised upon the acceptances of the Secretary of War than upon the vouchers of the department itself?

Answer. Your question would indicate that you had not understood my explanation.

Question. Were the acceptances never given for moneys earned, and so expressed upon the face of them?

Answer. I should say that no acceptance was ever given for money alreary earned, for that would be like borrowing $1,000 when you had the money already in bank.

Question. When Russell, Majors and Waddell had vouchers from the Quartermaster's department for money already earned under their contract, and had also acceptances of the Secretary of War covering the same money, was it in their power, under the circumstances of the arrangement, to have paid or not to have paid these acceptances?

Answer. If they had failed to pay them I do not know what action the department would have taken.

Question. Could they not have made the money from one quarter from the vouchers of the quartermaster's department and raised the money from another quarter upon the acceptances of the Secretary?

Answer. I have stated, I believe, in my testimony very fully that it was in the power of these gentlemen to apply any money that they received to these acceptances if they saw fit.

Question. I put the question again: was it not within the power of these contractors to have raised money upon the vouchers of the quartermaster's department for services under their contract, and at the same time to have converted to their use the acceptances of the Secretary of War?

Answer. I should say it was.

Question. Then do you know of any evidence to the department that these contractors had not used these acceptances for the purpose of raising money upon them, and at the same time held the vouchers of the Quartermaster's department?

Answer. They never held vouchers of the quartermaster, except *in transitu* from one office to another, for the purpose of raising money. The vouchers made out in Major Van Vliet's office in Leavenworth could not go to Washington except the work had been performed and the money paid or ready to be paid.

Question. Could not these contractors go to Washington for the payment of the vouchers?

Answer. Yes, sir.

Question. And when demanded was not the money to be paid upon the vouchers?

Answer. Yes, sir.

Question. Now, then, could not they have also used the acceptances of the Secretary of War, which they held for the purpose of raising money, at the same time?

Answer. Yes, sir; and I have no doubt they did, but for moneys yet to be earned.

Question. I confine my question to acceptances for moneys earned, and I ask whether the two did not run together?

Answer. No, sir; one was after date, and the other was at sight or on presentation. There is no possible analogy between the two things.

Question (by Mr. Thomas.) When these vouchers were presented did the department, on paying the money, require the acceptances to be produced, or did they pay it to Russell and leave him to take up the acceptances at his pleasure?

Answer. I only know in relation to one instance, and then the money was paid to me and I paid the acceptance myself.

Question (by Mr. Harris.) And was it not in the option of the contractors to apply the money to the acceptances or not, as they saw fit? Could not they have kept the acceptances and used the money also?

Answer. I judge they could.

Question (by the chairman.) Did Lea express surprise at the fact that a fraud in the Interior Department had been detected, or at the fact that the bonds had been used by Bailey in the manner in which they were?

Answer. I did not observe or hear any expression of the kind, to the best of my recollection.

Hon JOHN B. FLOYD, recalled.

Examination by Mr. Harris.

Question. I understood you that the usages of the government in connexion with the payments to be made under these contracts was, that the quartermaster at the point you named—I believe Fort Leavenworth—gave vouchers or certificates of the performance of service, and that the money earned was payable upon these vouchers at Fort Leavenworth, or at the Quartermaster's department here in Washington.

Answer. The idea I attempted to express was this: that the contracts provide for payments under them, and the manner in which such payments are to be made. What I intended to say was, that the payments to contractors and to all other persons having claims on the Quartermaster's department was made through the quartermasters. My recollection is that, under this last contract of Russell, Majors & Waddell, the payments were to be made at Fort Leavenworth, but any certificate for the performance of work would be paid either there or here.

Question. Then, any certificate of work performed under that contract would entitle the party holding it to payment either there or here in Washington?

Answer. Yes, sir.

Question. When these certificates were paid here, where were they paid?

Answer. By the Quartermaster's department, I suppose.

Question. Were they first presented to you for your indorsement or assent?

Answer. Never; nor did I ever hear of them; nor did I ever know of them; unless there was some dispute about some of the items.

Question. Then, for all the work absolutely done by these contractors, they were entitled to be paid, according to the usages of the department, absolutely by the quartermasters, without being presented for your indorsement or approval at all?

Answer. Certainly.

Question. You stated yesterday to the committee that the indebtedness to these contractors was never considered consummated until the work was actually done?

Answer. Yes.

Question. Had you any means of knowing, at any time when these acceptances in question were issued, whether these parties had been, in fact, actually paid for the whole amount of work done up to the time the acceptances were given?

WITNESS. The last $700,000 of acceptances do you mean?

Mr. HARRIS. No; I will take this particular acceptance, dated on the 13th of September, 1860, and which is an acceptance for $15,000, [handing it to witness.] Now the question is, whether, at the time that acceptance was given, these parties were, in fact, paid for all the work performed by them under their contract, up to that date.

Answer. I suppose that up to that date they had been paid, because as fast as they earned the money they received payment, of course.

Question. Was this considered by you as a conditional, or an absolute, acceptance?

Answer. I considered it a conditional acceptance; you will observe that in most of the others the language is different.

Question. Is not the acceptance you have in the language of an absolute acceptance of negotiable paper?

Answer. Probably so.

Question. At the time of the issue of this acceptance was it expected the government would be relieved from responsibility upon it, by its payment by the parties to whom it was given?

Answer. That was, at all times, the agreement and understanding. These acceptances were given to them for accommodation, and were put into a shape that would enable them to raise money for their business; and were to be taken up and paid by them. It was my conviction that they would be taken up and paid by these parties, and there were two grounds upon which I rested that conviction: the first was the money arising out of their business; and the next was their own individual resources, which I had been taught to believe, and did believe, were extremely large. The acceptances were given as a simple accommodation, to enable these contractors to sustain themselves.

Question. Then they were given for the purpose of keeping up these contractors, and based upon an appreciation of their personal means rather than any knowledge in the department of the amount of money due to them?

Answer. Upon that ground, and also upon a knowledge upon the part of the department of the amount of money under the contract it could control in case of difficulty about the payment—both.

Question. Do I understand, then, that you held that the acceptances drawn in this form, for value received, payable at a given date, and chargeable to the contract account of these parties, were acceptances which the department could at any moment revoke and annul, although in the hands of a *bona fide* holder or owner?

Answer. No, not when in the hands of a *bona fide* holder or owner.

If such an acceptance were to be presented by a *bona fide* owner at the department with the request to have it put on file, then a positive order would be made that the money arising from their work should be set aside for the payment of such acceptance.

Question. I understand, then, that when they were issued it was without any knowledge on your part that the moneys up to that time due these parties had not been paid to them in the ordinary way, and with the further understanding that unless the acceptances given were presented by a *bona fide* owner and registered in the department they could not be made available by the holder?

Answer. They would be subject to certain payment in the hands of the holder whenever he chose to have them registered in the department, and the order made that the money arising from the contract of these parties should be applied to them, but not until that was done. I never doubted but they would be used, as they had been used, in very large amounts in the ordinary routine of business, and that all concerned in them would be protected and taken care of by them under the agreement made with the parties who held the paper. What that agreement was I never knew and never desired to know.

Question. In case the holder of one of these acceptances presented it to the department and the department agreed to pay it in the manner you have stated, what course would the acceptance take on the books of the department; would it be registered?

Answer. Yes, sir.

Question. Would it be numbered?

Answer. It would be filed.

Question. What would be the indication upon the face of the paper that it had been so registered?

Answer. None that I know of.

Question. Is there any indication upon the face of that acceptance [handing one to witness] that it has been registered?

Answer. I think not. It never was registered.

Question. Look at the numbering upon its face and tell the committee what it indicates, and for what purpose it was put there.

Answer. It was done by a clerk in the department; the purpose I do not understand.

Question. Do you know whether or not it indicates its registration in the department?

Answer. I do not. I do not know what it means.

Question. Is the indorsement in red ink in the handwriting of the chief clerk of the War Department?

Answer. It is the handwriting of a clerk in the department, but not of the chief clerk.

Question. What is his name?

Answer. His name is Irwin.

Question. Will you be kind enough to explain the difference in the character of the two kinds of acceptances that I see here?

Answer. Yes, sir. I did it very fully yesterday, but I will do it again. One description of draft has the assurance of an absolute acceptance, and was given while I had the control of the funds arising from the work done. Desiring, as I have stated so frequently, to sustain these people, and it being represented to me by them that the acceptances of the other description, such as that you now hold in your hand, could be substituted to a large amount for those held by bankers, firms, and persons of wealth, who were disposed to extend an additional credit and longer indulgence to the contractors, upon that representation I changed the form of acceptances and made them payable when the work was done. It was upon the idea, as I stated yesterday, that these acceptances were only to go into the hands of bankers and firms holding the other acceptances that I gave them in large amounts in order to insure such a disposal of them, and to prevent their going upon the market.

Question. I understood you yesterday that every acceptance given by you to the contractors was to run against unearned money; was that rule applicable to both classes of acceptances?

Answer. All the acceptances I ever gave to these people were to run against money that was to arise from the execution of the work.

Question. Did you use the phrase unearned money?

Answer. I think likely; that is the same thing.

Question. I understood you further, that these acceptances had relation to moneys yet to be earned by them, and which were understood by you to be under the absolute control of the department. What do you mean by that?

Answer. I do not know as I can make my meaning any more explicit. I will say that if you ask if these contractors were disposed not to pay these acceptances into the hands of the men they had business with—men of whom I knew nothing whatever—whether they could draw the money from the quartermaster out there, put it into their own pockets, and refuse to pay these drafts into the hands of the men they had dealings with without any control of mine, I answer certainly they could.

Question. The first acceptance I handed you a short time since is number 78 and the next 90. Have you any knowledge of what has become of the acceptances intervening between those two?

Answer. I have not; I do not know, and never did know, where and when those acceptances have been paid. They have been given, exchanged, paid, and destroyed to the amount of several milions of dollars, from first to last. Until last September there never was any trouble about them; I said yesterday that it was July, but I was mistaken, I never heard a breath of trouble about these acceptances until last September. The contractors certainly had it in their power to do what you inquired about just now. I had no guarantee against that except two things: the first was that in doing so they would injure their credit; and the next was that it would break up their contract entirely, because as soon as I discovered that they had broken faith with these people and endeavored to get money on false pretences, I would make an order that all the earnings out of their contract should be disposed of in a particular way. To tell the truth, however, I never regarded the question in that point of view. It was from a different standpoint that I looked at it. I looked at it as the means of sustaining the contractors in a great work—a work which it is very difficult for persons not familiar with army transportation over the plains to comprehend; a work of infinite importance, as your folks will find out before six months from now; and to embarrass which is to produce greater confusion and to run greater risks of injury to the public service than could arise from any other cause whatever. And therefore, as a matter of administration, whilst the course I pursued was certainly not in conformity to the ordinary routine rules of the department, which would have saved me from probable public clamor, I felt that it was confering a substantial benefit to the public service, and I did it, and I would do it again, unless there was a law to prohibit it, which there is not.

Question. Do you know whether any of these acceptances went at any time into the hands of the Bank of the Republic of New York, and were discounted by them for the benefit of these indorsers?

Answer. I do not.

Question (by Mr. Case.) When these acceptances were destroyed or taken up was there any evidence of it in the department?

Answer. No, sir; unless there was evidence that they were overdue.

Question (by Mr. Harris.) Were they always taken up?

Answer. So far as I know, they were always taken up until September last, when the troubles began. Then, upon consultation with some of the creditors of Russell, Majors & Waddell, who came here to see me, it was generally understood that they would be able to arrange their affairs and go on with their business operations.

Question (by Mr. Morris.) I see that there are about $800,000 of these conditional acceptances made by you payable in 1861, if the money is earned. What assurance had you that these contractors would be able to perform their engagements to the government if they were forced in advance to hypothecate these acceptances for the purpose of raising money on them to pay old debts?

Answer. I had this assurance, if they could raise money to sustain their credit and keep their house on a business footing, that then, with the stock I knew they had on hand, and the facilities they possess for transportation, they would be in a condition to perform the work.

Question. What do you mean by keeping their house on a business footing?

Answer. I mean by that keeping it in credit, and such credit as it had and has had ever since I have been Secretary of War.

Question. Do you think the amount they will earn in 1861 will exceed the amount of those acceptances?

Answer. That depends on the policy of the succeeding administration. If the army is kept on the footing it has at present; if the Indian wars are prosecuted with the same energy, activity, and efficiency as they have been for the last two years, the amount of transportation will reach about that sum. But from the character of the paper the holder could not be misled, nor could any one else, because on the face of the paper itself nothing is to be paid unless the money is earned. Therefore, there is to be in the mind of the holder that confidence in the ability of these people to earn the money which would give the paper its credit.

FRIDAY, *January* 4, 1861.

WILLIAM R. DRINKARD sworn.

Examination by Mr. Harris.

Question. Mr. Drinkard, what is your position in the War Department?

Answer. I am chief clerk, sir.

Question. What is the character of your duties as chief clerk?

Answer. They are of a very general character. I am the medium of communication generally between the Secretary of War and parties who desire to see him. Papers that are to be submitted to him are generally passed through my hands.

Question. Are you familiar with the provisions of the contracts made between the War Department and Russell, Majors & Waddell?

Answer. I don't think that I am sufficiently familiar to give you a correct statement of their contents.

Question. How long have you been in the War Department?

Answer. Since the first of April, 1857.

Question. You are not, I suppose, familiar with the usages of the department in the matter of acceptances for parties who were contractors prior to that time?

Answer. No, sir.

Question. Do you know of any cases in which acceptances have been given to contractors by the Secretary of War since you have been in the office?

Answer. I know of none, except those given to the firm of Russell, Majors & Waddell under several of their contracts.

Question. They are, then, the only parties to whom such acceptances have been given to your knowledge?

Answer. Within my knowledge.

Question. Are you familiar with the acceptances given by the Secretary of War to that firm?

Answer. I have seen them generally, sir; I have seen a great many of them.

Question. Have any of them been drawn up by you?

Answer. None, sir.

Question. Have any of them been indorsed in any way by you?

Answer. None, sir.

Question. Have they ever been in your hands for any purpose whatever in connexion with your office?

Answer. Never, except to get the Secretary's signature—his acceptance.

Question. Have you at any time made memoranda of the date and tenor of any of those acceptances?

Answer. No, sir.

Question. Have any of them been handed to you at any time by the Secretary of War for the purpose of registration?

Answer. No, sir.

Question. Is there any register of any of these acceptances in the War Department, to your knowledge?

Answer. They are registered by a clerk in the War Department who occupies a room immediately opposite to mine.

Question. Do you know for what purpose they are registered?

Answer. They were registered simply for the purpose of keeping a memorandum of the dates, the amounts, and the time that they fell due.

Question. Was it the custom of the department for that registration to be made in the case of all acceptances given by the Secretary?

Answer. So far as I know anything of them, in the beginning of the transactions in reference to the acceptances, the Secretary of War desired that a register should be kept of them, and I selected a clerk in the department, who was a very intelligent gentleman, and wrote a fine hand.

Question. Was that Mr. Irwin?

Answer. Mr. Irwin, attached to the Secretary's office, was to keep a registry of these acceptances; or rather, in the first instance, copies of the acceptances were kept. I desired Mr. Irwin to keep copies, thinking they would furnish the best evidence of the acceptances.

Question. Are you aware that that habit of registration has been continued up to the issue of the last of these acceptances?

Answer. My impression is that a registration has been continued, but the particular form of it may have been changed.

Question. I understand you to say that that registration was at the instance, and by the direction, of the Secretary of War?

Answer. Yes, sir.

Question. And was to apply to all acceptances given by him in this connexion?

Answer. Yes, sir.

Question. Do you know Mr. Russell, of the firm of Russell, Majors & Waddell?

Answer. I do, sir.

Question. Did you see Mr. Russell at the War Office or elsewhere about the 13th of December, in connexion with any of these acceptances?

Answer. I think Mr. Russell was at the War Office about that time.

Question. Had he an interview with you, sir?

Answer. He generally had an interview with me when the went to the War Office.

Question. Had he on that occasion, in reference to the acceptances?

Answer. Yes, sir.

Question. Be good enough to state the character of that conversation, as nearly as you can. Did he come to the War Department to see you about it?

Answer. No, sir; he came to see the Secretary.

Question. He had a conversation with you?

Answer. He had a conversation with me.

Question. Be kind enough to state it.

Answer. He told me he desired to get some acceptances from the

Secretary of War, to make arrangements for his business transactions in connexion with his transportation; and I do not know that it was unlike other interviews that he had with me on the subject. He had difficulty in meeting the acceptances already issued, and he proposed to make some arrangement with the Secretary, the particulars of which I do not know, by which to meet his obligations arising out of the transaction about the acceptances and so forth.

Question. Did you understand it to be for the purpose of taking up the acceptances already due?

Answer. Yes, sir.

Question. In the nature of a renewal?

Answer. It was in the nature of a renewal, and of taking up acceptances overdue that had matured, and that he had not been able to meet. What the result of his interview with the Secretary of War was I do not know.

Question. Have there been, at any time, any of the acceptances issued by the department returned to the department and cancelled?

Answer. Some of them have been.

Question. Do you know what number and the amounts?

Answer. I could not speak positively about that; they were returned to Mr. Irwin, and he kept a memorandum of the cancelled acceptances.

Question. Do you know whether those cancelled acceptances are in the War Office?

Answer. I suppose they are, sir.

Question. Do you know Mr. Godard Bailey?

Answer. I do, sir.

Question. Had you any interview with him at any time in reference to any of these matured or overdue acceptances of the Secretary?

Answer. I had an interview with Mr. Bailey some time last summer.

Question. About what time?

Answer. I do not really know how to designate the time except from rumors which have recently reached me. I understand that it must probably have been about the month of July?

Question. Where was the interview?

Answer. At the War Department. As well as I can recollect the transaction, which I did not think of afterwards until within the last three weeks, I will repeat the substance of the conversation that passed between Mr. Bailey and myself upon that occasion. He came up to the War Department, and, finding that I had a good many gentlemen in my room, desired to speak to me privately, and I then took him on the floor above my room. He introduced the subject of these acceptances; said that he had understood that the Secretary of War had issued acceptances to Russell, Majors & Waddell to a large amount; that Mr. Russell was in a tight place in reference to money matters at that time, and there was a probability that some of these acceptances would be protested. He asked me what would be the effect of the protest of those acceptances upon Governor Floyd. I told him that I thought it would be very annoying to Governor Floyd; that it would disturb him greatly that any of his official papers should be protested before the public; that I supposed and firmly believed that the acceptances would be paid; that there was money coming due to Messrs. Russell, Majors & Waddell, under their contracts for transportation, sufficient to meet these acceptances; that up to that time none of them had been protested; that Mr. Russell had very promptly met all at maturity; and that while he might be pressed for money at that time I did not suppose he would be pressed so far as to be forced to submit to a protest. That was my opinion from previous transactions that Mr. Russell had had with the War Department. I stated to Mr. Bailey that I had understood Mr. Russell to be a man of large means and considerable wealth; that I believed him to be a business man and a man of honor and integrity; that I thought he would meet his obligations as he had done thus far to the War Department, and, therefore, I suppose he was perfectly responsible.

Question. Your conversation, then, was intended to give to Mr. Bailey the impression that these acceptances would be taken care of by Russell.

Answer. That was my impression. He then remarked that he did not know Mr. Russell, and cared nothing about him, but that he felt interested in Governor Floyd.

Question. Did he state why?

Answer. No, sir; he did not. He said then that if there was any doubt—any difficulty apprehended, so far as Governor Floyd was concerned, he was disposed to make an effort to protect him, that he had means which he could control, and that if he was entirely satisfied of Mr. Russell's responsibility, he thought he could make a negotiation with Mr. Russell by which he could relieve him. At that point of the conversation, I said to him, "I do not know anything about this, but you had better see Russell; he is in the building now." He desired me to introduce Mr. Russell to him. I took Mr. Russell up stairs and introduced him to Mr. Bailey; but I do not know anything of the conversation that passed between them. I cannot state this conversation between Mr. Bailey and myself more distinctly than in these general terms, because it passed out of my mind. I did not remember it again until, I think it was, last Thursday week.

Question. Did Mr. Bailey suggest to you that he feared the non-payment of these acceptances might make the resignation of Governor Floyd necessary?

Answer. No, sir.

Question. Did you suggest to him that you thought Governor Floyd would be compelled to resign if these acceptances were not met?

Answer. No, I did not, sir.

Question. You did not?

Answer. Not at all, sir.

Question. Was anything said in the interview between you about the probable resignation of Governor Floyd in case of their non-payment?

Answer. Nothing at all.

Question. Did Mr. Bailey indicate to you what was the character of the securities upon which he could negotiate to relieve these acceptances?

Answer. He did not, sir. My impression from the conversation was that Mr. Bailey was representing some friend who had means at his command, and who desired to make a money negotiation. I did not know the position that Mr. Bailey occupied in the Interior Department. I had heard that he was a law clerk to the Secretary of the Interior.

Question. Then I understand you to say, Mr. Drinkard, that one reason why you believe there was no risk of these acceptances not being met, was that there were moneys then due to these contractors which would probably be sufficient to meet them?

Answer. Yes, I supposed so, sir, and the principal cause of my assurance in the matter was the prompt manner in which these acceptances had been met. I had not heard a suspicion of a doubt about their being paid.

Question. Did you know anything about the state of the account from time to time of Russell, Majors & Waddell?

Answer. No; I did not.

Question. Was it not in the Quartermaster's department?

Answer. It was in the Quartermaster's department; most of the payments made to Russell, Majors & Waddell were made by the quartermaster at Fort Leavenworth, the eastern terminus of their transportation line.

Question. Those payments were made upon vouchers?

Answer. Those payments were made upon vouchers, generally speaking. Sometimes the requisitions would be made payable in Washington city. Sometimes the quartermaster at Leavenworth would send a requisition to the quartermaster general, and he would have a certain amount of money transferred to the quartermaster at Leavenworth on the books of the assistant treasurer at New York, and, upon that transfer, the quartermaster at Leavenworth would draw his checks in favor of Russell, and that is the reason, I suppose, why all the acceptances were made payable in New York.

Question. Then, as I understand it, the money earned by these contractors was paid either by the quartermaster at Fort Leavenworth in the way you describe, or, if not paid upon vouchers by him, by the quartermaster in Washington, Mr. Miller?

Answer. Yes, sir.

Question. Did you know from time to time the amounts paid by either of these quartermasters to Russell, Majors & Waddell?

Answer. No; I did not, sir.

Question. How did you know, then, that there were moneys due to them sufficient to cover these acceptances?

Answer. I did not know the fact, but that was my supposition.

Question. Might not, in point of fact, Russell, Majors & Waddell have been paid up to the date of their last earnings either by the quartermaster at Fort Leavenworth or the quartermaster here without your knowledge?

Answer. Oh, yes, they might have been paid it, but not in full under the contract, because the contract was a subsisting one; yet they might have been paid in full for the money earned.

Question. Then you had no means of knowing, in your office, whether they had or had not been paid up to the date of their last earnings either by the quartermaster at Fort Leavenworth or by Mr. Miller here?

Answer. I did not.

Question. Have you had any interview with Mr. Bailey since the one to which you have referred?

Answer. Not that I remember, sir.

Question. Has there been any correspondence with Mr. Bailey from the War Department?

Answer. None that I know of.

Question. Nor from yourself?

Answer. None, sir.

Question. Have you had any interview with Mr. Russell subsequent to the date of the conversation with Mr. Bailey to which you have referred?

Answer. Yes, I have. I saw him and had a conversation with him in December last.

Question. What was that conversation about?

Answer. It was in reference to further acceptances. He told me he desired to get those acceptances from the Secretary of War, to enable him to make some arrangement with parties who held acceptances then over due. I knew that he was embarrassed then, because a good many of the acceptances had been protested and the War Department had been informed of the protests.

Question. A good many of the acceptances had been protested in December?

Answer. Yes, sir. I think the first protest took place about the 27th of September.

Question. Do you know now the amount or the date of any of the acceptances of which the War Department had received notice of protest?

Answer. No, sir; I could not tell.

Question. What class of acceptances did those protests refer to?

Answer. They referred, as well as I remember, to the acceptances without condition.

Question. Where were they protested?

Answer. I think most of them were protested in New York; they were payable there.

Question. At what bank?

Answer. The Bank of the Republic.

Question. All of them at the Bank of the Republic?

Answer. I am not certain.

Question. Are those notices of protest in the War Department?

Answer. No, the notices of protest are not; but there are letters in the War Department informing the Secretary that certain drafts had been protested.

Question. You said the War Department had been advised of it by notices of protest.

Answer. Not by notices of protest, but simply by letters from the owners of the drafts.

Question. Are those letters on file in the department now?

Answer. They are.

Question. In whose charge are they—yours?

Answer. They are in charge of the record clerk.

Question. Who is he?

Answer. Mr. Lee.

Question. But they are at the disposal and under the control of the Secretary of War?

Answer. Yes, sir.

Question. Was what you have stated the whole of your conversation with Mr. Russell in December?

Answer. That is the substance of the conversation.

Question. Did he say anything to you then of this protested paper?

Answer. He said he would make arrangements for the protested paper.

Question. Did he say what the character of the arrangements was?

Answer. No, sir.

Question. Did he name Bailey to you in that conversation?

Answer. He did not.

Question. Did he say anything to you about these Indian securities?

Answer. He did not, sir.

Question. Did he name any person to you in that conversation from whom or by whom he expected to raise money to meet those protested acceptances?

Answer. No; he said simply that he expected to raise some money from friends in New York.

Question. Did he name them?

Answer. He did not.

Question. Nor did he say upon what character of securities he expected to raise it, but he asked for a renewal of some of these acceptances?

Answer. Yes, sir; or, rather, an additional amount of acceptances.

Question. Were these acceptances that he asked for given?

Answer. I cannot say that they were; they did not pass through my hands if they were.

Question. Then, to your knowledge, they were not given, nor any registration made of them if given?

Answer. I must say now that the registration was made a few days ago. Governor Floyd then handed me a list of acceptances which he had given.

Question. I understand you to say that the registration of these acceptances was made a few days ago?

Answer. I think I can say within the last eight or ten days.

Question. Within the last eight or ten days Governor Floyd handed you a memorandum of other acceptances?

Answer. Yes; the acceptances that he gave to Mr. Russell in December.

Question. Well, now, sir, did that memorandum refer to acceptances given to Mr. Russell after notice to the War Department of the protest of the prior acceptances?

Answer. Oh, yes, sir.

Question. They did?

Answer. Yes, sir.

Question. They were for the purpose, then, of enabling Russell to take up the overdue or unpaid acceptances?

Answer. I cannot say what the object was; the Secretary did not tell me.

Question. But the acceptances were subsequent to the protest to the War Department of the other ones?

Answer. Yes, sir; I so understand.

Question. Are you able to say what the amount of the acceptances so given was?

Answer. No, I could not say.

Question. What did you do with the memorandum that the Secretary gave you?

Answer. I handed the memorandum to Mr. Irwin, and he made record of it, and returned the memorandum to Governor Floyd.

Question. In the case of acceptances that were paid do you know what became of them in the department? What course they took?

Answer. They were cancelled generally.

Question. How do you mean cancelled? Marked "cancelled," or destroyed?

Answer. I think they were marked "cancelled" by Mr. Irwin on the list that he keeps. I do not think the acceptances were returned to the department.

Question. What evidence, then, had the department that they were paid?

Answer. The simple fact of the time for payment having passed.

Question. Without notice of protest?

Answer. Without notice of protest.

Question. And upon that they marked them "cancelled?"

Answer. Yes, sir, "cancelled."

Question. They cancelled them by marking them paid?

Answer. Mr. Irwin simply kept a list.

Question. Then did not the War Department consider that class of acceptances as binding upon the government?

Answer. I suppose so, sir.

Question. I understand you to say that they were acceptances by Mr. Floyd, and were not returned when paid to the department; but might, so far as you know, have remained in the possession of Russell, Majors & Waddell?

Answer. They might have been, so far as I know.

Question. It appears, then, that at the time the Secretary of War, according to the usage you have stated, gave acceptances to Russell, Majors & Waddell, he had no personal knowledge of the fact that the outstanding acceptances had been paid or returned?

Answer. In answer to that, I say that if he had any positive knowledge, I did not know it.

Question. Do I understand you, then, to say that if he had any knowledge upon the subject, it was knowledge confined to himself, and not apparent from the transactions upon the books of the department?

Answer. I did not know of any official knowledge; if he had any knowledge, it was personal and not official.

Question You say you had one conversation with Mr. Russell in December. Have you had any conversation with him since?

Answer. I have not; I have not seen him.

Question. Have you, from July last to this time, addressed any letters to Russell in reference to this transaction?

Answer. It is very possible I have.

Question. Do you recollect at whose direction those letters were addressed to him?

Answer. Sometimes I have written to him at the suggestion of the Secretary of War, but principally I would write to him when the Secretary received a notice of protest, and inform him of the fact.

Question. Then you wrote sometimes at the request of the Secretary of War, when the Secretary was informed of the protest of some of these drafts?

Answer. Yes, sir.

Question. Did you write to him upon any other occasion, and for any other purpose than that?

Answer. No, sir; except in reference to general matters of business, when he would direct letters to the Secretary or to myself, in relation to general business transactions relating to transportation, and then only giving him information or answering questions connected with that business.

Question. Did you, at any time, on your own motion, or by the direction of any other person, write to Russell any letters having any connexion whatever with these Indian trust bonds?

Answer. No, sir. I might as well say here that I did not know of the existence of those bonds until last Sunday night week.

Question. Is there any of the correspondence between Russell and the Secretary of War on file in the department now?

Answer. I do not remember.

Question. Is it the usage of the department to keep on file letters addressed to the Secretary of War?

Answer. Yes, sir; on official business.

Question. Any matters connected with these drafts would, I suppose, be considered official business?

Answer. I suppose so.

Question. Then, if the usage has been observed, these letters are on file in the department. In whose possession would they be?

Answer. I suppose any letters in reference to these drafts are on file, subject to the control of the Secretary of War. There are no letters on file, I suppose, addressed to Russell; I did not make any record of the letters I wrote to him calling his attention to these protested drafts.

Question. How many drafts were protested?

Answer. I do not know; I cannot state accurately, but all the letters received by the Secretary of War in reference to them are, I suppose, now in the War Department.

Question. Can you approximate to the number of drafts that were protested?

Answer. It is very difficult to do that; I do not like to make a surmise, when, I presume, the facts can be ascertained positively.

Question. But it occurred frequently.

Answer. A great many have been protested since the 27th of September last.

Question. And, of course, the fact of such protest was within the knowledge of the Secretary of War?

Answer. Yes, sir.

Question. Did you, during the month of December, and towards its close, telegraph to Mr. Russell in the city of New York?

Answer. I did.

Question. What was the purport of that telegraphic despatch?

Answer. The purport was that he should meet Mr. Latham at pier No. 1, I think it was, on the arrival of the Amboy boat.

Question. For what purpose, and why, did you desire him to meet Latham?

Answer. I added in that despatch, "it is vitally important to you to do so." In answer to the question why I did it, I say, I used that language, and sent that despatch, at the direction of Secretary Floyd. The object of the meeting I did not know; I simply used the words that the Secretary dictated.

Question. And you have no knowledge at all of the necessity for such meeting, nor of the purpose of the despatch?

Answer. I have not.

Question. Who is this Latham to whom you refer?

Answer. He is a gentleman who lives in the city of New York at this time; at one time he lived in Washington. He has been, for a part of the time during the last three or four years, attending to the private business of Governor Floyd.

Question. What is Mr. Latham's relation to the War Department?

Answer. He has no relation at all with the War Department.

Question. Does he hold any office in the War Department?

Answer. No, sir.

Question. Is he in the employ of the government in any way?

Answer. Not that I know of.

Question. Has he a desk in the War Department?

Answer. No, sir.

Question. Has he ever kept one there?

Answer. Not that I know of.

Question. Then you did not know Latham in any relation except his private relation to Governor Floyd?

Answer. No, sir.

Question. Did you receive any answer to that despatch?

Answer. No, sir.

Question. Did you have any communication from Latham subsequent to that despatch?

Answer. No, sir; Latham came on here.

Question. Did you see him?

Answer. I did.

Question. What conversation had you with him?

Answer. I cannot repeat it. The substance of the transaction in reference to these Indian trust funds had then been made public, and Latham had heard of it in New York.

Question. Did he tell you how he had heard of it?

Answer. No, sir.

Question. What else?

Answer. He told me that he had heard of it in New York; that parties had gone on to arrest Russell for connexion with the abstraction of the bonds in the Indian department; but he gave me no particulars connected with it. He did not tell me that he had had no conversation with Russell upon the subject.

Question. Had you no curiosity to ask him about it?

Answer. I had not. I had heard of the whole thing here. It seems that Latham got his information more from Washington than elsewhere, by rumors.

Question. Did or did he not communicate to you any source from which he had learned about this bond transaction?

Answer. I cannot say that he did. He told me he had a conversation with Russell, but I did not interrogate him.

Question. Did he refer to any other conversation with Russell?

Answer. He did not.

Question. Have you had any conversation with him since that time?

Answer. I have had several with him.

Question. Have any of them referred to these acceptances and these bonds?

Answer. Only in a general manner, and in reference to this whole transaction.

Question. Has he indicated to you the whereabouts of any of these bonds?

Answer. He has not.

Question. Have you had any conversation with Mr. Bailey since the one referred to by you in the War Department?

Answer. None whatever. I may have met Bailey casually, but have had no conversation with him in relation to business connected with the War Department. It was very seldom that I saw him.

Question. And I understand you to say that Russell has never intimated to you where any of these bonds are, or what use he has made of them?

Answer. I have never interchanged a word with Russell upon the subject. I did not know at all that he had them until I heard of it after this revelation was made.

Question. And Latham, upon his part, has never indicated to you any knowledge upon the subject?

Answer. No, sir.

Question. Nor Mr. Bailey?

Answer. No, sir.

Question. Then I understand from your testimony that so far as the earnings, up to any particular date, of Russell, Majors & Waddell, under these contracts, are concerned, they might have been paid by the quartermaster at Fort Leavenworth, or the quartermaster here, without the knowledge of the Secretary of War that they had been so paid; and that, so far as the acceptances given by the Secretary of War are concerned, there was no knowledge in the department of the fact of their payment, except such as may have been given by Russell himself; and that new acceptances were being given, from time to time, without the knowledge by the Secretary of War that the outstanding ones had been paid; and that, in point of fact, these parties might not only have collected their earnings from these quartermasters, but might also have retained to their use the outstanding acceptances for which, at the same time, they received new ones? Is that the substance of your testimony?

Answer. It is; that is a possible state of affairs. I do not know of its positive existence, but such a state of affairs might have existed under the circumstances.

Question. Here is a draft indorsed by Russell, Majors & Waddell, in the following words:

"$10,000. WASHINGTON CITY, *September* 19, 1860.

"Twelve months after date pay to our own order, at the 'Bank of the Republic,' New York city, ten thousand dollars for value received, and charge to account of our transportation contract of the 12th day of April, 1860.

"RUSSELL, MAJORS & WADDELL.

"Hon. J. B. FLOYD,
"*Secretary of War.*"

And indorsed in red ink on its face:

"No. 85.] WAR DEPARTMENT, *September* 19, 1860.

"Accepted.

"JOHN B. FLOYD,
"*Secretary of War.*"

Now is not that a positive acceptance?

Answer. It is what they call a positive acceptance, and for which the government is responsible, in contradistinction from a conditional acceptance.

Question. And in the course of business in the War Department is not an acceptance of this sort always paid, in the hands of a *bona fide* holder, if there are funds?

Answer. I should suppose so.

Question. Do you know, in connexion with any of this class of acceptances, that any necessity existed for a party holding them to notify the department that he held them and desired them to be paid, before the department considered itself bound to pay them, if they had funds?

Answer. I do not know that any such process is necessary.

Question. Do you know any reason why such a process should be necessary?

Answer. I do not. As I understand it, it was never expected that the department would take up these acceptances, but that these parties would receive their regular payments from the quartermaster at Fort Leavenworth, or from the quartermaster here, and with the funds they thus received they would take up these acceptances at their maturity.

Examination by the chairman.

Question. When did your acquaintance with Russell first commence?

Answer. I think it was some time in the fall of 1857.

Question. Did you, at any time thereafter, write any letter or letters to any persons urging upon them to loan these parties, Russell, Majors & Waddell, money or capital?

Answer. I think I wrote one letter.

Question. To whom, and when?

Answer. I am not positive as to the time, but it occurs to me it was about the time of the commencement of the issuing of these acceptances by the Secretary of War. I wrote a letter to the president of the Bank of the Republic—I am not entirely certain as to the individual, but I think it was the president of the bank—stating my opinion of the certainty of the payment of those acceptances from funds which the contractors would receive from the government. The Secretary of War wrote several letters of that kind, one, I think, to Mr. Belmont, and also to other parties; they are on file in the War Department. I think I stated generally in the letter, so far as I could, the process of receiving money by these contractors of the department on account of transportation, and based my opinion on the ability of the contractors to meet those acceptances from that process, and from the general amount of business they had to transact.

Question. Did you, in that letter, give any assurance to the Bank of the Republic that no acceptances would be given by the War Department unless the money was due to the contractors?

Answer. I do not remember that I did; I think it is possible. I think I stated that the acceptances then made were for money that was in process of being earned. According to the contract, as soon as the contractors receive notice of a certain amount of transportation to be carried from one point to another the department is considered bound to them for that transportation, whether he carries it or not, upon the principle that it subjects them to the expense of getting ready to take it; and there is a provision in the contract, that if the government does not require the transportation to be made the government shall make it good to the contractors.

Question. Your answer to my question is, that you do not remember to have written a letter of the character I referred to?

Answer. I wrote a letter, but do not remember precisely the contents of it.

Question. Have you given all the contents of the letter, so far as your recollection serves you?

Answer. I have.

Question. You say Governor Floyd wrote quite a number of such letters?

Answer. I think he wrote two or three.

Question. Do you recollect whether it was stated, either in your letter or in the letters of Governor Floyd, in order to give these acceptances credit and currency, that it was a rule of the War Department not to give those acceptances for over half the amount that was due to the contractors?

Answer. I do not remember.

Question. What was the character of those letters written by Governor Floyd?

Answer. I cannot give you the details. The object of the letters was to assure the parties to whom those acceptances were presented for negotiation that they would be safe in making the investment.

Question. Were those letters written by you as chief clerk?

Answer. No, sir; they were written by him, copied by the copying clerk in the department, and signed by the Secretary of War.

Question. And you think copies of all those letters are on file?

Answer. I think they are, in the War Department.

Question. Can you tell us who compose the firm of Russell, Majors & Waddell?

Answer. I think there are only three partners—Mr. Russell, Mr. Majors, and Mr. Waddell.

Question. Do you know whether any other person or persons shared in the profits of their contract?

Answer. I do not.

Question. Do you know whether Latham, or any other individual, received any bonus from them for attending to their business in the department?

Answer. I do not. I did not understand that Latham attended to Russell's business, or to the business of the firm; Russell generally attended to those matters himself.

Question. Mr. Latham, as I understand you, has been the private agent and confidential friend of Governor Floyd?

Answer. Yes, sir; for a part of the time that Governor Floyd has been here.

Question. Has Latham been in this city most of the time since Mr. Floyd has been Secretary of War?

Answer. He has been here a good deal.

Question. Do you know where their acquaintance commenced?

Answer. I think in this city, ten or twelve years ago; but I do not certainly know.

Question. Do you know of any officers of the government having paid off a larger amount of indebtedness, during his official term, than he received salary?

Answer. I do not.

Question. Do you know anything in reference to this transaction, other than what you have already disclosed, that would tend to throw any light upon the abstraction of these bonds?

Answer. I do not.

Question. When did your acquaintance with Bailey commence?

Answer. During this administration, but I cannot tell precisely when; I never had a very intimate acquaintance with him.

Question. Do you know him to be a man of means?

Answer. I do not.

Question. Do you know him to be without means?

Answer. I do not know anything certain about his history, either previous to or subsequent to his coming to Washington.

Question. I understood you to say that in the conversation you had with Bailey in regard to accommodating Russell, with a view to save the credit of the Secretary of War, the impression was left upon your mind that he was to receive means from some friend. Is that so?

Answer. I supposed he expected some friend, who had money, to assist him.

Question. Then did not you have the impression that he had no means of his own?

Answer. That was my impression. I did not suppose he intended a transaction upon his own account.

Question. What did he say to induce you to believe that he was to receive some money from a friend or friends?

Answer. Nothing, except the simple remark he made that he could control certain means. I did not ask him to make any explanation of the details. I did not regard it my business.

Question. And the inquiry did not suggest itself to your mind how Bailey was to command those means, or where they were to come from?

Answer. Not at all. The conversation with Baily made a very light impression on my mind, and I think it never again recurred to me until possibly week before last.

Question. How did it happen that Bailey and Russell met at the War Department at the time you introduced them?

Answer. I have not the slightest suspicion.

Question. Do you remember the day that introduction took place?

Answer. I do not.

Question. Fix the time as near as you can.

Answer. I could not fix the time at all, except for the fact that I have heard it rumored that Bailey came to the War Department in July last. There was no circumstance connected with it that left any impression upon my mind sufficient to base an opinion or surmise on, as to the day or particular time of the month.

Question. That was the only time you ever saw Bailey at the War Department?

Answer. No, sir; I had seen him at the War Department frequently before.

Question. Have you seen him there since?

Answer. I have not.

Question. Can you inform the committee whether Latham went to New York on the business of Governor Floyd, and in pursuance of the telegraphic despatch you sent to Russell to meet him?

Answer. I suppose he went to New York to see Russell.

Question. Did you have any conversation with him the day that despatch was sent?

Answer. I did not.

Question. How soon after did he return to this city?

Answer. I think he returned in two or three days.

Question. Before or after Russell was brought here?

Answer. I cannot say. I do not know but he came on the day that Russell did. I think he came on the same train, but I cannot say positively.

Question. Do you know what amount of money was paid to the contractors, Russell, Majors & Waddell, for the services they performed for the government during the past year?

Answer. I do not. The books in the quartermaster general's office will show.

GEORGE W. RIGGS sworn.

Examination by the chairman.

Question. Are you a banker in this city?

Answer. Yes, sir.

Question. Have you seen a list, published by the Secretary of the Interior, of bonds alleged to have been abstracted fraudulently from the Interior Department?

Answer. I have seen the list published in the papers.

Question. Do you know where any of those bonds are?

Answer. I am informed that five bonds that are now in the possession of my house in New York are of that kind; are of the same numbers as bonds on the advertised list. They are not my property, but they belong to another party.

Question. When were those bonds purchased?

Answer. I cannot tell you exactly.

Question. When were they purchased, and for whom were they purchased?

Answer. They were purchased by order for Captain Graham, of New York. I cannot give you the date without reference to the New York house. They were not purchased by me, but by our broker in New York, at the broker's board.

Question. For Captain Graham?

Answer. Yes, sir.

Question. Have they been delivered to Captain Graham, or are they still in the possession of your house?

Answer. They are held by my house for Captain Graham.

Question. Who is Captain Graham; is he a citizen of this place?

Answer. No; I do not think he is a citizen of this place. He is here now. He was originally a New Yorker, I think, or lived in New York.

Question. Is he in this city now?

Answer. He has been here within a day or two. I think he is in the city now. He goes backwards and forwards, but he is principally here.

Question. Do you know where he stays?

Answer. I do not, sir,

Question. Do you know what is his given name?

Answer. I think it is John, sir. I do not know that he has ever seen the bonds himself. I know as much about them as he does. It was a simple order to invest money in bonds, and they were bought for him at the broker's board, and are held for his account.

Question. On what day were they bought?

Answer. I cannot tell you. I think it was somewhere within two or three months past.

Question. Do you know anything about others of the bonds referred to?

Answer. No, sir; I do not know anybody who holds any of the bonds that are advertised. I know that bonds of the same numbers as some of those advertised are held by other parties, but they do not seem to be the same bonds, because the lost bonds have not coupons on them. I asked the district attorney whether the bonds lost had all the coupons cut off, and he told me they had. I then informed him that I had coupons of the same numbers sent to me for collection, and the conclusion is that the State of North Carolina had issued bonds of the same number, perhaps at different dates. I do not know that fact.

Question. What was the amount of those bonds?

Answer. $1,000 each; that, I believe, was the amount of each of the bonds stolen.

Question. Did I understand you to say that the bonds you purchased for Captain Graham were bought before the facts were disclosed in reference to the frauds?

Answer. Yes, sir; we have bought no bonds since.

Question. Are those all the bonds on the advertised list that you have any knowledge of?

Answer. I have been told there is one in the hands of Judge Dunlop of this city.

Question. You know of no other person or persons holding any of these bonds?

Answer. No, sir; I do not.

Question. Did you know Godard Bailey?

Answer. Yes, sir.

Question. Has he kept his banking account with you?

Answer. Yes, sir.

Question. What amount of money has he had on deposit within the last two years at one time?

Answer. I cannot tell you how much he has had on deposit at one time, but since this affair occurred I had the curiosity to look at his account, and I noticed that about $7,000 had been deposited by him since last July.

Question. $7,000 since last July?

Answer. In round numbers, about that. I first ran my eye over the ledger.

Question. Has he still that amount on deposit?

Answer. Oh, no; he did not leave it there, but kept drawing it out as he put it in. I do not know that he has got any money on deposit now. He may have a small sum. It is an ordinary deposit account, and I never looked at it. I trusted my clerk would not pay his checks without money; but since this affair I looked at it, and saw that that amount had been deposited.

Question. What was the amount of money deposited with you previously by him?

Answer. It was small generally. I do not know how much. Never much; his salary, perhaps.

Question. Please state the name of your clerk who keeps the deposit account.

Answer. Well, that depends upon which book you want.

Question. Mr. Bailey's deposit account?

Answer. The teller enters the cash received, and the bookkeeper keeps the ledger.

Question. What is the bookkeeper's name?

Answer. The bookkeeper's name is John Hunter.

Question. Do you remember whether Mr. Bailey has at any time brought drafts from any person or persons to your bank?

Answer. I do not often see what is done at the counters, as I am in a private room. I have seen Bailey at the counter, but never noticed particularly what he was doing. Since this affair occurred I have traced some of the deposits for my own curiosity.

Question. Please give us the information you have upon that subject.

Answer. There was one deposit I noticed of about twelve hundred and odd dollars. I do not remember the figures exactly. I did not know why I was summoned before the committee, and I did not bring any memorandum. I noticed that amount; I think it was in October; I may be mistaken about the date; it may have been later, but it was one of the last deposits. I saw that amount, and it was an odd sum, and I asked the teller to examine his book to see what it was—whether the book showed that it had been in money or in checks. Well, the way in which we keep our accounts is such that we found that on the night of the day on which that deposit was made we had in hand a check for that exact sum, and by reference to the book of exchanges next day—I mean the list of checks; we have no other book—I noticed that a check for that sum had been drawn and sent down to Suter, Lea & Co., and paid.

Question (by Mr. Harris.) A check of Bailey's?

Answer. We do not know that. I can only trace the amount. There was a check on hand at night for the amount of that deposit, and the next morning, on the list which we keep of the checks we give to our runners, I found one on Suter, Lea & Co. for the same amount.

Question. Corresponding exactly?

Answer. Corresponding exactly. I could not swear to the check, but there is proof in our office that a check for that amount went through our office to Suter, Lea & Co.'s.

Question. Had the bonds you purchased for Captain Graham the coupons off?

Answer. They had the January coupons off at the time we bought them.

Examination by Mr. Harris.

Question. Mr. Riggs, being a banker yourself, and, I know, one of very large business, I take it you are familiar with the operations of business in the stock board?

Answer. Yes, sir; I am not a member of the stock board, but I know how business is done there.

Question. Will you be kind enough to tell the committee whether a register is not kept at the stock board—say in New York—of all bonds that are bought in the stock board?

Answer. A register is kept in this way: It is like an auction. A certain list is before the President. He reads from that list, for instance, United States stocks of such a loan, and then some member offers to sell, and another to buy. There is a register of the transactions made at the board, but it does not specify what bonds are delivered; it merely states that such amounts were sold at such rates.

Question. It does not give the numbers of the bonds sold?

Answer. By the custom in New York the stock sold is deliverable next day, and that is a private matter outside the board between the brokers. The board has nothing to do with it, unless a member fails to make the delivery, and then he is reported as being delinquent.

Question. What I desired to know was whether, by any of the books kept at the stock board in New York, it can be ascertained whether any, and if so, which of these particular bonds were dealt with at the stock board?

Answer. I do not think it is possible to trace them in any way except by the books of private purchasers, for brokers frequently pass bonds without taking a note of them. They pass from hand to hand.

Question. How long has Godard Bailey kept an account with your banking-house?

Answer. I am not sure, but I think ever since he has been here.

Question. What length of time is that?

Answer. I think he came here soon after this administration came in. I only know the fact that my first acquaintance with Mr. Bailey was seeing him at the Interior Department when Mr. Thompson was Secretary.

Question. Have you any knowledge of his keeping an account with any other banking-house or bank in this city?

Answer. I have none. I never knew anything of Mr. Bailey's private affairs, except from the fact that he kept a deposit account at our office.

Question. Did you, at the time you made this private examination of his account for curiosity, glance over the whole of his account?

Answer. No, sir, I did not. I glanced so far as this, that I saw, I think, in July the first deposit which struck me as being too large for Mr. Bailey's means. I never had looked at his account before in my life.

Question. His account became a large account from about July?

Answer. His deposits became larger than they had been before.

Question. They became larger from July to an extent to attract your attention?

Answer. Not until after this affair; for we have so many accounts on the books that I seldom look at the private ones, except for a special purpose.

Question. But, after you did look at his account for curiosity, you found that, from July, his deposits were of a magnitude that excited your attention, in connexion with your impression of his means?

Answer. Yes, sir. The district attorney saw the account, and has a statement made from our books in his possession.

Question. You referred to a check for $1,200 on Suter, Lea & Co. I presume the books of Suter, Lea & Co. would, of course, show the details of that check?

Answer. They ought to, sir. The amount was about $1,200; it is on the paper furnished to the district attorney. At the same time I noticed that I found, I think, some time in July, a deposit, as nearly as I can remember, of nine hundred and odd dollars; I think $960. I asked the teller what it was, and, on reference to the book which the teller keeps at night in settling his cash accounts, I found, in the remittances to New York, one of $960, and no other sum of that amount in our transactions of the day, and then, on looking to my letter book, I found a certificate of deposit for that amount in the Bank of the Republic, in New York. That is the way we trace these things. I cannot swear positively that Mr. Bailey deposited that check; but I trace it as nearly as I can. I traced the check for $1,200 on Suter, Lea & Co. in the same way.

Question. Will you be kind enough to have made out for the com- account of Godard Bailey with your house, and inform yourself of the general character as to amount of the deposits made by him during the whole time that he has kept his account with your house, and bring with you to-morrow the books of your receiving teller, which will show the details of his deposits since July?

Answer. I will get all the information you require, as far as I can.

Question. Will you be kind enough to say whether you consider this acceptance a piece of negotiable paper?

"$15,000. WASHINGTON CITY, *Sept.* 13, 1860.

"Eight months after date pay to our own order at the Bank of the Republic, New York city, fifteen thousand dollars, for value received, and charge to account of our transportation contract of the 12th day of April, 1860.

"RUSSELL, MAJORS & WADDELL.

"To Hon J. B. FLOYD, *Secretary of War.*"

Indorsed: "Russell, Majors & Waddell."

On the face accepted as follows:

"No. 78.—WAR DEPARTMENT, *Sept.* 18, 1860.

"JOHN B. FLOYD, *Secretary of War.*"

Answer. I consider it in the form of a negotiable instrument.

Question. Have you at any time held paper of that description in your possession as banker?

Answer. I have in my possession two drafts accepted by the Secretary of War, which were sent to me for collection.

Question. Are they of the same character as this?

Answer. As near as I can remember, they are in the same form precisely. They had been protested for non-payment, in New York, I think, not by me.

Question. Have you collected them?

Answer. I sent them to the Secretary of War, or rather to the person I think acting as Secretary, in the Secretary's temporary absence, for payment.

Question. Were they taken up upon presentation?

Answer. No, sir.

Question. For what reason?

Answer. The information given to me was that they would be taken up by the agent of Russell, Majors & Waddell in New York, a man by the name of Simpson, I think. He is at the head of the Pony Express Company.

Question. Have you the drafts still?

Answer. Yes, sir.

Question. What are the amounts?

Answer. One is for $15,000, I think, and the other for $20,000. I am not certain, however, as to the amounts. I did not pay very particular attention to them, because it was not a matter that concerned me.

Question. From whom did they come?

Answer. I do not remember the name. From some one, I think, in Paducah, Ky.

Question. Will you bring these drafts with you before the committee to-morrow?

Answer. I will.

RICHARD B. IRWIN sworn.

Examination by the chairman.

Question. In what business capacity are you engaged at this time, and how long have you been so engaged?

Answer. I am, and have been since the 30th May, 1853, a clerk in the War Department?

Question. What position do you fill?

Answer. I fill the position of corresponding clerk in the office of the Secretary of War.

Question. What are the duties required of you as corresponding clerk?

Answer. My ordinary duties are to prepare letters for the signature of the Secretary of War.

Question. As corresponding clerk did you ever write any letters to the firm of Russell, Majors & Waddell, pertaining to their contract with the government?

Answer. I prepared no letters to them for the signature of the Secretary of War, except when a draft was furnished to me. I have copied drafts of letters addressed to them.

Question. Were the drafts prepared by the Secretary?

Answer. By him or by his chief clerk.

Question. Can you furnish the committee with a copy of such letters?

Answer. These letters are a part of the records of the department. I can obtain a copy if you wish it. The records are, however, not in my possession; they are in charge of the recording clerk.

Question. Have you occasionally been called on to discharge other duties than to write or copy letters?

Answer. Yes, sir; I have been occasionally called upon to perform duties of a miscellaneous nature.

Question. What were those duties?

Answer. They have been very numerous. If you will specify any particular duties to which you refer I will answer.

Question. Did you keep at your desk a registration of the amounts and character of the acceptances given by the Secretary of War to Russell, Majors & Waddell?

Answer. Yes, sir.

Question. Are those [handing the witness a bundle of acceptances] of the character you refer to?

Answer. [Examining one.] This has been registered by me; that is my handwriting.

Question. What part of it is in your handwriting?

Answer. The indorsement across the face in red ink is in my handwriting.

Question. Describe the drafts or acceptances which have been registered by you.

Answer. No. 78, an acceptance or draft dated September 13, 1860, for $15,000; No. 85, dated September 19, 1860, for $10,000; No. 110, dated October 11, 1860, for $7,000; No. 116, dated October 12, 1860, for $10,000; No. 120, dated October 30, 1860, for $10,000. These have all been registered, but not all by me; some of them were registered by another clerk in my absence.

Question. The drafts you have just described are unconditional acceptances?

Answer. Yes, sir; they seem to be in that form.

Question. You never then kept in your office a registration of drafts accepted by the Secretary of War payable out of moneys hereafter to be earned?

Answer. I cannot say that I have kept a register of all the drafts accepted from the beginning, except some of these which I see here.

Question. Have you in your office a registration of a draft dated December 13, 1860, for $135,000, accepted by the Secretary of War?

Answer. No, sir.

Question. Have you of a draft and acceptance, dated October 23, 1860, for $110,000?

Answer. No, sir.

Question. Have you of an acceptance, dated October 23, 1860, for $125,000?

Answer. No, sir.

Question. Have you of a draft, dated October 23, 1860, for $170,000?

Answer. No, sir.

Question. Have you of a draft, dated October 23, 1860, for $116,000?

Answer. No, sir.

Question. In whose handwriting are those acceptances?

Answer. They are altogether in Mr. Russell's handwriting, except the signature "John B. Floyd."

Question. Have you in your office any memorandum showing that these drafts were ever accepted by the Secretary of War?

Answer. No, sir. I have never before seen the acceptances, and have no memorandum of them except of the order cancelling them. All these drafts which have not been registered have been cancelled.

Question. When was that order entered?

Answer. I could not give the date without referring to the record.

Question. Did you cancel them?

Answer. The order was given by the Secretary of War.

Question. Did you furnish memorandums of these acceptances to the quartermaster general?

Answer. At first I did.

Question. When was that practice discontinued?

Answer. I do not remember. I suppose the records of the Quartermaster General's office will show.

Question. Why did you discontinue the practice?

Answer. I was told by the chief clerk that it was not necessary.

The examination was here suspended to enable the witness to bring before the committee certain written evidence.

SATURDAY, *January* 5, 1861.

GEO. W. RIGGS recalled.

Question (by Mr. Thomas.) Mr. Riggs, please state whether you have purchased bonds for the present and other Secretaries of the Interior, and in what manner the present Secretary has had his purchases made?

Answer. I have purchased, I think, most of the bonds held by the Department of the Interior which have been bought during the administration of Mr. Thompson. Previous to that I was never employed by the department for that purpose. Some time, I think, from July to October, 1857, Secretary Thompson sent for me and told me that there had been large land sales in the west, the money from which was, under treaties, to be invested for the benefit of certain tribes of Indians; he consulted with me in regard to future investments and employed me as a broker to make purchases on account of the department. I was in daily intercourse with him with regard to the purchases to be made, and he consulted with me as to how they could best be made. He examined the bonds on hand, and told me his object was to make the investment as safe as possible, and at the same time as profitable as might be for the Indians in whose interest it was to be made. We went into the market, but before purchasing

I always consulted Mr. Thompson with regard to the prices I should pay and the character of the bonds I should purchase. He told me he did not wish to buy too many of the bonds of any one State. I remember there was a pressure made to buy, for instance, the bonds of the State of Virginia, but I remember Mr. Thompson said he did not feel authorized to go further into the purchase of Virginia bonds, because he had a sufficiently large amount of those bonds already on hand for the Indians. He told me, moreover, that he did not wish to confine his purchase to any one State nor to any one section of country, but he wished to divide it between the different States. I purchased for him bonds of Missouri, North Carolina, Pennsylvania, Illinois, New York, Louisiana, Florida 7 per cents, Georgia, and Ohio, and as I bought them, I saw him daily, and consulted with him before making purchases. It was at a time when there was a great deal of financial distress, in 1857, and the bonds were bought on very good terms. I do not recollect the exact amount, but it was something like a gain, taking the bonds at their par value, on the amount invested of near $200,000. It was a discount saved to that amount on the bonds purchased divided among the States I have mentioned. I received instructions always never to buy too much of any one State. They would have been divided amongst all the States in the Union if it had not been impossible to secure the bonds of some of the States in market.

Examination by the ch a

Question. Since your examination yesterday have you referred to your books to ascertain the state of Godard Bailey's deposits in your bank, and can you furnish the committee with a copy of it, and also give such explanation as you are able to make in reference to the character of the deposits made, as to whether they were in money or in paper, and if the latter, of what description?

Answer. I have here a statement which purports to be the deposits of Godard Bailey with Riggs & Co., which is as follows:

Deposits of Godard Bailey with Riggs & Co.

January 4, 1860, by balance rendered	$7 17
January 5, 1860, by cash	150 00
January 26, 1860, by cash	160 00
January 30, 1860, by cash	150 00
February 4, 1860, by cash	45 00
February 27, 1860, by cash	500 00
February 28, 1860, by cash	160 00
March 3, 1860, by cash	62 65
March 7, 1860, by cash	100 00
March 10, 1860, by cash	519 37
March 19, 1860, by Marbury	588 47
March 27, 1860, by cash	200 00
March 30, 1860, by cash	150 00
April 11, 1860, by cash	20 00

April 20, 1860, by cash	$906 00
June 2, 1860, by cash	910 00
June 16, 1860, by cash	400 00
June 22, 1860, by cash	150 00
June 29, 1860, by cash	120 00
June 30, 1860, by cash	100 00
July 12, 1860, by cash	946 00
July 18, 1860, by cash	672 00
July 20, 1860, by cash	825 00
July 25, 1860, by cash	700 00
July 28, 1860, by cash	191 21
October 9, 1860, by cash	300 00
October 11, 1860, by cash	1,265 50
November 1, 1860, by cash	160 00
November 9, 1860, by cash	100 00
November 21, 1860, by cash	259 31
November 28, 1860, by cash	160 00
December 3, 1860, by cash	35 00
December 10, 1860, by cash	295 00

This account was taken by my book-keeper from the ledger this morning, and verified by me as to the amounts of deposits being correct, as they appear upon my ledger; the character of the deposits do not appear. They are placed in the ledger as cash entries; but I have with me some memoranda of an examination made this morning, previous to coming up here, which will explain several of the amounts. I did not have time to go over the whole list, and did not investigate any of the small sums. Supposing I should not have time to go through with the whole account, and that it was the later deposits to which you had special reference, I commenced at the end of the account and examined backward. The first deposit of any considerable amount (beginning at the end of the account) is on the 10th of October, for $1,265 50. I stated yesterday that the amount was about $1,200; and now to show the committee how I arrived at the data which I have, I will explain: On the 11th of October here is an entry in the ledger of $1,265 50. The book I have before me is the book kept by the teller, in which he puts down the items he has in his drawer every night, with the date of the transactions. Among the checks in his drawer on that day appears to have been one of $1,265 60, it was entered as 60 cents by the teller, though it appears in the ledger as 50 cents. The other book to which I then refer is the teller's collection book; it is a simple memorandum book, in which he puts down the amounts of the checks he hands to our runner every morning, and upon what bank or individual they may have been drawn. This book shows what checks were in the drawer on the preceding night. I find that on the 12th October, in the list of checks handed to our runner, was one of $1,265 50 on Suter, Lea & Co., presented that day, and which was the only check of that amount presented.

Question. Was that paid?

Answer. It was paid; at least I presume so. It would have been taken from Bailey's account if it had not been paid.

Question. You do not know by whom the check was drawn?

Answer. I do not; it merely appears as I have stated. The next amount which I examined is an entry, on the 25th of July, of a deposit of $700. On the 25th of July this book of my teller shows that a check was remitted to New York for $700. By reference to my letter book, which I did not bring up, I find that on the 25th of July we remitted the check of Suter, Lea & Co. to the Bank of America, on the Importers and Traders' Bank of New York, corresponding with the amount I have named, and the only check of that amount which it appears we received or remitted that day.

On the 20th of July there was placed to the credit of Mr. Bailey $825. On the 20th of July, by my teller's cash book, it appears there was in his drawer a check for $825. On the 21st of July, the next day, (the check having been received probably too late for transmission on that day,) we remitted to the Bank of America the check of Suter, Lea & Co. for $825.

On the 18th of July is a credit to Mr. Bailey of $672. By my teller's book there appears to have been in the drawer on that day a check for $672. On the next day, the 19th of July, a check for $672 appears to have been presented to Suter, Lea & Co., and paid. The deposits made on one day in checks are rarely presented till the next day, because we send our runner out in the morning and we cannot keep him going all day for each individual check as it appears.

On the 12th of July there was a deposit made of $946. By my teller's books the only item of $946 that appears on that day is a check remitted to New York. My letter book, which is a record of checks remitted, shows that on that day we remitted the check of William M. Peyton on the New York County or City Bank, I am not certain which, I believe for $946. I do not know who Mr. Peyton is.

On the 2d of June there was a credit for $910. The only item I see on the teller's account for that day of that amount was a remittance to New York. On that day, I find by my letter book, we remitted to the Bank of America, New York, a certificate of deposit in the Merchants' Bank of $910. I do not know to whom the certificate of deposit was issued.

On the 20th of April there was a deposit of $906. It appears that we had in our drawer on that day one check, or piece of paper, representing $906, and but one, that I see. On the next day, the 21st of April, we also remitted to New York a certificate of deposit in the Bank of the Republic for that sum. I had not time to go further into an examination of these items.

Question. All these several sums that you have specified here were entered to the credit of Godard Bailey?

Answer. They were, and placed in his bank book to his credit. I do not know of any one by the name of Bailey who made deposits in the bank at that time but himself.

Question. Are you able, this morning, to furnish the committee with the original acceptances of the Secretary of War, drawn by Russell, Majors & Waddell, to which you referred in your testimony yesterday?

Answer. Yes, sir; I have them here.

Question. Is this acceptance which you hand me, dated Washington, June 11, 1860, drawn by Russell, Majors & Waddell, due four months after date, payable at the Bank of the Republic, in the city of New York, one of the acceptances made by the Secretary of War, to which you referred?

Answer. Yes, sir.

Question. And this other acceptance I hold in my hand, dated Washington city, May 1, 1860, No. 5, for $15,000, payable six months after date at the Bank of the Republic, in the city of New York, drawn by Russell, Majors & Waddell, and accepted by the Secretary of War, the other acceptance to which you referred?

Answer. It is.

Question. Do you regard those acceptances as in the form of commercial paper?

Answer. The form of the drafts is that of ordinary negotiable bills of exchange.

Question. Were the drafts protested?

Answer. Those drafts came to us under protest from a bank in Kentucky, and I recognize the protests as in the usual form of protests in the city of New York.

Question. What bank in Kentucky sent them to you?

Answer. I forget, but it was a bank at Paducah, Kentucky; whether it was the Commercial Bank of Kentucky, or not, I cannot say. They were sent to us to present by us, for payment by the bank—I think the Commercial Bank of Kentucky, at Paducah.

Question. Did you present them for payment?

Answer. Not myself, but I sent my clerk to present them.

Question. Have they ever been paid?

Answer. No, sir; we were referred for payment to J. B. Simpson, No. 160 Fulton street, New York. It is proper that I should state that I understood the Assistant Secretary of War, or Mr. Drinkard, had been informed that there was money, or would be money there, by the time the drafts would reach New York, to take them up.

The following is a copy of the drafts, acceptances, and notices of protest:

"$10,000. WASHINGTON, *June* 11, 1860.

"Four months after date, for value received, pay to our own order, at the Bank of the Republic, New York city, ten thousand dollars, and charge to account of our contract for transportation, dated the 12th of April, 1860.

"RUSSELL, MAJORS & WADDELL.

"Hon. JOHN B. FLOYD.
"*Secretary of War.*"

Indorsed.

"Pay Jas. L. Dallam, cashier, or order.
"RUSSELL, MAJORS & WADDELL.

"For collection; pay Riggs & Co., or order.

"JAS. L. DALLAM, *Cashier.*"

Accepted, on its face, in red ink.

"WAR DEPARTMENT, *June* 12, 1860.

"Accepted.

"JOHN B. FLOYD,
"*Secretary of War.*"

"UNITED STATES OF AMERICA, }
"*State of New York,* } *ss:*

"On the thirteenth day of October, in the year of our Lord one thousand eight hundred and sixty, at the request of the Metropolitan Bank, I, Paschal W. Turney, a notary public, duly commissioned and sworn, dwelling in the city of New York, did present the original bill of exchange, hereunto annexed, to a teller at the Bank of the Republic, in the city of New York, (being the place where said bill of exchange is payable,) and demanded payment thereof, which was refused; whereupon I, the said notary, at the request aforesaid, did protest, and by these presents do publicly and solemnly protest, as well against the drawer and indorsers of the said bill of exchange, as against all others whom it doth or may concern, for exchange, re-exchange, and all costs, damages, and interest already incurred, and to be hereafter incurred, for want of payment of the said bill of exchange.

"In testimony whereof, I have hereunto set my hand, and affixed my seal, at the city of New York aforesaid.

"P. W. TURNEY,
"*Notary Public,* 110 *Broadway.*"

"$15,000. WASHINGTON CITY, *May* 1, 1860.

"Six months after date pay to our own order fifteen thousand dollars, for value received, at the 'Bank of the Republic,' New York city, and charge to account of our transportation contract of the 12th day of April, 1860.

"RUSSELL, MAJORS & WADDELL.

"Hon. JOHN B. FLOYD,
"*Secretary of War.*"

Accepted in red ink on its face.

"WAR DEPARTMENT, *May* 1, 1860.

"Accepted.

"JOHN B. FLOYD,
"*Secretary of War.*"

Indorsed.

"Pay Samuel & Allen, or order.
"RUSSELL, MAJORS & WADDELL."

"Pay James L. Dallam, cashier, or order.
"SAMUEL & ALLEN."

"For collection.
"Pay G. J. Seney, cashier, or order.
"JAS. L. DALLAM, *Cashier.*"

"UNITED STATES OF AMERICA, } ss:
"*State of New York,* }

"On the third day of November, in the year of our Lord one thousand eight hundred and sixty, at the request of the Metropolitan Bank, I, Joseph B. Varnum, jr., a notary public, duly commissioned and sworn, dwelling in the city of New York, did present the original bill of exchange, hereunto annexed, to the cashier at the Bank of the Republic, in the city of New York, (being the same place where the said bill of exchange is payable,) and demanded payment thereof, which was refused. Whereupon I, the said notary, at the request aforesaid, did protest, and by these presents do publicly and solemnly protest, as well against the drawer and indorsers of the said bill of exchange, as against all others whom it doth or may concern, for exchange, re-exchange, and all costs, damages, and interest already incurred, and to be hereafter incurred, for want of payment of the said bill of exchange.

"In testimony whereof, I have hereunto set my hand and affixed my seal, at the city of New York aforesaid.

"J. B. VARNUM,
"*Notary Public,* 110 *Broadway.*"

Question. Are those all the acceptances of the Secretary of War, of the kind, you have in your possession?

Answer. They are all I have now.

Question. You have been in the habit of receiving and collecting other acceptances of this character?

Answer. I never received, for collection, any of this kind, because they are payable in New York. I have had some of my own, but not exactly in this form. I think the first ever issued were negotiated by my house.

Question. Please describe, as near as you can, the form of those negotiated by your house?

Answer. I cannot do it exactly; but I was applied to, not by Russell, Majors & Waddell, but by an agent they sent, to negotiate a loan of $200,000. It was soon after the contract was made. I looked into the contract. An effort was made by the parties who came to me to procure money in New York. They failed to obtain it from the banks there on account of the irregularity of the paper. Application was then made to me. Suter, of the firm of Suter, Lea & Co., first came to me. Afterwards, by request, I called upon the Secretary of War; had the contract explained to me, and told the Secretary of War I could make the arrangement if satisfactory assurances were given to me that the Quartermaster's department should pay over the money into my hands. He asked me, as near as I can remember, what sort of acceptances I required. I then wrote, as near as I can remember, something of this kind: "This draft has been presented to the War Department, or to this department, and will be recognized according to its tenor." It was a draft to be paid out of the transportation money. Those drafts, to the amount of $200,000, I had recorded in the Quartermaster's department. They were payable, not at any bank in New York, but payable, like an ordinary assignment, at the treasury.

Question. Did you purchase those acceptances or advance the money on them?

Answer. I and my correspondents in New York advanced the money upon them.

Question. Were they to be paid out of money then earned by the contractors, or thereafter to be earned?

Answer. The representation made to me—and I believe it was a true one—was that the wagons had started, or were about to start; that, according to the terms of the contract, there was a certain sum to be paid when the wagons had gone a certain distance; that a quartermaster was to be at that post prepared to pay off a certain amount; that when they had proceeded a certain distance further there was to be another quartermaster to pay a sum which would be due there. The understanding I had was that the money, if not earned, was being earned at the time.

Question. Would you have purchased those acceptances unless you were satisfied, by the representations made to you at the War Department, that the money had already been earned, or was in the process of being earned?

Answer. No, sir; not unless I was very certain that the money would be paid at maturity of the drafts, and the only way to pay it was by the money earned by the wagons, which were about starting, if they had not already started. The acceptance was conditional. It was not, in fact, an acceptance. I did not venture to ask the Secretary for an acceptance, for I did not think it right that he should accept; but I wrote, as I stated, that the draft would be recognized according to its tenor. My object was that I should have a hold upon the Quartermaster's department that he should pay me instead of the parties drawing the drafts. I received assurances from the Secretary of War that they would be paid.

Question. By whom did the Secretary of War say they were to be paid?

Answer. He assured me, in general terms, that I should be paid, but he did not say by whom.

Question. Were those drafts the first paper of the kind ever issued by the War Department, so far as you are apprised?

Answer. They were the first I knew of, and the first I ever saw, and I presume they were the first of the kind.

Question. Had you any conversation at that time with the Secretary of War as to whether he would make acceptances on sums thereafter to be earned by the contractors?

Answer. No, sir.

Question. Did he intimate that he would accept drafts of that character?

Answer. No, sir. My conversation was solely in reference to this single amount they wanted to raise at that time. He was anxious to facilitate the contractors, and told me I should certainly be protected; that at any event I should be paid.

Question. You relied as much, or more, upon the verbal assurance that you should be paid as upon any written obligation?

Answer. Not altogether; for my reliance was upon the contract, and the certainty that the money would be earned.

Question. If I understand you, you say you had the personal assurance of the Secretary of War that you should be paid out of the money that was being earned upon the contract, and that he would see that you were protected at all events?

Answer. Yes, when the money was earned. I understood that there would be no difficulty about the transfer of the money to me; that it would be regarded as a transfer of that much money as it was earned by Russell, Majors & Waddell; that there would be no objection to the form of the transaction.

Question. Do you know of any additional facts than you have already disclosed, pertaining to these transactions of Russell, Majors & Waddell with the Department of War, which are material to be stated or known?

Answer. I do not. After the first transaction, when drafts were presented to me for discount, I refused to discount them.

Question. Please state if other drafts were presented to you, and, as near as you can, the time, and the character of the drafts.

Answer. Subsequent to this first transaction application was made to me for further discounts, and in one instance, I know, drafts were exhibited to me, but I declined touching them, not liking their form. They were in the form of the drafts sent to me from Kentucky, payable at the Bank of the Republic, in New York.

Question. Were any drafts of any other form presented to you?

Answer. Not that I remember.

Question. Please name to the committee the name of the brokers in New York who purchased a portion of these bonds?

Answer. Cammann & Co., of New York, as brokers, purchased them for us.

THOMAS J. D. FULLER sworn.

Examination by Mr. Morris.

Question. Are you the Second Auditor of the Treasury.

Answer. I am.

Question. As such officer, does the duty devolve upon you to pass upon the accounts of the Indian trust fund in the Interior Department?

Answer. Those accounts were sent to me as Auditor, by the Secretary of the Interior, for auditing.

Question. When was the last account sent you?

Answer. It was received on the 14th day of December, 1860.

Question. Have you those accounts with you?

Answer. I have.

Question. Have you passed upon them yet?

Answer. I have not.

Question. Have you examined them sufficiently to know whether they cover the January interest upon the bonds held as Indian trust fund, and whether they show that all the bonds heretofore purchased by the government for that fund were, at the time the account was presented, in the Department of the Interior?

Answer. The account current and accounts of the various trust funds show upon their face what they purport to be. These accounts, sent to me on the 14th of December, embrace the account of bonds, and not the account of interest. It was proposed by the Secretary that the bond account should be settled distinct from the interest account. When they were received I addressed a communication to the Secretary of the Interior, desiring him to furnish a statement of the interest account before settling the bond account, as the bond account would form a basis of computing the interest account, and serve as a check. With the bonds came a communication from the Secretary of the Interior and from the Commissioner of Indian Affairs.

Question. You have not, then, passed upon the bond account, for the reason that the interest account has not been rendered to you?

Answer. No action has been taken upon the bond account, because I was waiting the receipt of the interest account.

Question. Have you the bond account with you; if so, please state to the committee the particulars of it.

Answer. By the account the Secretary charges himself with stocks received from various times from July, 1857, to November 30, 1860, to the amount of $3,396,241 82.

Question. Does the account purport upon its face to give a detailed statement of all bonds held by the Secretary of the Interior in trust for the different tribes of Indians?

Answer. There is nothing to show that this covers all the bonds in his possession except that he renders it as his bond account.

Question. Do you know who made out that bond account for the signature of the Secretary?

Answer. I am not acquainted with the handwriting. It purports to be signed, as you can see here, by Godard Bailey. I believe it to be his signature, but in whose handwriting the account current is made out I do not know.

Question. Does the body of it appear to be in the same handwriting as the signature?

Answer. I think not, sir.

Question. In what capacity is it signed by Godard Bailey?

Answer. As disbursing clerk.

Question. Who presented that account to you?
Answer. I think it came through a messenger of the Interior Department.

R. J. ATKINSON sworn.

Examination by Mr. Harris.

Question. Do you hold a position in the State Department; and if so, state what it is?
Answer. I am Third Auditor of the Treasury Department.
Question. Can you furnish to the committee, from your office, the amounts paid to Russell, Majors & Waddell upon their contracts with the War Department during the year 1860; and if so, please produce before the committee such statement?
Answer. I can.

RICHARD B. IRWIN recalled.

Examination by the chairman.

Question. Have you made an examination of the records in your office; and if so, can you state to the committee the aggregate amount of the uncancelled drafts of Russell, Majors & Waddell which were accepted by the Secretary of War?
Answer. From a statement which I have prepared from the original memoranda, it appears that the aggregate amount of acceptances on account of both contracts uncancelled was $5,339,395.
Question. Please state, also, the amount of the cancelled drafts of the same parties which were accepted by the Secretary of War?
Answer. It appears from the same statement that the cancelled drafts amounted to $840,000.
Question. What drafts do you refer to when you speak of cancelled drafts?
Answer. Drafts which have been returned to the War Department and cancelled there.
Question. Are the uncancelled drafts still outstanding?
Answer. As to that I have no knowledge at all.
Question. Is there anything on the records of the War Department to show where those drafts are, or what has become of them?
Answer. There were notices of protest received from some of the holders.
Question. And that is all the information you have upon the subject?
Answer. We have occasionally received notices that certain parties had discounted them.
Question. By letter?
Answer. Yes, sir.
Question. Are the drafts to which you referred in your testimony yesterday included in your statement of the amounts of the cancelled and uncancelled drafts to-day?
Answer. The statement which I have produced before the committee to-day shows only such drafts as have been registered. The drafts

which I referred to yesterday as not having been registered by me are not included in that statement at all.

Question. What is the aggregate amount of those drafts referred to in your testimony yesterday as not having been registered?

Answer. $798,000.

Question. Please state to the committee the aggregate amount of the cancelled and uncancelled acceptances, the record of which you have in your office, and also including the amount of the acceptances, of which you have no registration in the War Department.

Answer. The amount of the cancelled and uncancelled drafts is obtained by adding the amount, which I have stated as uncancelled, to the amount which I have stated as cancelled, which makes $6,179,395. The whole amount of registered and not registered is obtained by adding to the latter amount $798,000, making a grand total of $6,977,395.

Question. Please to state how the registration of the acceptances was kept in the War Department.

Answer. They were kept on separate sheets, which were filed together.

Question. Were the entries made upon those sheets of paper at the time of the acceptances, or subsequently?

Answer. They were made at the time that the drafts were accepted; that is to say, some of them were made after their signature by the Secretary of War, and some of them before their signature by the Secretary of War.

Question. Is the paper that you now furnish to the committee an accurate copy of the order of cancellation by the Secretary of War, and the drafts to which it referred?

The following is the paper alluded to:

The following acceptances of drafts drawn by Russell, Majors & Waddel, having been obtained by false representations, are hereby cancelled, viz:

No.	Accepted.	Dated.	Time.	Amount.
78	September 18, 1860	September 13, 1860	8 months	$15,000 00
85	September 19, 1860	September 19, 1860	12 months	10,000 00
90	October 10, 1860	October 1, 1860	10 months	10,000 00
99	do	October 8, 1860	do	10,000 00
110	October 13, 1860	October 11, 1860	do	7,000 00
116	do	October 12, 1860	do	10,000 00
120	do	October 13, 1860	do	10,000 00
Not numbered	October 26, 1860	October 22, 1860	Not specified	110,000 00
	do	October 31, 1860	do	125,000 00
	do	October 23, 1860	do	143,000 00
	do	do	do	170,000 00
	do	do	do	115,000 00
	December 13, 1860	December 13, 1860	do	135,000 00
				870,000 00

JOHN B. FLOYD, *Secretary of War.*

WAR DEPARTMENT, *December* 26, 1860.

Answer. The paper which I have just handed to the committee is a correct and examined copy of the original order, and the drafts therein referred to as cancelled appear to be the identical drafts first shown to me by the committee.

Question. Has any order of cancellation of acceptances been made upon the records of the War Department other than those embraced in this paper?

Answer. Not to my knowledge.

PETER LAMMOND sworn.

Examination by the chairman.

Question. Mr. Lammond, please state to the committee what position you occupy in the Interior Department?

Answer. Disbursing clerk of the department, and likewise requisition clerk. I have charge of the appropriation ledger, and issue all the requisitions signed by the Secretary of the Interior on the treasury.

Question. Are you acquainted with Godard Bailey?

Answer. I am, sir.

Question. Has he been engaged in the department during the last three or four years.

Answer. He was appointed, according to the pay-roll, on the 1st of July, 1857, according to the information given me.

Question. Can you inform the committee what his habits were?

Answer. Well, sir, I was not acquainted with him enough outside of the office to know what his habits were?

Question. Is there any record or memorandum in your department showing the amounts that have been paid to him, from time to time, for his services other than those as clerk?

Answer. The books in the office show that moneys have been advanced and paid to him on settled accounts.

Question. Other than his salary?

Answer. Yes, sir.

Question. Was he at any time within your knowledge sent as an agent or commissioner to Minnesota to transact certain business with Indian tribes?

Answer. He was, sir.

Question. What amount was paid him for that service?

Answer. Well, under the instructions he would be paid ten cents a mile for travel, and three dollars a day for every day's detention on business.

Question. Do you know how long he was gone?

Answer. He was gone about six weeks, I think, perhaps a little more.

Question. What do the books in your office show to have been the aggregate amount paid to him for that service?

Answer. The books in our office will not show that. That may be ascertained by referring to the accounts when settled in the Second Auditor's office.

Question. Have you a memorandum by which you can furnish that information to the committee?

Answer. I think I can furnish the information. One account was settled November 22, 1858, Report No. 7612, which will show the transaction. In November, 1859, another account was settled, Report No. 8667; July 20, 1860, Report No. 33. July 21, 1860, there was advanced to him $1,287 58—that account has not yet been settled; July 26, $1,000, in the same way, and November 1, $259 31. That is the last record we have in our office of any moneys charged to him.

Question. Were the several sums of money to which you refer paid him on account of his services in going to Minnesota?

Answer. Not all for services in Minnesota, I presume, but services in other places.

Question. What other services?

Answer. He went to California one time.

Question. How long did he remain in California?

Answer. His commission and instructions to go to California were dated July 2, 1858, and I will give the committee the compensation he was to receive for that trip, if necessary.

Question. What was it?

Answer. He was to receive ten cents per mile for travelling expenses, and five dollars per day for every day's detention on business.

Question. Do the several sums you have specified embrace the aggregate amount of the expenses and compensation paid to him for the several services to which you have referred?

Answer. I do not know that these would include the whole. I will explain to the committee, if they will allow me the privilege of doing so. When a man is sent out upon service—he may be sent out by the Commissioner on Indian Affairs or the Secretary—he may be directed to draw upon the superintendent of Indian affairs. The superintendent takes this man's receipt. That receipt is a voucher to him when his accounts are settled at the treasury, credited to him, and charged to the agent. And when a requisition is issued for the amount due the agent, that requisition is only for the amount due him, although he may have had a great deal more money.

Question. In what department can we find the exact state of his accounts?

Answer. You will find them in the Second Auditor's office.

Question. What time was it that he went to Minnesota?

Answer. It was some time last summer or fall. I think it was in July or September, but I cannot fix the precise date.

Question. Can you tell when he went to California?

Answer. Yes, sir; his commission and instructions were dated July 2, 1858, and he sailed a few days after that.

Question. Was he drawing his pay as a regular clerk in the Department of the Interior during the time he was engaged in performing the services to which you have referred?

Answer. He drew his pay from the date of his appointment up to the end of November last.

Question. Can you inform the committee whether he drew upon the government any drafts while he was in Minnesota or California?

Answer. I have a memorandum here taken from the books of the department: "October 20, 1858. Draft drawn to the order of Stickney & Scollay on the Commissioner of Indian Affairs for $50, dated St. Louis, October 10, 1858." That draft was, of course, paid, and charged to him as an advance.

Question. Are there any other drafts?

Answer. No others that I could find. I examined the records very carefully, but that was the only one I could find.

Question. Did any person go with Mr. Bailey to Minnesota or to California by appointment of the Secretary of the Interior?

Answer. Young Mr. Barksdale—John A. Barksdale—went with him to Minnesota. I do not know that he went with him by appointment, but I presume so.

Question. Was there any other person who went with him, to your knowledge, either to California or to Minnesota?

Answer. No, sir, none to my knowledge.

Question. Have you any knowledge that he drew drafts, other than those drawn on the government, upon any persons in this city during his absence either in Minnesota or California?

Answer. No, sir.

Question. Where were these bonds kept in the Interior Department?

Answer. They were kept in a large iron safe, and at one time the safe was in the room that I occupy in the department.

Question. Where was it removed to?

Answer. It was removed to the room that was occupied by Mr. Bailey, across the passage from where I am.

Question. At what time?

Answer. As near as I can recollect, two years ago—after he took charge of that branch of business.

Question. Have you any knowledge of any person or persons, at any time, being locked up with Mr. Bailey in that room where the safe was?

Answer. I have heard such rumors, but I was not cognizant of the fact myself.

Question. Did Mr. Bailey frequently keep the room locked, and exclude other persons.

Answer. As I had very little communication with him for the last year, and was seldom at the room except on business, I never saw the room locked myself. I may have gone to the room and found the door locked, but I did not know when it was locked. I never asked the question.

Question. Do you know whether Wagner was frequently in that room with Bailey when the door was locked?

Answer. I do not know that. I know he was frequently in the room with him.

Question. Did they appear to be very intimate?

Answer. Yes, sir.

Question. Has Mr. Bailey been in the Interior Department within the last few days for the purpose of demanding payment of arrearages of salary due him?

Answer. He was in the department some day last week; I cannot tell what day. He claimed his salary up to the date of his removal from office.

Question. When was that removal made?

Answer. On the 22d day of December last.

Question. Please state what occurred at that time?

Answer. I was sent for by the Secretary; Bailey was in the room, and the Secretary told me he supposed Bailey was entitled to his compensation up to that date. Being off my guard, I went into the room I occupied to make a calculation of the amount due him; but while I was doing that it occurred to me that, being a defaulter, he was not entitled to payment. I notified the Secretary of that. The Secretary sent for Bailey and told him I had raised that question.

Question. What did Bailey say?

Answer. Mr. Bailey stood up, in a dignified manner, and said: "Mr. Secretary, you make me out a thief, and that does not make me a defaulter." I refused to pay the salary.

Question. In whose custody was he at that time?

Answer. The custody of the marshal or assistant marshal.

Question. Did you pay the arrearages of salary due him?

Answer. I did not.

Question. Are you acquainted with Russell?

Answer. I am not.

Question. Do you know anything about Mr. Bailey's means or his circumstances?

Answer. If my memory serves me, he told me he was considerably in debt; that he was worse off than nothing. I think he told me he owed $9,000.

Question. What was the amount of salary paid him?

Answer. Two thousand dollars per annum.

Question. Is he a man of family?

Answer. He has a wife and two or three children.

Question. Was he married when he came here?

Answer. Yes, sir.

Question. When did he tell you he was about $9,000 in debt?

Answer. It must have been in September, 1857, or about that time.

MONDAY, *January* 7, 1861.

JOHN THOMPSON sworn.

Examination by Mr. Conkling.

Question. Where do you reside?

Answer. I reside in Brooklyn.

Question. What is your business?

Answer. My business is editor.

Question. Of what?

Answer. Of the Commercial Reporter.

Question. Is that your only business?

Answer. I have no other regular business.

Question. Have you any other business whatever?

Answer. I do other business occasionally, such as broker and negotiator.

Question. Are you connected with any firm?

Answer. I am not.

Question. Have you sons, bankers here?

Answer. I have.

Question. What are their names?

Answer. One's name is Samuel C. Thompson, and the other's name is Frederick F. Thompson.

Question. And their banking-house is where?

Answer. Corner of Wall and Broadway, New York.

Question. Is that under the Bank of the Republic?

Answer. Yes, sir.

Question. Have you read in the newspapers a notice and description published of certain bonds or State stocks alleged to have been abstracted from the Interior Department in Washington?

Answer. I have read a notice, but failed to discover any description.

Question. Did the notice which you read contain the number of each bond?

Answer. The notice which I read purported to contain the number of each bond, but, as far as my investigation went, it did not contain correct numbers of the bonds.

Question. How did you arrive at that discrepancy?

Answer. By comparing one bond with the list and finding it to be a published number. I then went with an attorney to parties through whose hands the bond had passed, and found that it had been in this city for more than two years.

Question. What was the number of that bond?

Answer. It was 926.

Question. What state?

Answer. North Carolina.

Question. For what amount?

Answer. One thousand dollars.

Question. Dated when?

Answer. Dated 1856, I believe.

Question. Payable when?

Answer. I cannot give a positive answer to that question. I may be wrong in my memory, but I think it was payable in 1886.

Question. At the Bank of the Republic?

Answer. I did not notice.

Question. Where is that bond now?

Answer. It is in the office of my sons, I believe.

Question. Who holds it?

Answer. They hold it.

Question. Who owns it?

Answer. They own it.

Question. When did you first see it?

Answer. Within fifteen days past.

Question. How came you to see it then?

Answer. When the announcement was made that there were bonds abstracted from the Indian bureau, my sons and myself examined the bonds which we had in the office; that is how I came to see it.

Question. Was that previous to the publication of what purported to be a description of the missing bonds?

Answer. It was on the day that the first publication made its appearance in the Herald of this city. We examined the bonds before any numbers had been made public to see what we had. Then we examined the bonds after the numbers appeared, to see if we had any of the abstracted bonds.

Question. And did you find any bonds corresponding in number with any of those published except the one you have spoken of?

Answer. No, sir.

Question. When did your sons obtain that bond?

Answer. It was a very few days before the announcement was made that bonds had disappeared from the Interior Department.

Question. Did you obtain it separately, or as one of several bonds obtained in the same transaction?

Answer. They obtained ten bonds in the same transaction.

Question. From whom?

Answer. From a broker by the name of Williams.

Question. What is his first name?

Answer. I do not remember.

Question. Where is his office?

Answer. His office is in Wall street; I do not remember the number.

Question. A member of a firm?

Answer. He is a member of the Board of Brokers; he has no partner.

Question. When were these ten bonds obtained? Can you fix the date?

Answer. I cannot.

Question. What was the transaction in which they were obtained? Were they purchased at the stock exchange, or purchased privately of an individual?

Answer. Purchased at the board, I suppose. We gave an order to purchase ten North Carolina bonds—that is, my sons did; I was knowing to the transaction.

Question. What figure was paid?

Answer. It was about 80; it may have been a fraction over or less.

Question. Was there any variation in the price of the ten bonds?

Answer. They were obtained at one purchase and at one price.

Question. This purchase, then, was made at so much per cent. upon the bonds; there was no variation in the valuation of any particular one of these ten bonds?

[The witness here stated that he was present without counsel, but he believed the committee had no right to inquire into individual transactions.]

Question. Was the price paid for these ten bonds uniform as to each bond, or did it vary?

Answer. It was a uniform price for the whole of the bonds?

Question. Who was the attorney with whom you went to make investigations on this subject?

Answer. His name is Center.

Question. What is his first name?

Answer. That I cannot remember.

Question. To what parties did you go?

Answer First, to Smith & Patrick.

Question. Brokers?

Answer. Brokers, bankers, or commission merchants, I believe.

Question. Where?

Answer. In Wall street.

Question. How came you to go there?

Answer. Because we were told that they had obtained the ten bonds which we bought from the Merchants' Bank.

Question. From them to whom did you go?

Answer. To the President of the Merchants' Bank.

Question. What is his name?

Answer. His name is Silliman.

Question. Did you trace them back to him?

Answer. We showed him this bond, and he said it was beyond question one of the bonds that he had passed over to a gentleman connected with an Alabama railroad running into Georgia, or to Smith & Patrick; he did not explain to which gentleman he had passed it.

Question. Did you understand from him from whom he had received it?

Answer. He said it had been in his trunk for more than two years,

Question. He held it as an individual, then, and not for the bank?

Answer. He held it as an individual in trust for southern parties.

Question. Did he tell you what southern parties?

Answer. He did.

Question. Who were they?

Answer. I do not remember.

Question. Do not you remember anything about them, where they were or how many?

Answer. The amount was some $70,000 or $80,000 that he held for them, I believe.

Question. Did he tell you from what State?

Answer. I think he said Alabama.

Question. Did he name the parties as a bank, or as individuals?

Answer. Neither; I do not remember whether the parties were connected with a bank or not; he named them as individuals; but whether as individuals acting in any official capacity, I do not know.

Question. Have you ever seen any other bonds answering to the published description?

Answer. I do not know whether I have or not.

Question. What is your belief?

Answer. My belief is that I have.

Question. Where?

Answer. At our office, or at the office of my sons; I say our office for convenience sake.

Question. When first?

Answer. I should think six or seven weeks ago.
Question. To what amount?
Answer. $25,000.
Question. In whose hands?
Answer. They were in my hands.
Question. Whose before that?
Answer. In the hands of a man by the name of Simpson.
Question. His first name?
Answer. I do not know.
Question. His business?
Answer. All the business I could fix on him was a borrower of money; I never knew him to do anything else.
Question. Where does he reside?
Answer. In this city, I suppose.
Question. Had he any place of business here?
Answer. He had a place of business in Nassau street.
Question. Do you know what number?
Answer. I do not know.
Question. What business was conducted in his office?
Answer. I do not know.
Question. Have you ever been into it?
Answer. Yes, sir.
Question. What business was done there, as far as you could ascertain?
Answer. I could not well devise any particular business that was done there.
Question. Was it the practice of medicine?
Answer. It might have been and it might not.
Question. Do you know where Mr. Simpson is?
Answer. I do not.
Question. When did you see him last?
Answer. I have not seen him since about the time I saw these bonds.
Question. Do you know whether he is a married man?
Answer. I do not.

[The witness here complained of the course of questioning on the part of the committee. He said he was willing to disclose what he knew of the transaction, which was nothing, but he did not wish to be dragged into the disclosure of individual transactions.]

Question. When did you first know Mr. Simpson?
Answer. I should think it was two years ago.
Question. Where?
Answer. In New York.
Question. What was your business with Mr. Simpson at the time you speak of?
Witness. These two years?
Mr. Conkling. During the time you have known him.
Answer. I have talked with Mr. Simpson about borrowing money, and about making negotiations on various species of paper occasionally, for two years past.

Question. What was your particular business with him at the times when you went to his office?

Answer. I went to see if he wanted to buy a certain piece of paper.

Question. At that time did you know what Mr. Simpson's business was?

Answer. I had understood that he was the financial agent in New York of Russell, Majors & Waddell.

Question. You had no doubt about that?

Answer. I had no doubt that his office was the place where their business was done.

Question. Who did you see, at either of these times when you visited his office, besides Simpson himself?

Answer. I cannot tell.

Question. Do you know William H. Russell?

Answer. I cannot say that I do. I should not know him if I were to see him to-day.

Question. You have had interviews with him?

Answer. I have merely seen him. As I said, I should not know him if I were to meet him now. I never had any business with him at all.

Question. Have you seen a description of the acceptances of the Secretary of War relating to this matter?

Answer. I think I have seen one or two pieces of paper of that description.

Question. The acceptances themselves?

Answer. Yes, sir.

Question. When did you first see acceptances predicated on the transportation contracts of Russell, Majors & Waddell—acceptances of John B. Floyd?

Answer. It was some time since; I cannot fix the date.

Question. As near as you can?

Answer. I think it was a year or more since.

Question. In whose hands?

Answer. I cannot say with certainty whose hands I did see them in; and I may be a little mistaken about having seen any of that particular class of paper at all; my mind may have confused it with another class of paper of a similar class.

Question. What other class?

Answer. Acceptances of the Secretary of the Navy.

Question. Given to Russell, Majors & Waddell?

Answer. No; given to another man.

Question. According to the best of your recollection, in whose hands were these acceptances?

Answer. I think I have seen Floyd's acceptances in the hands of Simpson.

Question. To what amount?

Answer. $10,000.

Question. Can you fix the date?

Answer. A year or more ago, I should say; it is very indefinite in my mind.

Question. Have you seen any of these acceptances since?

Answer. I have not, to the best of my recollection; I have not seen any of that description of paper lately.

Question. At the time Simpson showed you this $25,000 in bonds you have spoken of, had you seen any bonds similar in character before?

Answer. I had seen bonds similar in character, and had no suspicion that these were not of a legitimate character.

Question. You saw them in Simpson's hands?

Answer. No, not before, but at the time I mentioned; I saw also bonds of another State.

Question. To what amount?

Answer. $25,000 of the bonds of a State of which numbers are given as being the bonds taken from the Interior Department, and $25,000 of the bonds of another State which the department has not given any numbers of.

Question. What State was that?

Answer. The State of South Carolina.

Question. Any others?

Answer. No, sir.

Question. He showed you bonds to the amount of $50,000 in all?

Answer. Yes, sir.

Question. Will you fix the date as near as you can?

Answer. I cannot fix the date; I should think six weeks ago.

Question. Have you any entry about it on your books?

Answer. There is an entry in the books of the office of my son's from which I could fix the date to my own satisfaction.

Question. Is it an entry relating to $25,000 only or to the whole $50,000?

Answer. The whole $50,000.

Question. Have you seen the entry?

Answer. No, I have not.

Question. Do you know that there is one?

Answer. No, I do not.

Question. Did you not say there was an entry on the books by which you could fix the date?

Answer. No, I did not say any such thing; I said I thought there was an entry there; I think so still.

Question. What makes you think there is an entry there?

Answer. Well, I do not know; I believe there was a transaction in the office which would involve an entry on the books.

Question. What was that transaction?

Answer. It was the loaning to Simpson of a sum of money.

Question. How much.

Answer. I forget

Question. State the amount, if you please, as near as you can.

Answer. Somewhere between $20,000 and $30,000.

Question. On what?

Answer. State bonds.

Question. This $50,000 you have mentioned?

Answer. Yes.

Question. Were the bonds left there?

Answer. They were.
Question. On what time was the loan made?
Answer. On call.
Question. But no other security taken?
Answer. No, sir; or I should say there was a note taken, if you call that security.
Question. Whose note?
Answer. Simpson's.
Question. A note on time?
Answer. A note on demand; that is my impression.
Question. Then it was a call loan, as you term it?
Answer. Yes, sir.
Question. Do you know how long, in fact, it run?
Answer. A few days.
Question. Do you know when the money was paid?
Answer. When the bonds were given up.
Question. When was that?
Answer. After a few days.
Question. When, as near as you can?
Answer. I think I have fixed the date of the whole transaction already as near as I can.
Question. I repeat the question: please state as near as you can when these bonds were given up.
Answer. Six or seven weeks ago, I should think.
Question. Is that as near as you can come?
Answer. As near as I can come without the books.
Question. Was the money paid then?
Answer. It was.
Question. In money?
Answer. In checks, I think.
Question. Whose checks?
Answer. I do not remember.
Question. Presented by Simpson?
Answer. Or by somebody on Simpson's behalf.
Question. Were you there when the bonds were taken away?
Answer. I was there that day; I do not know whether I was there when the bonds were taken or not.
Question. Do you know who took the bonds away?
Answer. I do not.
Question. Who, as you understood it, took them away?
Answer. The person who paid the money.
Question. My question was, as to whom you understood took the bonds away.
Answer. I do not understand who took them away.
Question. Which son transacted this business?
Answer. I think it was my son Frederick.
Question. Who made the loan to Simpson?
Answer. My sons made it; I advised with them.
Question. Were you present at the time when it was made?
Answer. I was.
Question. For whom was this money borrowed by Simpson?

Answer. For himself, as far as appears by his transactions with us.

Question. For whom was it in fact?

Answer. I do not know.

Question. Do you know where these bonds are now?

Answer. I do not.

Question. Have you seen them since the publication of this notice?

Answer. I have not.

Question. When did you see Simpson last?

Answer. I do not think I have seen Simpson since about the time that loan was paid, some six weeks ago.

Question. Have you heard from him since?

Answer. I have heard people speak about him.

Question. You have heard from him in no other way?

Answer. No.

Question. Who else was acting here as the agent of Russell, Majors & Waddell?

Answer. I do not know of anybody.

Question. Have you seen at any other time any bonds answering to the published description, other than the $25,000 bond of South Carolina stock and the $25,000 of Missouri stock?

Answer. No.

Question. Were the coupons cut off from the entire $50,000?

Answer. Yes, sir.

Question. What is the name and place of business of the broker who succeeded you in this operation with Simpson?

Answer. I do not know, except by hearsay.

Question. What is the name of the broker, as you understood, who succeeded you in this operation?

Answer. William T. Coleman & Co.

Question. What street and number?

Answer. Wall street; I do not know the number.

Question. Cannot you recollect, upon reflection, who the Alabama parties were for whom the president of the Merchants' Bank held these bonds in trust?

Answer. I cannot; they were strange names to me.

Question. No recollection at all about it?

Answer. No, sir.

Question. For what purpose did Simpson at first show you the acceptances of John B. Floyd?

Answer. I do not remember much about it.

Question. Where did he show it to you?

Answer. At my office.

Question. Your editorial office do you mean?

Answer. It is all the same.

Question. The office in which your sons do business?

Answer. Yes, sir.

Question. Can you fix more definitely than you have done the date?

Answer. I cannot, for I paid no attention to it of any consequence.

Question. Do you not remember the purpose for which he showed them to you?

Answer. The purpose was to negotiate them and raise money.

Question. How many pieces of paper of that description did he hold that you saw?

Answer. I do not say that he showed me more than one.

Question. Do you recollect the amount of that?

Answer. I believe it was $10,000.

Question. Did he state whether he had more or not?

Answer. I do not think he did.

Question. What amount did he want to procure or negotiate for?

Answer. He wanted to procure what he could upon that piece of paper.

Question. Only upon that one piece?

Answer. That is all that I have any recollection of.

Question. He never proposed a negotiation larger than that one to you?

Answer. Not on that kind of paper to me.

Question. To what party did you refer when you spoke of the Secretary of the Navy having given acceptances to another person?

WITNESS. I do not know that I am under examination on anything except what pertains to this transaction in relation to these bonds.

Question. The question I propound to you is this: state the name of the party to whom you have referred as the person to whom the Secretary of the Navy gave acceptances?

(On the request of the witness the question was furnished to him in writing.)

WITNESS. The question being foreign to the subject under investigation, I decline to answer.

Question. Have you consulted as to what questions you should and what questions you should not answer before this committee?

Answer. I have not.

Question. Have you consulted in reference to your rights before this committee with any person?

Answer. I have not.

Question. You have consulted counsel about the matter of these bonds?

Answer. About the matter of one bond I have.

Question. And you understand what your legal rights are as to that?

Answer. I do not know anything about legal rights; I consulted in reference to it.

Question. When did you see any acceptance of the Secretary of the Navy?

Answer. I must, in consistency, decline to answer that question.

Question. What did you mean by your answer respecting acceptances given by the Secretary of the Navy?

Answer. I meant just what I said.

Question. What was that?

Answer. That I had seen acceptances given by the Secretary of the Navy as well as by the Secretary of War.

Question. To what amount?

Answer. $10,000, and I think $20,000.

Question. When did you see them?

WITNESS. I must decline answering.

Question. In whose hands did you see them?
WITNESS. I must decline answering.
Question. At what time did you see them?
WITNESS. I decline answering.
Question. How came you to see them?
WITNESS. I must decline answering.
Question. State the circumstances under which you saw them?
WITNESS. I must decline answering.
Question. Was any person present when you saw them?
WITNESS. I must decline answering.
Question. How often have you seen acceptances of the Secretary of the Navy?
WITNESS. I must decline answering.
Question. To what amount in all have you seen such acceptances?
WITNESS. I must decline saying more upon that subject than I have already said.
Question. Do you stand, Mr. Thompson, in any position of confidence or trust in regard to these acceptances of the Secretary of the Navy?
WITNESS. I must decline answering.
Question. Upon what contract or consideration were these acceptances of the Secretary of the Navy given?
WITNESS. I must decline answering any more questions upon that subject.
Question. Have you ever had any contract with the Navy Department?
Answer. I never have.
Question. Any interest in any contract?
Answer. No, sir.
Question. Have you in your possession any acceptances of the Secretary of the Navy?
Answer. I have not.
Question. Have you had at any time?
WITNESS. I must decline answering that question.
Question. Have you ever seen acceptances of the Secretary of War in the hands of any person, except Simpson?
Answer. I do not think I have.
Question. Why do you answer with that qualification?
Answer. I do not remember that I have seen any.
Question. When did you first know that bonds had been removed from the custody of the government?
Answer. I do not even know now that bonds have been removed from the custody of the government.
Question. When as a matter of information?
Answer. When it first became a matter of public notoriety through the newspapers.
Question. Do you know Latham?
Answer. I do.
Question. How long have you known him?
Answer. Ten years I should think.
Question. Do you know where he is?

Answer. I do not.

Question. When did you see him last?

Answer. Last Thursday, I think.

Question. Where?

Answer. In our office.

Question. Do you know where he is now.

Answer. I do not.

Question. Did you ever see any paper or memoranda relating to these acceptances of John B. Floyd?

Answer. I never did.

Question. Did you ever have any correspondence in reference to them?

Answer. I never did.

Question. Did you ever see any statement or letter from the Secretary of War concerning them?

Answer. I cannot give a satisfactory answer to that question; it is my impression that I have, and that is about all I can say about it.

Question. From whom?

Answer. Written by Mr. Floyd himself.

Question. To whom?

Answer. I cannot say.

Question. Who showed it to you?

Answer. The whole thing is based upon such a frivolous impression that you cannot catch me in making any definite statements in relation to it.

Question. According to the best of your recollection, who showed you that letter from Secretary Floyd?

Answer. I cannot give any satisfactory answer.

Question. What was the paper you referred to just now as one you thought you had seen?

Answer. My mind is foggy in relation to some paper written by one of the Secretaries of the present administration.

Question. Have you had correspondence with any of the present heads of the departments.

Answer. I have not.

Question. Have you seen an extensive correspondence with them?

Answer. I have not.

Question. Have you seen any.

Answer. I have seen some letters in relation to certain acceptances, I think.

Question. A good many of them?

Answer. Not many.

Question. Now, to the best of your recollection, what was the paper or papers referred to by you which you thought you had seen?

Answer. They were letters.

Question. Written or purporting to be written by Secretary Floyd?

Answer. I cannot say positively; I think they came from the War or Navy Departments.

Question. Where did you see them?

Answer. In our office, I believe.

Question. Who brought them there?

Answer. I cannot say.

Question. Your best recollection as to who brought them there?

Answer. My recollection is, that they were brought there by Mr. Simpson, Mr. Latham, or Mr. Thompson.

Question. What Thompson?

Answer. Not any Thompson connected with our house; I believe his name is Ambrose W. Thompson.

Question. What is his business?

Answer. I do not know.

Question. Do you know where he lives.

Answer. I do not.

Question. Did you ever see him?

Answer. Yes, sir.

Question. Where was this?

Answer. If the thing took place, it must have been something like a year ago; but I have been so uncertain about the thing transpiring at all, that you must let me have the benefit of the uncertainty.

Question. Do you mean the committee to understand that you do not know that you ever saw letters from the War or Navy Departments.

Answer. I mean them to understand that I think I have seen them.

Question. Have you any doubt that you have seen letters from one place or the other?

Answer. I have some doubt.

Question. Have you any doubt that you have seen letters purporting to come from the War or Navy Departments?

Answer. I have very little.

Question. Have you any?

Answer. I have no doubt that I have seen letters which purported to come from one or the other.

Question. Then why did you say that if the thing happened, it happened something like a year ago?

Answer. Because the transaction is very unsettled in my memory.

Question. When was it that these letters, purporting to come from one office or the other, were shown to you?

Answer. Something more than a year ago.

Question. That is the transaction you referred to when you said they were brought by Simpson, Latham, or Thompson?

Answer. Yes, sir.

Question. How many letters were there?

Answer. I do not remember that I saw more than one or two.

Question. How many letters were shown to you purporting to come from the War Office or the Navy Office?

Answer. I cannot say whether there was one or two.

Question. Not more than two?

Answer. I should think not more than two; I should think two were enough to cover the whole ground.

Question. According to the best of your recollection, did these letters come from the War Office or the Navy Office?

Answer. I cannot draw in my mind an intelligible answer to that question.

Question. Have you no recollection as to which department they came from?

Answer. No positive recollection.

Question. Have you any recollection at all as to which department they came from?

Answer. My impressions are, that I have seen letters from both departments.

Question. At different times?

Answer. I should think at different times, but it is drawing on an imperfect memory to answer these questions at all.

Question. From which department first did you see letters?

Answer. I cannot say.

Question. Were there letters from both departments shown to you by the men you have mentioned?

Answer. I have mentioned these men as the most likely, the most probable men who have shown me such letters.

Question. Is it the best recollection you have that these are the men who have shown the letters to you?

Answer. It is the best memory I have on that subject.

Question. What did you mean when you said you thought there were not more than two letters, because you considered two ample to cover the whole ground?

Answer. I meant that the exhibition of two such letters was sufficient to inspire confidence in certain pieces of paper. The Bible, I believe, speaks of three witnesses being required; but I considered two such witnesses, coming from a department of the government, as sufficient.

Question. That is what you meant?

Answer. Yes, sir; I think that ought to be sufficient to inspire confidence.

Question. What were these two pieces of paper that confidence was to be inspired in?

Answer. I cannot remember the wording of the paper.

Question. I ask what it was?

Answer. It was a written piece of paper.

Question. Is that the only answer you can make?

Answer. I do not remember the wording, and, therefore, I cannot say what it was.

Question. Is that the best answer you can give to the question what this piece of paper was?

Answer. It was what we call an acceptance.

Question. Whose acceptance?

Answer. The acceptance of a Secretary of a department.

Question. Which department?

Answer. Either the War or Navy, I cannot tell which.

Question. In whose favor?

Answer. I do not remember.

Question. Have you no memory whatever in whose favor these acceptances were?

Answer. I have no remembrance in whose favor they were.

Question. None whatever?

Answer. None whatever.

Question. Who presented them?

Answer. I cannot say who presented them, any further than to say that the three names I mentioned are the persons most likely to have shown them to me.

Question. Did the same persons showing the letters present the acceptances?

Answer. I think the letters and acceptances were all together.

Question. Attached to each other?

Answer. No, not attached to each other, but in the same budget.

Question. What was the amount, as near as you can give it, of these acceptances?

Answer. I think some $10,000; from $10,000 to $20,000.

Question. Do you know how many different pieces of paper there were?

Answer. Not certainly.

Question. How long ago was it.

Answer. A year or a year and a half.

Question. Did you ever on more than one occasion see these letters, or any such letters?

Answer. I cannot say.

Question. Who was present when the letters were shown you?

Answer. I do not know; I do not remember the transaction well enough to give any more details about it.

Question. Were your sons present?

Answer. I think not.

Question. Neither of them?

Answer. I think not.

Question. Were these letters shown to you privately?

Answer. Not particularly so; they consider everything private in Wall street.

Question. Were these letters shown to you (I put this question to refresh your recollection) by one person, and no other person present at the time, or by more than one person?

Answer. My impression is, that there were no other persons present than the parties showing the letters and myself.

Question. Did the party showing you the letter consist of more than a single person?

Answer. I do not think there was more than one person at a time.

Question. Then do you mean that these letters were shown to you, successively, by different persons?

Answer. It is my impression that I have seen some of the letters, and papers or acceptances, in the hands of different parties.

Question. At different times?

Answer. Yes, sir. I want you to understand that I give that merely as my impression.

Question. You have named three persons that you think are those, or among those, who showed you acceptances; can you name persons in addition to those three in whose hands you saw those acceptances?

Answer. I cannot.

Question. These three embrace the catalogue?

Answer. These three embrace the catalogue, according to the best of my recollection.

Question. You refused to loan money upon these letters and acceptances?

Answer. I did.

Question. How many times did you refuse?

Answer. Two or three.

Question. Did you ever see or receive other letters in reference to them?

Answer. Not that I know of.

Question. Do you know where any of the bonds are, or perhaps are, except the one in the hands of your son?

Answer. I know a minister of the Gospel who came down to the office and said he had two.

Question. Who is he?

Answer. I shall not tell you.

Question. You decline to tell that, do you?

Answer. I do.

Question. When did you receive this information that you have just now related?

Answer. Two or three days after the list was published.

Question. The amount of those bonds, I suppose, was $1,000 each.

Answer. Yes.

Question. Does that clergyman reside in this city?

Answer. I believe he does.

Question. Did he tell you what the numbers of his bonds were?

Answer. He did not.

Question. Did he tell you what State they were on?

Answer. Yes; he did.

Question. What State?

WITNESS. I decline to answer.

Question. Do you know where any other of these advertised bonds are?

Answer. I do not.

Question. Have you any information?

Answer. I have not.

Question. Do you know what became of the bonds placed by Simpson in Coleman's hands, or transferred to him by your son?

Answer. I do not; I never knew where they went to.

Question. Have you no information from Latham where any of these bonds are?

Answer. Not a particle.

Question. Nor from any other person?

Answer. No, sir.

Question. Nor where they have been since they were taken from the department?

Answer. Only hearsay.

Question. Have you any information as to where any of the bonds advertised now are, or where they have been at any time since their abstraction was made public?

Answer. I have not.

Question. Have you no information directly or indirectly.

Answer. I have heard that a man by the name of Anderson, of St. Louis, held a large amount of them.

Question. Who did you hear that from?

Answer. I cannot say.

Question. Do you not know who told you that?

Answer. I cannot say who it was.

Question. Where else, according to your information, are there any of these bonds?

Answer. I have been told that there was a large lot of these bonds in the hands of Duncan, Sherman & Co. at one time.

Question. Who told you that?

Answer. I am equally in default about who told me that. I cannot get at the sources of these stories at all, they were so thick and so much talked about at the time.

Question. Where else, according to your information, are there any of these bonds?

Answer. I have been told that there was a lot of them in the hands of M. Morgan & Son, in William street.

Question. Where else?

Answer. We were told that there were some of them in the custody and keeping of the president of the Bank of America, and that these had been bought by Buchanan within the last six months, to tell the whole story.

Question. Where else?

Answer. I do not remember any more of these street rumors that I can tell you.

Question. Have you neither knowledge, information, nor advices of any kind as to the present or recent whereabouts of any more of these bonds?

Answer. I have not further than as the street rumor was that Richard Schell had been the medium of putting large amounts of them upon the market. Whether it was so or not I cannot say.

Question. Do you still refuse to name the clergyman who you mentioned as holding two of these bonds?

Answer. I refuse to give his name.

Examination by the chairman.

Question. You have said that $50,000 of the bonds you saw in possession of Simpson had the January coupons off?

Answer. Yes, sir.

Question. Was your attention directed to the fact that they were off; and if so, what induced you to notice it?

Answer. My son observed to me that these bonds had their coupons off, and I looked and saw it to be so.

Question. Did you call Simpson's attention to the fact that the coupons were off the bonds?

Answer. We did.

Question. What reason did he assign why they were off?

Answer. He did not assign any reason, but evaded giving any reason.

Question. I understood you to say that he said there was a particular reason for it.

Answer. No; I could not have said exactly that. I asked him why he did not sell the bonds instead of holding them, and he said there was a particular reason why he would rather keep them than to sell them.

Question. He did not assign any particular reason why the coupons were off, but when asked the question he evaded answering?

Answer. Yes, sir.

TUESDAY, *January* 8, 1861.

G. B. LAMAR sworn.

Examination by the chairman.

Question. Please inform the committee what your present position is in the Bank of the Republic?

Answer. I am president of the Bank of the Republic, and have been since the 15th of May last.

Question. Has that bank had any business transactions since you have been connected with it with Russell, Majors & Waddell; and if so, please state the nature and character of them?

Answer. The bank has at different times discounted notes and drafts from Russell, Majors & Waddell, and some drafts coming from St. Louis, indorsed by Anderson & Co., for Russell, Majors & Waddell, and others accepted by the Secretary of War, Governor Floyd. I am not sure that any of the latter description have been discounted since May last. Without referring to the books of the bank I cannot tell certainly whether they have been or not.

Question. Will you state the date and amounts of the acceptances you discounted either of Russell, Majors & Waddell, or of the Secretary of War?

Answer. I could not without reference to the books of the bank.

Question. Has the bank in its possession any written communications from the Secretary of War pertaining to these acceptances?

Answer. It has a letter dated in 1858.

Question. Can you furnish the committee with that letter?

Answer. It is in the possession of the cashier; he will furnish it to you.

Question. Have you any letter from any other person connected with the War Department referring to the same subject-matter?

Answer. Not that I know of.

Question. Do you know whether there is a letter in the possession of the bank from Mr. Drinkard, the chief clerk in the War Department?

Answer. I do not know; it is possible there may be such a letter; if so, I will instruct the cashier when he comes before the committee to bring it with him.

Question. You are not certain that you have held any of the acceptances of the Secretary of War since you have been president of the bank?

Answer. No, sir, I am not certain that we have.

Question. Have you seen in the Constitution newspaper, published at Washington city, a list of the bonds said to have been abstracted from the Interior Department?

Answer. Not in that paper. I have seen such a list in other papers.

Question. Have you in your bank any of these bonds?

Answer. Not one that I know of.

Question. Had you at the time that publication was made or just previous?

Answer. Not that we know of.

Question. Did you ever have them?

Answer. I have no reason to believe we have ever had any of these bonds in our possession except in a single instance. We did on one occasion have bonds which we suspect may have been among those abstracted from the Interior department; I think, in the latter part of October.

Question. How many?

Answer. Twelve, I think.

Question. Can you furnish the committee with a statement showing the date and number of these 12 bonds, and the State which issued them?

Answer. No, sir; we never keep a memorandum of such particulars. A person came in and got a loan of $9,000 on 12 of those bonds. He afterwards came and paid the money and took up the bonds.

Question. Who was the person that hypothecated them?

Answer. His name was Simpson.

Question. You have no memoranda or register in your office showing the numbers?

Answer. No; we never keep any record of the numbers of bonds pledged as collateral security in that way; we just put the bonds away with the note.

Question. Do you know what Simpson did with the bonds after he took them up?

Answer. No, sir; I have no idea.

Question. Do you know Simpson?

Answer. Yes, sir; I have known him for the last six months.

Question. What has been his business?

Answer. He generally transacted the business of Russell, Majors & Waddell at the bank.

Question. Do you know where he is now?

Answer. I do not. He was in the bank a few days ago and told us he was going to Europe. He said he was very much broken down in health; and he looked as though he was very far gone with consumption.

Question. How long ago?

Answer. Two or three days, or one or two days before the explosion about the knowledge of this robbery.

Question. Have you ever seen in the possession of any other corporation or individuals any of the bonds referred to?

Answer. I am not aware that I have seen any of them.

Question. Have you any knowledge which leads you to believe that any person or persons or corporation has any of these bonds in their possession?

Answer. I have no positive knowledge.

Question. Have you any knowledge?

Answer. I have only a suspicion arising from various circumstances.

Question. Please state to the committee what you know on that point.

Answer. I do not know whether I ought to state suspicions, because it might be doing injustice to other people. I do not know any fact; it is a mere suspicion that has crossed my mind since the facts have been made public.

Question. Please state the facts upon which you found your belief that you may have a knowledge of what became of some of the bonds.

Answer. In the month of August I commenced buying Tennessee bonds as a matter of speculation, supposing large quantities of them would be wanted for banking purposes in some of the western States. Some other gentlemen engaged in the same business. We found the market supplied with bonds so abundantly that we at last desisted from the purchase, because we saw no chance of their rising. We were surprised that so many bonds were continually coming into market for sale, and we could not imagine where they came from.

Question. Did you ascertain?

Answer. We ascertained that Clarke, Dodge & Co. were throwing a large amount of these bonds upon the market.

Question. Did Russell, Majors & Waddell do their business in this city through your bank since the time you became president?

Answer. I think they did a great deal of it; I do not know that they did all.

Question. Will you be kind enough to furnish to the committee a statement showing the acceptances of the Secretary of War discounted at your bank for these parties?

Answer. I will ask the cashier to bring it with him when he comes before the committee.

Luther C. Clark sworn.

Examination by Mr. Harris.

Question. Have you seen, at any time, any of the bonds alleged to have been abstracted from the Interior Department.

Answer. I suppose I have, a great many; I know we have two of them in our house.

Question. What is the name of your house?

Answer. Clark, Dodge & Co.

Question. Have you seen the descriptive list of those bonds that has been published by the Secretary of the Interior?

Answer. I have never examined it with any degree of care. A

great many State bonds are bought and sold by our house, probably amounting to $3,000,000 or $4,000,000 since this thing commenced, and it is probable that a number of thousand of these bonds have passed through our hands; probably some of them several times, but I do not know.

Question. You have no memorandum or description of these bonds?

Answer. We intend to keep the numbers of most of the bonds that pass through our hands, but we have never compared the list furnished by the Secretary of the Interior with our books, and that list would not be conclusive in any event, because some of the bonds are issued by letters, and there would be different bonds of the same number issued by the same State.

Question. Would the number and letter correspond?

Answer. The bonds of some of the States are issued in this way: A particular class of bonds is called A, and numbered consecutively, beginning with 1; another class is called B, and numbered in the same way; of course there would be a No. 1 of letter A, and a No. 1 of letter B.

Question. But each of the bonds would differ in letter or in number?

Answer. Yes, sir.

Question. Are you able to say that you have none of these bonds in your possession now?

Answer. None except the two I have mentioned.

Question. You have a description of them?

Answer. Yes, sir, a full description is given in our answer.

Question. What answer; has there been an injunction served upon you?

Answer. Yes.

Question. Have you no further knowledge in relation to the bonds?

Answer. No more than I have seen in the papers.

Question. You do not know any parties who probably have them?

Answer. No; there are parties wanting to buy some of them; a party yesterday wanted to sell some real estate and take these bonds in payment.

Question. Have you ever seen, or have you any knowledge of any acceptances of the Secretary of War in connexion with the contract of Russell, Majors & Waddell?

Answer. I have seen these acceptances a great many different times, but I do not think I ever bought any of them. I sold some two or three years ago, but I have not sold any within the last year.

Question. Do you recollect the character of the acceptances you saw; whether they were based upon the future earnings of these parties, or whether they were in the ordinary form of negotiable paper?

Answer. There was a paragraph—some words attached to them which I cannot remember. If I could see a specimen of the two kinds I could tell. I remember one was shown to Mr. Cisco, the assistant treasurer, and he said that they amounted to an acknowledgment on the part of the government that the service had been performed.

Question. Do you recollect whether those presented to you were negotiable in their character?

Answer. All were that I saw.

Question. You did not purchase any of them?

Answer. I did not.

Question. Do you know in whose hands they were when they were presented to you?

Answer. I believe they were all indorsed by Russell, Majors & Waddell. Some of them, I think, came direct from Mr. Anderson, of St. Louis.

Question. Not through any intermediate party here.

Answer. I believe not; if they did, they came for his account.

Question. Did you ever see any letter or memorandum in writing from any officer of the government in relation to these acceptances?

Answer. I have not.

Question. Have you any recollection of the date or amount of any of these acceptances?

Answer. Not of the date; the amount, I think, was $10,000 each, or it may be $20,000. I recollect that I sold to the amount of $20,000 on one occasion, but whether in one or two pieces of paper I am not certain.

Question. What was the gross amount?

Answer. This is the only transaction I remember, and I am almost certain this was in two acceptances of $10,000 each.

Question. And you think this transaction was a couple of years since?

Answer. I should think all of that.

Question. Have you any recollection of the time on which they were drawn?

Answer. I have no special recollection; my impression is that the time was four months.

Question. Do you know where they are now—what has become of them?

Answer. They were all paid.

Question. Those that you sold were paid.

Answer. Yes.

Question. Do you know by whom?

Answer. They were made payable at the Bank of the Republic.

Question. Here is a draft which reads as follows:

"$10,000 WASHINGTON, *October* 12, 1860.

"Ten months after date pay to our own order, at the Bank of the Republic, $10,000, for value received, and charge the same to our transportation contract of the 12th day of April, 1860.

"RUSSELL, MAJORS & WADDELL.

"Hon. JOHN B. FLOYD,
"*Secretary of War.*"

(In red ink across the face:)

"No. 116.] WAR DEPARTMENT, *October* 13, 1860.

"Accepted.

"JOHN B. FLOYD,
"*Secretary of War.*"

(Indorsed:) "RUSSELL, MAJORS & WADDELL."

Looking at that paper are you able to say, to the best of your recollection, that it is of the character of the acceptances which you negotiated?

Answer. That is my impression.

Question. Do you consider such paper as that negotiable paper?

Answer. I do.

Question. Do you know any matter or thing connected with these acceptances that you have not stated to the committee?

Answer. I believe nothing.

Question. Do you know any matter or thing connected with these acceptances, or with the bonds referred to, which you have not stated?

Answer. I do not know anything further, of my own knowledge. I know I have heard it stated, upon pretty good authority, that there were existing facts and circumstances that would tend to throw doubt as to the correctness of the list of bonds published by the Secretary of the Interior.

Question. What?

Answer. I know this fact in connexion with it. There were bonds which we sold bearing the same numbers contained in the published list. A party who had purchased some of these came to us and said they were included in the published list. He wanted to know where we got them? I went to the bank from which we got them, and the president told me that the bonds could not be among those abstracted from the Interior Department, for he obtained them from a corresponding bank in North Carolina, and that he was certain that they came direct to that bank from the State treasurer.

Question. What bank was that in New York?

Answer. It was the Continental Bank.

Question. Will you be good enough to state the name of the party to whom you sold these bonds?

Answer. It was a broker who bought them, at least we delivered them to him, but I have no doubt that he bought them for somebody else. In fact I do not know who we did sell them to.

Question. To the best of your knowledge, who was the party you sold them to?

WITNESS. Do you want the name of the broker.

Mr. HARRIS. Yes.

Answer. I do not know. I could give you his name by going to my office.

Question. Do you know the name of any other party than the broker who was connected with this transaction?

Answer. The party who came to see me was interested in them at that time. I do not know whether he is interested in them now or not.

Question. Will you please state his name?

Answer. His name is F. P. James.

Question. Does he live in this city?

Answer. He is living in the city this winter.

Question. I repeat the question I put some time ago: Have you given us all the knowledge in your possession in relation to the subject-matter of our investigation?

Answer. I believe I have.

Question. I ask you this question in addition: Is the practice an unusual one to sell bonds without the coupons attached to them?

Answer. They are very frequently sold without the coupons attached to them.

RICHARD SCHELL sworn.

Examination by the chairman.

Question. What business are you engaged in?

Answer. I am a broker and speculator.

Question. Do you know John B. Floyd, Secretary of War?

Answer. Yes, sir.

Question. Do you know William H. Russell?

Answer. Yes, sir.

Question Do you know J. B. Simpson?

Answer. Yes, sir.

Question. Have you had any business relations or connexions with either of these parties pertaining to the contract of Russell, Majors & Waddell with the government?

Answer. No, sir; neither directly nor indirectly, in any way, manner, or shape.

Question. Have either of the parties named, or their agents, called upon you to assist them, at any time, in consummating any business transaction, or to effect a loan of money?

Answer. I have here an account, which I will put in evidence if you wish it, of all the transactions I have ever had with them.

Question. Please state the nature and character of your connexion with these parties in consummating the business transactions referred to in this account?

Answer. I was dining at this hotel. I met Russell, and he said to me, "It has been a very tight day for money to-day." He said he wanted to borrow money on the security of State bonds. I told him I would lend him money on that security; that I would get him all he wanted. I then left him.

Question. What time was that?

Answer. I do not remember the date, but I think it was November 12 or 13; because here, on the 14th, I see he comes to me, or at least his agent, Simpson, applied to me the next day or two after, and wanted to borrow money of me on State stocks. He made the application for a loan of $25,000 on $32,000 of North Carolina 6 per cent. stocks, which he gave me, and I loaned him the $25,000. On the 16th of November there was a sort of a panic, and I required $4,000 additional bonds as margin. On the same day he came into the office and wanted to borrow money on Missouri 6 per cent. stocks. Money was very tight that day. I told him we could not negotiate in Wall street; but I finally said, "I could get you $12,000 on 20 Missouri sixes, if you will allow the parties to sell them." "Well," said he, "you can make sale of them for me." I did sell them, and obtained 71¾ or 72 less the coupons for January, which were off. The next day, the 17th, I sent for $4,000 additional margin on the North Carolina sixes, which he gave to me, and which made $40,000 worth of North Carolina stock, on which I had loaned or borrowed for him $25,000. Then I said to him, "Now I sold $20,000 of Missouri sixes for you yesterday; now I will take that sale and loan you the money for sixty days, at 2½ per cent. commission and 7 per cent. interest." Said he, "I would rather do that." "Very well," said I, "I will do it." Then the sale of Missouri sixes was my sale. On December 11 I sold these $20,000 of Missouri sixes, at the market price for the day, which, in looking over the stock list for that day, I find was 64. I settled with him at 64 per cent., which made $12,800, less coupons off, $600, and less ¼ per cent. brokerage, $50, leaving the amount $12,150. Then I allowed him return interest and commission on the loan for 60 days, $220, making the net worth for him $12,370. I had loaned him $12,000. Now, then, we come to November 20. On that day—I cannot be very positive in regard to these matters, but I think I am right—I made him an additional loan on $25,000 worth of North Carolina 6 per cent. stocks, of $15,000, for 63 days, 7 per cent. interest off, and 2½ per cent. commission, and then brokerage for obtaining money, besides $125, making $500 in commissions in all, and $183 75 interest. On December 12 he called at my office and gave me a check certified, I think, for $14,877 50, to take up the loan on $25,000 worth of North Carolina sixes; or, rather, he gave me his check, and I sent to have it certified. On the 20th of December he called and gave me a check for $24,833 41, which was, I think, to take up the $40,000 worth of North Carolina sixes. These are my transactions with him.

Question. Can you furnish the committee with a particular description of the bonds that Simpson left to be hypothecated?

Answer. No, sir; I cannot. I have never been in the habit of keeping an account in numbers of such bonds; but I will tell you what I can if it will be of any service to you. The broker who sold these $20,000 of Missouri sixes wrote me a note stating that, by looking at the advertisement of the Secretary of the Interior, he found that the numbers of those bonds corresponded with the numbers advertised. I do not, however, know that fact of my own knowledge.

Question. What is the name of that broker?

Answer. Ward, Campbell & Co.

Question. Had the bonds to which you refer the January coupons off.

Answer. The $20,000 of Missouri sixes had.

Question. And the others?

Answer, I do not know; I did not look at them specially; my impression is that some of these North Carolina bonds for April, 1861, had the April coupons on; I cannot state positively, however.

Question. Are the bonds you have described the only ones you ever received from Simpson?

Answer. Yes, sir, all I have ever received.

Question. Did you ever receive any directly from Russell?

Answer. No, I never have.

Question. How did the interview occur at first between you and Simpson or Russell?

Answer. I was here all the afternoon.

Question. Did they call upon you?

Answer. No, the meeting was accidental; I was here dining; I do not know but what I met him in the hall; I met Russell, and I do not know but what Simpson was with him.

Question. Was it Simpson or Russell who spoke to you about borrowing?

Answer. Russell.

Question. And Simpson came to you afterwards at the instance of Russell?

Answer. That I do not know, and have no right to say; I have no doubt, however, of the fact.

Question. Did either of them, at the interview which took place at the St. Nicholas hotel, express a wish or desire to negotiate a larger amount of bonds than that afterwards presented.

Answer. Simpson did.

Question. What amount.

Answer. I think it was $50,000 worth; that loan on $20,000 of Missouri sixes he wanted to make $50,000; but things had come to such a pass in Wall street that I would not go beyond $20,000 on account of the tightness in Wall street that day.

Question. What was the aggregate amount of the loan he desired to make?

Answer. He did not express the amount.

Question. Did Russell say to you that he had $20,000 Missouri sixes upon which he was desirous of raising money?

Answer. Not to the best of my recollection. At the time I held this conversation with him I was in hopes he might want some $300,000 or $400,000; for as money was at that time I could have made some $6,000 or $7,000 out of the operation; I did not care how large an amount.

Question. Have you ever examined the description of bonds published by the Secretary of the Interior as having been fraudulently abstracted from his department?

Answer. I have examined it generally, but not with precision, because I had no interest in it. From that general examination I came to the conclusion that no bond in my possession was embraced in the list.

Question. You say you have made a general examination of the list, *i. e.*, so many Missouris, so many North Carolinas, so many Tennessees, &c.?

Answer. Yes, sir.

Question. Can you now state to the committee whether you ever saw any of these bonds to the best of your recollection?

Answer. No, sir.

Question. Do you know where any of them are?

Answer. No, sir.

Question. Have you never met with them in the market?

Answer. I do not think I have.

Question. Did Simpson or Russell state from what source the bonds came that they offered?

Answer. No, sir; I never asked a question.

Question. And they never made an allusion to them?

Answer. No, sir.

Question. Did you know Simpson well?

Answer. I had seen him in Russell's office.

Question. Did you know what his resources were?

Answer. I did not know, except from the money which he paid. He gave pretty good checks, and I sent and got them certified; and when he made loans he brought the securities in, and such as I considered pretty good securities.

Question. Did Simpson, at any time subsequently to your first interview at the St. Nicholas to which you have referred, urge upon you to take a larger amount of the bonds than you did take?

Answer. Never, except in the single instance I have mentioned of $50,000 of Missouri sixes.

Question. Do you know what he did with the bonds you returned to him?

Answer. No, sir; I have got my own impressions; but I could not swear what he did with them.

Question. Upon what are those impressions founded?

Answer. I merely saw sales at that period of North Carolina sixes.

Question. Who made that sale?

Answer. That I do not know.

Question. Who was the broker that sold them?

Answer. I was not a member of the board, and therefore did not go to inquire.

Question. Would an inspection of the books kept by the board of their transactions afford any specific information as to their numbers and dates?

Answer. I should think not.

Question. Please state the aggregate amount of bonds you received from Simpson.

Answer. I received $65,000 of North Carolina State sixes and $20,000 of Missouri sixes; that is all.

Question. Do you know where Simpson is?

Answer. I do not.

Question. When did you last see him?

Answer. About a week ago.

Question. Then you have no knowledge, either directly or indirectly, which will enable you to state where any of the bonds are which were abstracted from the Interior Department?

Answer. No, sir.

Question. And have had no such knowledge at any time?

Answer. No, sir, no further than what I have told you of these

$20,000 Missouri sixes, which were sold, and that I only know from the broker.

Question. Have you ever seen any drafts drawn by Russell, Majors & Waddell upon the Secretary of War which had his acceptance upon them?

Answer. I may have seen them; I never have dealt in them at all; I never owned one; my impression is that I have seen one, but still I cannot swear positively.

Question. In whose hands were they, if you ever saw them?

Answer. That I do not know; if I have ever seen them I cannot tell in whose hands.

Question. Have you ever had any conversation with Russell in reference to these bonds, except what you had here in this hotel?

Answer. I went into the office of Russell to see Simpson; he was not in; I said to Russell that I understood North Carolina sixes were down to 60, and, if that was so, I should require further margin.

Question. What was his reply to that?

Answer. That Simpson would see me; but he did not see me, for the reason that when I came to examine closely I found I had made a mistake of 10 per cent. on the price of the bonds.

Question. Russell seemed to know what bonds were meant?

Answer. I suppose so.

Question. You knew Simpson to be Russell's agent?

Answer. Oh! yes; I suppose so.

Question. You informed the committee, I believe, that you borrowed money upon the bonds that Simpson left you from other parties?

Answer. Yes.

Question. Please state the names of those parties?

Answer. I borrowed money of the United States Trust Company upon North Carolina sixes; I also borrowed money of the Manhattan Savings Institution.

Question. Can you state the dates?

Answer. It was within ten days of the dates when I made these loans.

Question. Did you let him have your own money when you received the bonds?

Answer. No; I borrowed the money.

Question. Where did you borrow the money?

Answer. I borrowed it of different parties; I borrowed some of Daniel Torrence.

Question. Of what other parties?

Answer. I borrowed $4,000 or $5,000 of the Bank of the State of New York on some of these bonds.

Question. Did you leave any of the bonds with Torrence as collateral security?

Answer. Yes, sir.

Question. Did you borrow of any other person or institution?

Answer. I gave some of the bonds to Shuchardt & Gebhard.

Question. Are these all the persons you can remember to have borrowed of?

Answer. Yes, sir.

Question. Did you subsequently repay the money and take the bonds away?

Answer. Yes, sir.

Question. What did you do with them?

Answer. I gave them to the Manhattan Savings Institution and to the United States Trust Company for the loan which was made.

Question. About how long after you received them from Simpson did you do that?

Answer. I think within ten days.

Question. Did you take them up from these institutions subsequently and deliver them to Simpson?

Answer. I did.

Question. These were the North Carolinas?

Answer. Yes.

Question. How about the Missouri bonds?

Answer. I took them to some broker for sale; he advanced me the money on them and sold them.

Question. Do you know whether the persons or institutions you have named as having these bonds kept a record of them?

Answer. Only from what I learned in reference to the Missouri sixes from Ward, Campbell & Co., who informed me that they had received letters stating that the $20,000 Missouri sixes were among the number advertised by the Interior Department. I do not know the fact, but I have no doubt they were.

Question. Did you see Russell in this city after he was arrested?

Answer. No, sir.

Question. Or immediately before?

Answer. No, sir.

Question. Did you see Simpson about the time Russell was arrested?

Answer. I saw him that afternoon; I stopped at his office, and said I, "What does this mean?" said he, "I don't know anything about it."

Question. And you have not seen him since?

Answer. I have seen him once.

Question. Was there nothing else said in the conversation you had with Simpson?

Answer. No, sir.

Question. You say you saw him in his office, and asked—referring to Russell's arrest—"What does this mean?" What object had you in going into his office and asking that question?

Answer. You know I had made loans on North Carolina sixes and Missouri sixes, and I did not know how it was going to affect me.

Question. Had you any knowledge or information from Russell or the Secretary of War that one was drawing and the other receiving acceptances?

Answer. I did not, except from the fact that at one time the matter was talked of and seemed to be a matter of public notoriety. I never had any transactions in reference to them myself.

Question. Did you ever receive any letter from Secretary Floyd, or any other person in the War Office, relating to the drafts of Russell, Majors & Waddell upon that office?

Answer. No, sir.

Question. Then you state to the committee that you have no knowledge of any business transaction between the Secretary of War and Russell, Majors & Waddell other than that derived from general information?

Answer. No other; not in any manner or shape, directly or indirectly, except what I derived from the public prints.

Question. Did you ever hear any person say he held acceptances of the Secretary of War, such as reference has been made to?

Answer. No, sir; I have heard other people say they knew somebody who held them, but that I cannot give you as evidence.

MATHEW MORGAN sworn.

Examination by the chairman.

Question. Please state to the committee whether you have ever seen a description of the bonds said to have been fraudulently abstracted from the Interior Department at Washington, which was published by direction of the Secretary of the Interior?

Answer. I have seen two bonds. These two bonds bore the numbers advertised.

Question. In whose hands were they?

Answer. They were the only ones I have seen, and they are in the hands of Captain Porter now. They were purchased for him. I cannot remember exactly the date of the purchase.

Question. Can you state the numbers?

Answer. I can. Captain Porter commanded a ship which I was interested in, and asked us to purchase North Carolina bonds for him. We purchased two bonds bearing the dates of 873 and 875.

Question. Does Captain Porter still hold these bonds?

Answer. Yes, sir; at least he did the other day.

Question. Had these bonds the January coupons on when you purchased them?

Answer. Yes, sir. He has collected the coupons since the 1st of January.

Question. Please state the place and time of purchasing these bonds as near as you can.

Answer. I could not give an idea of the time, except that it was some time after the election, which took place on the 6th of November. It was at a period when they were very much depressed, and therefore I know it must have been after the election.

Question. What did you pay for them?

Answer. I think it was 75 or 76.

Question. Have you any knowledge, direct or indirect, where any of the balance of these bonds are?

Answer. None whatever.

Question. Are you a broker in this city?

Answer. No.

Question. What is your business?

Answer. They call me a banker. My principal business is dealing in foreign exchange, and the purchase of securities for foreign account. We purchase them for anybody who comes and directs us, however; but we do the business that comes to us in this way through a broker.

Question. Please state the name of the broker who purchased these two bonds.

Answer. Ward & Co. They purchased them, however, from another broker.

Question. Where are they?

Answer. I believe their office is No. 56 Wall street.

Question. Have you ever seen any drafts drawn by Russell, Majors & Waddell, and accepted by him?

Answer. I have seen one or two, but it must have been more than twelve months ago. We buy domestic bills of exchange, and notes, drafts, &c. I think that paper was offered to me, but I do not recollect now by whom, or any of the particulars; I only recollect that there was such paper offered in the market, and that I was asked if I would purchase some of it.

Question. Do you remember who called upon you to get you to purchase some of this paper?

Answer. I do not.

Question. You never purchased any of the paper yourself?

Answer. No; and I will not be positive that I have ever seen it. I recollect the circumstance that it was proposed to me to purchase some of it.

Question. Do you know J. B. Simpson?

Answer. No. It is possible that I may know him when I see him, but it could not be said that I know him.

Question. Do you know whether it was he who offered you the drafts referred to?

Answer. I do not think it was him. You understand that when they come into market with paper of that description, there are a great many brokers who endeavor to make a commission by going about and offering the paper. It is so common a thing for brokers to come into my office to offer bills, drafts, notes, and such things, that it is very seldom that I recollect it, unless there is something peculiar about it.

Question. If the January coupons had been off the bonds would you have purchased them?

Answer. I think not, without an explanation as to what had become of them.

Question. You would have considered the absence of the coupons as a badge of fraud?

Answer. It would have led at any rate to asking the question what had become of them, and why they were taken off.

JOHN H. GARLAND sworn.

Examination by Mr. Harris.

Question. Are you a broker?
Answer. Yes, sir; a stock broker.
Question. Have you ever seen any descriptive list of certain bonds of States fraudulently abstracted from the Interior Department?
Answer. I have seen some bonds that were represented to be lost, by advertisement in the papers.
Question. Have you in your business had any transactions in any way connected with these bonds?
Answer. I have had bonds of that description coming to me from members of the board; bonds bought and sold at the board of brokers and delivered to me by brokers.
Question. Do you remember what they were, and to what amount?
Answer. It would be impossible to specify without referring to my books. I could give you the whole list of bonds which have passed through my hands by referring to my books. These bonds, I suppose, were in the street, and passing through the hands of the brokers during the whole time after they were abstracted. It is possible that some of them may appear upon my books half a dozen times.
Question. Do you know any persons connected with these transactions other than brokers?
Answer. Not a human being. I have sold bonds for parties who are not members of the board, in the street. I have sold bonds to Peters, Campbell & Co., and these bonds were delivered. Whether they were bonds of that description I cannot tell, because my attention was not directed to them at the time.
Question. Have you any knowledge indicating where any of these bonds in question may be now?
Answer. I sold some of these bonds to a certain party in the street.
Question. How long ago?
Answer. Since the advertisement appeared.
Question. Will you state the name of that party?
Answer. Jerome Fitzhugh & Co.
Question. Is that the only case that will enable you to speak of the whereabouts of any of these bonds?
Answer. That is the only case. These bonds were in my possession on the morning the advertisement, stating the numbers of the stolen bonds, appeared. There were either nine or ten of them.
Question. Do you recollect what State?
Answer. I do not.
Question. Can you furnish the committee a memorandum of the particulars in regard to the bonds by reference to your books?
Answer. I can.
Question. Is there any other case in which you have any idea of where bonds are now?
Answer. There is not. I know nothing concerning the bonds except in the way of my business; in the way of a broker doing business

on the street. The only party who ever came to me in reference to these particular bonds was Peters, Campbell & Co., a party outside of the board, as I have stated.

Question. I understand you to say that neither directly nor indirectly have you any knowledge, except in the instances you have stated, as to who may have possession of any of these bonds?

Answer. Emphatically.

Question. Have you ever dealt in or seen the acceptances of the Secretary of War in favor of Russell, Majors & Waddell?

Answer. Never. I do not know the parties.

Question. Do you know Russell?

Answer. I never have seen him.

Question. Do you know J. B. Simpson?

Answer. I do not.

Question. Do you know Robert Latham?

Answer. I have known a man by that name, formerly connected with a bank in Washington some three or four years ago, but I do not think I have laid my eyes upon him for twelve months.

Question. Have you ever had any transactions with him in connexion with these acceptances?

Answer. I never have had a transaction with Latham in my life.

Question. Is there any matter connected with these bonds or acceptances of the Secretary of War, within your knowledge, directly or indirectly, that you have not communicated in this investigation?

Answer. None whatever.

Question. Do you know of whom you purchased the nine or ten bonds to which you have referred?

Answer. I have a memorandum on my books showing of whom I purchased them.

Question. I understand you that the party who purchased them of you purchased them with a full knowledge of the facts connected with this abstraction?

Answer. Certainly.

Question. And purchased them at a less rate than other bonds of the same State sold for on the same day?

Answer. Yes, sir.

Question. They purchased them with a full knowledge that they had been published as having been abstracted from the Interior Department?

Answer. Unquestionably they bought them with that knowledge, under the belief, I suppose, that the government would make no reclamation, and that they would make a very good speculation by it.

WILLIAM T. COLEMAN sworn.

Examination by Mr. Conkling.

Question. You are a broker in this city?

Answer. Yes, sir; a commission merchant and broker. We do not claim to be brokers, however; we are commission merchants.

Question. Commission merchants in what business?

Answer. We are in the shipping business, and dealing in merchandise generally. We also deal in bills of exchange and in money.

Question. Are you a member of a firm doing business here?

Answer. I am.

Question. Of what name?

Answer. William T. Coleman & Co.

Question. Do you know J. B. Simpson?

Answer. Yes, sir.

Question. How long have you known him?

Answer. I do not recollect—for two or three years.

Question. Have you at any time received securities from Simpson during the last year?

Answer. Yes, sir.

Question. When first?

Answer. I have been doing business with him for the last two or three years in securities.

Question. When did you, if ever, first receive from him any State stocks?

Answer. In October last, if I recollect right.

Question. What were they?

Answer. The first that we received were some Tennessees and some South Carolinas, on which we negotiated a loan for him.

Question. What amount of bonds of each?

Answer. $25,000 of each.

Question. The January coupons on or off?

Answer. The first January coupons off.

Question. Explain, if you please, the transaction in which you received these bonds.

Answer. Simpson came to me and wanted to borrow money for 90 days, or four months; I told him I would lend him what he wanted on call; he said that did not answer his purpose; that he could get what he wanted on call, but he wanted to carry the loan over into the new year, or into February; he came to us, knowing that we loaned money, and did that kind of business; I told him we could not spare the money ourselves for anything more than a short time, but I thought if he wanted it I could negotiate it for him; I went to one of my banks, but they did not want to loan for a long time, State bonds not being a kind of security they liked; I then went to a trust company and they readily took them.

Question. Which company?

Answer. The United States Trust Company. I proposed giving them Simpson's name, and merely act as broker in the premises. They did not know him, but they knew us, and said we could have what we wanted in our own name, he being a stranger. I reported to Simpson and told him we should have to charge 1 per cent. commission for the use of our name, but I would rather he would procure the money in his own name; that if he would go directly to them I would introduce him; he said he did not know them; did not know as they would accept his name if he went. After trying to induce us to take a smaller commission, he asked me to close the transaction, and I went and did so.

Question. Giving the Trust Company what besides the bonds?

Answer. A stock note, as it is called.

Question. Whose note?

Answer. Our own.

Question. What amount of bonds did you have?

Answer. $50,000.

Question. What was the amount of the note?

Answer. $35,000.

Question. What were the bonds left with them?

Answer. They were, if I recollect, $25,000 South Carolinas and $25,000 Tennessees. In a short time, as the political excitement rose, the South Carolinas were not liked. There was something said between the company and ourselves about substituting other bonds. I mentioned it to Simpson, and he said he would give us North Carolinas, which he did, exchanging $25,000 of one for $25,000 of the other.

Question. When was that?

Answer. I cannot give the date.

Question. As nearly as you can.

Answer. It was during November. There was afterwards a decline in all these securities, and the Trust Company called on us for a margin. We responded and called on Simpson, and Tennessees declining he gave us North Carolinas, so that it finally resulted in the company holding 50 bonds of the State of North Carolina, besides the margin which we paid in.

Question. What margin did you pay in?

Answer. Between $3,000 and $4,000.

Question. Does that complete the transaction?

Answer. It completes it up to the denouement about the bonds.

Question. What then?

Answer. I saw Simpson and asked him what he could do in the premises. He said he could not do anything; that he was an innocent party acting in good faith; he was satisfied that Russell would do what would be satisfactory to us. I told him that we were merely agents, and that we had no interest in the matter, except to serve him; that we knew Russell pretty well, and I would like him to give me some other securities. He said he would see. The Trust Company called on us, and we paid them the whole amount in cash, they not liking to hold these bonds as security. I then consulted my counsel in the matter, and we proposed writing to the Secretary of the Interior or Attorney General, but, after discussing the matter finally, did not. I was afraid they would not appreciate our frankness and plain statement of the facts. I did not know but we should be published in the newspapers as holders of these bonds; we were willing to tell all we knew to a committee or any responsible authority, but did not want to go into the newspapers.

Question. Then the bonds are now remaining in your hands?

Answer. In the hands of my counsel; I gave them to him.

Question. Who is he?

Answer. Daniel Lord.

Question. Did you examine the published numbers of the bonds abstracted from the Interior Department?

Answer. I looked over the list, but did not examine it particularly.

Question. Will you state whether the present 50 bonds you hold correspond with the numbers published?

Answer. I can furnish you the numbers by going to my office, if you wish it. My cashier looked them over and told me that the numbers of these bonds were included in the published list. I have not looked at them myself particularly.

Question. Did the Tennessee bonds you held correspond with the published numbers?

Answer. I never looked. I take it for granted, without going into the details, that all these bonds came from the Interior Department.

Question. You knew Simpson at the time of this transaction as the agent of Russell, Majors & Waddell?

Answer. Yes, sir.

Question. And supposed he was acting on their behalf?

Answer. Yes, sir.

Question. Have you ever seen any other bonds than those you have spoken of, corresponding with the published description?

Answer. Not to my recollection.

Question. How long after the publication of the notice by the Secretary of the Interior before you purchased these bonds of the Trust Company, and gave them the money?

Answer. The same day.

Question. The same day of the publication of the numbers of the bonds?

Answer. The same day or the next day. They called on me, and the money was paid

Question. The publication you refer to is the notice with the numbers of the bonds attached?

Answer. Yes, sir.

Question. Do you know what became of the Tennessees and South Carolinas?

Answer. We returned them to Simpson.

Question. What became of them after that?

Answer. I do not know.

Question. Since this transaction that you speak of, when you loaned the money, have you had any moneyed transactions with Simpson?

Answer. No, sir.

Question. Do you know where he is?

Answer. No, sir.

Question. When did you last see him?

Answer. I last saw him on the Saturday previous to this publication. I called at his office, but did not see him; then my cashier called upon him.

Question. Will you state what your cashier informed you that Simpson agreed to do?

Answer. He said that Simpson told him he had made other negotiations of the same sort.

Question. Did he say with whom?

Answer. He did not say.

Question. Do you know with whom?

Answer. I do not. And he said he was using every effort he could to satisfy the parties, and make them good.

Question. Did he agree to substitute other securities for these?

Answer. He proposed to substitute the acceptances of the Secretary of War, I believe.

Question. Did that complete the message which your cashier brought you?

Answer. That was the general tenor of it. He was to see Simpson the next morning in regard to the matter. Simpson told him he would make it good; that it was all right; that it was perfectly straight, or should be made so.

Question. Did you see him the next morning?

Answer. No, sir; and my cashier did not see him. In the meantime I had thought the matter over, and concluded that the bonds were better than the acceptances, if anything. I consulted with my counsel, and he agreed with me that it would not do to give them up. If there was anything wrong about them, we concluded we would not give them up except to the department, or with the consent of Simpson. I went myself the next day and tried to find Simpson, to get some additional security, and see what he would do. I went to his office and went to his residence several times. I took the matter in hand, but could not find him.

Question. Where was his residence?

Answer. Up town somewhere. I looked it out in the directory. I think in East Twenty-fourth or fifth street; I have forgotten the precise locality.

Question. Did you ever see any of the acceptances of either of the heads of the departments?

Answer. Yes, sir.

Question. Whose?

Answer. Floyd's. I have seen a great many of them.

Question. When first?

Answer. I cannot tell you when first; a long while ago.

Question. Acceptances in favor of Russell, Majors & Waddell?

Answer. Yes, sir.

Question. In favor of any other parties?

Answer. Not to the best of my recollection.

Question. In whose hands?

Answer. In the hands of different people. In the hands of Simpson; in the hands of John J. Anderson & Co, of St. Louis, here; and I think in the hands of a dozen people.

Question. For what purpose were they shown?

Answer. Negotiation.

Question. Did you ever buy any of them?

Answer. No, sir.

Question. Did you ever hold any of those which have been celled?

Answer. Yes, sir.

Question. For what purpose?

Answer. I have made negotiations upon them.

Question. For whom?

Answer. For Simpson.

Question. For what amount?

Answer. I made one negotiation for $35,000 or $40,000 on them, and on the note of Holliday & Russell, during the summer, perhaps in July or August last, and I think I made similar negotiations previously, but I do not remember them definitely. I know that John J. Anderson wanted me to take some of them and to enter into negotiations with us upon them, but we never did. We have received them from different people. Our correspondents in the west have sent them to be placed to their credit. We have had them in our possesion many times, but never bought one. We always regarded them as irregular, and yet, from what I heard, I supposed they would be paid.

Question. Did you ever see any letters from Secretary Floyd?

Answer. Never; I heard there were letters, but I never saw them.

Question. When last did you see any of these acceptances?

Answer. I cannot tell; not long ago.

Question. As near as you can.

Answer. Within three months.

Question. Did you in the month of December last, ultimo?

Answer. I do not recollect having seen any as late as that.

Question. When did you first know of these acceptances being protested for non-payment?

Answer. I never knew of their being protested for non-payment, or heard of it until the last six months. I think we held some at the time.

Question. Have you had any transactions with Wm. H. Russell during the last six months?

Answer. No, sir; I think he has been in our office about business never consummated; we have had no moneyed transactions with him.

Question. Have you had any conversation with him in reference to this transaction?

Answer. Never.

Question. Have you seen Russell since the exposure of the abstraction of the bonds?

Answer. No, sir.

Question. Do you know where any of these abstracted bonds are, except those you hold?

Answer. No, sir.

Question. Have you any information in reference to the whereabouts of any of them?

Answer. No, sir.

Question. Do you know where any of them have been at any time since the abstraction?

Answer. No, sir.

Question. Have you any information?

Answer. No, sir; I would add that we sold four North Carolina bonds and got the money a short time before this notice came out for account of Simpson. Simpson gave us an order to close out the whole of them the week previous to this announcement, and our broker had sold $35,000 of them, but they were deliverable some time afterwards. The next week the announcement came out, and the transaction was cut off—so that we stand now as sellers of $35,000 of these bonds which have not been delivered.

Question. But the four bonds sold for cash were delivered?

Answer. Yes, sir.

Question. And you still hold $50,000 of them?

Answer. Yes, sir.

Question. These four being margin above that?

Answer. Yes, sir.

Question. Was that the only margin above $50,000 in these bonds?

Answer. Yes, sir.

Question. Is there any other fact about these bonds that you know which you have not disclosed to the committee?

Answer. Nothing, except that they came to us in what seemed to be perfect good faith. We received them in perfect good faith and presented them.

Question. Is there any point to which I have not interrogated you about which you know in reference to these bonds?

Answer. No, sir.

Question. To whom were these acceptances sold?

WITNESS. The $35,000 transaction?

Mr. CONKLING. Yes.

Answer. There were three pieces of paper, either of which was considered good, placed in the hands of C. K. Garrison. The money was paid and the acceptances handed back.

Question. One of these papers was the acceptance of John B. Floyd?

Answer. Yes, sir.

Question. Is that the only acceptance of his which you have negotiated?

Answer. I cannot say; we have had so many friends coming to us with almost every description of security. I suppose, generally speaking, we have had these acceptances offered to us a hundred times. They have been the most common thing in the market imaginable. Before doing anything in them I went to the Bank of the Republic, to the American Exchange Bank, and to the Metropolitan Bank. I asked the cashier of the American Exchange Bank if he could do anything for one of these correspondents in the way of discounting this paper. He said they received nothing else from the west but that paper; that their entire remittances from the west had been in that paper, and they did not want any more.

Question. Name the party who said that.

Answer. I think it was the cashier of the American Exchange Bank. It was the cashier of one of the banks I have mentioned.

Question. Do you know of any parties who now hold acceptances of John B. Floyd?

Answer. I do not.

Question. And you do not know what has become of the large floating mass of acceptances which were circulating here?

Answer. No, I do not. Simpson nearly always told me whenever I saw him that if any of my friends wanted to buy that paper to negotiate for him. I told him we had no faith in them at all. We regarded the thing as an irregular transaction altogether, but that was between the Secretary of War and them. He has frequently asked me to enter into some transaction in them, but I always told him it was of no use to offer them any more. He said they could not dispose of them; that they had to fortify them by their "reserved corps," by every other means in their possession.

Question. Did he ever explain to you the circumstances under which the Secretary of War gave these acceptances?

Answer. Oh! yes; he went into a full explanation of all the circumstances.

ALEXANDER CAMPBELL sworn.

Examination by the chairman.

Question. What is the firm with which you are connected?

Answer. Ward, Campbell & Co.

Question. In what business is the firm of which you are a member engaged?

Answer. We are bankers and commission brokers. One branch of our business is to purchase and sell stocks on commission.

Question. Have you seen the publication made by the Secretary of the Interior in reference to certain bonds belonging to the Indian trust fund alleged to have been stolen from his department.

Answer. Yes, sir.

Question. Have you any of those bonds on hand?

Answer. No, sir.

Question. Do you know of any person or persons who have?

Answer. I do.

Question. Please state what you know on that subject.

Answer. I did not expect that question to be asked, and therefore I cannot give you all the particulars that I ought to be able to tell you. The only knowledge I have has accrued since the appearance of that advertisement. We have been notified by parties from whom we have bought bonds that they have had delivered to them some of the numbers of these bonds.

Question. Give the numbers and the parties?

Answer. I cannot give that; I will give you all the information I have. The only knowledge I have is, that I find by my books that there were $21,000 Missouris and either $4,000 or $5,000 North Carolinas of these bonds, of which we have been notified. I do not remember whether we discovered any Tennessees among our friends or not. We bought, for instance, for George Smith, of Chicago, Tennessees, North Carolinas, Missouris, and all kinds of State stocks. I think he has notified us that about $21,000 of Missouris were included in the published list. I cannot tell whether he had any Tennessees or not. We bought also for a bank in Washington, which has notified us of $4,000 or $5,000 North Carolinas as being among these bonds.

Question. Do you remember the name of that bank?

Answer. No, I do not. Let me say that these bonds were all bought in the market and the stock board for orders from our customers. The bonds were received, paid for, and delivered.

Question. Do you know who had the bonds sold in market?

Answer. Oh! no; I have not the least idea. We bought them in open market, and received them from the different brokers of whom we bought them.

Question. What are the names of the brokers of whom you bought them?

Answer. I cannot inform you without referring to my books.

Question. Will the statement you propose to furnish the committee, setting forth the number, character, and denomination of the bonds you have dealt in, embrace all the knowledge you have with reference to the bonds contained in the published list?

Answer. Yes, sir.

Question. State what other knowledge you have.

Answer. This is the point to which I supposed my testimony was required. We have sold bonds, and among them are some issued by the State of Missouri to the Iron Mountain road, the numbers of which are included in the list published by the Secretary of the Interior, amounting to $20,000.

Question. Will you give the numbers of those bonds?

Answer. Yes, sir; they are 1870, 1872, 1873, 1874, 1875, 1876, 1877, 1878, 1880, 1884, 2037, 1808, 1809, 1879, 1882, 1883, 2039, 2040, 2041, 2042. On the 16th of November, 1860, we sold for Richard Schell these 20 Missouri bonds, for which we paid him in advance of the sale, *i. e.*, we advanced money before the meeting of the board. We advanced him $12,000 on the 20 bonds. We sold them at the second board, and delivered them the following day, giving a check for the balance due him of $1,250, I think it was. We sold the bonds in open market: $9,000 to H. A. Johnson & Co., $5,000 to E. Whitehouse & Son, and $6,000 to Carpenter & Vermilye; all at 72 per cent., less the January coupon.

Question. Was the January coupon off from all these bonds?

Answer. Yes; it was cut off.

Question. These bonds, of which you have given a description as having sold, were not a part of the bonds that you purchased for Smith and other customers?

Answer. No. These are all the bonds contained in that list of which we have any knowledge of having sold to anybody. All I have to say about this transaction in selling the bonds is, that it was in the regular course of business. We paid for the bonds before we sold them, in fact. We sold them legitimately in open market at the price of the afternoon; and as to the purchases, of which I shall send you a statement, they were all bought in open market, in the usual course of business, on orders from our clients, without any knowledge or information, or suspicion of any sort or kind, that there was anything wrong about them. All these transactions occurred previous to the publication of these bonds by the Secretary of the Interior, and all in entirely good faith.

Question. Are you in possession of any information, either directly or indirectly, with reference to any other of the published bonds than those you have described?

Answer. None whatever of the slightest.

Question. Have you ever had any business transactions with J. B. Simpson in reference to bonds?

Answer. No, sir. I do not know him.

Question. Or with Wm. H. Russell?

Answer. No. I do not know him. When I say "I," I speak of my house; and when I say "I do not know him," I mean that the firm does not know him.

Question. You are distinct in your recollection that you know of no other person or persons or institution holding a portion of the published bonds?

Answer. I do not. Of course we have no knowledge of what may have passed through our hands, but I have no information of any sort or kind where any of the other bonds are.

Question. Have you ever seen in the market drafts drawn by Russell, Majors & Waddell upon the Secretary of War, and accepted by him?

Answer. Not since the first and only ones that I ever did see, which was some time in the year 1858, I think. We were asked to negotiate some of them.

Question. By whom?

Answer. That is more than I can tell you—it is too long ago. We were asked in reference to them, but had nothing to do with them.

Question. Do you know of any person or institution now holding any of these acceptances?

Answer. I do not.

Question. Have you ever learned from any other person that they were held by parties in this city?

Answer. I have no knowledge of it at all. We have been asked at some time, by one of our correspondents in Boston, I think, what such a paper would be sold at. We replied that we could not tell them, and declined to say anything about it.

Question. What is the name of your correspondent in Boston?

Answer. There was a mere casual reference to the matter in the correspondence, which attracted no notice, and I really cannot say who was the correspondent.

The following communication was subsequently received from the witness:

NEW YORK, *January* 9, 1861.

SIR: The published bonds bought by Ward, Campbell & Co., and alluded to in my testimony yesterday, are as follows:

November 27, 1860, of W. R. Travers, $1,000 Missouri bond, No. 2769, issued to N. M. railroad $1,000

December 4, 1860, of Clark, Dodge & Co., $5,000 Missouri bonds, issued to Pacific Railroad Company, Nos. 5306 to 5310	$5,000
December 5, 1860, of P. & F. Jaudon, $15,000 Missouri bonds, issued to Pacific Railroad Company, Nos. 5197 to 5200, 5231 to 5241	15,000
In all, 21 Missouri bonds, for George Smith, of Chicago......	21,000
December 22, 1860, of J. Brandon & Son, $5,000 North Carolina bonds, Nos. 300 to 303, each $1,000, per account of Richard Smith, cashier, Washington	4,000
And No. 317, resold by us to Trevor & Colgate	1,000
	5,000

Your obedient servant,

A. CAMPBELL.

Hon. J. N. MORRIS,
Chairman Committee U. S. H. R.

ROBERT H. LOWRY sworn.

Examination by Mr. Case.

Question. Will you state what your business is in New York.

Answer. I am cashier of the Bank of the Republic.

Question. How long have you held that position in the bank?

Answer. Nearly seven years.

Question. During that time state what knowledge you have of any negotiations you have had at your bank of the acceptances of John B. Floyd, Secretary of War.

Answer. I can only state, in a general way, that we have discounted them to a very large amount, probably to the amount of three-quarters of a million in two and a half years.

Question. As near as you can recollect, when was the first time when the acceptances were offered to you.

Answer. The first time such acceptances were discounted by the bank was the 6th of May, 1858.

Question. For whose benefit were they discounted?

Answer. Russell, Majors & Waddell.

Question. Were all the discounts of these acceptances for their benefit?

Answer. No, sir; they may, however, have been all directly or indirectly for their benefit, but we took them from brokers and other parties who had them discounted.

Question. What was the amount of the acceptances which you discounted on the first occasion?

Answer. Two acceptances of $50,000 each, which were severally due September 4 and October 4 of that year.

Question. What was the character of those acceptances?

Answer. They were conditional. It has been only within the last fifteen or seventeen months that Secretary Floyd accepted unconditionally.

Question. What was the condition attached to these acceptances?

Answer. They stated that they would be due upon the fulfilment of a certain contract to Russell, Majors & Waddell, the sum named in the instrument which he agreed to pay to the holder of the paper chargeable to such an account.

Question. Did you have any communication or correspondence with the Secretary of War relative to the payment of these acceptances?

Answer. We had no reciprocal correspondence.

Question. Did you receive any communication from the Secretary?

Answer. Yes, sir; we received a letter, of which the following is a copy:

WAR DEPARTMENT,
Washington, May 1, 1858.

GENTLEMEN: As this department will be indebted to Russell, Majors & Waddell to a large amount, I have accepted five orders, two calling for the sum of one hundred thousand dollars each, and three for fifty thousand dollars each—all but two orders of the last-named amount having been negotiated.

These acceptances will be promptly paid in pursuance of their tenor. If you will advance the money upon their assignment of the orders to you, I will see that the funds shall be applied to their payment.

I am, gentlemen, very respectfully, your obedient servant,

JOHN B. FLOYD,
Secretary of War.

The PRESIDENT AND DIRECTORS
Of the Bank of the Republic, New York City.

Question. Do you know at whose instance that letter was written?

Answer. It was written at the instance of Russell.

Question. Please explain the circumstance under which the letter was written.

Answer. This letter was obtained from Floyd at the suggestion of the president of the bank, in order to satisfy him and the board of directors of the security of the acceptances.

Question. Will you state the reason why you desired something from him?

Answer. Because we were not satisfied as to the validity of such acceptances, although we were otherwise satisfied with the responsibility of the drawers.

Question. Please state whether you had other communications from any person connected with the War Department with reference to these acceptances.

Answer. There was a communication written, I believe, in reply to a letter of the president of the bank upon the subject.

Question. From whom was that communication?

Answer. From W. R. Drinkard, chief clerk of the War Department.

Question. Can you furnish a copy of that communication?

Answer. The following is a copy, underscored as in the original:

WASHINGTON CITY, *July* 4, 1858.

MY DEAR SIR: Yours of yesterday was received this morning. Being Sunday, I have not access to the books or officers of the War Department, and therefore cannot give as good a reason for my opinion if I were at this moment differently situated. I have not the slightest doubt that the acceptances of the Secretary of War, discounted by your bank for Messrs. Russell, Majors & Waddell, will be promptly paid at maturity. If there had been *any* doubt on that point, the Secretary of War would not have *accepted* them; and before accepting them, he consulted fully and freely with the officer in charge of the quartermaster's department as to the propriety and safety of such an act.

Let me give you one idea which may possibly not have been brought to your notice. The *contract* between the department and Russell & Co. provides that for all transportation they may be required to do they shall be previously *notified* by the department, and if, after being notified, the department should not need the transportation, still Russell & Co. *are to be paid*. The reason of this is obvious, because on receiving the notice the contractors of course go to work at once to make their arrangements. Now, it so happens that Russell & Co. *have already received the notice for nearly all the transportation they have contracted to do*, and therefore they have an indisputable and a certain claim to their pay. Besides this, it is very certain that the government will require all the transportation that has been contracted for.

Further, although their bills of lading have not been received, I feel sure that Russell & Co. have *already carried* at least five times the amount of all the acceptances that have been given to them. In a word, I consider those acceptances as good and as promptly convertible into coin at maturity as any government security, or any paper you may have presented at your counter.

These gentlemen have a high reputation for personal and business integrity, and I feel assured your experience will enable you to add yours to this general testimony.

I am, dear sir, very truly yours,

W. R. DRINKARD.

JAMES T. SOUTTER, Esq.,
President Bank of the Republic, New York City.

Question. You say you discounted these two acceptances of $50,000 each?

Answer. We discounted one of them at the time for Russell, Majors & Waddell; the other was discounted by another party, who had it re-discounted at our bank.

Question. And that one was discounted before this letter of the 4th of July was received?

Answer. It was discounted subsequent to the receipt of Floyd's letter, but prior to the receipt of Drinkard's.

Question. That acceptance was paid at maturity?

Answer. Yes, sir; all of them in fact—every acceptance we took.

Question. Were they paid by the Secretary?

Answer. Not directly, but through Russell, Majors and Waddell; the paper was retired by treasury drafts and warrants, and by quartermasters' or paymasters' drafts.

Question. How recently have you discounted any of the drafts of Russell, Majors & Waddell?

Answer. The last one we discounted on the 26th of April, and that was paid on the 26th of July.

Question. Have you a statement showing the number of acceptances?

Answer. I have a statement of the discounts made for them and for other parties outside as near as I could arrive at it from a hasty glance at our books. I think we discounted from May, 1858, to April, 1860, these acceptances to the amount of $725,000, all of which were promptly paid at maturity; not one of them laid over for a day.

Question. Have you any of these acceptances now?

Answer. Not a dollar; and we have not had, to the best of my recollection, fortified by an examination of our books, since the 26th of July of last year.

Question. I ask you whether, in connexion with the negotiation of any of these acceptances, you have received at any time collateral security in the shape of bonds?

Answer. We have not.

Question. Do you know personally anything of the negotiation or sale or hypothecation of these bonds alleged to have been abstracted from the Interior Department.

Answer. No knowledge whatever.

Question. Have you seen the list of those bonds published by the Secretary of the Interior?

Answer. I have just seen it; I have never scrutinized it.

Question. Your bank has no interest in it?

Answer. It has no interest in Russell, Majors & Waddell, or in these bonds to the extent of one cent directly or indirectly, and never has had an interest in any of these bonds.

Question. Do you know J. B. Simpson?

Answer. Yes, sir; I do.

Question. How recently have you seen him?

Answer. I think it was about two weeks since.

Question. Since the publicity of this matter?

Answer. No, sir; previous to that; he said he was going to Europe for his health, which was very much broken down; in fact, he did look so. It was on Friday that I saw him, and he was to sail in the steamer which left the next day.

Question. You say this paper was retired by paymasters' drafts or treasury notes: were they forwarded to you by the paymasters themselves?

Answer. No, sir; they were generally deposited by Russell, Majors & Waddell, through their collectors or servants, or remitted from Leavenworth city.

Question. Your communication was with Russell, Majors & Waddell?

Answer. Yes, or with Smoot, Russell & Co., at Leavenworth, Kansas.

WEDNESDAY, *January* 9, 1861.

HECTOR MORRISON sworn.

Examination by the chairman.

Question. Please state whether you are in company with any other person or persons, and the kind of business you are engaged in.

Answer. I am in business in the city, and constitute one of the firm of E. Whitehouse, Son & Morrison; we are stock and exchange brokers and bankers.

Question. Do you know William H. Russell?

Answer. No, sir.

Question. Do you know J. B. Simpson?

Answer. Yes, sir.

Question. Have you had any business transactions with him?

Answer. Yes, sir.

Question. Please state the nature and character of these transactions.

Answer. On the 9th of November last we loaned him $15,000.

Question. Upon what security?

Answer. On North Carolina State bonds.

Question. Were they hypothecated with you?

Answer. Yes, sir.

Question. Did he retire them?

Answer. They were retired, and the loan was paid on the 30th of November. I think the loan was paid by Mr. Schell, or, at least, that it was paid by his certified check. Both parties, however, were present at the time it was paid.

Question. To whom were the bonds delivered; to Mr. Simpson or Mr. Schell?

Answer. I think Mr. Schell took them. The delivery was intended to be to Mr. Simpson, but I think Mr. Schell took them. I will, however, not be positive in relation to the matter.

Question. Do you know what became of these bonds afterwards?

Answer. No, sir.

Question. Have you ever examined the published list of bonds, made by the direction of Secretary Thompson, purporting to have been abstracted from his department?

Answer. I have, partially.

Question. Were any of the bonds referred to, in the transaction you have named, a portion of these bonds?

Answer. I have not a record of the numbers of those bonds, and I therefore could not tell.

Question. Were the January coupons off from the bonds you received?

Answer. I cannot be positive, but I think they were not.

Question. I would like you to be certain upon that point.

Answer. I cannot; nor have I any definite recollection on the subject. I think if they had been incomplete I should not have received them as security; that is all I can say.

Question. You would have regarded the bonds as incomplete with the coupons off?

Answer. Yes, sir; though it is not a very unusual circumstance.

Question. Would you regard it as a suspicious circumstance?

Answer. Oh! no, sir; they are very frequently cut off and discounted by persons wanting money.

Question. Have you ever had any business transaction with Mr. Simpson, other than that you have stated?

Answer. No, sir.

Question. Did you understand from Mr. Simpson that he was transacting that business for his own account, or for some other person or persons?

Answer. I supposed it was for himself. He gave his own note—his individual note.

Question. Do you know whether he was acting for Russell, Majors & Waddell in that transaction?

Answer. I do not.

Question. When did you last see Mr. Simpson?

Answer. I have no recollection of seeing him since the day he paid that loan.

Question. You do not know where he is now?

Answer. I do not.

Question. Have you any knowledge, directly or indirectly, which enables you to furnish the committee information of the whereabouts of any of the bonds abstracted from the Interior Department?

Witness. According to that list of numbers?

Mr. Morris. Yes.

Answer. I think I have.

Question. Please state your knowledge.

Answer. I think I know where there is one of the Missouris. It was purchased by us, and belongs to the Merchants' Benevolent Association of this city. It was purchased by them for an investment.

Question. Is that the only one you have any knowledge of?

Answer. I might, from our books, trace others, but I do not know of any others now. There is one circumstance I would like to state to you. I sold a very large amount of North Carolina bonds belonging to one of the banks in Tennessee; I sold them for the Merchants' Bank of this city. In the fall of 1857 we made a loan to the State of Alabama, receiving, as security, North Carolina bonds corresponding with these numbers and with the numbers contained in the published list, and in the meantime they have not been out of the possession of the Merchants' Bank, except for a short time it may be in one of the savings banks of this city.

Question. Do you know the letter of these bonds?

Answer. I do not.

Question. Have you ever seen any drafts drawn by Russell, Majors & Waddell on the Secretary of War, and accepted by him?

Answer. I cannot tell; I think I have seen such acceptances.

Question. In whose favor?

Answer. I do not remember.

Question. When and where did you see those acceptances; in whose hands were they?

Answer. I can only speak from recollection; I think about two years ago Mr. Simpson applied to us to make a loan.

Question. To make a loan upon those acceptances?

Answer. To make a loan on an acceptance; I cannot tell whether there was more than one; I think there was, but I did not see but one. It must have been more than two years ago.

Question. Is that acceptance the only one you recollect to have seen?

Answer. I think that he had more than one, but I did not see them.

Question. Did you purchase it?

Answer. No, sir.

Question. Did you advance money on it?

Answer. No, sir; we declined to take it. We doubted whether it was legal.

Question. Have you detailed to the committee all the knowledge you have respecting these acceptances?

Answer. I think I have. I have several times been asked questions in regard to them, but that is to the best of my knowledge the only time I have seen one of them.

Question. Have you stated to the committee all the knowledge you have respecting these published bonds; if not, please add to what you have already stated?

Answer. I have stated all that I am able to state from memory.

Question. Will your books furnish any additional information?

Answer. They show the numbers of the bonds that have passed through the office, from whom they were received, and to whom they have been delivered.

Question. Have you ever examined your books to see whether any numbers correspond with those of the published bonds?

Answer. Our clerk has.

Question. Did he find any of them to correspond with the published numbers?

Answer. He did.

Question. How many?

Answer. A great many. I cannot tell how many; a large number, including those North Carolina bonds which I have mentioned.

Question. Can you state what you did with the bonds corresponding with the published bonds in number?

Answer. We delivered them to the parties for whom we purchased them.

Question. Who were those parties?

Answer. I cannot state without reference to our books.

Question. Will you furnish to the committee a statement of the facts referred to by you?

Answer. I will.

Question. You say it is a very common thing to find bonds in the market with the coupons off?

Answer. Yes, sir.

Question. When they are presented to you in the market for sale, do you not regard it a matter for explanation?

Answer. No, sir. It has been a very common thing, and is not regarded as anything unusual, for the reason that they are frequently cut off to borrow money upon. We have received them from strangers.

The following statement, above referred to, was subsequently handed in by the witness:

North Carolina.

July 23.—13, 15, and 11, received from G. Wedtfeldt, Hallett & Co.; delivered to Ward, Campbell & Co.

July 24.—318, received from G. Wedtfeldt, Hallett & Co ; delivered to Mervin & Kunz.

August 3.—203, 296, 297, received from Meigs & Greenleaf; delivered to George Ellis.

August 4.—203, (same bond as above,) received from George Ellis; delivered to Mervin & Kunz, August 21.

August 21.—317, received from G. Wedtfeldt, Hallett & Co.; delivered to A. D. Williams, August 21.

August 23.—316, received from G. Wedtfeldt, Hallett & Co.; delivered to C. Kowalski, August 23.

August 24.—236, 237, received from Clark, Dodge & Co.; delivered to E. W. Hewitt, August 25.

September 13.—32, 33, received from Ward & Co.; sent to W. W. Boardman, New Haven.

September 20.—51, 52, 53, 54, received from Merchants' Bank; delivered to H. T. Morgan & Co.

September 21.—60, 62, received from Merchants' Bank; 60 delivered to T. Ketchum & Co.; 61 delivered to L. Thomas & Co.

October 22.—604, received from F. W. Worth ; delivered to C. H. Raberg.

November 24.—125, received from Lockwood & Co.; delivered to E. W. Hewitt.

December 4.—178, 179, 180, received from Meigs & Greenleaf; delivered to E W. Hewitt.

December 13.—191, 106, 99, 98, 97, received from Clark, Dodge & Co.; delivered to E. W. Hewitt.

Tennessee bonds.

October 17.—210, received from Merchants' Bank, New York ; delivered to Clark, Dodge & Co., October 17.

November 6.—828, received from W. & J. O'Brien ; delivered to E. H. Hewitt.

December 8.—5389, 5390, received from P. & F. Jaudon ; delivered to John Sneden.

Missouri bonds.

November 17, 1860.—Iron Mountain, 1870, 1872, 1873, 1874, 1875, received from Ward, Campbell & Co.; 1870, 1872, 1873, 1874, 1875, delivered to Weeks & Co., November 19.

November 22, 1860.—Iron Mountain, 2007, 2008, 2006, 2013, 2014, received from W. R. Travers; 2007, sent to L. Cooper, Philadelphia, December 8; 2008, 2013, delivered to H. Toland & Son, December 13; 2006, 2014, delivered to H. T. Morgan & Co., December 12.

November 30, 1860.—Iron Mountain, 1868, received from Clark, Dodge & Co.; delivered to L. G. Wilkins, December 1.

December 14, 1860.—Iron Mountain, 2010, received from J. R. Garland; sent to L. Cooper, Philadelphia.

December 15, 1860.—Hannibal and St. Joseph, 1831, received from P. & F. Jaudon; delivered to L. A. Colin, December 17.

December 17, 1860.—Hannibal and St. Joseph, 1821, received from Mervin & Kunz; purchased for the Merchants' Benevolent Society.

HOWELL L. WILLIAMS sworn.

Examination by the chairman.

Question. Please state to the committee what is your business in this city.

Answer. Merchant.

Question. Wholesale merchant?

Answer. General shipping and commission merchant; also wholesale dealer in produce. Cotton and sugar are my principal articles of trade in the latter line of business.

Question. Are you doing business principally on your own account, or in connexion with others?

Answer. In connexion with others.

Question. Have you, as an individual, or the house with which you are connected, examined a published list of bonds, made by direction of the Secretary of the Interior, purporting to have been abstracted from the Interior Department?

Answer. I have not; I have seen such a list in the newspapers, but I have not gone over it to examine it.

Question. Have you any knowledge of these bonds?

Answer. No, sir.

Question. Did you ever see any of them?

Answer. Not to my recollection; I do not own any; the concern with which I am connected does not own any, nor do they hold any State stocks at all now.

Question. Do you know J. B. Simpson?

Answer. I do not; I may know who he is when I see him, but I have no recollection of him now.

Question. Have you ever seen any drafts drawn by Russell, Majors & Waddell on the Secretary of War, and accepted by him?

Answer. I have.

Question. Please state when and where you saw these acceptances, and in whose hands they were.

Answer. I saw one in November, 1859, and I think I have seen two or three others. I saw it in the hands of a gentleman from St. Louis, indorsed, if I mistake not, by the State Bank of Missouri. I will not be positive, however; I am not sure who was the St. Louis party.

Question. Was it a gentleman by the name of Anderson?

Answer. I think it was Anderson; that is my impression.

Question. What was the amount of the acceptance?

Answer. $15,000.

Question. Do you know what became of it?

Answer. Yes, sir; I bought it, and was paid for it.

Question. From whom did you receive it?

Answer. I received my pay from the Bank of the Republic; I received a check payable there, and which was certified by that bank.

Question. Do you remember the date?

Answer. No, I do not; I recollect I bargained for it on the 2d of November. I got it, I think, on the 5th, and it was due in eighty days from the time I bought it.

Question. Is that the only acceptance of the kind you recollect to have seen?

Answer. I recollect to have seen others, but I did not take any particular note of them. This is the only one I ever bought. I had them offered to me afterwards, but I declined buying. This was in November, 1859, please recollect, not 1860.

Question. Can you state to the committee whether you have within your knowledge such information as to lead you to believe that any person or persons, or institution, in the city of New York now holds any portion of the abstracted or published bonds?

Answer. Not the slightest.

Question. Or any of the acceptances referred to?

Answer. No, sir. In the case of the acceptance I speak of, I went to Mr. Cisco and asked him about it. He said there was no doubt about their being paid. There were two kinds of acceptances. I would not buy until I had that assurance from him.

Question. Did Mr. Cisco state the reasons which induced him to believe these acceptances would be paid?

Answer. None, except that the money was coming to these parties.

Question. Did he state that the money was coming to these parties?

Answer. He said he had no doubt the money would be paid. He said there were other bills which were drawn differently, but he had no doubt that this one charge for $15,000 would be paid.

Question. Did he state what induced him to make that statement to you?

Answer. There was a difference in the wording of the drafts.

Question. Was that the reason?

Answer. One of the reasons, I suppose.

Question. Was there any other?

Answer. I do not recollect of any other.

Question. Did he state to you who he supposed would pay it?

Answer. He did not.

Question. Who did you understand would pay it, from what he said?

Answer. He had seen the draft himself payable at the Bank of the Republic. I showed him the draft, and he said it would be paid.

Question. My question was, who did he say he expected would pay it?

Answer. He did not say.

Question. Who did you understand would pay it, from what he did say?

Answer. I understood that the Bank of the Republic would pay it. It was payable there, and, if protested at all, it must be protested by the Bank of the Republic.

Question. You do not mean that, because a draft is made payable at the Bank of the Republic, it would necessarily follow that the Bank of the Republic would pay it?

Answer. It is the presumption, when a bill is made payable at a particular bank, that the money is there to pay it at maturity.

Question. Then it was your understanding that the draft being made payable at the Bank of the Republic, it would be paid at that bank if the parties drawing it, or accepting it, had the funds there to pay it at maturity?

Answer. Yes, sir; it was presumed they would pay it.

Question. Are you acquainted with William H. Russell?

Answer. I am not; I do not know any one in the concern. If I have seen him I do not know it.

Question. Did I understand you to say that your acceptance was made payable at the Bank of the Republic?

Answer. It was.

Question. Do you mean that the acceptance written across the face of the draft made it payable at the Bank of the Republic, or that the draft was made payable at the Bank of the Republic, and then accepted by the Secretary of War?

Answer. I presume it was Russell's draft which made it payable there.

AUGUSTUS E. SILLIMAN sworn.

Examination by the chairman.

Question. State, if you please, the business in which you are engaged in this city.

Answer. I am president of the Merchants' Bank.

Question. How long have you been president of that bank?

Answer. I think it is about three years; I have been attached to the bank a great many years.

Question. As director?

Answer. No, sir; in various capacities, from clerk up to cashier, and finally president.

Question. Do you know J. B. Simpson?

Answer. No, sir.

Question. Do you know William H. Russell?

Answer. No.

Question. Do you know whether the bank of which you are president has ever done any business with either?

Answer. I do not think they ever have.

Question. Have you seen an advertisement in the newspapers setting forth a description of certain bonds alleged to have been fraudulently abstracted from the Interior Department?

Answer. I have seen such a list and run my eye over it, but not closely nor with any care. I looked to see whether a North Carolina bond which we had had in our possession, No. 926, was contained in the list, and I found that it was.

Question. Have you any knowledge of the whereabouts of any of these bonds at this time?

Answer. No, sir.

Question. You do not hold any of them?

Answer. Not that I am aware of. I did hold bonds for the State of Alabama, which were delivered up some six weeks ago, and the institution with which I am connected holds none at all now that I am aware of, and I should probably know it if it did.

Question. Have you any knowledge, directly or indirectly, as to where or by whom any of these bonds are now held?

Answer. None. It is proper to say that some of the bonds which we held were of the same numbers contained in the advertised list.

Question. Do you refer to North Carolina bonds?

Answer. Yes, sir.

Question. Do you remember whether the bonds to which you refer were designated by letters, such as "A," "B," "C?"

Answer. I do not know that I ever looked at the bonds.

Question. Do you remember the dates of them?

Answer. I do not. The particular bond held by the Thompsons, which is said to have come from me, was drawn, if I mistake not, in favor of the commissioner of the State of Alabama.

Question. Is that the bond to which you refer in a former part of your testimony?

Answer. Yes, sir.

Question. Please state the particulars in reference to it?

Answer. I know nothing about it, more than this: Mr. Thompson came to me with this bond, which had come from me, to ascertain how long it had been in my possession. I gave him the information, for several years. It was in my possession, with others, as a special deposit. I do not know the numbers, though I could, by referring to my books, ascertain the numbers delivered up at that particular time. These are only a portion of the bonds I held in my possession.

Question. You know the fact that that bond had been in your possession for some years?

Answer. I know that it must have been in my possession for at least two years prior to the robbery.

Question. Have you ever seen any drafts drawn by Russell, Majors & Waddell upon the Secretary of War, and accepted by him? If so, please state all the knowledge you have pertaining to them?

Answer. We have had at several instances within a few years, I do not know whether one, two, or three, acceptances of Mr. Floyd offered to us for discount. Who they were signed by, or what was their character, I cannot now state. I have some general information that it was in connexion with some western transportation contract, but it was a character of security that we did not care to have anything to do with. I have no recollection of any of the particulars about it at all.

Question. Did the bank with which you are connected buy any of them?

Answer. No, sir.

Question. Do you know who holds any of them now?

Answer. No, sir.

Question. Have you stated to the committee all the knowledge you have, directly or indirectly, relating to the bonds said to have been abstracted from the Interior Department, and of the acceptances made by the Secretary of War?

Answer. Yes, sir; I recollect that in two or three instances these acceptances have been offered to us, but it is not the character of security that is recognized by the Merchants' Bank in its business.

Question. On the 2d of July, 1860, Riggs & Co., bankers at Washington, remitted to New York a certificate of deposit on the Merchants' Bank for $910. Can you state to the committee in whose favor that certificate was issued?

Answer. We can do it without difficulty by reference to our books.

The certificate was subsequently received by the committee, of which the following is a copy:

$910. MERCHANTS' BANK,
New York, June 1, 1860.

Joseph H. White has deposited in this bank nine hundred and ten dollars to the credit of himself, payable to his order on the return of this certificate.

J. D. VERMILYE, *Cashier*.

GEO. ACHENBACH, *Teller*.
No. 1140.

Indorsed.

Pay to the order of Godard Bailey.

JOSEPH H. WHITE.

Pay to the order of Riggs & Co.

GODARD BAILEY.

Pay Bank of America, New York, or order.

RIGGS & CO.

CHARLES A. MEIGS sworn:

Examination by Mr. Case.

Question. Please state what is your business in this city?

Answer. It is that of a commission broker—buying and selling stocks and bonds on commission.

Question. How long have you been engaged in that business?

Answer. About six years.

Question. Have you seen an advertisement, purporting to come from the Secretary of the Interior, describing certain bonds alleged to have been abstracted from his department?

Answer. I have.

Question. Have you looked over the numbers?

Answer. I have.

Question. Can you state to the committee any personal knowledge in regard to any of these bonds—whether they have been in your possession?

Answer. I have ascertained that several of these bonds have passed through my hands in the way of business; I have been buying and selling these bonds among other securities very freely.

Question. Have any of them passed through your hands or been offered to you since the announcement of that publication?

Answer. None have passed through my hands, and I have not seen any.

Question. Can you state what amount in all, so far as you can identify them by the numbers, have passed through your hands?

Answer. My answer to that would be mere guess work. I should say that $20,000 or $30,000 of these bonds have passed through my hands; I think my attention has been called to these different numbers to something like that extent.

Question. Have you any recollection in reference to these particular bonds as to whether they had their January coupons off or not.

Answer. Not in respect to particular bonds. We bought and sold bonds with the January coupons off, and the fact of their being off from particular bonds would not be a circumstance that would attract my attention.

Question. You do not know, then, whether these bonds were of this description or not?

Answer. I have received bonds of these numbers with the January coupons off, previous to the publication of this advertised list.

Question. Are you engaged in business alone?

Answer. There are two partners. The firm is Meigs & Greenleaf.

Question. Will you state to the committee whether at this time your house holds any of these bonds?

Answer. We are holding some of these bonds at this time, belonging to our clients.

Question. To what amount?

Answer. We now hold ten of these bonds.

Question. On what State.

Answer. Missouri.

Question. Can you state to the committee about what time they were purchased?

Answer. Yes, sir; they were bought on the 22d day of December.

Question. From whom?

Answer. From John R. Garland. They were bought at the board of brokers, on the 22d, and paid for on the 24th day of December.

Question. Have you the means of knowing from whom Mr. Garland received them?

Answer. I have not.

Question. On whose account do you hold these bonds?

Answer. They are held for the account of C. W. Purcell & Co., Richmond, Virginia; bought by their order and paid for by their money.

Question. Have you any personal knowledge of the whereabouts of any other of these bonds?

Answer. I have not.

Question. Have you seen, at any time, any of these alleged acceptances of the Secretary of War?

Answer. I never have seen them.

Question. I will ask you this question: Have you, since this publication by the Secretary of the Interior, received from your correspondents letters stating that bonds held by them and purchased by you were a portion of the abstracted bonds?

Answer. Yes, sir; I have received letters stating that the numbers of bonds held by the writers were among those advertised.

Question. Can you inform the committee from whom you have received such letters?

Answer. Yes, sir; I can state the names of two parties who have given me such information; the only ones that occur to me now. One is a gentleman in Schenectady, by the name of Mitchell, and the other a gentleman by the name of Sanders, of Haydenville, Massachusetts. These are the only two that I can recollect.

Question. What amount of bonds?

Answer. That I do not recollect. From one to three bonds in each case.

Question. Please state whether you sold the bonds to them before the publication of this list?

Answer. I did. Since the publication of the advertised numbers, they are not taken.

R. Bayles sworn.

Examination by the chairman.

Question. In what business are you engaged in this city?

Answer. I am the assistant cashier of the American Exchange Bank.

Question. Have you ever read a publication made by the Secretary of the Interior giving a statement of certain bonds alleged to have been abstracted from the Interior Department?

Answer. I have seen such a list published over the signature of Moses Kelly, as chief clerk of the Interior Department.

Question. Have you compared that list with the bonds in possession of the bank with which you are connected; and if so, do you find any of the advertised bonds in your possession?

Answer. Such an examination has been made, and the bank does not hold any such bonds.

Question. Did the examination made of your record show that you have held any such bonds since the 1st of July last; and if so, what amount, where did you get them, and to whom did you deliver them?

Answer. To the best of my knowledge and belief the records of our bank show that we have not held any such bonds.

Question. Do you know of any institution in this city, or of any person or persons holding any of the bonds referred to?

Answer. I do not.

Question. Have you any knowledge, directly or indirectly, which will enable you to state to the committee where any of the bonds are?

Answer. I have not.

Question. Have you ever seen any drafts drawn by Russell, Majors & Waddell on the Secretary of War, and accepted by him, on account of transportation?

Answer. I have.

Question. When did you see them?

Answer. At various times, in the bank of which I am assistant cashier.

Question. Have you any of them on hand now?

Answer. I cannot say positively.

Question. What is your impression or belief?

Answer. I have no knowledge of any.

Question. Do you remember when you first received the acceptances referred to?

Answer. No, sir; I do not.

Question. When did you receive the last of the acceptances referred to?

Answer. I could not give the date.

Question. Did your bank purchase or discount any of them?

Answer. My impression is that they were lodged there for collection.

Question. Are they in the possession of the bank yet?

Answer. I think they have been returned under protest.

Question. To whom returned?

Answer. To the best of my recollection they were returned to the Farmers' Bank, Missouri.

Question. Do you remember the dates and the amounts of the acceptances?

Answer. I do not.

Question. State, as near as you can, the number, dates, and amount.

Answer. I have no recollection about the date. The amounts were, I think, $10,000 each. I could not say how many there were, but I think more than one.

Question. Were they hypothecated with your bank?

Answer. They were not.

Question. Have any drafts of the kind been hypothecated there?

Answer. To the best of my knowledge there have not.

Question. Fix the time, as near as you can, when the acceptances were protested for non-payment.

Answer. Some time in the month of December is as near as I can come to it.

Question. Do you know J. B. Simpson?

Answer. I do not.

Question. Or William H. Russell?

Answer. No, sir.

Question. Did your bank ever have any business transactions with either of them?

Answer. Not to my knowledge.

Question. Have you stated to the committee all the knowledge in your possession relating to the bonds alleged to have been abstracted from the Interior Department, and also relating to the acceptances of the Secretary of War?

Answer. I have. I desire to correct one statement. I said none of the acceptances were discounted at our bank. I recollect now that they were discounted in one or two cases by the bank.

Question. For whom were they discounted?

Answer. For the Bank of Lexington, Missouri.

Question. Have they paid the amount of the acceptances to your bank since they were protested?

Answer. They have.

Question. As far as you know, then, the Bank of Lexington still has these acceptances in its possession?

Answer. As far as I know.

JAMES G. KING sworn.

Examination by the chairman.

Question. Will you inform the committee what is your business in this city?

Answer. I am a banker.

Question. Are you connected with any incorporated institution?

Answer. No, sir; we are private bankers; the firm is James G. King & Sons.

Question. Have you seen and examined a certain publication containing a list of bonds alleged to have been abstracted from the Interior Department?

Answer. I have seen an advertisement, published originally, I think, in the New York Herald, and signed by Moses Kelly, chief clerk of the Interior Department, containing a list of certain bonds alleged to have been abstracted from the Interior Department—Missouris, Tennessees, and North Carolinas. I have not seen another publication, which was promised, of some other North Carolina bonds, which are also missing.

Question. Have you any of the bonds referred to in your possession?

Answer. I have; or rather my firm has bonds in their possession, the numbers of which correspond with the advertised numbers.

Question. Of what State?

Answer. Missouri.

Question. Will you state to the committee the numbers and amount?

Answer. Yes, sir. My firm have five bonds, of $1,000 each, Missouri six per cents, issued to the North Missouri Railroad. The numbers are 2770, 2771, 2772, 2774, and 2775. They also have five bonds of $1,000 each Missouri six per cents, issued to the Pacific Railroad, the numbers of which are, 4887, 4888, 4889, 4890, and 5242. I did not examine this statement with the bonds before me, but I have no doubt it is correct.

Question. When did you purchase these bonds, and of whom did you purchase them?

Answer. I will explain that my brother, who is a member of the board, purchased these bonds. He is not well to-day, or he would have come up here. They were bought, the first five, on the 20th of November, of Messrs. Ward & Co., of this city; the second lot was bought of Messrs. Peyton, Frank & Jaudon, on the 5th of December.

Question. Had the bonds to which you refer the January coupons off?

Answer. They had at the time of delivery. They were bought at the board, and allowance was made for the January coupons.

Question. Do you know who had them sold?

Answer. I know no more than that of those I bought of Peyton, Frank & Jaudon. I have heard nothing, and they have said nothing further upon the subject. They do not know, I suppose, of whom they purchased them. Ward & Co. informed me that they sold those we purchased of them for account of the Nassau Bank, of this city.

Question. Have you any knowledge of any bank, or of any person or persons holding any other of the bonds contained in the published list?

Answer. No, sir. We have had our securities examined, and do not find any others except those I have mentioned.

Question. Have you given the committee all the information that you have, directly or indirectly, in your possession, in relation to the bonds embraced in the published list?

Answer. I have. I will say that I have not examined whether we have any Missouri bonds in our possession except those, but I do not think we have.

Question. Have you ever seen any drafts drawn by Russell, Majors & Waddell upon the Secretary of War and accepted by him?

Answer. I do not think I have ever seen one of those drafts. They have been mentioned to us to inquire whether we would purchase them, but I do not think I ever saw one of them.

Question. Do you know the name of any party or parties who now hold them?

Answer. I do not.

Question. Do you know J. B. Simpson?

Answer. I do not.

Question. Did you regard the fact that the coupons were off the bonds as a badge of fraud sufficient to put purchasers upon their guard?

Answer. No, sir; I think it is quite a usual circumstance to sell bonds with the accruing coupons cut off. Sometimes they are cut off by parties wishing to raise money on them by having them discounted. I should not consider that as any indication of fraud. At all events, it would not strike me as unusual.

Question. Have you the bonds to which you refer in market, since the publication of the list was made?

Answer. I have not. We sold these bonds previously, but we have delivered others instead.

THURSDAY, *January* 10, 1861.

FREDERICK F. THOMPSON sworn.

Examination by the chairman.

Question. Have you seen or read a publication embracing a description of certain bonds alleged to have been abstracted from the Indian trust fund at Washington?

Answer. I have read an advertisement in the papers—no separate publication—I have simply read the list in the Herald. I have also read a list of the bonds on which an injunction was served upon our house.

Question. Have you made an examination of your books so as to enable you to state to this committee whether you have any of those bonds on hand?

Answer. We have one bond according to the Herald publication. We have none of the stolen bonds on hand.

Question. Describe the bond you have?

Answer. It is a North Carolina bond, and is in the Herald list. The number is 916, I think, but I will not be certain. But in the list published in the Constitution, which list I have not read myself, it is not, I understand, contained at all. As we know where the bond has been for the last two years, I say it is not one of the stolen bonds.

Question. Have any of these bonds passed through your hands since July last? And if so, please give us a description of them?

Answer. Not to my certain knowledge. No, sir.

Question. Have you a belief that any of them have passed through your hands since that time?

Answer. I have a belief that we loaned a sum of money on some of those bonds in October last. From the circumstance of the January coupons being off, I believe we have had some of those bonds; the numbers I do not know; we kept no account of them.

Question. State the amount of bonds hypothecated for that purpose, by whom hypothecated, and the amount of money loaned on them?

Answer. On the 16th day of October, or thereabouts, Mr. Jerome B. Simpson came into our office and borrowed a sum of money. He borrowed $35,000 on $25,000 Missouri bonds, and $25,000 South Carolina bonds. He gave us his note for the amount. Before giving a check for the amount I examined the bonds and found they had the January coupons cut off, I asked him why that was done, and he said they were retained by the parties for whom he was making the loan. He made the loan in his own name; I did not ask him, that I remember, who he made it for. On the 29th day of October, or thereabouts, at any rate near the end of October, we called upon Mr. Simpson to pay us the loan. He paid the money, or rather he said that his check would probably not be good, and at his request I took the bonds, and went down the street with him. William T. Coleman gave me their check for the amount. I gave him the bonds, and Mr. Simpson executed to them another note, I think.

Question. Is that the only transaction of the kind you ever had with Mr. Simpson?

Answer. Yes, sir; the only one I can remember, certainly the only one within the last six months. Mr. Simpson has several times wanted to borrow money on bonds, but we have never loaned except on that occasion.

Question. Do you know whether Mr. Simpson was transacting business on his own account, or as the agent of another?

Answer. It was generally in his own individual name.

Question. Did you ever hear him say he was the agent of Russell, Majors & Waddell?

Answer. I always understood he was when he signed for them. We always understood that he negotiated the New York end of their business.

Question. That he was their agent here?

Answer. Yes, sir.

Question. Do you know anything about his individual means?

Answer. No, sir, nothing whatever.

Question. When did you first become acquainted with him?

Answer. I think I first became acquainted with him about a year and a half ago; but it would be impossible to state with any precision, as he has been in and out of the office a great deal, when I did first become acquainted with him.

Question. Do you know where he is now?

Answer. No, sir; I have not seen him for several weeks.

Question. Have you any knowledge, direct or indirect, where any of the bonds are published in the list prepared by the direction of the Secretary of the Interior?

Answer. No, sir.

Question. Have you ever seen any of those bonds other than those you have described?

Answer. I do not know that I have seen any of them, because I do not know the numbers. These are the only ones I suspected of being among the stolen bonds. The one we still have in our possession I have stated is not one of those bonds.

Question. Of whom did you purchase that bond?

Answer. I do not know.

Question. When did you buy it?

Answer. That I do not know either.

Question. Have you offered it for sale since the publication of the list?

Answer. No, sir; not to my knowledge.

Question. Have you ever heard any person or persons say they had any of these bonds? If so, give us the name of such person or persons, or corporation.

Answer. No, sir, I have not.

Question. Was that bond bought on your own account, or for some correspondent?

Answer. For ourselves.

Question. Is there any written correspondence in your office between yourselves and Russell, Majors & Waddell, Jerome B. Simpson, or the Secretary of War, relating to business transactions?

Answer. No, sir; relating to nothing. I do not think we have got the signatures of any of these parties excepting, perhaps, that of Simpson to notes or checks.

Question. Have you ever seen any drafts drawn by Russell, Majors & Waddell on the Secretary of War and accepted by him?

Answer. No, sir.

Question. Do you know of any corporation, person, or persons, who now have any such acceptances in their possession?

Answer. No, sir; I have heard of such acceptances, but I have never seen one, that I am aware of. I have seen in the newspapers that a bank down in Lynn, Massachusetts, had some of them, but I do not know where they are.

Question. Have you given this committee all the information you have in reference to the bonds and acceptances referred to?

Answer. I believe I have.

Question. You know of no matter or thing pertaining to them that you have not stated?

Answer. No, sir.

STEPHEN L. MILES sworn.

Examination by the chairman.

Question. With what bank are you connected in this city?

Answer. With the City Bank.

Question. In what capacity?

Answer. As an accountant.

Question. How long have you been connected with that bank?

Answer. About ten years.

Question. Will you state whether there was transmitted to you, on or about the 12th of July, 1860, the check of Wm. Peyton?

Answer. We have no account with any person by that name; neither have we received any check of his that we can trace at all.

Question. Have you examined the published list, authorized to be made by the Secretary of the Interior, of certain bonds alleged to have been abstracted from the Interior Department?

Answer. I cast my eye over it, but not with a view of examining it at all.

Question. Do you know where any of the bonds embraced in that list are?

Answer. No, sir.

Question. Did you ever see any of them?
Answer. Not that I have any knowledge of.
Question. Did you ever see any drafts drawn by Russell, Majors & Waddell upon the Secretary of War, and accepted by him?
Answer. No, sir.

ROBERT W. LATHAM sworn.

Examination by the chairman

Question. Please inform the committee in what business you are now engaged, and in what business you have been engaged for the last two or three years.
Answer. I am engaged as an agent or attorney for any person who chooses to employ me, and have been for several years—since 1855, I believe.
Question. Do you mean by the word "attorney" to be understood that you are engaged in the practice of the legal profession?
Answer. No, sir.
Question. What do you mean by it?
Answer. I simply mean that if you give me the power of attorney to act for you I would do so.
Question. Have you been engaged as the agent or attorney, in the sense in which you use the term, of John B. Floyd, late Secretary of War, within the last three or four years?
Answer. I was engaged for him in business up to May, 1859, I think, when I retired from his business.
Question. From what time?
Answer. From about the time he commenced his term of office as Secretary of War.
Question. Was the character of the business he intrusted to you of a public or private nature?
Answer. He never intrusted to me any public business at all; I never had anything to do with his public affairs.
Question. Then you were his private attorney?
Answer. Yes, sir.
Question. What was the nature of the business you transacted for him?
WITNESS. You would find the nature of my business in my testimony before the Haskin committee, I think.
Question. Please answer the question.
Answer. I attended to any private business that he wanted me to; his coal mines, or any of his other private affairs.
Question. Did you receive and pay out money for him?
Answer. Yes, sir.
Question. To what amount?
Answer. I cannot say.
Question. State the amount as near as you can.
Answer. I could not give you any particular idea about the amount I received and paid out.
Question. Was it as much as $25,000?

Answer. Yes, sir; while I was agent for him it was more than that amount.

Question. How much more?

Answer. I could not tell how much more without looking at my books.

Question. Was it as much as $50,000?

Answer. I could not say how much it was without examining my books.

Question. Can you tell by an examination of your books?

Answer. I probably might do so, though some of my accounts I have not got.

Question. Was it as much as $50,000?

Answer. My answer to that is, that I could not say without an examination.

Question. Could you not say whether it was as much as that?

Answer. No, sir.

Question. Can you inform the committee whether it was more than that?

Answer. No, sir; I could not.

Question. Have you your books so convenient that you could refer to them?

Answer. I have not.

Question. Where do you keep your books?

Answer. I do not have a regular set of books.

Question. Then you keep memoranda of your business transactions instead of books?

Answer. I make memoranda.

Question. Have you, then, memoranda of these transactions that you can refer to and give the committee definite information in regard to the subject-matter of their inquiry?

Answer. No, sir; unless I went into a calculation, I could not answer.

Question. To what books did you refer when you stated that you could not make an answer without examining your books?

Answer. I referred to my books and memorandums. I have a book in which I keep my memorandums and accounts, but I have not, as I said, a full account of my dealings with Mr. Floyd.

Question. Did you keep your business transactions with him in your recollection, without making any entry of them at all?

Answer. No, sir.

Question. Was your authority to transact his business of a general or specific character?

Answer. At one time it was of rather a general character, but he generally gave me specific directions in reference to each transaction?

Question. Was that authority in writing or verbal?

Answer. I do not think I ever had any written authority from him.

Question. Do you mean to be understood as saying that it was sometimes a general and sometimes a specific authority?

Answer. I say that it was sometimes very general, but that he usually gave specific directions when any particular matter was to be attended to.

Question. Did he intrust to you the management of his business generally, without limit?

Answer. Oh! no, sir.

Question. What business, then, did you transact for him?

Answer. Any business that he wished me to.

Question. What was that business? Please inform the committee more definitely than you have done upon that point.

Answer. If he wanted me to raise $1,000, he would ask me if it could be done.

Question. And you would negotiate the monetary matter for him?

Answer. If I could.

Question. Have you or not received and paid out within the last four years a large amount of money for John B. Floyd?

Answer. I ceased to be his agent in May, 1859. We then had a difficulty, a dispute, or a falling out—in fact, a very bad falling out—and I threw up his business entirely and ceased to be his agent.

Question. You have not answered my question.

Answer. I am coming to that. You say in the last four years. I have stated that I did receive, by borrowing, and pay out for him, a considerable sum of money, and I said that I supposed it to be near $25,000.

Question. Was it not much larger than that amount?

Answer. It may have been.

Question. What is the best of your recollection upon that point?

Answer. I have no idea, and could not speak definitely without going into an examination of my accounts, or of my memoranda, as I have them upon my books.

Question. Did he pay you commission upon the business you did for him?

Answer. No, sir, not usually.

Question. Were you employed at a salary of so much per annum?

Answer. He promised to pay me a salary for attending to his business, but he had not been able to do so at the time I left him.

Question. What was the amount of that salary?

Answer. He first proposed to pay me $4,000 per year.

Question. Where are the books and memorandums you refer to, containing a statement of the business transactions you had with Mr. Floyd?

Answer. I suppose I could get them.

Question. Will you be kind enough to do so, and refer to them, so that you can give the committee definite information touching the matter of which I have inquired?

Answer. I must say that there must be some other authority to require me to render an account of my private transactions. They have nothing at all to do with the government.

Question. Will you make out that account and furnish the committee with it?

Witness. When will the committee want it?

Mr. Morris. As soon as possible.

Answer. I suppose I could make them out.

Question. You have not yet answered my question as to where the books and memorandums are?

WITNESS. I answered by saying I supposed I could get them.

Question. My question is, where are they?

WITNESS. I must ask the committee to excuse me from answering.

Question. Do you decline answering the question?

WITNESS. Do you decline to excuse me from answering?

Mr. MORRIS. I do.

WITNESS. Then I must say that, believing the subject of the question is one with which the committee has nothing to do, I must decline to answer.

Question. Do you keep these books or memoranda in Washington, or at your residence in this city?

WITNESS. In reference to the accounts or books containing the accounts of my private business with Governor Floyd, or anybody else, I decline to answer.

Question. Did you keep the memoranda to which you refer in Washington or in the city of Brooklyn?

WITNESS. I decline to answer.

Question. Have you now got these books and memoranda referred to in your possession?

WITNESS. I decline to answer.

Question. Have you these books or memoranda now in this (your) house, or about your person?

WITNESS. I decline to answer.

Question. Do these books or memoranda show from whom you received money for Mr. Floyd, and to whom you paid it?

WITNESS. I decline to answer.

Question. Have you paid any money for John B. Floyd?

Answer. If I received money from Mr. Floyd, and paid off an account against him, I suppose it is an indebtedness.

Question. Do I understand you to desire that the committee shall so construe your answer as that you have paid off indebtedness for Mr. Floyd?

Answer. Certainly; if I received money for him, and appropriated it to his accounts, I paid off indebtedness.

Question. Did you, in point of fact, do that?

Answer. I did.

Question. From whom did you receive that money?

Answer. I cannot tell now from whom I received money; I do not know what particular item is alluded to.

Question. Any money that you received?

Answer. I have borrowed money from various parties.

Question. Who did you borrow from?

WITNESS. I decline to answer.

Question. To whom did you pay moneys received for Gov. Floyd?

WITNESS. I decline to answer.

Question. On what account did you pay money for Governor Floyd?

WITNESS. I decline to answer.

Question. On what securities did you raise the money for Governor Floyd to which you refer?

WITNESS. I decline to answer.

Question. Were the securities on which moneys were raised placed in your hands by Governor Floyd, or by some other person or persons?

Answer. I have no recollection that anybody ever placed any security in my hands to raise money for Governor Floyd except Governor Floyd himself.

Question. What was the character of the securities which he placed in your hands on which he desired you to raise money; were they notes, bonds, or what were they?

Answer. Governor Floyd usually placed in my hands his own notes, sometimes indorsed by his brother-in-law. On one occasion I had a large amount of Virginia bonds placed in my hands to raise money on.

Question. Which brother-in-law do you refer to?

Answer. Colonel Preston.

Question. You referred to Mr. Floyd's usually putting his own notes in your hands for the purpose of raising money upon them, do you desire to be understood that he at any time placed other paper in your hands, such as bonds or securities other than the Virginia bonds to which you have alluded?

Answer. I do not.

Question. Did you, in fact, raise money upon the securities which Governor Floyd placed in your hands?

Answer. I sometimes did and sometimes did not.

Question. Did you receive money at any time upon these securities?

WITNESS. I decline to answer.

Question. Do you know whether Governor Floyd ever paid these notes?

Answer. He has not paid all the notes on which I raised money for him, I do not think.

Question. Has he ever paid any of them?

Answer. I expect he has.

Question. Inform the committee which notes he has paid and which notes remain unpaid.

Answer. I cannot do that.

Question. Do you mean to be understood by your last answer as saying that you have no information in your possession which will enable you to answer the previous interrogatory, or that you decline to answer it?

WITNESS. I decline to answer.

Question. Did you, in fact, raise money upon securities placed in your hands by persons other than Governor Floyd, which money was used for his account?

Answer. I do not know that I ever raised any money for him upon securities placed in my hands by other parties than himself.

Question. Do you know of any person or persons who had transactions with the War Department who have paid to Governor Floyd, either directly or indirectly, any money or other consideration?

Answer. I know of no party at all who has had transactions with the War Department who has paid Governor Floyd any money or other consideration.

Question. Have you or not been the medium through which money, at different times, has been paid to Governor Floyd by persons having transactions with the War Department?

Answer. I know of no person or persons having dealings with the War Department who has paid any money through me to Mr. Floyd.

Question. Do you know of any person or persons through whom Mr. Floyd has received money from those having tranactions with the War Department?

Answer. I have no knowledge of any such person.

Question. To the best of your knowledge and belief, have you information which will enable you to respond definitely to the last preceding interrogatory?

WITNESS. I decline to answer the question.

Question. Have you ever been engaged by any person or persons to transact business for them at the War Department? and if so, please state the names of the persons who thus engaged you, and the nature and character of the engagement you entered into.

WITNESS. I decline to answer.

Question. Have you at any time been employed to obtain contracts of any nature or character from the War Department by any person or persons while John B. Floyd was Secretary of War?

WITNESS. I decline to answer.

Question. Have you at any time received a commission or compensation from any person or persons desirous of obtaining contracts from the War Department?

WITNESS. I decline to answer.

Question. Have you at any time received commissions or compensation for service indicated in the last preceding interrogatory, which commissions or compensation you divided with any person or persons?

WITNESS. I decline to answer.

Question. If you did divide with any person or persons any commissions you received for such services, state to the committee the name or names of the person with whom you so divided.

WITNESS. I decline to answer.

Question. Have you spent a considerable portion of your time in Washington city since John B. Floyd was Secretary of War? and if so, have you frequently been at the War Department?

Answer. I have spent a considerable portion of my time in Washington city, and, when there, have been frequently at the War Department.

Question. Have you been engaged by any person or persons to obtain contracts from any other than the War Department?

WITNESS. I decline to answer.

Question. Do you know what the pecuniary circumstances of John B. Floyd were at the time he became Secretary of War?

WITNESS. I decline to answer.

Question. Was he in embarrassed circumstances?

WITNESS. I decline to answer.

Question. State whether you have in your possession, either directly or indirectly, any knowledge of the money paid or used by Governor Floyd since he has been Secretary of War.

WITNESS. I decline to answer.

Question. Can you inform the committee whether John B. Floyd had not a large amount of mortgage or other indebtedness upon his real estate in Virginia or elsewhere at the time he was appointed Secretary of War?

Answer. I cannot.

Question. Can you inform the committee whether he had not a large amount of indebtedness of any other character or kind at the time of his appointment?

Answer. I have no knowledge of the extent of John B. Floyd's indebtedness at the time he was appointed Secretary of War.

Question. Do you know whether it was large or small?

Answer. I do not know the amount or extent of it.

Question. State, to the best of your knowledge, the amount or extent of it.

WITNESS. I decline to answer.

Question. How much indebtedness has Governor Floyd paid off since he has been Secretary, as far as you know, directly or indirectly?

WITNESS. I decline to answer.

Question. Do you not know, either directly or indirectly, that he has paid off a large amount of indebtedness?

WITNESS. I decline to answer.

Question. If he has paid off a large amount of indebtedness since he has been Secretary of War, from whence did he receive the money, as far as you have any knowledge, directly or indirectly?

WITNESS. I decline to answer.

Question. Do you know, and if so, please state to the committee, whether John B. Floyd has used in and about his business money since the time he was appointed Secretary of War?

Answer. Of course he must have used money in his business.

Question. State the amount as near as you can?

WITNESS. I decline to answer.

Question. Was the amount large or small, as far as you know, directly or indirectly?

WITNESS. I decline to answer.

Question. State what business John B. Floyd has been engaged in since he has been Secretary of War that would require the use of money to any considerable amount.

Answer. He has been engaged in the salt and coal business.

Question. Where?

Answer. In Kentucky and Virginia.

Question. Has that business been carried on pretty largely or not?

Answer I do not know to what extent it has been carried on. There are large mines.

Question. Have you ever been at the mines?

Answer. Yes, sir.

Question. And to the salt springs or wells referred to?

Answer. Yes, sir.

Question. Then you can state that the business is a small or a large one. Do you know how many hands were employed?

Answer. I have no knowledge on that subject, but I have understood that there have been from 50 to 60 hands employed and sometimes less.

Question. Who was engaged in that business with Mr. Floyd as partners, either silent or otherwise?

Answer. I think one of his brothers was living there and managed the business.

Question. Had you any interest in the business?

Answer. Not a dollar.

Question. Where are these mines?

Answer. They lie in Virginia and Kentucky. The river divides them.

Question. What river?

Answer. The Big Sandy.

Question. Has he been engaged in the construction of dams and other improvements in that river for the purpose of making a slackwater navigation to his mines and springs?

Answer. He has been trying to do so, I believe.

Question. Has there not been a large amount of money laid out for that purpose?

Answer. Not that I know of.

Question. When did you first become acquainted with John B. Floyd?

Answer. Some ten or twelve years ago, as well as I remember.

Question. Where?

Answer. In Washington city.

Question. Have you been engaged in transacting his business, more or less, since you first became acquainted with him?

Answer. I never was engaged in transacting any of his business until he employed me.

Question. When did he first employ you?

Answer. I think it was in February, 1857.

Question. Have you been on terms of intimate social relationship with him since you first became acquainted with him?

Answer. Yes, sir; or rather I was on intimate terms socially with him up to May, 1859.

Question. You spoke of having some trouble with him about that time, what was it?

Answer. We had a misunderstanding and a separation of the intimate relationship we held previously.

Question. Did that trouble originate out of monetary transactions?

Answer. The difference between us was outside of monetary affairs.

Question. Did it grow out of social or business relations?

WITNESS. I decline to answer.

Question. Have you been on speaking terms with Governor Floyd since the difficulty occurred to which you referred?

Answer. I have.

Question. When did you last see him?

Answer. I think I saw him last just before I left the city of Washington, which was, I think, on the morning of the 31st December.

Question. Did you have an interview with him at that time?

Answer. Yes, sir.

Question. State the nature and character of that interview?

Answer. It was upon general subjects.

Question. Was nothing said between you at that time in reference to any business or official transaction?

Answer. No official transaction was referred to, and I have no recollection of any business transaction. It was of a private character, nothing affecting the government in any way.

Question. Where did the last interview you had with Governor Floyd take place?

Answer. At his house, in Washington city.

Question. Did he send for you to go and see him, or did you go there voluntarily?

Answer. He did not send for me.

Question. How happened you to go there at that time?

Answer. I could not say.

Question. Was it a social or a business call?

Answer. I was going off to New York, and I called before I went to see him.

Question. Do you mean by the last preceding answer that your call was of a social character?

Answer. I merely called as I was going to New York.

Question. To pay him your respects?

Answer. No, sir.

Question. What was the object of your call there?

Answer. To see him and converse with him in reference to any matter that might come up.

Question. Who was present at that interview?

Answer. His wife may have been; I do not recollect.

Question. Did the conversation between you relate to public or private matters?

Answer. We talked about secession, as well as I recollect, the dissolution of the Cabinet, &c. I do not remember the particulars.

Question. Did you talk about anything else?

Answer. I think the subject of the abstraction of bonds from the Interior Department was talked of.

Question. What was said about that?

Answer. It was just talked about in general terms.

Question. What was said?

Answer. I could not tell.

Question. Who introduced the subject of the abstracted bonds?

Answer. I do not recollect. It was the general subject of conversation with everybody I met with in Washington about that time.

Question. Did he state to you in that conversation any particulars in regard to the abstraction of the bonds?

Answer. He did not.

Question. You say the conversation in regard to the bonds was general. Can you not give some of the particulars of that conversation?

Answer. I cannot.

Question. Can you give the committee any particulars in reference to the balance of the conversation?

Answer. No, sir; I only stayed there a short time. I think I was there not more than fifteen minutes.

Question. Did you leave immediately for New York on the close of that conversation?

Answer. I left by the afternoon train at 3 o'clock, or thereabouts.

Question. At what time were you at Governor Floyd's house?

Answer. About 9 or half-past 9 o'clock in the morning.

Question. Have you stated to the committee, as nearly as you can, all the particulars of the conversation which took place between you and Governor Floyd on that occasion?

Answer. I have.

Question. You know, then, of no matter or thing connected with or growing out of that interview which you have not detailed to the committee?

Answer. No, sir; I have no special recollection of the conversation, and I could not state it more definitely than I have. It was a short interview.

Question. Did you have any other interview with Governor Floyd on that day?

Answer. I did not.

Question. Was the conversation you had with him on that day the first conversation you had with him on the subject of the abstracted bonds?

Answer. It was not.

Question. When was the first conversation upon that subject?

Answer. A few days before.

Question. How long?

Answer. I think I had a conversation with him on the Friday night before Christmas day.

Question. Had you any other conversations with him relative to the abstracted bonds except those to which you have referred?

Answer. I had two conversations with him relative to the abstracted bonds, though the first was of a vague and unsatisfactory character, and could hardly be said to be upon the subject of the bonds. Governor Floyd asked me if I knew of any trust fund in the hands of Bailey in the Interior Department which he could use. I answered promptly that there was none. He then asked me what dealings Russell & Bailey could have. I answered that I knew of nothing except to speculate in Indian lands. There the conversation ended, and I heard nothing further from him at the time.

Question. When was that conversation?

Answer. I think this conversation was on Thursday. On Friday night I informed him that I was going to New York. He then intimated to me that there was great difficulty with Bailey & Russell—a serious affair—and he wished me to see Russell on Saturday night in New York, and get him to come on to Washington city as soon as possible, and to ascertain if I could what were the facts of the case. I came on to New York and saw Russell. He told me he had received bonds from Bailey, and that he had until next June to return them, but that he would go on to Washington immediately and attend to it.

That was on Saturday night. On Monday morning Russell was arrested.

Question. This conversation, you say, occurred on the Friday night before Christmas?

Answer. As well as I remember.

Question. Had the facts in regard to the abstracted bonds then been made public upon the street?

Answer. Not that I know of.

Question. Did you learn the facts first from Governor Floyd?

Answer. He threw out these intimations to me on Friday night.

Question. Did you go back, on Saturday morning, to have another interview with Governor Floyd about the abstracted bonds?

Answer. I did not.

Question. I understood you to answer a preceding interrogatory, by stating that you saw Governor Floyd about 9 o'clock in the morning?

Answer. That was more than a week afterwards.

Question. What time on Saturday did you leave for New York?

Answer. I left in the 6 o'clock, a. m., train.

Question. You have stated to the committee that, in pursuance of the request of Governor Floyd, you met Russell—where did you meet him?

Answer. He was telegraphed to meet me at the wharf, as I landed with my wife in New York.

Question. Why was it necessary for him to meet you there?

Answer. It was late in the evening when I got in, and I did not want to go away up to his house, or wherever he stayed. I did not know exactly where he stayed.

Question. So that the only interview you had with Russell before he was arrested was on your return to New York, Saturday night?

Answer. I went up to his office, on Monday morning, to ascertain when he was going to Washington, and he was arrested while I was standing there.

Question. Have you received from Governor Floyd or Russell any letters or despatches since your last interview with each?

Witness. I decline to answer.

Question. If you have received any such letters or despatches, have you them now in your possession; and if so, please state the nature of their contents?

Witness. I decline to answer.

Question. How long have you known William H. Russell?

Answer. I have known him, I suppose, about two and a half years?

Question. Have you ever transacted any business for him with the War Department?

Witness. I decline to answer.

Question. Have you ever negotiated for him any State bonds or stocks?

Answer. Not to the amount of a dollar. I never saw any of the bonds he had, and never had anything to do with them—or heard of them until what I have related occurred.

Question. Do you know who has negotiated any bonds or stocks for him?

Answer. Collector Schell told me he had. He is the only one who has told me so. I have heard a good deal floating around about them.

Question. Have you answered the interrogatory as fully as you can?

Answer. I think I have.

Question. Do you know whether he hypothecated any bonds or securities at any time with any person or persons, or banking institutions?

Answer. I have seen Mr. Simpson in at Thompson's, but I do not know anything about their hypothecation or present position.

Question. Did you ever see one of them?

Answer. I never saw nor handled one of them in my life.

Question. Were you ever connected in any way with any business transaction pertaining to the bonds, if you did not see or handle them?

Answer. None whatever. I tried my best to ascertain, when I was in Washington, and here in New York, who were the parties who knew anything about these bonds; and, after the best investigation I could make, I could learn of no one, except Russell, Bailey, and Colonel Luke Lea. They were the only three who knew anything about it?

Question. How did you know Colonel Luke Lea was connected with the transaction?

Answer. Colonel Luke Lea told me that suspicion rested upon several persons in reference to who was the party between Russell and Bailey; that he had known of the transaction, and he went up and told Mr. Thompson himself that he knew it.

Question. When was this interview between you and Lea?

Answer. It was in the cars going to New York some time ago, at least some few days ago.

Question. Do you know where any of the abstracted bonds are?

Answer. No, sir, I do not.

Question. Have you any information, directly or indirectly, which will enable you to inform the committee where any of the bonds are?

Answer. I have not.

Question. Have you seen drafts drawn by Russell, Majors & Waddell upon the Secretary of War, and accepted by him?

Answer. Yes, sir, I have seen them.

Question. Where did you see them first?

Answer. I think I saw them with Russell.

Question. To what amount did he hold them?

Answer. I do not know.

Question. Do you know what he did with them?

Answer. I do not.

Question. Did you ever see them in the hands or possession of any one else except Russell?

Answer. I do not know; but I think I have seen them in the hands of Mr. Souter, of the Bank of the Republic. I will not be positive.

Question. In the hands of any other person or persons?

Answer. I do not recollect. I think I have seen them in Simpson's hands. I am not much acquainted with Simpson, and I could not state positively.

Question. Do you know where Simpson is?

Answer. I do not.

Question. When did you last see him?

Answer. I saw him at the time Russell was arrested, and I think I have not seen him since.

Question. Did you have any conversation with him at that time in reference to this matter?

Answer. No, sir; he was in a great state of excitement. Russell had to be taken away, and he went with him. He said that when he read the newspapers of the morning stating that bonds had been stolen he did not know that Russell was implicated.

Question. Where did he go with Russell?

Answer. He went from his office to the marshal's office, I suppose.

Question. Who telegraphed Russell to meet you at the wharf?

Answer. I think Colonel Drinkard telegraphed him.

Question. Do you remember to have read one of the acceptances of the Secretary of War? and if so, state as nearly as you can the purport of it.

Answer. I think I have read one through, but I do not recollect, and could not state the purport of it.

Question. Did Russell ask you to assist him in raising money upon them?

Answer. Yes, sir; he asked me about fifteen months ago to assist him in raising money upon them.

Question. Did you do it?

Answer. Yes, sir; I did what I could.

Question. What commission did he pay for your services?

Answer. He never paid me a cent; he offered to give me a commission for my services, but not having succeeded in making a negotiation to meet his limits I did not get it.

Question. Did he ever pay you any money for aiding him in business transactions?

Answer. He has.

Question. What were the business transactions you aided him in for which he paid you money?

WITNESS. I decline to answer.

Question. Did he engage you to induce the Secretary of War to make acceptances?

Answer. Why, the acceptances were given before I knew anything about them.

Question. Did you negotiate or aid him in any way in getting facilities from the War Department.

WITNESS. I decline to answer.

Question. When did you first see the names of Russell, Majors & Waddell, or either of them, on Governor Floyd's paper?

Answer. I have no recollection of seeing their names on any of his paper except these acceptances.

Question. When did you first know of any business or pecuniary transactions between John B. Floyd and Russell?

Answer. I knew that Mr. Russell had engagements or contracts at the War Department two or two and a half years ago.

Question. Is that the first you know of any dealings between them?

Answer. If I am not mistaken as to the time when I became acquainted with Russell, it was after my knowledge of his dealing with the War Department.

Question. Do you know of any business transaction between these two parties other than those relating to his contract for transportation?

Answer. I know of no other transactions between them.

C. A. Macy sworn.

Examination by Mr. Harris.

Question. Will you be good enough to state with what bank you are connected?

Answer. I am cashier of the Park Bank.

Question. Have you seen the published list of bonds alleged to have been abstracted from the Interior Department.

Answer. I saw the list published in the Herald.

Question. Have you seen, or have you now in your bank, any of the bonds embraced in that list?

Answer. I think not.

Question. Do you know where any of those bonds are?

Answer. I do not.

Question. Have you ever seen or negotiated any of the acceptances of John B. Floyd, late Secretary of War, given to Russell, Majors & Waddell.

Answer. I do not remember that I have.

Question. Have you had frequent business transactions with these parties?

Answer. I have not.

Question. Do you know J. B Simpson?

Answer. I do.

Question. Were any acceptances of the Secretary of War offered to you for discount?

Answer. I think we have received some of them for collection, and perhaps for discount?

Question. Will you furnish the committee with a statement of whatever transactions your bank has had in these acceptances?

Answer. I will send such a statement to the committee.

The following communication was subsequently received from the witness:

The Park Bank, *New York, January* 15, 1861.

Dear Sir: Enclosed I hand you a list of acceptances of the late Secretary of War which have been forwarded to this bank for collection during the past year.

I also enclose a copy of a draft which this bank held for collection, received from the Bank of Mutual Redemption of Boston, that became due 13th instant, and was protested for non-payment. We hold one more for $10,000, due January 21, dated June 18, at 7 months, number 45; indorsed by T. L. Smith, cashier, to H. P. Shed, cashier of Bank of Mutual Redemption, from whom we received it.

I find from our books we discounted an acceptance of like character on the 23d of August, 1859, for $10,000, which became due, and was paid, November 1, 1859.

This was discounted for the St. Louis Building and Savings Association.

All of the acceptances were drawn, I believe, by Russell, Majors & Waddell.

Yours, respectfully,

CHARLES A. MACY, *Cashier.*

ISAAC N. MORRIS, Esq.

The following is a list of notes forwarded to the Park Bank for collection, with the name of the bank from whom received, date of maturity, and whether paid or protested:

Bank	Place	Date	Amount	Status
		1860.		
Bank of Mutual Redemption,	Boston,	Feb. 5,	$10,000;	paid.
Do	do	Mar. 11,	5,000;	paid.
Do	do	Apr. 18,	10,000;	paid.
Do	do	May 20,	10,000;	paid.
Do	do	June 11,	5,000;	paid.
Do	do	June 18,	15,000;	paid.
Do	do	July 22,	10,000;	paid.
Do	do	July 23,	10,000;	paid.
Do	do	Aug. 15,	10,000;	paid.
Do	do	Aug. 22,	5,000;	paid.
Do	do	Aug. 27,	10,000;	paid.
Do	do	Sept. 19,	15,000;	pro. & rt'd.
Do	do	Oct. 1,	5,000;	paid.
Do	do	Oct. 29,	10,000;	paid.
Do	do	Nov. 17,	10,000;	pro. & rt'd.
Do	do	Nov. 22,	10,000;	pro. & rt'd.
Do	do	Dec. 17,	15,000;	pro. & rt'd.
		1861.		
Do	do	Jan. 13,	10,000.	
Do	do	Jan. 21,	10,000.	
		1860.		
Hide & Leather Dealers' Bank,	Boston,	Oct. 9,	10,000;	pro. & rt'd.

"$10,000. WASHINGTON CITY, *July* 10, 1860.

"Six months after date pay to our own order at the Bank of the Republic, New York city, ten thousand dollars, for value received, and charge to account of our transportation contract of the 12th day of April, 1860.

"RUSSELL, MAJORS & WADDELL.

"To Hon. J. B. FLOYD, *Secretary of War.*"

Accepted as follows:

"No. 47.—WAR DEPARTMENT, *July* 16, 1860.

"JOHN B. FLOYD, *Secretary of War.*"

MONDAY, *January* 14, 1861.

WILLIAM H. RUSSELL called.

The CHAIRMAN. Mr. Russell, your counsel have doubtless apprised you of your rights. You are under a criminal prosecution, and I deem it my duty to state to you that the committee do not propose to require you to answer any questions. If you choose voluntarily to do so you can, but if you do not prefer to do it, as indicated to you, you can withhold your answers.

Mr. RUSSELL. I am anxious to make a full statement in regard to the bonds. I claim to be an honest man, and would prefer to make out a statement of the whole transaction in writing, and have you spread it at length on your records. I ask that as a favor from the committee. I am under a criminal prosecution, and think it is due to me that I should be permitted to make a full statement, though I do not fear the result of the criminal prosecution. If the committee prefers the statement made verbally I will make it in that way, but I should like to make one in writing.

The witness was then sworn.

Examination by the chairman.

Question. Are you the William H. Russell of the firm of Russell, Majors & Waddell, who held contracts with the War Department for the transportation of army provisions?

Answer. I am, sir.

The following paper was handed to the witness, who examined it:

WASHINGTON, D. C., *December* 13, 1860.

We have acknowledged to have received from Godard Bailey, on the 13th of July last, and at various times subsequently, the following bonds, viz:

Missouri 6's	$370,000
North Carolina 6's, (January and July)	296,000
North Carolina 6's, (April and October)	61,000
Tennessee 6's	143,000
Making a total of	870,000

which we agree to return to the said Godard Bailey, or to his assigns, on demand.

As collateral security for the return of the above-described bonds we have deposited with the said Godard Bailey acceptances of the Hon. John B. Floyd, Secretary of War, to the amount of eight hundred and seventy thousand dollars.

RUSSELL, MAJORS & WADDELL.

Deliver the above-described bonds to the Secretary of the Interior.

GODARD BAILEY.

Question. Is that your signature Mr. Russell?

Answer. It is, sir.

Question. You signed that receipt?

Answer. I did, sir.

Question. When and where did you first become acquainted with Godard Bailey?

Answer. I first became acquainted with him in the War Department.

Question. Who introduced you?

Answer. Colonel Drinkard.

Question. What is his given name?

Answer. I think William R.

Question. Is he chief clerk of the War Department?

Answer. Yes, sir.

Question. On what day was that?

Answer. That I cannot say positively. It was somewhere in the neighborhood of the middle of July; I do not remember the date, but I think that it was a little prior to the middle of July.

Question. When and from whom did you first learn that he had in his possession certain bonds or State stocks?

Answer. That is a question which I cannot answer definitely. I learnt it in the city of New York, on Wall street. Mr. Bailey had been there on several occasions dealing in stocks, and in this Chiriqui expedition. I did not even get his name right.

Question. Can you give the name of the person or persons from whom you first learned that he had these bonds?

Answer. I do not think I could. It was the general talk on Wall street. Mr. Bailey had been there dealing in some Florida stocks. How or from whom he got them, or whose they were, I do not know.

Question. Who told you that Bailey had been there dealing in Florida stocks?

Answer. That is the same question I replied to a moment ago. I could not tell you definitely the particular person; it was common rumor on Wall street. I heard it more especially in connexion with the Chiriqui matter.

Question. Did you learn any particulars in reference to the rumors to which you refer as to the Florida bonds and the Chiriqui bonds or securities, as they call them?

Answer. The common rumor in New York was in connexion with Mr. Yulee and some railroad—I do not know what; I never inquired into the particulars; but Mr. Yulee's name was connected with it in some way.

Question. How about the Chiriqui securities?

Answer. Well, he had them there for sale. I do not know how he got them. I can give you a fuller explanation as to the Chiriqui matter.

Question. Who is your agent in New York?

Answer. Mr. Jerome B. Simpson.

Question. Can you tell us where Mr. Simpson now is?

Answer. I cannot.

Question. When did you last see or hear from him?

Answer. The day I left New York.

Question. Have you received no letter or despatch from him since that time?

Answer. No, sir; I have received a letter from my attorney in New York saying that Mr. Simpson had gone to Kansas, but where he is now I cannot tell you.

Question. From whom did you receive that information?

Answer. From Mr. Borden, my attorney. Mr. Simpson is the vice-president of the Pony Express Company, with which I am connected, and he thought that my arrest would ruin our business and he went west. I have not seen him since I left New York.

Question. Can you tell us where the bonds are that you received from Mr. Bailey?

Answer. I cannot, sir.

Question. Have you got any of them in your possession?

Answer. I have not, sir.

Question. Do you know whether they have been sold or hypothecated?

Answer. I think they have, sir.

Question. All of them?

Answer. Yes, sir.

Question. What portion have been sold and what hypothecated?

Answer. That I cannot tell you. This man Simpson attended to all the business. I think most of them were sold.

Question. Do you know who holds them?

Answer. I do not, sir. I have a general idea who holds some of them. I do not know it of my personal knowledge.

Question. Can you inform the committee who holds them?

Answer. I can give you my impression. I do not know positively who holds them.

Question. Let us have your impression?

Answer. I am inclined to think that Mr. Richard Schell, of New York, owns some of them.

Question. Who else?

Answer. Well, I think the United States Trust Company holds some.

Question. Who else?

Answer. My impression is Lee, Higginson & Co., of Boston.

Question. Who else?

Answer. The Shoe and Leather Bank, of New York; I know of no other persons or institutions holding them.

Question. Please inform the committee the amount of these bonds held by each of the persons and institutions to which you have referred.

Answer. That is more than I can tell you, sir.

Question. Give us your impression upon that point?

Answer. Well, I think Lee, Higginson & Co. hold 41; my impression is that Mr. Schell holds 20; I think the United States Trust Company hold an amount covering $25,000—perhaps 30 bonds; and I suppose the Shoe and Leather Bank hold 12. That is all I know of.

Question. Did you sell those bonds yourself or hypothecate them, or were they sold or hypothecated by your agent or agents?

Answer. I sold twelve to the Shoe and Leather Bank. That is the only transaction I made.

Question. Were they the only ones you sold yourself?

Answer. That is all I now recollect.

Question. Who were the balance sold by?

Answer. By Mr. Simpson, or rather he had it done by brokers. I do not know by what brokers.

Question. Did you receive these bonds from the hands of Godard Bailey?

Answer. I did, sir.

Question. And delivered them to Jerome B. Simpson?

Answer. Yes, sir.

Question. As your agent?

Answer. We officed together; he was our general agent, and I was working with him.

Question. Is he your agent or one of your firm?

Answer. He is the agent of Russell, Majors & Waddell.

[At this point Mr. Russell renewed his request for time to submit a written statement, and was answered by the chairman, after consulting the committee, that he could have any length of time he desired. Further interrogatories were then withheld, and Mr. Russell retired.]

J. A. WILLIAMSON sworn:

Examination by the chairman.

Question. Please inform the committee whether you are engaged in the Interior Department, and if so, what desk you occupy and how long you have been there?

Answer. I was for six years in the General Land Office; I was then transferred, by order of the Secretary, to the assistant appeals desk; I revised the decisions of the Commissioner of the General Land Office; that situation I held until the first day of January last. On the 24th day of December, at my residence in Georgetown, I read the Baltimore *Sun*, and to my surprise discovered the information relative to the abstraction of these bonds. I immediately hurried down to the department; on my arrival there I was met with an order to go, in company with Messrs. Lammond and Beard, into Mr. Bailey's room, which was next to my own room, and there take charge of all the government property, make a thorough examination of everything, and report the result of our labors. We did so, and made a report to the Secretary, which I believe you have before you.

Question. Were you present when the safe was opened by the Secretary?

Answer. No, sir; I was not. It was opened, if I mistake not, on Saturday night.

Question. Can you inform the committee whether the safe in which these bonds were kept had a double set of keys?

Answer. Yes sir; we discovered a double set of keys in the course of our investigation.

Question. Is it usual for safes to have double sets of keys?

Answer. Well, I cannot say personally from my own knowledge, but I have been told by my brother-in-law, who is an agent for these safes, that it is. In regard to these keys, permit me to say that one set of them was made of composition and the other, I think, of steel. Immediately after we went into the room, Mr. Beard took the coupons which belonged to these abstracted bonds and called them off to me, and I took a list of them; Mr. Kelly started that afternoon with a copy of that list; the original I have in my desk. Immediately after we got through with that work Mr. Lammond, Mr. Beard, and myself took the packages, examined them closely, and numbered them, and I made an inventory of the sum, and found that the safe contained $2,525,241 82; we then made up our report of the whole contents of the safe, signed it, and handed it to the Secretary. On the 1st day of January I received an appointment from the Secretary of the Interior detailing me to the charge of that room, and appointing me also a disbursing officer, and I am now on work connected with that business, such as collecting interest which is overdue.

Question. When you took charge of that room and made the examination, how many bonds did you find had been abstracted?

Answer. Well, sir, I should say, before I answer you that question, and before I go into Mr. Bailey's abstractions, that there was an Indiana bond missing, and the Secretary told me thoroughly to investigate the matter. I did so, and I found that in 1857 or 1858, I think, Mr. Bailey had addressed a letter to the Hon. Mr. Fitch, of the Senate, relative to the non-payment of interest upon a certain set of bonds issued in favor of the Wabash and Erie canal, but that letter was a private letter of Mr. Bailey. Secondly, I could not find any recognition by Mr. Fitch of the reception of such bonds on our files; I immediately told the Secretary that that would have to be inquired into in justice to Mr. Fitch. He told me to use all the means in my power, and suggested that I should go down and see Mr. Bailey. I went down, and Mr. Bailey informed me that he had received the letter, but said it was not a public letter, and that is the reason why I have not put it on file. After some persuasion, he said that he was willing to file it in justice to Dr. Fitch, and in order to save him. "But," said he, "I will not put it into your hands, nor into the hands of any other person to file for me. I must come up and do it myself." I reported the facts to the Secretary when I returned, and he requested the marshal to bring Mr. Bailey up. In the meantime Dr. Fitch called upon the Secretary and informed him of this transaction, and requested that he should address a letter calling upon him (Dr. Fitch) for a statement of the facts. I addressed that letter to Dr. Fitch, and received his answer containing a statement of these facts, which are now on file in the department. Mr. Bailey was brought up, and filed the letter of Dr. Fitch, acknowledging the reception of that bond, which I have now on file in the department. That is all I have to say in regard to the Indiana bond. That bond has not yet been returned to the department. But Dr. Fitch is making all the search he can for it, according to his statement. And here I should say that Dr. Fitch states that he received the bond for the purpose of getting a description in order that he could make inquiries in reference to it in Indiana, in regard to the probability of the interest being paid, &c. That is about all I know in regard to that one bond. Now, in regard to Mr. Bailey's operations, I find that taking out the $870,000, confessed to have been abstracted by him, and adding to it what we have on hand, including the Indiana bond, it balances exactly what should have been in the safe.

Question. You have stated, Mr. Williamson, that you occupied a room adjoining the one occupied by Mr. Bailey; can you inform the committee whether at times Mr. Bailey kept the door of his room locked while himself and others were in there?

Answer. I cannot say that it was locked, but it certainly was shut.

Question. Who was in the habit of visiting the room occupied by Mr. Bailey?

Answer. Well, sir, I have seen Mr. Luke Lea go in there sometimes. I have also seen Senator Rice go in there; and then I have seen attorneys having business with the department, as I supposed, go in there.

Question. Was Charles G. Wagoner in the habit of going in there?

Answer. Well, sir, he has been in the habit of going in there since this excitement, but not previous to it. In regard to keeping the door shut, Bailey's habit or custom was, when he was cutting his coupons off in January and July, the interest being payable then, to keep his door shut besides the times I have mentioned.

Question. Have you given the committee all the information you have pertaining to the bonds abstracted and the circumstances attending their abstraction?

Answer. Yes, sir; I have.

R. J. ATKINSON recalled.

Examination by the chairman.

Question. Can you furnish the committee with the information which you supposed the other day you had in your possession showing the payments made to Russell, Majors & Waddell, on account of army transportation, under their contracts with the War Department?

Answer. Yes, sir.

I have caused a statement to be prepared in my office of payments made to Messrs. Russell, Majors & Waddell, on account of transportation contracts, during the years 1858, 1859 and 1860, as appears by the vouchers in accounts of disbursing officers on file in my office, and the result is as follows:

1858.—Payments by Captain S. Van Vliet, assistant quartermaster of the United States army, at Fort Leavenworth, Kansas Territory.........	$2,425,378 35
Payments by Captain M. S. Miller, assistant quartermaster, at Washington city..........	712,213 65
	3,137,592 00

(In addition to the above, the sum of $209,104 60 was paid by Captain Miller to "Majors & Russell," and $14,644 38 by Captain Van Vliet to "Majors & Russell.")

1859.—Payments by Captain Van Vliet at Leavenworth..........	$1,010,731 84
Payments by Captain Miller at Washington..	126,899 50
	1,137,631 34

(In addition the above, the sums of $36,771 17 were paid by Captain Miller to "Majors & Russell," and $10,074 92 to "Brown, Russell & Co.," "Brown & Russell," "Jones & Russell," and "Majors & Russell.")

1860.—Payments by Captain Van Vliet, at Leavenworth, up till the 1st of October..............	$252,681 91
Payments by Captain Miller, at Washington, up till the 1st of October......................	65,934 91
	318,616 82

(In addition to the above, the sum of $89,402 23 was paid by Captain Miller to "Majors & Russell.")

Question. Can you furnish the committee with an abstract showing each payment made to Russell, Majors & Waddell, and the particulars of each payment?

Answer. I can; and the abstracts herewith submitted, numbered 1, 2, 3, 4, 5, and 6, contain the information you inquire, giving the date of each payment, the officer by whom made, the time when made, and to whom the payment was made.

Question. State whether or not there are not items in these accounts that are suspended, and whether any of them have been noted for rejection; and if so, what items?

Answer. In abstract No. 2, of payments by Captain Miller in 1859, there are payments to the amount of $9,626 44 that have been disallowed by the accounting officers. In abstract No. 6, of payments by Capt. Miller in 1860, there are payments to the amount of $27,390 80 that are noted for disallowance in my office, but the account has not yet been reported to the Comptroller. A voucher for payment of $54,250 has not yet been acted on, and another voucher for $69,656 09 has also not been acted on. There are a few other small items disallowed, which are noted in the abstracts furnished and above referred to.

By Mr. CASE. What is the nature of the voucher for $69,651 09?

Answer. It is in the nature of an extra allowance for transportation, made by the Secretary of War. I could not give the facts in detail without reference to the papers in my office, but if the committee desire I can furnish them.

By Mr. CASE. Can you give particulars as to any other items?

Answer. Of the items of $9,626 44, disallowed as above, and

$27,390 80, noted for disallowance, a considerable portion is for payments made under the same authority, on account of claims which, on examination in my office, showed had already been paid, and being a double payment was of course disallowed.

TUESDAY, *January* 16, 1851.

JAMES T. SOUTTER sworn.

Examination by Mr. Harris.

Question. Are you vice-president of the Bank of the Republic, New York?

Answer. I am.

Question. Have you seen a list in the papers purporting to be a list of certain bonds abstracted from the Interior Department?

Answer. I have.

Question. Have you ever seen any of those bonds?

Answer. Yes, sir.

Question. Be good enough to state under what circumstances you saw those bonds?

Answer. I have seen bonds which I presume were some of those bonds, because they bore the same numbers.

Question. Were they all of the same State?

Answer. Yes, sir.

Question. Of what State were they and what were their numbers?

Answer. They were Tennessee bonds, but I cannot state the numbers of them.

Question. For what amount?

Answer. $19,000.

Question. Were they presented to you for purchase?

Answer. No, sir.

Question. Under what circumstances did you see them?

Answer. They were presented to me for loan.

Question. By whom?

Answer. By J. B. Simpson. I desire to say that they were presented to me as an individual, and not as an officer of the bank. The bank never had any of them, I believe.

Question. Did you effect a loan?

Answer. I loaned $15,000 upon them.

Question. Where are those bonds now?

Answer. They are in my possession.

Question. You do not recollect the numbers?

Answer. I do not.

Question. Were they all Tennessee bonds?

Answer. Yes, sir.

Question. Are those the only bonds of the published list you ever saw?

Answer. There were some bonds brought to me by individuals in Wall street, since the publication and advertisement, that had numbers corresponding to those in the published list. What the numbers were I do not know. They were brought to me by persons who had bought them in the streets, and, fearing that they should lose them, came to me with them for advice. Whether they were the same bonds I cannot say. I am convinced that some of them were not, though they had the same numbers.

Question. Were the coupons off the bonds you invested in?

Answer. Yes, sir; some of the bonds which were presented to me by alarmed persons had the January coupons on, and I felt satisfied that they could not be any of the bonds specified in the published lists.

Question. You say some of the bonds had the January coupons on, and from that circumstance you were satisfied they were none of the bonds contained in the published list?

Answer. I thought so.

Question. Do you know where these bonds are?

Answer. I do not; they were presented to me by transient individuals.

Question. Have you ever seen any of the acceptances of the Secretary of War, John B. Floyd?

Answer. Yes, sir.

Question. When did you see any such acceptances?

Answer. I have seen them off and on for two years.

Question. In whose possession were they?

Answer. In the possession of Russell.

Question. Of the firm of Russell, Majors & Waddell?

Answer. Yes, sir.

Question. Under what circumstances did you see them?

Answer. They were brought to me for negotiation, and to the bank as well.

Question. Did you negotiate any of them?

Answer. Yes, sir.

Question. Do you recollect the character of the acceptances?

Answer. I do not.

Question. Do you know that there were two classes of bonds?

Answer. Yes, sir.

Question. Were they for money earned?

Answer. One class was for money earned and the other class was for money to be earned.

Question. Which class did you negotiate?

Answer. I am inclined to think I negotiated some of both.

Question. Did you negotiate any amount of them?

Answer. Yes, sir; a large amount.

Question. What amount?

Answer. I do not know, but I think over $100,000.

Question. How long ago was your first transaction with Russell in regard to these acceptances?

Answer. I think it must have been in the year 1857 or 1858; it was not earlier than 1857, and it might have been in 1858.

[A paper, of which the following is a copy, was handed to the witness:

$10,000. WASHINGTON CITY, *October* 12, 1860.

Ten months after date, pay to our own order, at the "Bank of the Republic," New York city, ten thousand dollars, for value received, and charge to our transportation contract of the 12th day of April, 1860.

RUSSELL, MAJORS & WADDELL.

Hon. J. B. FLOYD,
Secretary of War.

Indorsed.

No. 116. WAR DEPARTMENT, *October* 13, 1860.

Accepted.

JOHN B. FLOYD,
Secretary of War.]

Question. Look at that paper, and see if that is one of the class of acceptances which you negotiated?

Answer. I do not think it is. Its language is, "charge to our transportation contract of the 12th day of April, 1860." Now, I have been an invalid to a date beyond that and in my bed.

[A paper, of which the following is a copy, was handed to the witness:

$115,000. WASHINGTON CITY, *October* 23, 1860.

Out of any monies becoming due to us for army transportation in the year 1861, under our transportation contract of the 12th day of April last, pay to our own order one hundred and fifteen thousand dollars, for value received, and charge to our transportation account for moneys earned in 1861.

RUSSELL, MAJORS & WADDELL.

Hon. J. B. FLOYD,
Secretary of War.

Indorsed.

WAR DEPARTMENT, *October* 26, 1860.

Accepted, payable according to its terms.

JOHN B. FLOYD,
Secretary.]

Question. Look at that paper, and say whether it is of the character of those you negotiated?

Answer. I think not.

Question. Did any one but Russell, upon any occasion, present those acceptances to you?

Answer. They were frequently brought to me by persons who held them.

Question. Had you any conversation or correspondence with Mr. Floyd, or with any one connected with the War Office, in relation to those acceptances?

Answer. I think I had. Such letters are in the possession of the cashier of the Bank of the Republic, and I believe they have already been laid before the committee.

Question. That is the only correspondence with the War Department that you recollect of?

Answer. It is.

Question. Did that satisfy you to negotiate the acceptances?

Answer. It did.

Question. You understood that the department would see that they were paid?

Answer. Yes, sir.

Question. Are you able to say what was the amount of the acceptances that you spoke of as having been seen by you about the year 1857?

Answer. No, sir. I can only say that they were more than $100,000, and I should think probably they were as much as $200,000.

Question. Do you speak now of those presented at one single time?

Answer. No, sir; but of the gross amount.

Question. Were all of those that you negotiated paid?

Answer. Yes, sir.

Question. Were the acceptances presented to you for negotiation all from the War Department?

Answer. They were.

Question. Do you know where Mr. Simpson is?

Answer. I do not.

Question. Are you able to indicate any person in whose possession any of these bonds are at this time, or in whose hands they are likely to be?

Answer. I cannot; but there were certain three or four parties who had, or professed to have had small amounts of them; but who they were I do not remember. They were unknown to me.

Question. Have you any one of those acceptances which you negotiated about 1857 in your possession; or are they all paid?

Answer. They are all paid.

Question. Try to give the committee the tenor of one of those acceptances, as near as you can?

Answer. I should think they were precisely like the first acceptance you handed to me, up to the words "value received."

Question. In what respect did they differ from that?

Answer. I think they then went on to state, "out of money due them" in certain months, naming the months. That is one class. The other class was to be paid out of moneys to become due "under our contract."

By Mr. Thomas:

Question. State the terms and manner of making the loan to Mr. Simpson on the $19,000 of bonds.

Answer. About the 8th of October I loaned Simpson $15,000 on $19,000 of Tennessee bonds, for his note, without other security, at simple interest, seven per cent.

General J. E. JOHNSTON recalled.

Examination by the chairman.

Question. The committee have been furnished by Mr. Atkinson, Third Auditor, with a statement showing the amount of money paid at different times to Russell, Majors & Waddell, on account of their army transportation contracts, up to the 1st of October, 1860. Will you be good enough to state, if you can, what amount has been paid to them by the government since that date, as nearly as you can?

Answer. The requisitions of the officer paying those accounts amounted, for the whole year, to $488,000. A little more than $65,000, besides, was paid in the city of Washington. That last sum is included in the Third Auditor's statement. The amount of the requisitions for payments at Fort Leavenworth was $488,000 for the year 1860. The difference between the amount of those two sums and that given by the Third Auditor will give the amount of the requisitions for the last quarter of the year.

Question. Please examine the statement of the Third Auditor, and tell us the amount of that difference?

Answer. $318,616 82 is the sum reported by the Third Auditor as paid up to the end of the third quarter of last year. The amount of the requisition from Fort Leavenworth is $488,000. To that should be added $65,934 91, which was paid here. Subtract the Auditor's statement from the amount of those two sums, and you have the amount for the last quarter, which is $235,318 09, the sum paid since the 1st of October. We have not yet the evidence of the payments, because they are due after the end of December, and the officer, who has large accounts to make up, is allowed three weeks from the beginning of January to make up the account; so that we shall not get them until February. I ought to state that about the 12th of December I ordered that officer to pay no more to Russell, Majors & Waddell, and I shall not be able to say whether any part of that requisition was withheld until I receive his account. There could have been, however, a very small portion. The amount of his requisition for December was $22,000 only, and possibly $22,000 of the sum I have given here may have been withheld.

FRIDAY, *January* 18, 1861.

General J. E. JOHNSTON was recalled, and testified as follows:

Examination by Mr. Harris.

Question. Are you able to furnish the committee with the information you were asked for when you were before the committee on a former occasion?

Answer. Yes, sir. On that day I asked Captain Van Vliet, by telegraph, to report to me the amount of his payments to these contractors, Russell, Majors & Waddell, made during the last quarter of the year 1860. His reply has been received.

Question. Have you the papers with you giving you that information?

Answer. Yes, sir. The following is the reply received from Captain Van Vliet:

"FORT LEAVENWORTH, *January* 17, 1861.

"The amount of my payments to Russell, Majors & Waddell, during the last quarter of eighteen hundred and sixty, was one hundred and seventy-five thousand eight hundred and sixty-four dollars and twenty cents; the last payment was made November twenty-sixth.

"STEWART VAN VLIET,
"*Captain, Assistant Quartermaster.*

"General J. E. JOHNSTON, *Quartermaster General.*"

"A true copy.

"J. E. JOHNSTON,
"*Quartermaster General.*"

I have also here a statement of Captain Van Vliet's monthly estimates of the amounts required to pay for the services of these contractors, which is as follows:

Amounts estimated for by Captain S. Van Vliet to pay for transportation of stores to and in New Mexico, and Forts Larned, Wise, and Riley.

1860.		
February	$8,879 46	
May	12,579 85	
June	52,276 93	
July	84,543 72	
September	121,943 39	
		$280,223 35
October	123,670 14	
November	62,063 66	
December	22,662 79	
		208,396 59
		488,619 94

Due, $23,750 49, of which $17,134 20 is on indorsed bills of lading received at Fort Leavenworth.

Question. I observe that these estimates of Captain Van Vliet show for October, 1860, the amount of $123,670 14; for November, $62,063 66; for December, $22,662 79, making an aggregate of $208,396 59, and the statement of Captain Van Vliet shows th payment, during the last quarter, of $175,864 20. I observe that Captain Van Vliet says that the last payment was made on the 26th of November. Do you know what additional amount was earned by them, or was paid to them, at the close of the quarter ending the 31st of December?

Answer. Yes, sir; the amount earned by them is $23,750 49.

Question. Then I understand you that the whole amount known to be due them up to the close of the quarter ending December 31, 1860, was $199,614 75?

Answer. Yes, sir.

Question. Will you state whether the whole amount was paid; and if not, how much of it was retained?

Answer. The sum of $23,750 49 has been retained in consequence of this transaction; an order for that purpose having been given by the Secretary of War on the 12th of December.

Question. Are you able to state whether these payments which were made, together with the amount ascertained to be due and retained under that order, cover the whole indebtedness of the department to those parties under their contract, on the 31st of December.

Answer. No, sir; they are contractors for transportation, also, in New Mexico, and they may have done additional service during the quarter, the account of which has not been rendered.

Question. Can you inform the committee the probable amount that may be due them on that branch of the service?

Answer. No, sir.

Question. Can you give an approximate amount?

Answer. No, sir. There is an Indian war going on in New Mexico, so that things have not been going on there as usual. Under ordinary circumstances I could give an approximate amount.

Question. Can you tell the committee about the amount the government owed them, or was likely to owe them, on the 31st December, 1860?

Answer. I do not think it could have much exceeded the estimates furnished by Captain Van Vliet for the three months of October, November, and December, as has been before stated.

Question. Are you able to tell the committee whether the accounts of these contractors with the government prior to the last quarter were settled or not?

Answer. I cannot, precisely. Frequently after they are paid for one quarter, sometimes two or three months subsequent a particular bill of lading is brought from some other fort to Fort Leavenworth and paid.

Question. Does that make any material difference?

Answer. Not much.

Question. Do you know whether, prior to this quarter, any large amount of money was due and unpaid to these contractors.

Answer. No, sir.

Question. Do you think any large amount was due?

Answer. I think not.

Question. What sum due to them would cover the probable amount remaining unsettled prior to the last quarter?

Answer. In the matter which the quartermaster's department decides, they have scarcely ever had a draft at any time much exceeding $100,000—probably from $100,000 to $120,000. All these accounts are paid almost invariably on presentation. Sometimes there is a little delay in getting the money.

Question. From your best knowledge of the facts are you able to state whether any amount of money, or what amount, is now due under the contracts of these parties with the government?

Answer. I do not know of any except the sum of $23,760 49, heretofore referred to. I have very little doubt, however, that a few thousand dollars will be found to have been earned the last quarter in New Mexico.

Question. Are you able to state, approximately, the earnings of these parties for the year 1861?

Answer. It will be just about what it was in 1860.

Question. Which was?

Answer. Which was very nearly, including what was paid here, $540,000. I am giving that sum without attempting to add the payments made in the different places.

TUESDAY, *January* 15, 1861.

HENRY BEARD sworn.

Examination by the chairman.

Question. Are you in the Interior Department?

Answer. I have been in the Interior Department since the 1st of June, 1857. I was a clerk in the Indian office from May, 1853, up to the 1st of June, 1857.

Question. Have you had anything to do with the Indian trust bonds?

Answer. I had charge of that branch of business in the Indian office in connexion with other business, being head of the finance division.

Question. Up to what time?

Answer. From about the 1st of July, 1853, until after the 1st of July, 1857.

Question. Who succeeded you in the charge of those bonds?

Answer. They were delivered to Mr. Godard Bailey by order of the Secretary of the Interior.

Question. Did you keep an account of the bonds that were in your charge?

Answer. Yes, sir.

Question. What did that account specify?

Answer. I will state. In 1853 schedules were made of all the bonds in the chest. The bonds were examined by a committee designated by Secretary McClelland, in November, 1853, and compared with those schedules. Duplicate copies of them, I think, were transmitted to the Department of the Interior. The rough drafts were merely upon slips of paper. I think those rough drafts were lost before I left the Indian office. Those which were formally transmitted to the Indian Department ought to be there on file. That was in 1853. I think that there were no purchases of stocks after that time and during Secretary McClelland's administration. By referring to a memorandum I can state more accurately; but I think there were no purchases of stocks or stock transactions of any importance from

November, 1853, up to August or September, 1857; so I think there were no essential changes in the stocks on hand. The list of stocks on hand in November, 1853, is as follows.

Question. Is that a detailed account of the stocks then in hand?

Answer. It is not a descriptive list, but a memorandum of the quantity and a general description I will state, generally, that in 1853 the chest was examined and the contents of it ascertained and reported to the Department of the Interior.

Question. Can you state, from any memorandum in your possession or of your knowledge, the aggregate amount of the bonds in hand for the Indian trust fund in November, 1853?

Answer. I can, with accuracy. There were:

Maryland five and six per cent. stocks	$172,749 82
Virginia six per cents and guaranteed	796,800 00
Michigan six per cent. coupon bonds	64,000 00
Indiana five per cent. coupon stocks	70,000 00
Kentucky five per cent. coupon bonds	183,000 00
Tennessee five per cent. stocks, (part certificate and part coupon)	395,000 00

(I can state, from recollection, that $250,000 of this Tennessee stock was certificate stock, and the balance coupon stock.)

Missouri five and a half per cent. stocks	63,000 00
Missouri six per cent. coupon bonds	100,000 00
Arkansas five per cent. (certificates)	3,000 00
United States loan of 1847	58,050 00
United States loan of 1842	193,280 00
Total	2,098,879 82

Question. Do you know whether any record was kept of the numbers and amounts or lettering of each of those bonds?

Answer. About that time, or shortly before, descriptive lists were prepared by myself and others and transmitted from the Indian office to the Department of the Interior, under cover of official communications.

Question. What was the character of such lists?

Answer. They described all these bonds and stocks specifically.

Question. As how?

Answer. In this way, for instance: Certificate stocks of Richmond and Danville Railroad Company, guaranteed by the State of Virginia, issued at such a date, redeemable at such a time, six per cent. interest, $13,500; interest payable semi-annually at Richmond, and the number and the party to whom issued.

Question. About what time did you leave the Indian office?

Answer. I went into the Interior Department on the 1st of June, 1857.

Question. And left it when?

Answer. I left the Indian office on the last of May, 1857.

Question. Was that the time you gave up these bonds to Mr. Bailey?

Answer. No, sir.

Question. When did you give them up to Mr. Bailey?

Answer. In the Indian office the charge of this business fell to my supervision. Before I left there there had been some conversation between the chief clerks of the two offices and myself in relation to the transfer of this business to the Interior Department, but it had not been arranged; and about the time I have stated I was myself transferred to the Department of the Interior, and had the key of the chest at the time. I retained the key of the chest until September or October of that year. I am not positive now of the exact date, but I attended to the collection of the July interest in 1857. It was attended to some time after it fell due.

Question. By you?

Answer. Yes, sir.

Question. When did you give up the key of the chest?

Answer. The last of September or the first part of October, 1857.

Question. Who did you give the key to?

Answer. I delivered it, by order of the Secretary of the Interior, to Godard Bailey.

Question. At the time of the delivery of the key of the chest to Godard Bailey had you a detailed account of all the securities in the chest?

Answer. The lists which had been transmitted from the Indian office were, many of them, then on the files of the Interior Department, to my certain knowledge; I cannot positively swear that they were all there, because I did not examine them; I saw them there, and knew what they were without examination.

Question. When you made the transfer of that chest to Mr. Bailey did you then go over the securities that were in the chest?

Answer. Yes, sir; they were examined.

Question. Did you examine them?

Answer. I was not willing to give up the key without a full examination; they were examined by Mr. Bailey and myself, and, I think, Mr. Lester.

Question. Did you find them to correspond with any detailed list previously made out; and, if so, what list, and where is it?

Answer. They were not examined by a detailed list, but examined as to the amount, and whether they answered the general description, and whether all the coupons were there; that was the kind of examination that was made. It did not occupy more than one day probably. The bonds were not checked off by the formal lists. I will state further that I have been informed that Secretary McClelland, when those lists were received by him in 1853, addressed the different banks at which the interest was payable, and informed them of the number and description of the stocks.

Question. Are the committee to understand you as saying that at the time you transferred the custody of these bonds to Mr. Bailey the chest contained all the bonds that ought to have been in it according to the previously prepared lists?

Answer. Yes, sir; and quite a number that had been bought afterwards, which I can state to you.

Question. State the stocks that were in the chest at the time you made the formal transfer.

Answer. I can state positively so far as Secretary McClelland's account was concerned; beyond that I may not be able to.

There were of bonds that had been held in Secretary McClelland's time:

United States six per cents	$251,330 00
Virginia six per cents	796,800 00
Missouri five and a half per cents	63,000 00
Missouri sixes	100,000 00
Tennessee fives and sixes	395,000 00
Kentucky fives	183,000 00
Indiana fives	70,000 00
Arkansas fives	3,000 00
Maryland fives and sixes	172,749 82
Total	2,034,879 82

This was the amount of stocks held when Secretary McClelland left office; but shortly before I delivered the key of the chest to Bailey $41,138 was delivered to the State of Maryland, to be redeemed, which left an actual balance of those old stocks in the chest of $1,993,741 82. At that time Mr. Bailey executed a receipt to me; I am unable to state exactly what that receipt covered—whether it covered the stocks and the key. He executed a receipt; that receipt was filed by me, with a communication addressed to the Secretary of the Interior, about the 10th of October, 1857, with a request that it be filed in the department. Secretary Thompson had purchased certain stocks prior to the 10th of October and after Secretary McClelland left office, and those stocks were in the chest when the key was delivered to Bailey. I am not able to say positively what they were, but I believe that the following is a description of some of them:

North Carolina bonds (six per cent.)	$245,000
Missouri bonds	75,000
Tennessee	6,000
Georgia	2,000
Florida seven per cents	50,000

A communication was addressed to the Secretary of the Interior by me, about that time, containing a more accurate description of these bonds.

By Mr. Case:

Question. Who was the predecessor of Mr. Bailey in the office he held?

Answer. I believe Mr. Ashton White.

Question. What is that office called in the department?

Answer. It is now called "Appeal Clerk, Indian Business."

Question. Had it been known by that name before Mr. Bailey assumed the place?

Answer. I do not know.

Question. Had the person who is now called appeal clerk, at any time prior to Mr. Bailey's appointment, had the custody of these bonds?

Answer. No, sir; he had not.

Question. Had they always been in the Indian bureau prior to that time?

Answer. Yes; with the exception of the anomalous state of affairs that I have explained to you.

By Mr. THOMAS:

Question. I understood you to say, Mr. Beard, that the stocks in hand in 1853, when you took charge of them, amounted to $2,098,879 82?

Answer. No, sir; that is not exactly accurate.

Question. Well, what was the amount?

Answer. On the 23d of Nov., 1853, the amount was $2,098,879 82.

Question. I understood you to say that in 1857, when you delivered over this fund to Mr. Bailey, the stocks amounted to $2,034,879 82?

Answer. No, sir; $1,993,741 82 of the old stocks and the new purchases made by Secretary Thompson, which had been placed there in August or September, 1857, before I delivered the key to Mr. Bailey. The $2,034,879 82 I stated as the balance on hand when Secretary Thompson came into office.

Question. What is the cause of the difference between the two amounts you have named?

Answer. I can explain that. $64,000 of Michigan stocks was redeemed before Secretary McClelland left office, and the money remained in the treasury uninvested; this is the difference between the stocks on hand November 23, 1853, and March 4, 1857.

Question. And $41,138 of Maryland stocks went to be redeemed?

Answer. Yes, sir, after Mr. Thompson became the Secretary, and before I delivered the key to Bailey.

Question. During the time you had charge of the chest, or at any time since you have been connected with the department, have any exchanges of stocks been made?

Answer. There were some exchanges of this kind while I had charge; some stocks fell due and were reinvested in others. There had been exchanges made by Secretary Stuart before I had charge, as I understand from the records and books, but Secretary McClelland made no changes, except to reinvest and exchange stocks that had fallen due; and I think these exchanges occurred in July and August, 1853. The stocks that were on hand March 4, 1857, were identically the same certificates and bonds that were in the chest in November, 1853.

Question. Have you examined the chest since this defalcation came to light?

Answer. Yes, sir; in December, 1860.

Question. State what you found the contents of the chest to be in stocks and bonds.

Answer. $2,525,241 82. The amount of Virginia stocks was the same as in 1853 and 1857, and the stocks were the same, or represented the same indebtedness The Kanawha Canal Company failed, and the State of Virginia, since 1857, issued certificates in lieu of the coupon bonds of that company; otherwise it was the same stock. The five and a half per cent Missouri stocks now in the chest are the same which were there in 1853 and 1857. The 69 Indiana five per cent. coupon bonds are the same, and have identically the same numbers, as 69 of the 70 referred to in my former statement. The 183 five per cent. Kentucky bonds are the same, I can state from old acquaintance with them; and the Arkansas five per cents, the United States six per cent. stocks, and the Maryland stocks are also the same. In relation to the others, I am unable to state, excepting that $125,000 Tennessee five per cent. certificates have been there a long time. I ought to say that search has been made in the department for the communication I addressed to the Secretary of the Interior in 1857, in which I enclosed Bailey's receipt, but it has not been found. I ought also to state that when I had charge of that chest there were other gentlemen who knew the contents of it, and sometimes opened it, as well as myself. Mr. Luther Smoot knew the contents of it in 1853, and Mr. W. W. Dennison was well acquainted with all its contents in 1855, 1856, and part of 1857.

Question. Where is Mr. Dennison now?

Answer. He is in Nebraska, I think. Perhaps I ought to say, too, that the stocks were examined when I took charge of the chest, in July, 1853, by Mr. Luther Smoot, Mr. James J. Miller, and myself.

JOHN J. BOGUE sworn.

Examination by the chairman.

Question. Please state to the committee your place of residence, and your business?

Answer. I reside in Georgetown, D. C.; and am a grocer.

Question. Have you seen a publication, caused to be made by the Secretary of the Interior, of certain bonds alleged to have been abstracted from the Interior Department?

Answer. Yes, sir.

Question. Have you any of those bonds in your possession?

Answer. Yes, sir.

Question. State to us the number and character of the bonds which you have in your possession?

Answer. I have numbers 1885 and 1886 of Missouri bonds.

Question. Of $6,000 each?

Answer. Yes, sir; I think I have number 1881 also; but I am certain of the two numbers I have stated.

Question. From whom did you purchase those bonds?

Answer. I wrote to Mr. Daniel Torrance, a friend of mine in New York, and he purchased them for me.

Question. When?

Answer. On November 21, 1860. I wrote to him to buy them,

and he wrote me that he had bought them, and I sent him a draft on New York. The coupons had been torn off, and he gave me credit for that. I sent him money to pay for coupons and all, supposing that the coupons were attached to the bonds, and he sent me back $90.

Question. What did you pay for those bonds?

Answer. Sixty-eight cents on the dollar; I had the money idle, and I used it as an investment.

Question. Do you know of whom Mr. Torrance purchased them?

Answer. It seems that he purchased them from William & John O'Brien, of 29 Wall street, New York.

Question. When?

Answer. On November 21, 1860, the same day he sent them to me.

Question. Do you know anything further in relation to the abstracted bonds?

Answer. No, sir; I have seen the publication of the list; that is all.

Question. Have you ever seen any drafts drawn by Russell, Majors & Waddell on the Secretary of War, and accepted by him?

Answer. No, sir; I know nothing at all concerning those parties.

James Chestney sworn.

Examination by the chairman.

Question. Please state to the committee what business you are engaged in.

Answer. I am a clerk in the Pension office, but am at present engaged as an assistant in the office of the clerk of appeals from the Indian office and Patent Office. Mr. Bailey was clerk of appeals from the Patent Office and the Indian office, and was also disbursing clerk of the Indian trust fund. My desk was in his room, and immediately close to the iron safe that contained the trust fund. I am at present engaged as an assistant to Mr. Williamson, who succeeded Mr. Bailey.

Question. Can you give the committee any information in regard to those bonds alleged to have been abstracted from the Interior Department?

Answer. I cannot, sir; I am very glad of the opportunity of being called here, as it were, to vindicate myself, because it has been suggested to me that worthy persons have said: "Mr. Chestney, being in the room with Mr. Bailey and where the safe was, ought to have known something of this abstraction." I am charmed to have an opportunity of saying that Mr. Bailey was a gentleman of about thirty years of age, Mr. Chestney was sixty and over, so that there was no sympathy or companionship between Mr. Bailey and him.

Question. Do you know whether Mr. Bailey at certain times kept the door of that room shut?

Answer. Very frequently; but rather to avoid interruption when he was engaged in some business that I supposed required calculation on his part.

Question. Were you in the room at the time he kept the door shut?

Answer. Oh! yes, sir; I have been there frequently when he kept the door shut. He might have been there in the evenings, and I suppose he was, because I often discovered that my desk had been used by some person, and I suppose with his approbation, because a person could hardly go in there without his knowledge.

Question. Who were in the habit of coming to that room to see Mr. Bailey?

Answer. Well, very frequently gentleman that I did not know; I do not recollect anybody particularly, except other gentleman who were clerks in the Indian office, and who, I supposed, had some business with him.

Question. Did you ever see Luke Lea there?

Answer. Oh, yes; he has a lame leg, I believe. What struck me as singular in those days was that occasionally Mr. Lea called towards 3 o'clock, about the time we were to leave; that struck me as a little singular.

Question. Do you know Mr. William H. Russell?

Answer. I do not.

THURSDAY, *January* 17, 1861.

WILLIAM MCKIM sworn.

Examination by Mr. Harris.

Question. Have you seen a public list or any list of certain bonds for the Indian tribes abstracted from the Interior Department?

Answer. I have seen such a list, but have never examined it.

Question. Have you seen any of the bonds described in that list?

Answer. No, sir.

Question. Have you had any negotiations connected with any of these bonds, or any bonds that you believe to be included in that list?

Answer. No negotiations. We purchased some bonds which we believe to be in that list.

Question. Can you state to the committee the amount and character of the bonds?

Answer. So far as I know, which information I get from others, for I have never examined them myself, we purchased $10,000 Missouris. I am not certain whether all of them are in that list, but I believe they are.

Question. Do you know whether the January coupons were off these bonds at the time of that transaction?

Answer. They were off when we received them. We purchased them in New York a few days before the 1st of January.

Question. From whom did you purchase them?

Answer. These were purchased from Trevor & Colgate, brokers, in New York.

Question. Is that the only instance in which you have encountered any of these bonds?

Answer. I was just trying to recollect. I think there was a $1,000 Tennessee bond in another purchase made at another time for another person. I have neglected to examine into it, but I just remember some person in the office speaking of it.

Question. Have you ever seen any of the acceptances of John B. Floyd, late Secretary of War?

Answer. No, sir; I never saw and never heard of them until the recent publications

Question. Did you purchase these bonds for your house or for some other person or persons?

Answer. We purchased them on an order for a customer of ours.

Question. As an investment?

Answer. Yes, sir.

Question. For whom did you purchase them?

Answer. Considering that this is to some extent a violation of our relation with the party for whom we purchased, I would prefer not to answer, but being required by the committee to do so, I reply that it was for Mr. Thomas Swan, of Baltimore.

Question. Does he still hold them, or do you hold them for him?

Answer. They were handed over to him, and I presume he still holds them.

Question. Does that include the Tennessee bond?

Answer. No, sir; only the $10,000 Missouris.

Question. For whom was the Tennessee bond purchased?

Answer. I cannot answer without referring to my books. It was purchased on an order from a customer, but I cannot say who.

Question. Do you know of any person or persons who hold any other of these bonds?

Answer. No, sir; I do not recollect hearing of any person or persons who hold them.

WILLIAM FISHER sworn.

Examination by the chairman.

Question. Will you inform the committee whether you have any knowledge of the bonds, or any portion of them, alleged to have been abstracted from the Interior Department?

Answer. Yes, sir; we purchased some of these bonds, or some which have been reported to us as being among those abstracted.

Question. Please give a description of them.

Answer. We purchased $4,000 Missouri stocks, which have been reported to us by our customers as contained in the list of abstracted bonds.

Question. Are they the only ones you have purchased?

Answer. They are all that have been reported to us, and all that we are aware of.

Question. Have you any knowledge, directly or indirectly, where any of the other bonds contained in that list are?

Answer. I have heard that some other parties held these bonds, but I have no positive information or personal knowledge on the subject.

Question. Please give the committee what information you have in reference to other parties holding the bonds.

Answer. I have heard as a mere report that Townshend Scott and John S. Gittings have purchased these bonds. I have no knowledge, except the mere report in respect to Mr. Gittings. I believe Mr. Scott told me himself he had purchased some of them.

Question. Did he state how many?

Answer. I think he said $5,000.

Question. Had the bonds you purchased the January coupons on?

Answer. No, sir; I think they had not. Here is an account for one, in which it is stated that the coupon is missing, and in which our broker in New York has credited us with the amount of $30. In the other cases nothing is said, but I am under the impression the January coupons were off.

Question. Did you purchase the bonds on an order or for your house?

Answer. On an order.

Question. For whom did you purchase them?

Answer. I should prefer not to give the names; but being required by the committee, I state that we purchased $3,000 of them for R. D. Gaither and $1,000 for B. Atkinson.

Question. Did they buy them as an investment?

Answer. Yes, sir.

Question. Do they hold them now?

Answer. Yes, sir; at least, I suppose they do.

Question. Do they reside in Baltimore?

Answer. Yes, sir.

Question. Have you ever seen any orders drawn by Russell, Majors & Waddell on the late Secretary of War and accepted by him?

Answer. No, sir.

Question. And you know nothing about those acceptances?

Answer. I do not.

MARTIN LEWIS sworn.

Examination by the chairman.

Question. Please inform the committee whether you have seen any of the bonds alleged to have been abstracted from the Interior Department.

Answer. I got $6,000 Tennessee bonds for a party on the 7th of December, five of which were found to have numbers contained in the list published by the Secretary of the Interior.

Question. State the names of the parties for whom you purchased them.

Answer. Being required by the committee to give the names, I answer, Lowdnes, Thompson & Co., of Baltimore.

Question. Did they buy them for an investment?

Answer. They did.

Question. Have you any knowledge of the whereabouts of any others of these bonds?

Answer. I have not.

Question. Do you know whether the parties for whom you purchased these bonds still hold them?

Answer. I believe they do; I am not certain.

Question. Have you ever seen any drafts drawn by Russell, Majors & Waddell upon the Secretary of War and accepted by him?

Answer. I have not.

Question. Did the bonds you purchased have the January coupons on?

Answer. I bought for this party $6,000 Tennessee bonds, five of which had the January coupons off, and these five were among the stolen bonds.

GEO. W. RIGGS recalled.

Examination by the chairman.

Question. Please inform the committee whether you have seen, and if so, in what time and what amounts, orders drawn by Russell, Majors & Waddell upon the late Secretary of War, and accepted by him, in which either the dates or amounts were left blank?

Answer. I have seen drafts in which the amounts and the dates were inserted; but the time which they were to run left blank. For instance, the word "months" would be written, but the number of months not put in the draft. They were acceptances, dated, the committee will understand, and commencing, instead of "one," "two," or "three months," with the word "months." These have been offered to me; but I could not mention the date or number, because no record was made. They were merely offered, and refused by me. As I have said, I do not remember the number of acceptances; and I think they differed in amount.

Question. How many of these acceptances do you think you saw?

Answer. I really cannot tell the number. They were offered to me only once—I should think two or three of them.

Question. By whom were they offered?

Answer. They were offered by Mr. Suter, of the house of Suter, Lea & Co. They were offered to me to be negotiated; but I declined to do anything with them.

Question. You speak of the time being left blank. Did Mr. Suter say he was at liberty to fill in the time according to the arrangement that he made with you?

Answer. I do not remember the exact words, whether he said he was at liberty or I was at liberty, but he said they could be filled up, if I would take them, so as to make the time two, four, or six months, as I pleased. In other words, if I would discount them, I had the privilege of selecting the time they were to run.

C. G. WAGNER sworn.

Examination by Mr. Harris.

Question. Where do you reside?

Answer. In Washington, temporarily.

Question. What is your position or occupation?

Answer. None, just now. I have been engaged in the Department of the Interior. I have been in the government service since 1854, I think. My connexion with the government was first in the Pension office, until the coming in of this administration. I then received an appointment, and was out in Minnesota from that time until, I think, February last.

Question. Have you at any time been connected with the Indian office?

Answer. No, sir.

Question. Do you know Godard Bailey?

Answer. I do, very well. He is one of my blood relations, and a very close one.

Question. Do you know whether Mr. Bailey had, in the Indian department, in his possession, or under his control and custody, the funds held for the Indian tribes?

Answer. I only know by hearsay. I know that he was the clerk having in charge the Indian bonds; but further than that, as to what in particular he had charge of, or what were his duties, I know not.

Question. Has he made any communication to you in relation to those trust funds?

Answer. Yes, sir.

Question. When?

Answer. It was the day before Mr. Thompson, the Secretary of the Interior, returned from North Carolina.

Question. About what date?

Answer. Some time in December—about the 19th or 20th, I should think.

Question. What was the nature of that communication?

Answer. Some time in December, the exact date I do not remember, (there is a letter bearing a memorandum of mine showing the date,) Bailey called at my room. I was then chief clerk in the Census bureau. He called at my room and said to me, "here is a communication which I desire you to place in the hands of Mr. Thompson five days before he retires from office." We were intimate; necessarily so. I was educated with him, and brought up in his father's family. I had had several conversations with him relative to his resigning his position, and he had said repeatedly that there was a matter of honor connected with that matter. He brought me that paper and requested that I should deliver it five days before Mr. Thompson retired from office. I took it to mean five days before the 4th of March. I received it, and made a memorandum on it, presuming it contained an explanation in regard to his resignation, and threw it in my desk. The letter remained in my desk until some short time before—a day or two days—Mr. Thompson returned from North Carolina. About one o'clock on that day I was sitting in my room, with some gentleman in my office, and Bailey came in and said, "I wanted to see you this morning; I have laid a letter on your table, have you got it?" I told him I had not. After I got through with the interview with the gentleman on business, I went to the desk and took up this letter; or rather it was a little note. I do not remember what the note said, but the purport of it was this: "I have had reason to change my mind as to the delivery of the letter placed in your hands some days ago, and request you to deliver it to Mr. Thompson immediately after his return;" and something was said about his honor being concerned. I was much engaged in my business—sometimes I am detained late at it—but as soon as I got my supper I went around to Bailey's house. I said to him that the note I had received that morning was of such a character that it required some explanation.

Question. Where is that note?

Answer. In Mr. Thompson's hands, I believe. I did not put the note in his hands, but I know he had or has it. All the papers I received went into Mr. Thompson's hands. The interview I had with Bailey then was in the presence of his wife. I said to him that the character of the note was such that it required an explanation from him before I could be the bearer of a sealed note, from the simple fact that there was an allusion made to his honor. That was sufficient for me, and I required an explanation. He said he would give me an explanation. This, I think, was the night before Mr. Thompson returned; but the memorandum upon the letter will establish the date. I may say here that my connexion with Bailey was very intimate; I have nursed him like a brother, and have had him in my arms when he was not more than three days old. He said he regretted to have to say to me that he had parted with $870,000 of bonds which were in his charge. I gave him an answer. I told him I would rather have paid for his coffin. He said to me, "that letter I gave to you"—I had it in my hand—"that letter is my confession, and I have placed it in your hands, because, in the difficulties by which I am surrounded, I know of none that I have a right to come to sooner than yourself, and I desire you to deliver that letter." I told him that, without any desire upon his part, I should undoubtedly do it. I next morning went to Mr. Kelly, chief clerk in the Interior Department, and asked him when Mr. Thompson was expected back. I was anxious to know, for I was determined that the letter should go into his hands. In that conversation with Bailey, I said further to him, "while I feel deeply what you have done, I want to know whether you have any intention of getting out of the way; if so, I will even now see that you are taken care of." He said he had no such intention at all. After that interview, and the assurance that he would not get out of the way at all, I left him with the determination to deliver the letter.

Question. Did you deliver the letter?

Answer. No, sir; I kept that letter, as well as the other note, and the next afternoon—I think it was Saturday—as soon as I heard of Thompson's arrival in the city, I got an early tea and went to Bailey's room, saw him, and said to him, "I am on my way to Thompson's to deliver that letter; would it not be as well for you to accompany me?" He said he did not think it necessary; that he would be at home, and that he was not going anywhere. I went up to Mr. Thompson's residence; he was out. I returned to Bailey's house, stated to him that I had been up there, but that Mr. Thompson was out; that I would set there awhile, and then return by and by. He said "It is of very little importance whether you go or not. I think that Thompson is now at the President's, and is in full possession of the whole matter." I sat and talked with him, and then went into some particulars. I felt anxious, and I asked him some questions. I did not know what was in his letter further than that it was his confession of having converted those bonds. As he had thrown himself upon me as a friend, I could not give him any assistance unless he made a clean breast of the matter to me, as he had to Mr. Thompson. He then told me that he had not received the first dollar for his own benefit. I am not in the habit of using profane language, but I will give the language I used. I asked him if he had grown to be such a damned fool as to risk his character for other men, and to tell me that he had not received a dime of benefit? I told him I thought it was one of the most remarkable cases of disinterested friendship. He told me that John B. Floyd, of whom I think he is a nephew by marriage, had been a friend to him, and had come in between himself and the starvation of his wife and children in getting him that situation. I know the fact that when Bailey came here he was poor. He did not at all allude to dates, but he told me that when he parted with those bonds, or a portion of them—if I am not mistaken, he told me it was $150,000—it was in this way: that he was approached by an individual—he did not name him then——

Question. Did he name him afterwards?

Answer. Yes, and I will give his name now. He told me afterwards that Luke Lea was the man. He told me that the individual had approached him; that there were certain acceptances of John B. Floyd that were about to be protested in New York; that he (Lea) wanted him (Bailey) to assist him (Lea) in saving that protest—to assist in saving Floyd's credit. I cannot give the exact words Bailey used, but my impression is that the conversation was this, that he wanted him to assist him by loaning him those bonds.

Question. Did the conversation of Bailey produce the impression upon your mind that Lea suggested to him the use of those Indian trust bonds in his custody as a means of raising money for the purpose of protecting the acceptances of Floyd?

Answer. Undoubtedly so; and more than that, he said they would be returned to him in ninety days.

Question. Did he say whom Lea named as a co-operator in the transaction?

Answer. He did not. The whole confession was of such an interest to me to know where the guilt was, that I charged my memory with it, and am distinct in my recollection. I then asked him, "Have you anything from John B. Floyd that will stand between you and harm in this matter?" He said he had nothing, except that he had the acceptances of John B. Floyd, as Secretary of War, to the amount of $870,000. He said "that he was not satisfied that this was a matter in which Mr. Floyd was at all concerned or anxious for, and that he went up to the War Department to see Governor Floyd; that he found Governor Floyd in an interview with Lieutenant General Scott, and that that interview lasted a long time; that he then went to Drinkard, the chief clerk, a man that he had reason to believe knew all of Governor Floyd's business, and asked Drinkard as to the correctness of those papers I have spoken of going to protest. He said he was told it was so."

Question. Do you recollect whether he told you that Drinkard told him if they were not lifted Floyd would be compelled to resign?

Answer. He was emphatic in that part of his language. I do not say that Drinkard told Mr. Bailey this, but this expression was used: "if it is not done, Floyd will be obliged to leave the cabinet in disgrace." That language was emphatic, and in those words. Drinkard assured him, he said, that the condition of things was as they had been represented to him in reference to those papers; and if I remember aright—and that is a point I have been trying to settle in my mind—he said he was then introduced to Russell by Mr. Drinkard, and they had an interview in the third story of the War Department.

Question. In what story is Drinkard's office?

Answer. I do not know. My recollection now is this, as to what Drinkard said at the time of the introduction, that he, Bailey, could rely upon Russell as as honorable gentleman, and would do all he said he would do. It was an indorsement of Russell by Drinkard.

Question. Was that the substance of the conversation?

Answer. It is; but there was other conversation. He said that there was a promise by Russell that these bonds should come back in 90 days, and that whatever was done had to be done by three o'clock that day, so that Russell could proceed to New York and prevent the protest; and that he went to the office and delivered the bonds at that time.

Question. Did you subsequently deliver the note to Mr. Thompson?

Answer. I did not. As I told you, I returned from my visit to Mr. Thompson's residence when I found he was not at home, and was waiting at Bailey's quarters, intending soon to return. But Bailey told me it was of no importance whether the note was delivered or not, as Mr. Thompson was in full possession of the contents of it. While sitting there, Mr. Rice, the senator from Minnesota, came in, and I delivered the letters to Rice, as he, it appears, had been up to Mr. Thompson's; I delivered them to Mr. Rice in Mr. Bailey's room; that was the last I saw of them.

Question. Did you deliver them to Mr. Rice with Bailey's assent?

Answer. Bailey was there, and told me to deliver them to Rice, and I did so.

Question. Have you had any conversation with Mr. Luke Lea on the subject?

Answer. I do not know him. I have seen Mr. Lea once, I think, some years ago, when I kept a bank account at his establishment.

Question. Had you any conversation with Mr. Bailey subsequent to the one which you have detailed?

Answer. I have seen him once or twice since at the jail.

Question. Have you had any further conversation with him in reference to these bonds?

Answer. I have not, sir.

Question. Have you had any conversation or interview relative to these bonds, or to these transactions in any of their phases, with any other parties?

Answer. I have not, sir.

Question. Has Mr. Bailey at any time stated to you whether he knew where any of these bonds were?

Answer. I think, though I will not be certain of it, that, in the interview at his house, he said that he did not know. I asked him, cursorily, where the bonds were, and he said he did not know where they were.

Question. He stated to you that the sum he first gave to Mr. Russell was $150,000?

Answer. That is my impression.

Question. Did he give you any explanation of the subsequent increase in the amount of bonds abstracted?

Answer. He did, sir.

Question. State what it was.

Answer. It was something to this effect: I said "you have only accounted for $150,000, but here is $870,000; how was the amount increased?" The impression on my mind is this: that he stated that when the time came for returning the $150,000 they were not returned; they had reduced in value in the market, and as he had taken $150,000 to save his friend, he went on and took more until the amount increased from time to time to $870,000.

Question. Did he say to you that he ever sought an interwiew with Mr. Floyd after the first occasion when he took the bonds?

Answer. On the night to which I have referred, when I went to him for an explanation of his note, he said that he had either written a note to Mr. Floyd, or that he had had an interview with him.

Question. What was the tenor of that interview?

Answer. I do not know that he went into any details; he merely stated the fact that Mr. Floyd knew of this thing.

Question. Can you state whether it was Mr. Luke Lea or Colonel Drinkard who gave Bailey the impression that if these acceptances were not paid Mr. Floyd would have to leave the cabinet in disgrace?

Answer. I cannot.

THOMAS R. SUTER sworn.

Examination by Mr. Harris.

Question. Were you served with a subpœna to bring with you certain books of your banking house?

Answer. Yes, sir; I was yesterday.

Question. Have you brought those books with you?

Answer. No, sir.

Question. Will you state the reason.

Answer. The reason I did not bring them was because there was nothing in them that bears upon this bond transaction whatever, either directly or indirectly.

Question. Is there anything upon your books to show any of your transactions with Godard Bailey?

Answer. Nothing whatever, sir; not a scratch of the pen.

Question. Have you ever had any transactions in your banking house with Godard Bailey?

Answer. Yes, we have casually, as we have had with you or anybody else.

Question. Will you state what the character of such transactions was?

Answer. Well, if my recollection is right, on one occasion when he wished to pay some money to Riggs & Co., and did not wish to take the money up there, we took the money and gave him a certified check, so as to save him the trouble of taking the money up there. Where he got the money I did not know; it was none of my business to inquire.

Question. Do you recollect what the amount of that transaction was?

Answer. I do not.

Question. Do you recollect whether it was about, or above, or below, $900?

Answer. I do not recollect the amount at all.

Question. Do you recollect what time it was?

Answer. I do not.

Question. Do you keep a memorandum of your certified checks?

Answer. None, of that irregular kind. They are generally destroyed; I do not know whether this one was destroyed. My instructions to the teller are to destroy them, as they are merely given out for the accommodation of transient customers.

Question. Have you had other transactions with Godard Bailey in connexion with certificates of deposit on any bank?

Answer. No, sir.

Question. Have you made any collections for him, or remitted any paper for collection on his account to New York?

Answer. None that I am aware of.

Question. Has Mr. Luke Lea private transactions in your banking establishment, or are his transactions and those of the house all blended?

Answer. He has a great many private transactions that I know nothing about.

Question. Do any of these appear upon the books of your banking house?

Answer. No, sir.

Question. Does he keep private books of his own for these transactions?

Answer. No, sir.

Question. Have you seen, at any time, any of the bonds fraudulently abstracted from the Interior Department?

Answer. No, sir. I never knew anything about that transaction—any more than you did—until I saw it published.

Question. Did you ever negotiate any of the bonds.

Answer. No, sir; never.

Question. Do you know where any of them now are?

Answer. I never saw any of them.

Question. Do you know anything of any acceptances of the late Secretary of War, Mr. Floyd?

Answer. Oh, I have seen them often.

Question. Have you negotiated any of them?

Answer. I do not recollect now whether I have done so or not; I am not certain. I have taken some of them to Mr. Riggs's for negotiation.

Question. But you never negotiated any of them yourself?

Answer. No, sir.

Question. Who offered them to you at the time they were presented to you?

Answer. Mr. Russell.

Question. Were you aware, from any source, of the operations between Mr. Russell and Mr. Bailey in these bonds, until their public development?

Answer. Never; I did not dream of such a thing.

Question. When did you last see Mr. Bailey in your banking establishment?

Answer. I do not recollect; he did not come there often; I have a very slight acquaintance with him; what transactions were done with him were done at the counter.

FRIDAY, *January* 18, 1861.

WILLIAM H. RUSSELL reappeared.

Examination by Mr. Conkling.

Question. Who drew this paper?—(the statement presented and asked to be filed on a former occasion by the witness.)

Answer. The paper was drawn by the assistance of my attorneys and myself.

Question. Who did draw it in fact?

Answer. Colonel Thompson and Mr. Bradley.

Question. When was the original draft of it made?

Answer. It was made the night after I asked your permission.

Question. And when was it completed?

Answer. It was completed on the 16th.

Question. To whom was it shown or read?

Answer. Mr. Akers, a friend of mine in Missouri, read it.

Question. Was it shown to Colonel Lea?

Answer. He has never seen it.

Question. To whom else?

Answer. It has not been shown to anybody, save to the attorneys who helped me to get it up and to Mr. Akers. I have read small parts of it to one or two of my friends—parties having nothing to do with this suit.

Question. To Governor Floyd?

Answer. No, sir.

Question. To Mr. Bailey?

Answer. No, sir.

Question. To Mr. Lea?

Answer. No, sir; I say positively that no party connected in any manner with this suit has seen it or heard of it from me, directly or indirectly.

Question. Who, in July last, held the outstanding acceptances to which you have reference in this paper?

Answer. That is a question I cannot answer. Some of them were held by banks in St. Louis, and some by Boston and New York bankers.

Question. I refer to the particular set of acceptances on which you received the first lot of $150,000 in bonds from Bailey.

Answer. I cannot tell; they went into the hands of agents in St. Louis and of our friends in Boston and New York. I kept a list of those maturing, but I do not know who held them; they were all made payable at the Bank of the Republic.

Question. What were the bonds which you received in the first instance from Bailey?

Answer. I think they were Missouris and Tennessees—mostly Missouris, according to my recollection.

Question. Were there any Florida bonds among them?

Answer. Not on that occasion.

Question. How did you dispose of the bonds which you first received from Bailey?

Answer. I did not dispose of the $150,000 all at that time; they were disposed of, as I said, to raise money.

Question. On what date did you receive them?

Answer. Somewhere between the 12th and 15th of July; I cannot tell precisely; I have no memorandum to refer to; but my recollection is, that it was between those two dates.

Question. Where did you receive them?

Answer. I received them at my room at Potentini's.

Question. Who was present?

Answer. I do not think anybody was present; but I am not sure.

Question. What proportion of these bonds were Tennessees, and what Missouris?

Answer. I think there were $90,000 Missouris.

Question. And the residue Tennessees?

Answer. Yes, sir; that is my impression.

Question. Coupons on or off?

Answer. I do not recollect.

Question. Was anything said in that interview between you and Bailey, or had there been at any time, about the January coupons of these bonds?

Answer. Not a word.

Question. How many interviews had you with Bailey?

Answer. Three.

Question. At that time?

Answer. Oh, no; I had only one interview at that time.

Question. How many interviews had you had with him at the time the first bonds were delivered to you?

Answer. Only one.

Question. Which was where?

Answer. At the War Department.

Question. Had you never seen him before?

Answer. Never.

Question. Nor had any communication with him?

Answer. I did not know there was such a man living before.

Question. Were the bonds delivered to you on the first day you saw Bailey?

Answer. They were.

Question. And how long after you had first met him?

Answer. I suppose it was probably three or three and a half hours.

Question. Was any agreement made between you and him in reference to interest, commission, or compensation for the use of these securities?

Answer. Not a particle; no question was asked, and nothing said.

Question. How soon afterward did you leave the city?

Answer. I left by the afternoon train for New York.

Question. Carrying these bonds with you?

Answer. Yes, sir.

Question. Did you carry any other securities with you at the time?

Answer. I did not.

Question. What did you do with these bonds?

Answer. I left them with my agent in New York for the purpose of hypothecation and raising money.

Question. When did you deliver them to him?

Answer. The next morning after I arrived in New York.

Question. Who was the agent to whom you delivered them?

Answer. Jerome B. Simpson. He is in the same office, and was the agent of our house; he had the control and management of our money matters in New York.

Question. You handed them to him?

Answer. Yes, sir.

Question. With what direction?

Answer. To raise money upon, to hypothecate, and to pay the acceptances of the Secretary of War.

Question. Anything else?

Answer. No, sir.

Question. You suggested to him the name of no party with whom to hypothecate?

Answer. No, sir. I consulted with him as to where we could get the money.

Question. You gave him no direction as to the party, the terms of hypothecation, or the time?

Answer. Yes, sir. I gave him the time, which must not exceed 90 days.

Question. And then what did you say to him?

Answer. I gave him the bonds, and told him to raise money on them to pay the acceptances of the Secretary of War. I wished him to go to parties who had money they would loan upon the bonds.

Question. What else did you say to him?

Answer. I do not know what else. We had a general conversation about the mode of getting money, and where we could get it.

Question. Is that all you told him, by way of direction, as to the disposition of those bonds?

Answer. Yes, sir.

Question. Did you go with him to negotiate them?

Answer. I went to one or two places.

Question. Where did you go with him?
Answer. I went to the Chatham Bank, I think it is; I am not certain as to the name; I could give the locality of it.
Question. Was that a bank at which you did not borrow.
Answer. We did borrow at that bank.
Question. Did you place any of these bonds there?
Answer. Yes, sir.
Question. How many?
Answer. I think fifty.
Question. Which bonds?
Answer. I do not recollect.
Question. They were a part of the $150,000 which you first received from Bailey?
Answer. Yes, sir.
Question. For how long did you place them there?
Answer. 90 days; or rather, I think there were two notes given—one for 70 and the other for 90 days.
Question. Stock notes?
Answer. Yes, sir.
Question. You gave them stock notes?
Answer. Yes, sir.
Question. Whose notes?
Answer. Russell, Majors & Waddell's.
Question. And the terms of the notes were such as, in default of payment, gave them the right to sell the bonds?
Answer. Yes, sir.
Question. At 90 days?
Answer. Yes, sir; or rather, as I remarked before, I think there were two notes—one at 70 and the other at 90 days.
Question. What did you do with the residue of the bonds?
Answer. Mr. Simpson hypothecated them to raise money.
Question. With whom?
Answer. I think some of them were hypothecated with the bank with which we do business—the Continental Bank.
Question. How long did they have them?
Answer. I do not know; I presume I did know at the time, but I have forgotten.
Question. Did you give them a stock note?
Answer. Yes, sir.
Question. Your note?
Answer. Yes, sir, I think so; I am not certain.
Question. And what did you do with the residue?
Answer. They were hypothecated by Mr. Simpson to raise money. I do not know with whom.
Question. Did you give your note and sign it yourself in each case?
Answer. I do not think I did, but I am not sure.
Question. Do you know whether any of them were placed with any one without the note being given?
Answer. I think some of them were placed in that way, or that Mr. Simpson gave his individual note for them.
Question. Have those notes which you gave been taken up?

Answer. Yes, sir, long ago.

Question. Where are they?

Answer. I do not know. Mr. Simpson has charge of our business in New York.

Question. How were these notes taken up—by the sale of bonds, or by being retired by you?

Answer. I think those notes were taken up with money without reference to the bonds at all.

Question. Then the bonds were retired?

Answer. Yes, sir, upon that occasion.

Question. The whole of the $150,000?

Answer. I am not sure whether they were all taken up or not; my impression is that most of them were.

Question. They were retired, then, at the maturity of the notes?

Answer. I think this bank, which I call the Chatham Bank, sold a portion of theirs.

Question. Which bank do you speak of now; the one in Sherman's building?

Answer. No, sir.

Question. The bank over in the Bowery?

Answer. No, sir; but in that direction. It was not on Chatham street, but between Chatham and Broadway.

Question. We will call it, then, for this purpose, the Chatham Bank. You say they sold some of their bonds?

Answer. I think they did.

Question. How many?

Answer. I do not know.

Question. According to your best recollection.

Answer. I am inclined to think we settled with that bank, and there were between seven and ten thousand dollars of money paid them at the maturity of those two stock notes, and for the residue the bonds were sold.

Question. In selling those bonds to pay the notes, did the bonds fall short of par so as to leave a deficit of seven or ten thousand dollars?

Answer. The bonds fell short of par as a matter of course.

Question. I only want to know if they sold for what they would bring, and you paid the deficit?

Answer. Yes, sir, that is so.

Question. How much did the bonds fall short?

Answer. I do not know.

Question. You know that some of the bonds were taken up?

Answer. Yes, sir.

Question. Do you know why certain of these bonds were taken up and others not?

Answer. I do not know, except perhaps Simpson thought he could sell them better.

Question. Do you mean to say that so far as you had the money to retire those bonds you did, and the residue you let them sell?

Answer. Yes, sir.

Question. Now, speaking of that portion of the $150,000 of bonds which you retired, what next was done with them?

Answer. They were sold.

Question. By whom?

Answer. Through the agency of Mr. Simpson.

Question. Were they sold by Russell, Majors & Waddell as your bonds?

Answer. Yes, sir; through our agent, Mr. Simpson.

Question. At what figure?

Answer. I cannot tell; the price varied so rapidly from time to time that it was hard to keep the run of the matter.

Question. Have you the means of ascertaining the figure at which they were sold?

Answer. None, except by applying to the brokers who sold them.

Question. Can you inform the committee of the aggregate sum you received for the $150,000 of bonds?

Answer. If I knew the amount of each class of bonds I could tell.

Question. You know you had $150,000 in all; you had $90,000 in Missouris, which would leave $60,000 of Tennessees; that classifies them.

Answer. I received about $97,000.

Question. Within what time were the last of those $150,000 of bonds sold; by what time did you part with the last of them?

Answer. They were sold in the month of December, or in the latter part of November, that is, the Missouris; I think they were sold in November.

Question. Then all of the $150,000 you held were sold in the latter part of November or in December?

Answer. I think they were.

Question. On what day in December were the last of those $150,000 of bonds sold?

Answer. That is more than I can tell.

Question. As nearly as you can recollect?

Answer. They were sold prior to the 10th of December.

Question. Is that as near as you can state?

Answer. It is.

Question. To whom did you sell late in November or in December any of those $150,000 of bonds?

Answer. I did not sell any personally.

Question. Russell, Majors & Waddell held the bonds, and of course they sold them; to whom did they sell in November or in December any of them?

Answer. I do not know.

Question. Through whom was the business done for you?

Answer. Through Simpson.

Question. When did you receive any bonds from Bailey again?

Answer. I do not recollect the date.

Question. Come as near to it as you can.

Answer. I think it was in September.

Question. Do you know what day in September?

Answer I cannot fix the date; I think that was the month.

Question. On the occasion of receiving the first bonds from Bailey, were any papers executed by you?

Answer. I gave him the note of Russell, Majors & Waddell for the par value of the face of the bonds, $150,000.

Question. With interest?

Answer. Without interest.

Question. Payable where?

Answer. Payable, I presume, in Washington; it was dated in Washington.

Question. Where is that note?

Answer. It is torn up; when we exchanged again we tore it up.

Question. Did you execute any other papers?

Answer. Not at that time.

Question. Did you see Bailey again until you received bonds from him the second time?

Answer. No, sir; I saw him, say to-day, and got the bonds to-morrow; it was all on the same occasion. I think he had gone to the west in the meantime.

Question. That was in September?

Answer. It was.

Question. Had he ever written to you in the meantime?

Answer. No, sir.

Question. Or you to him?

Answer. No, sir.

Question. Did you communicate with him through any other person?

Answer. I think not.

Question. Or he with you?

Answer. No, sir.

Question. Not between the first and second getting of the bonds?

Answer. I think not.

Question. Did you ever communicate with Colonel Lea in reference to this $150,000 of bonds before you got any others?

Answer. I did not see Lea from the time I got the first until I got the second.

Question. Did you hold any communication with Lea in reference to these bonds between the time you got the first and the time when you got the second?

Answer. No, sir.

Question. State as near as you can the day you came to see Bailey the second time.

Answer. I cannot be more positive than to state that it was in the month of September.

Question. Cannot you say it was in the forepart of the month?

Answer. It might have been the middle of the month.

Question. Did you come from New York to see him?

Answer. I saw him at my rooms at Potentini's, in this city. I addressed him a note upon my arrival here.

Question. And when did he come to see you?

Answer. I arrived in the morning, and I think he came to see me the following evening.

Question. Did he see you alone?

Answer. I presume we conversed alone. My room was full of friends.

Question. What took place between you and him then?

Answer. I told him of my condition and distress; that I could not take care of the bonds he gave me, and that they would be sold at a sacrifice; that I came to Washington to get more aid to take care of them. In that conversation, and after a long talk, he told me the position of the bonds, what they were, and what fund they belonged to.

Question. That was the third talk you had with him?

Answer. It was.

Question. Begin with the first conversation you had with Bailey, and detail it—the first conversation you ever had with him.

Answer. Mr. Bailey was introduced to me at the War Department by Mr. Drinkard. He asked me if certain acceptances of the Secretary of War were due, and what would be the consequence of their going to protest. He asked me if the reports he had heard of the disastrous consequences of such a protest was true. I told him that I believed the reports which had been related to him, as to the consequence of a protest to the War Department, Secretary Floyd, and the army transportation, was true. He told me he had heard it from Mr. Lea and Mr. Drinkard. He asked me if the acceptances were in danger of going to protest, and if the report he had heard from Lea and Drinkard, in regard to the consequences upon the War Department and the army transportation, was correct. He told me he heard that from Lea in the first instance, and that Lea represented that he got that statement from me; that Lea told him that I had negotiated acceptances of the Secretary of War; that I was not able to protect them, and that if they were dishonored, Mr. Floyd would be disgraced; and not only that, but that it would break up the army transportations and supplies. He also said he had got the same information from Drinkard. He asked me if those were the facts, and asked my opinion in regard to the disgrace of Secretary Floyd, and his retiring from the cabinet. I told him they were literally true, and I feared the consequences. His reply to me was that his mind was made up. I asked him what his mind was made up to, and if he could aid me. He said he could; that he had some State securities that I could have to raise money on, and that such a state of things as the ruin of Secretary Floyd must not be permitted. I told him I was willing to make any sacrifice, if sacrifice would save Floyd in this thing. He said that, for his part, he wanted no sacrifice; that he had some State securities he would let me have. He appointed a time to meet me at my room to give them to me; that he would go and get the bonds and meet me at 2 o'clock, in time to enable me to go to New York that evening, as the paper would mature in New York the next day. At 2 o'clock he met me at my room with the bonds or stock.

Question. Is that all the conversation?

Answer. It is all.

Question. Did no other persons participate?

Answer. No, sir.

Question. Is there anything you can remember which you have not detailed?

Answer. There is not. He came to my room with those bonds about 2 o'clock, and told me he required me to give him our note for them at ninety days; and that if I did not return the bonds in ninety days he would make us pay the full par value of them. I was so confident that I could do so that I took the risk. He then required that I should only hypothecate them, and return them in ninety days.

Question. Was there anything else in that conversation?

Answer. No, sir. There may have been some general conversation, but I do not recollect.

Question. What did you do then?

Answer. I gave him the note, took the bonds, and took them to New York with me.

Question. Come now, if you please, to the third interview, which, you say, was at Potentini's.

Answer. As I said before, that was in September, and, I believe, prior to the middle. I came to Washington, and was here a day or two before I addressed him a note advising him of the condition of things, thinking I could get money from the government. I wrote him a note asking him to call and see me, and on the following evening, I think it was—I got in in the morning—he came to my room according to my request, when I had a full conversation with him in regard to what I had done with the securities. I do not know that I can detail the conversation. I told him I came back to Washington in an embarrassed condition; that our firm was in an embarrassed condition; that those securities were hypothecated, some on short date, and that they were liable to be sold; and that in addition thereto, we had other acceptances of the Secretary of War to protect; and that owing to the state of the finances of the country, and especially of the west, we could not raise money. I asked him if he knew of any way in which he could aid me. He then told me that these bonds belonged to the government, and were held in trust for the Indians.

Question. What followed that?

Answer. He told me it was necessary to save those securities; that it was utter ruin to him if they were not saved. In response to that, I gave him to understand that I could not save them. He then proposed to give me additional aid to take care of those acceptances of Governor Floyd's. I had mentioned to him that there were other acceptances maturing, which it was necessary to take care of.

Question. Did you tell him to what amount?

Answer. I told him the amount.

Question. What was it?

Answer. To the best of my recollection, it was about $300,000. He proposed to give me bonds even then, when I knew what they were, to protect those out, and to save them from sale, and also to save the additional acceptances of the Secretary of War. I finally consented to take them.

Question. What further occurred in that interview?

Answer. Nothing more than his getting the bonds and bringing them to me, and taking our paper for them.

Question. He did not bring them that evening?

Answer. No, sir, but the next day.

Question. What time next day?

Answer. I cannot say what hour; some time during the day; time enough to take them to New York that evening.

Question. Where did he bring them to you?

Answer. At my room, at the same place.

Question. How many did he bring, and what bonds?

Answer. I think there were 387 bonds.

Question. What bonds were they?

Answer. To the best of my recollection they were Missouris.

Question. How many Missouris?

Answer. I cannot recollect.

Question. Tell as near as you can.

Answer. I do not know. I think they were Missouris, South Carolinas, and Floridas.

Question. How many Floridas?

Answer. To the best of my recollection there were 120 or 130.

Question. That made up the 387?

Answer. Yes, sir.

Question. What did you give him, if anything?

Answer. I gave him Russell, Majors & Waddell's paper. I took up the $150,000 note, and gave him one for $387,000.

Question. Were the coupons off or on those 387 bonds?

Answer. I think they were left on. I am not positive.

Question. Did any other paper pass between you?

Answer. Not upon that occasion. I may be mistaken; I may have given him a receipt; I do not now recollect. I think it probable I did give him a receipt, specifying the bonds of each class.

Question. Was there any agreement as to what disposition you should make of those bonds?

Answer. I was to hypothecate them.

Question. Any particular time mentioned?

Answer. It was agreed that they should be returned before the 4th of March; and if I was forced to allow them to be sacrificed, I was to return an equivalent amount of bonds of the same class.

Question. How came the 4th of March to be the limit fixed for their return?

Answer. It is all supposition on my part how he came to fix that day.

Question. Did *he* fix the 4th of March?

Answer. I think he did.

Question. Did you know why?

Answer. From his conversation I supposed it was because he was going out of office then.

Question. What did you do with those bonds—take them to New York?

Answer. Yes, sir.

Question. Did you take any other securities from here at that time?

Answer. I do not think I did upon that occasion. I cannot say positively.

Question. Did nothing occur between you and Bailey at that time in reference to interest, commissions, or payment.

Answer. Not a word.

Question. What did you do in New York with those bonds?

Answer. I hypothecated some of them. I could not use the Florida bonds at all.

Question. How many did you hypothecate?

Answer. I cannot answer that.

Question. According to the best of your recollection?

Answer. There were 120 or 130 of the Florida bonds I could not use. A portion of the South Carolina bonds were not hypothecated.

Question. How many did you hypothecate?

Answer. I suppose about two hundred.

Question. With whom did you hypothecate them?

Answer. I cannot tell you.

Question. Have you no means of knowing?

Answer. A portion of them were hypothecated with Lee, Higginson & Co., of Boston.

Question. How many with them?

Answer. I suppose about sixty.

Question. For what time?

Answer. I do not recollect. I recollect that the paper became due in January.

Question. Did they advance the money upon them to you?

Answer. Yes, sir, through Simpson.

Question. How much upon those sixty bonds?

Answer. Forty thousand dollars, less the discount upon the notes.

Question. What was done with the residue of the two hundred you hypothecated?

Answer. I cannot say.

Question. Have you no means of knowing?

Answer. Not now.

Question. Did you keep no account, which showed?

Answer. I kept none. Simpson kept the only account which was kept.

Question. What account was kept of these transactions?

Answer. I suppose Simpson had a list of sales when sold.

Question. Were regular entries made on books?

Answer. I think not.

Question. Upon what was the entry of these transactions made?

Answer. I do not think there was anything except a memorandum.

Question. Upon loose pieces of paper?

Answer. Yes, sir.

Question. Did you keep any account of your transactions with Bailey?

Answer. None.

Question. Did you make any entry of your transactions with Bailey?

Answer. No, sir.

Question. Did you direct no entries to be made of them upon your books?

Answer. I did not.

Question. How long have you been a business man?

Answer. Ever since I went into a store in 1828.

Question. Since that time have you been in business?

Answer. Yes, sir.

Question. And a partner in a banking house, among other things?

Answer. A partner in one, but I did not have anything to do with it?

Question. And you have now no means by which you can inform yourself who were the parties that received those two hundred bonds, except the sixty which Lee, Higginson & Co. received?

Answer. I have no means. I have a general impression of who some of the parties were with whom they were hypothecated.

Question. Who were they?

Answer. I think a portion of them were hypothecated through Wm. F. Coleman, of New York, with the United States Trust Company.

Question. How many?

Answer. I do not recollect.

Question. Were there forty?

Answer. I do not recollect. This was done through Coleman, at the request of Simpson. I know it only from hearsay or rumor.

Question. You hypothecated two hundred bonds, sixty of them with Lee, Higginson & Co.; now I want to inquire how many of the remaining one hundred and forty bonds Wm. F. Coleman negotiated with the Trust Company?

Answer. I think Coleman got $25,000 upon the bonds. I have had no account current from Simpson.

Question. Aside from those which Wm. F. Coleman negotiated, what became of those one hundred and forty bonds?

Answer. Some were negotiated through E. S. Darling & Co.

Question. How many?

Answer. I do not now remember.

Question. Who else?

Answer. Simpson negotiated some with J. T. Soutter, president of the Bank of the Republic, New York.

Question. How many did he leave with him?

Answer. I do not know the number of bonds; but I think he got $15,000 of money from him.

Question. Anybody else?

Answer. I think he got some from Duncan, Sherman & Co.

Question. How much; how many bonds?

Answer. I do not know.

Question. In all, if I understand you, you used at that time two hundred of those three hundred and eighty-seven bonds. What became of the Florida bonds?

Answer. I brought them back to Bailey.

Question. When?

Answer. I think it was early in October.

Question. That was the next month?

Answer. Yes, sir.

Question. Why?

Answer. I could not use them.

Question. Did you try to use them?
Answer. Yes, sir.
Question. With whom?
Answer. I cannot tell any particular party. There was no market for them.
Question. Why could you not use them?
Answer. They were worth nothing, I suppose.
Question. And you brought them back the next month?
Answer. I think it was early in October.
Question. What did you do with them?
Answer. I gave them to Bailey, and received other bonds in exchange.
Question. What did he give you in exchange?
Answer. To the best of my recollection he gave me North Carolina bonds.
Question. How many Florida bonds did you return to him?
Answer. Some one hundred and twenty thousand or one hundred and thirty thousand dollars' worth.
Question. And he delivered to you an equivalent amount of North Carolina bonds?
Answer. Yes, sir.
Question. At the same time that you returned those Florida bonds to him did you return anything else to him?
Answer. I think I returned some bonds of South Carolina.
Question. How many?
Answer. I cannot say.
Question. Did you return all the South Carolina bonds you did not succeed in using?
Answer. Yes, sir.
Question. And you cannot state to the committee the number of South Carolina bonds you returned?
Answer. I do not think any of the South Carolina bonds were used except those which Lee, Higginson & Co. bought.
Question. State the number of South Carolina bonds you returned?
Answer. I cannot.
Question. What did you receive in exchange for the South Carolina bonds you returned.
Answer. My impression is that I received the same that I did for the Florida bonds.
Question. North Carolina bonds?
Answer. Yes, sir.
Question. Where did you receive those?
Answer. I do not recollect whether at his rooms or mine.
Question. Was it at one or the other?
Answer. Yes, sir.
Question. Had you ever had any interview with Bailey up to that time except the three you have detailed?
Answer. I have not.
Question. Have you ever been in his office?
Answer. Never in my life.
Question. You never have seen a safe where those bonds were kept?
Answer. No, sir.

Question. Who suggested North Carolina bonds to be given in exchange?

Answer. I think I did.

Question. Did Bailey state to you what bonds he had that you could select from?

Answer. I do not think he did upon that occasion.

Question. You received from him then 120 or 130 North Carolina bonds in exchange for Florida bonds, and received an additional number of bonds for the South Carolina bonds you returned, but you cannot tell how many. Can you tell how much, in all, you returned to Bailey at that time?

Answer. I cannot. I only made the exchange of what I brought over from New York.

Question. What did you give him at that time, if anything?

Answer. I may have exchanged the receipts he held.

Question. And gave him no new paper?

Answer. No, sir.

Question. Was anything said as to commissions, interest, or compensation?

Answer. No, sir.

Question. Neither directly nor indirectly?

Answer. No, sir.

Question. What did you do with those bonds?

Answer. I carried them back to New York.

Question. What did you do with them?

Answer. They were used there to raise money, as I had raised money before.

Question. In the same way?

Answer. Yes, sir.

Question. By hypothecating them?

Answer. Yes, sir.

Question. Were any of them sold?

Answer. No, sir; they were hypothecated.

Question. Up to this time, October, none of them had been sold?

Answer. Some of the Missouris had been.

Question. Some of the original $150,000 of bonds?

Answer. Yes, sir.

Question. Were they sold to this Chatham bank, as we call it, upon the maturity of the note?

Answer. Yes, sir.

Question. There had been no bonds sold up to October, except those by this bank?

Answer. There were nothing but Missouris sold.

Question. You hypothecated these in October?

Answer. Yes, sir.

Question. When did you see Bailey next?

Answer. I think it was the 12th or 13th of December.

Question. This, then, if I understand you, is the first interview you had with Bailey after October?

Answer. The first personal interview.

Question. Did you receive letters from him before that?

Answer. I did, in the month of September, after I got the second lot of bonds.

Question. Is that the first time you received a note from him?

Answer. Yes, sir.

Question. Where did you receive it?

Answer. I do not recollect; I presume in New York.

Question. Where is it?

Answer. It may be with my papers in New York, but I may have torn it up. I do not recollect. I think it most likely I tore it up.

Question. How long a letter was it?

Answer. My recollection is it was short, urging me to be sure to take care of and return the bonds.

Question. Is that all you recollect about it?

Answer. That was the tenor of it.

Question. Did you receive any other letter from him up to December?

Answer. I think I received two or three notes of a corresponding character, urging me to take care of the bonds.

Question. And you received no other communication up to December?

Answer. No, sir.

Question. For what purpose did you come here in December?

Answer. I came here to get the privilege to sell those I had hypothecated, to save us from ruin, in consequence of the market going down, and to get further aid to take care of the acceptances of the War Department, and to make further arrangements with Bailey.

Question. What day did you come here?

Answer. I cannot state positively; about the 12th of December.

Question. What did you do first when you got here in reference to seeing Bailey?

Answer. I sent for him.

Question. Did he meet you?

Answer. He came to my room.

Question. What took place?

Answer. I told him the condition I was in—the danger of losing the stock—and my fear that they would be sold at a sacrifice on a declining market. I asked him if I could not sell them all, and buy in again after the market declined, as the best way to get them returned. We thought we could do so, with that and other resources we expected to command. I explained to him, in addition thereto, that there was some paper of the War Department maturing; that all our accounts had not been adjusted and allowed at the department; and if I did not protect my credit the credit of the War Department would suffer and be disgraced. I told him if I did not protect myself I could not take care of the bonds finally. He then told me if I would get the acceptances of the Secretary of War to the amount of the bonds I had already received, and the additional amount I required to protect the whole thing—our credit and all—he would give me an additional amount to do that thing with. I had suggested that the amount would be $350,000. I told him that $350,000 would enable me to protect the whole thing and get the bonds all back. By the way, I should say he proposed to give me an additional amount of bonds to extend the matter to the first of June, if I got the acceptances of the Secretary of War. I procured the acceptances.

Question. What further occurred between you and Bailey at that time?

Answer. Nothing that I know of pertinent to the case.

Question. I omitted to ask you whether the bonds you received in exchange for the Floridas and South Carolinas had at that time coupons on or off.

Answer. I think they were off.

Question. When were they taken off.

Answer. Before he gave them to me.

Question. By whom?

Answer. The bonds were brought to me with the coupons off.

Question. Was any remark made about it at the time?

Answer. He explained to me that he had taken them off so that if they were sold it would give us to the first of June to get the bonds back.

Question. That suggestion was never made until you came to exchange bonds with him?

Answer. I think that was the occasion.

Question. When this exchange was made $350,000 of the bonds had been negotiated by you, had they not?

Answer. I suppose about that amount.

Question. Did you ever exchange bonds with Bailey more than once?

Answer. That was all.

Question. Returning now to the December transaction, what did you do upon the termination of that interview between you and Bailey?

Answer. I secured acceptances of the Secretary of War, which were sufficient, with the amount I then had in my pocket.

Question. How many had you in your pocket?

Answer. I do not recollect; about $100,000.

Question. When had those bonds been given?

Answer. I think they were given in October; that is my impression.

Question. At the time you were on to exchange the bonds?

Answer. I do not recollect whether it was upon that occasion or not?

Question. How many in addition did you procure from the Secretary of War?

Answer. Over $700,000.

Question. What did you do with them?

Answer. I gave them to Bailey, and he gave me bonds which, with what I had, amounted to $870,000, and I gave him a receipt.

Question. What bonds did he give you?

Answer. I think most of them were North Carolinas; some of them were Missouris.

Question. How many in number?

Answer. Three hundred and thirty-three.

Question. Did Bailey tell you how long those Florida bonds had been there?

Answer. I do not think he did.

Question. Did he tell you how the department bought them?

Answer. Not then.

Question. When did he tell you that?

Answer. I heard him speaking of it in the prison; not in a private conversation with me, but speaking publicly, and not privately.

Question. What did he tell you as to the source of those Florida bonds?

Answer. My impression is that they bought them of Mr. Yulee.

Question. Did he say when?

Answer. No, sir; it was only a general conversation, not addressed to me.

Question. Did he say at what figure they bought them?

Answer. I do not think he did.

Question. Did he say how many they had of them in all?

Answer. My impression is that it was one hundred and thirty-two.

Question. Did he tell you how the bonds came to be purchased of Mr. Yulee?

Answer. He did not tell me that at all.

Question. Did you hear him state how they came to be purchased of Yulee?

Answer. I recollect hearing him talk about it, but I cannot explain exactly what he said. I heard him state in jail, in conversation with others, that he had had those bonds in New York to hypothecate and raise money on, but that he could not do it.

Question. You say you heard him say in the jail that those one hundred and thirty-two Florida bonds in the department were purchased from Yulee, and that he, before their purchase, had had them in New York, and had attempted to raise money on them by hypothecation or otherwise, and could not do it?

Answer. Yes, sir.

Question. Did he state to you how soon after he attempted to raise money upon them the department took them?

Answer. He did not.

Question. Did he state to you when they were purchased?

Answer. He did not. In his conversation he referred to a railroad in Florida.

Question. He said he was trying to raise money for a railroad?

Answer. Yes, sir.

Question. Were they railroad securities?

Answer. Yes, sir; my impression is that they were railroad bonds. I do not know whether they had the State guarantee or not.

Question. Do you know the name of that railroad?

Answer. The Fernandina railroad.

Question. Where was the receipt drawn which you gave Bailey for the bonds? I mean the last receipt you gave him.

Answer. It was drawn at his house, I presume.

Question. In December?

Answer. Yes, sir.

Question. Were you at his house?

Answer. I was.

Question. Where was his house?

Answer. Well, sir, I think it was on F street. I think he had rooms at the Lafayette House.

Question. Had you ever been in his rooms before?

Answer. On one occasion, which I referred to.

Question. Only once before?

Answer. That is all.

Question. Who drew the drafts and acceptances which you gave him at that time?

Answer. I did.

Question. Both the drafts and acceptances, leaving nothing in blank but the name of Mr. Floyd; or was it only the drafts you drew?

Answer. There was but one paper in all.

Question. The acceptance was one thing, the draft another thing?

Answer. I think I wrote the acceptances myself.

Question. At that time who held the matured acceptances of Governor Floyd?

Answer. They were held by various persons; they were floating. I merely had a list of the times of maturity.

Question. What did you do with that last batch of bonds?

Answer. I applied them, as I did the others, to raise money.

Question. Did you place any of them yourself, personally?

Answer. I think I gave twelve of those bonds to the Shoe and Leather Bank; that is all I sold personally.

Question. Did you place any yourself?

Answer. I sold twelve to the Shoe and Leather Bank; that was all; I did not place any others; I do not remember that I did.

Question. By whom were they placed? I speak now of the 333 bonds last received.

Answer. They were sold by different brokers.

Question. Do you mean that the whole 333 were sold without being placed previously?

Answer. They were all parted with on sale in the first instance.

Question. Do you know who bought them?

Answer. No, sir.

Question. How much did you receive for the 333 bonds?

Answer. That is more than I can tell you.

Question. As near as you can tell.

Answer. If I only knew the class of stocks I could give a more definite estimate of the value received for them; I suppose it was about $234,000.

Question. What was done with the money?

Answer. It was used in paying out debts.

Question. When were these 333 bonds sold?

Answer. Right away; as soon as I could get them upon the market.

Question. By what day?

Answer. I suppose by the 20th of December.

Question. Can you be more definite than that?

Answer. By the 22d; that was Saturday.

Question. Can you be more definite than that?

Answer. No, sir; I was arrested on Monday morning, and I had no more business to do after that.

Question. When you returned to New York with the 333 bonds, what other bonds had you remaining in your possession?

Answer. I had none.

Question. Do you mean that you had parted on sale with all the bonds you had received from Bailey previous to your coming here in December?

Answer. I think they were all parted with except those which were hypothecated.

Question. And you continued to make sale of these bonds down to the Saturday previous to the Monday on which you were arrested?

Answer. I do not think any were sold on Saturday, but up to that day; I am not certain that any were sold on that day; I think there were some sold.

Question. When did you first know that this matter was likely to be made public?

Answer. I knew it on the morning that I was arrested.

Question. How?

Answer. Mr. Smoot came over and told me it; it was in the papers, but I had not read it.

Question. Mr. Smoot is your partner?

Answer. Yes, sir.

Question. Was that the first intimation you had of it?

Answer. Yes, sir.

Question. That was on Monday morning?

Answer. Colonel Lea wrote me prior to that there was danger of there being an exposure; I think he wrote me on Friday.

Question. What did he write?

Answer. The condition Bailey was in, and the probability that he would expose the matter, and that I had better come on and see him.

Question. What time did you receive that letter?

Answer. I got it on Saturday.

Question. What time of day?

Answer. In the morning.

Question. How many bonds had you then on hand?

Answer. I do not recollect precisely; not many.

Question. Had you some?

Answer. Yes, sir.

Question. How many, according to your best recollection?

Answer. I think I had on hand, then, 25 or 30.

Question. Which bonds?

Answer. I do not recollect.

Question. Did you dispose of them during that day?

Answer. Mr. Simpson disposed of them during that day.

Question. What was done with the money you got for them?

Answer. He made payments, I think, that day; there was a little money left when I was arrested; I do not know what has been done with it; it was not in my name; it was in Simpson's name in the bank.

Question. How many of these bonds remain hypothecated? And I use that word now to distinguish it from parted with on sale.

Answer. I think there were but two lots.

Question. Which two lots?

Answer. The one with Lee, Higginson & Co., and one with the United States Trust Company.

Question. That is $100,000 in all?

Answer. About that.

Question. About $40,000 with the Trust Company, and $60,000 with Lee, Higginson & Co?

Answer. I think so.

Question. Do you know where any of the residue of those bonds are?

Answer. I do not.

Question. Have you no information about that?

Answer. I have not.

Question. Now, sir, will you explain to the committee how it was, if no reference was made to the coupons till October, that the coupons were procured and returned from so many of these bonds?

Answer. Mr. Bailey told me the danger of an exposure if the coupons were left on and sold upon them; I think he explained that to me at the time he told me what the bonds were; that was my second trip here.

Question. Did Bailey apprise you of the necessity of reserving the coupons at the time of your obtaining the second lot of bonds from him?

Answer. He did; he then told me I must be very sure to get them back before the 1st of January, and he would be very much obliged to me if I would get them back immediately; he said if they were hypothecated, that I must take them up and take off the coupons and then re-hypothecate them.

Question. But the coupons were not cut from them then?

Answer. No, sir.

Question. Did you procure the coupons from that second lot of bonds, and also from the first lot?

Answer. I procured the coupons from all those I had had.

Question. Including the $150,000 of bonds first received?

Answer. Yes, sir.

Question. How did you procure the coupons from the $150,000 of bonds?

Answer. It was done by taking up the loan, taking off the coupons, and then renewing the loan with the same parties or with somebody else.

Question. Were all the bonds previously parted with retired for the purpose of resuming the coupons?

Answer. I think they were.

Question. And then negotiated again?

Answer. Negotiated or sold.

Question. And when did you first make a return of any coupons to Bailey?

Answer. I think it was when I came back to exchange the Florida bonds.

Question. How many coupons did you give him then?

Answer. I do not recollect; some fifty, I believe.

Question. Did you give him the coupons of all the bonds you had previously received?

Answer. Not at that time.

Question. Did you, from time to time, give him the coupons upon all the bonds that you had received?

Answer. Yes, sir.

Question. When did you first receive bonds without coupons?

Answer. I am not certain that it was on my second trip. I think he gave me bonds in the second lot with coupons on, but I am not positive.

Question. Had the bonds you received in exchange for the Florida and North Carolina bonds the coupons on or off?

Answer. I think that was the first time he took the coupons off.

Question. And then the last lot you received had the coupons off?

Answer. Yes, sir.

Question. Were coupons procured from any bonds other than those you received from Bailey in order to take the place of those you had received from Bailey and had parted with?

Answer. No, sir; they were the identical ones I believe. That was my instruction, and I believe them to have been so. Simpson got them all back.

Question. When did you first become a contractor with the War Department?

Answer. In 1847 or 1848.

Question. Have you been such contractor from time to time since?

Answer. Every year.

Question. When did you first receive from any head of the War Department acceptances such as we have been speaking of?

Answer. I first received them from Mr. Floyd in 1858.

Question. What time in 1858?

Answer. I think it was in March.

Question. How long had you then known Governor Floyd?

Answer. I was introduced to Mr. Floyd in December, 1857.

Question. By whom?

Answer. I do not recollect.

Question. By Latham?

Answer. No, sir.

Question. Can you state by whom?

Answer. I am under the impression that one of my delegation went there with me.

Question. When did you first have any business transaction with Governor Floyd?

Answer. I had an interview with him in relation to a contract in December, 1859. I had interviews with him often, and as early as December, 1857.

Question. How soon after that did you become a contractor under the new contract?

Answer. I think the contract was concluded finally on the 16th of January.

Question. Is that the contract which subsists now?
Answer. No, sir.
Question. When did Mr. Floyd first give you an acceptance?
Answer. I think in the month of March, 1858.
Question. Where did it occur?
Answer. At the War Department.
Question. To what amount did Governor Floyd accept for you upon the first occasion?
Answer. I think it was $400,000.
Question. State the tenor of those drafts and acceptances.
Answer. They were conditional drafts upon our earnings under the contract.
Question. Were they for so much money, to be paid out of the first earnings?
Answer. I do not think any period of maturity was fixed. It was a draft against our first earnings.
Question. Was it accepted absolutely or conditionally?
Answer. I do not remember. I think there was no condition of acceptance. The draft itself was conditional, paying the money as we earned it.
Question. Do you know what you did with that $400,000 of acceptances?
Answer. I know what I did with a portion of it.
Question. What?
Answer. I discounted $100,000 with August Belmont, of New York. I think it was $100,000.
Question. What was done with the residue?
Answer. I discounted some with the Bank of the Republic.
Question. Were those acceptances numbered or lettered?
Answer. I do not recollect. I do not think they were.
Question. What account did you keep of them?
Answer. I kept a memorandum of them as though they were our own notes.
Question. Did you enter it in your books?
Answer. Yes, sir; in our own books at home.
Question. Where?
Answer. At Leavenworth, in Kansas.
Question. Do you keep a regular set of books there?
Answer. Yes, sir.
Question. Was there any entry made of it in books elsewhere?
Answer. Not by me. I presume the War Department kept an account.
Question. Did your firm keep an account of all the acceptances given you by Governor Floyd?
Answer. They kept an account only of those we used. Those not used I always had in my own possession. They were received and drawn payable at the Bank of the Republic.
Question. All of them?
Answer. Yes, sir; we have taken care of them invariably ourselves.
Question. To what amount does your account show that you have used the acceptances of Governor Floyd in all?

Answer. I suppose it shows several millions.

Question. State as nearly as you can, of your own knowledge and recollection, the amount of acceptances of Governor Floyd shown by that account to have been used by you?

Answer. I have got but an idea about it. It was very large; I cannot tell how large; I believe it exceeds $3,000,000.

Question. Does it not exceed four millions?

Answer. I do not recollect.

Question. Does it not exceed five millions?

Answer. I judge not. It is all impression upon my part.

Question. Can you state that you have not used his acceptances to an amount exceeding $6,000,000?

Answer. I do not think I have.

Question. How much less than six millions will you say was the amount?

Answer. I will not fix the amount; I know it was very large; I know it was millions.

Question. Will you fix any amount short of six millions which you can say covers it?

Answer. I do not believe it reaches four millions.

Question. I ask you whether you can name any sum short of $6,000,000, which you say will cover the amount you have used of Governor Floyd's acceptances?

Answer. I say I do not believe it will reach four millions.

Question. Will you state what amount of acceptances you have received from Governor Floyd and not used?

Answer. I cannot tell you. I have got some, but how many I do not know; I do not think the amount is very large.

Question. Have you received any acceptances from Governor Floyd which you have not used, aside from those which now remain in your possession?

Answer. No, sir.

Question. What is the amount, as near as you can state it, of Governor Floyd's acceptances remaining unused within your control?

Answer. I think it is less than $200,000.

Question. Has Governor Floyd given you any acceptances since the occasion, in December, when you procured them to be given to Bailey?

Answer. No, sir. I have not seen him or conferred with him in any way since.

Question. When you delivered the $870,000 of acceptances to Bailey, had you, in your hands, acceptances of anything like the amount of $200,000 besides?

Answer. I had not; not here.

Question. Where were they?

Answer. In New York and St. Louis.

Question. Can you name any amount of money which you say now is due upon these contracts?

Answer. I cannot; but I believe the trains are not all in.

Question. Can you say that there is one cent due?

Answer. I believe there is.

Question. You cannot say positively that anything is due; you believe there is, but you do not know how much?

Answer. If our trains are all in, and our accounts settled, I do not know it.

Question. When does your last contract expire?

Answer. Next December—on the last day of 1861.

Question. You know, I suppose, about what the *maximum* of your earnings under that contract will be?

Answer. That will be governed by circumstances.

Question. Do you know the range within which the *maximum* of your earnings will be?

Answer. I do.

Question. Will you state the *maximum* of unearned money to accrue by the last of December, 1861?

Answer. As near as I can state it, it is five or six hundred thousand dollars.

Question. Can you state to the committee to what amount you have paid the acceptances of Governor Floyd?

Answer. I cannot.

Question. Can you state to the committee within half a million of dollars the amount of acceptances of Governor Floyd which you have paid?

Answer. No, sir; I cannot. We have certainly paid upwards of $3,000,000, and probably $3,500,000, upon Governor Floyd's acceptances, and cancelled them, or retired them.

Question. Does $3,500,000 cover the amount?

Answer. I cannot say positively.

Question. Will you name a sum which you can be positive does cover the amount?

Answer. I am sure we have paid and cancelled $2,000,000.

Question. Are you sure you have paid and cancelled three millions?

Answer. Well, I am pretty confident in my own mind that we have.

Question. Can you state any amount larger than that which you are confident in your own mind was paid and cancelled?

Answer. No, sir.

Question. Did you pay and cancel Governor Floyd's acceptances to an amount larger, at the outside, than $3,500,000?

Answer. I think three and a half millions will cover the sum. I am very confident in my own mind that it will.

Question. Do you mean to say that, aside from the acceptances used, and aside from the $200,000 of acceptances still remaining in your possession, Governor Floyd gave you acceptances?

Answer. Yes, sir.

Question. What was done with those?

Answer. I returned them unused to the department, and they were cancelled.

Question. To what amount in all, as near as you can state?

Answer. I think they must exceed $200,000.

Question. How much would they exceed $200,000?

Answer. I cannot say.

Question. As near as you can?

Answer. I think they exceeded $250,000.

Question. The acceptances which you returned to the department unused were acceptances which had matured in your pocket?

Answer. Yes, sir.

Question. Where are the two or three million dollars of acceptances which Russell, Majors & Waddell have retired?

Answer. I suppose they are at home.

Question. In whose possession do you suppose they are?

Answer. At our office in Leavenworth.

Question. And who is the partner in charge there?

Answer. Majors, and Waddell, occasionally.

Question. And all that have been retired are there as vouchers?

Answer. I suppose they are.

Question. Have you paid any of Governor Floyd's acceptances since the 12th of December, 1860?

Answer. Yes, sir.

Question. To what amount?

Answer. I do not know. I should think to the amount of sixty or eighty thousand dollars.

Question. Will that cover it?

Answer. I think it will.

Question. Where are those you have paid since the 12th December?

Answer. I cannot tell you. Simpson has them among his vouchers to settle with the firm.

Question. That was no part of the $200,000 you had in your possession?

Answer. No, sir.

Question. To whom were those sixty or eighty thousand dollars of payments made?

Answer. I do not know; they are floating in the market.

Question. How do you know they were paid to the amount of sixty or eighty thousand dollars?

Answer. Simpson had a list of all payments lying before him on his desk, and I saw it every day. I saw some of the paper which was taken up afterwards.

Question. Have you in your possession or under your control any paid acceptances of Governor Floyd?

Answer. I cannot say that they are in my possession. They were when I was arrested.

Question. Are they in New York and in Washington?

Answer. Yes, sir.

Question. What compensation was Bailey to have in this transaction?

Answer. Nothing in the world from me.

Question. What was Bailey's compensation?

Answer. Nothing was said about it by me to Bailey or by him to me.

Question. What was the compensation really that Bailey was to have?

Answer. Nothing in the world.

Question. You had no expectation of giving him any equivalent or present?

Answer. I may have had a reservation in my own mind, after the thing was got through with; nothing was said about it.

Question. You think you had it in your own mind though?

Answer. I think it likely I had a kind prompting to him at the time, as the man was kind to me. I thought so on the first occasion, but towards the latter part of the matter I did not have it.

Question. Did you make Bailey at any time any present?

Answer. No, sir.

Question. Have you never made him any present?

Answer. Nothing that I recollect, and nobody made him any present on my account.

Question. Has he not received anything?

Answer. No, sir.

Question. Is he not going to receive anything on your account?

Answer. No, sir.

By Mr. Morris:

Question. Did you ever, directly or indirectly, pay to any person any consideration, or make to any person any present, for services rendered to you connected with your business with the War Department?

The witness declined to answer the question, and asked permission to consult with his counsel before giving his final decision.

The committee granted his request, and thereupon the examination of the witness was suspended for the present.

Wednesday, *January* 23, 1861.

Frederick P. James sworn.

Examination by the chairman.

Question. Where do you reside and what is your business?

Answer. I reside in New York city and am a banker.

Question. Have you ever seen a letter written by the Secretary of War, John B. Floyd, relating to acceptances made by him in favor of Russell, Majors & Waddell?

Answer. I cannot say positively whether I have seen it or not.

Question. What do you know about its contents?

Answer. I have been told of its contents.

Question. By whom?

Answer. By James T. Soutter.

Question. Please tell the committee what he said to you relating to the contents of said letter, and where that conversation took place?

Answer. The conversation took place the morning after there was a publication in the papers that the Bank of the Republic had some of the Indian fund stolen bonds. He said he had a draft of $15,000 which was protested, and the only one he had; that with that draft he had a letter from the Secretary of War, in which the Secretary said he had issued, or was about to issue, acceptances in favor of Russell, Majors & Waddell, but that at no time should he issue those acceptances to exceed one-half of the amount which he knew of his own knowledge was actually due to the parties for services already performed.

Question. Had you any further conversation at the time referred to by you, or at any other time, with Mr. Soutter, in reference to the bonds alleged to have been fraudulently abstracted from the Interior Department? and if so, please give us the whole of those conversations.

Answer. He said that the Bank of the Republic had never had one of these bonds, never had loaned upon them, nor had received one of them, to the best of his knowledge; that he (Mr. Soutter) was of the impression that he once loaned $15,000 to a man, on eighteen of them, and that the man had paid the loan, and that he was of the impression that that was all he had ever seen or known of the bonds, either directly or indirectly; that he could not think of any other bonds he had had which related to this Indian trust fund.

Question. State whether he gave you the name of the person from whom he received those eighteen bonds?

Answer. I think he said it was Simpson—a man I never had heard of before in connexion with business.

Question. Did he say anything to you, in any conversation you had with him, whether he had ever seen or held any other acceptances except the ones you have referred to, made by the Secretary of War, John B. Floyd, in favor of Russell, Majors & Waddell?

Answer. I think he said he had had some before, but that they had been paid always.

Question. Did you understand Mr. Soutter to say, in that conversation you had with him, that he held the acceptance referred to in his own right, or for the Bank of the Republic?

Answer. He said positively it was not for the Bank of the Republic; but whether it was his individually, or belonged to the people he was dealing with, he did not say. He said positively that the Bank of the Republic had none of the stolen bonds, or of the acceptances of the Secretary of War.

Question. Do you know where any of the abstracted bonds are? And if so, who holds them?

Answer. I think we have had them pass through our hands, and we know whom we purchased them for. We purchased some bonds, but I do not know whether they were any of the abstracted ones or not, though some of them bore the same numbers, for we have the best reason to believe that the numbers were not correctly published. We purchased of Clark, Dodge & Co. ten North Carolina bonds, numbering from 226 to 235 inclusive, and of those numbers 234 and 235 are advertised as being stolen bonds.

By Mr. Thomas:

Question. When were those bonds issued?

Answer. I do not recollect.

Question. Did those bonds have the coupons on?

Answer. My impression is that they had the coupons on. We also purchased three Missouri bonds, the numbers of which—1823, 1632, and 1631—were among those advertised.

By Mr. Morris:

Question. Had they the January coupons on?

Answer. We purchased five bonds, three of which came in with the coupons off. I do not know whether they were these three or not.

By Mr. Case:

Question. What was the date of that purchase?

Answer. The 14th of December, 1860.

By Mr. Morris:

Question. Whom do you mean when you say *we* purchased?

Answer. F. P. James & Co.

Question. Did you purchase the bonds to which you have referred for yourselves or for other persons?

Answer. We purchased them for the Passaic County Bank of New Jersey—that is, the three last ones.

Question. Did you ever hold any of the orders drawn by Russell, Majors & Waddell upon the Secretary of War, and accepted by him?

Answer. No, sir; we always refused to take them.

Question. Do you know of any other person than Mr. Simpson who holds any of those orders?

Answer. I do not, of my own knowledge; I cannot say positively, but I have heard that there is about a hundred thousand dollars of them held by the different banks in Dover, New Hampshire. One notary last night told me that he had protested $200,000 of those War Department drafts.

Question. Can you give me the names of those banks?

Answer. I cannot; one was a savings bank in Dover.

Question. Give the name of the notary who protested $200,000 of those acceptances?

Answer. I cannot recollect; he is the notary for the Metropolitan, and, I think, for the Continental Bank of New York; he is here in town.

Question. Have you any other knowledge, directly or indirectly, other than that you have communicated to the committee, relative to the bonds and acceptances? If so, please communicate it to the committee.

Answer. I do not know of anything in particular; all these protested bonds are recorded in the different notary's books in New York; they have a record of every name, indorser, and everything of that kind.

William H. Russell reappeared.

Mr. Morris. Mr. Russell, the committee was careful, before administering the oath to you, to apprise you that if you took the oath and testified, you must do so voluntarily and entirely at your own election; that you were not required by the House or the committee to answer any question or to make any statement whatever touching the matter whereof the committee is charged to inquire. You declared your desire to testify on those terms; we deem it fair now to repeat the same caution; your examination may now be waived, if you desire, wholly or in such part as you choose; and in the event of your so electing, any or all parts of your evidence will be expunged and held for naught.

In order the more fully to renew the admonition heretofore given you as to your rights, we call your attention to the following section of an act of Congress that you may determine whether you are willing to testify further on the same terms as heretofore.

There was then handed to the witness an act of Congress approved January 24, 1857, entitled "An act more effectually to enforce the attendance of witnesses on the summons of either house of Congress, and to compel them to discover testimony."

After reading the same, the witnessed answered as follows:

Answer. I am no lawyer, and know nothing about my rights—not enough to protect myself or take care of myself in this case; and as I asked the other day, I now ask the privilege of consulting my counsel about it.

Question. State to the committee what your decision is?

Answer. I would like time to confer with my counsel, to suggest to him what you have laid before me.

Question. How long a time do you desire?

Answer. Until to-morrow morning.

Mr. Conkling. You understand the meaning and effect of the section to which you have been referred, do you not?

Answer. Yes, sir, generally.

Question. You did understand it before reading it now, did you not?

Answer. Yes, sir, in general.

Question. You understood it before being examined in the first instance, and had had it all explained before appearing before the committee, had you not?

Answer. Yes, sir.

[The witness then desired that the committee would give him time to consult his counsel to decide upon the matter. The committee informed the witness that he could have such time as suited his convenience; whereupon the witness suggested to-morrow morning, and that time was granted him.]

Ashton S. H. White sworn.

Examination by the chairman.

Question. Are you a clerk in the Indian bureau?

Answer. I am.

Question. Do you know anything in regard to the Indian trust fund bonds, or have you heretofore known anything in regard to them?

Answer. Nothing; except that I knew they were in existence, and I have seen some of them.

Question. Did you ever have them in your charge?

Answer. Never.

Question. Are you familiar with the description of the bonds?
Answer. I cannot say that I am; I have never seen them but once.

By Mr. CASE:

Question. Are you the predecessor of Mr. Godard Bailey?
Answer. I am; he occupies the same desk I did, but these bonds never were in the custody of any officer in the office of the Secretary of the Interior until Mr. Bailey was appointed.
Question. In what department were they held previous to that?
Answer. In the Indian office.
Question. What particular officer or clerk had them in charge?
Answer. They were taken from the custody, in the Indian office, of a clerk named Henry Beard.
Question. What office did he hold there?
Answer. He held the office of chief of the finance division in the Indian office.
Question. And always, up to that time, the bonds had been held by that officer?
Answer. They were in the custody of the Commissioner of Indian Affairs, Mr. Beard being his subordinate.
Question. When Bailey was appointed your successor the additional duty of the custody of those bonds was imposed upon him by Secretary Thompson?
Answer. Yes, sir; by giving to him the trust fund account to settle.
Question. For what reason?
Answer. Prior to that time there had been but one disbursing clerk for the whole Department of the Interior. At the time of Bailey's appointment three disbursing clerks were appointed, and this additional duty of the custody of those bonds, and the Indian trust fund account, was given to Mr. Bailey. I presumed it was done with the view to give him the additional amount of $200 per annum, making his salary $2,000. I received but $1,800.

FRIDAY, *January* 25, 1861.

GEORGE W. RIGGS recalled.

Examination by Mr. Harris.

Question. Has your house been in the habit of purchasing all the bonds for the government which they have purchased?
Answer. For the Indian bureau, on the occasion of this investment; I do not know what other bonds the government has purchased recently.
Question. Did you purchase all the bonds for the Indian fund on behalf of the Interior Department?
Answer. I cannot say certainly, but I believe they nearly all passed through my hands.
Question. Do you know what amount, in all, you purchased for the department on this occasion?

Answer. I could not answer without reference to my books.

Question. About what?

Answer. I cannot tell; a very large sum.

Question. Two or three millions?

Answer. Oh, no; not that amount. I think not above $1,000,000.

Question. You stated in your former examination that, among others, you purchased Florida bonds: will you be good enough to state what class of bonds they were—whether for railroad, or for what purposes?

Answer. They were bonds issued, I think, to defray the expenses of Indian hostilities in that State.

Question. Were they all of that class?

Answer. Yes, sir. I sold no railroad securities to the department. In my purchases for that fund were included some Tennessee railroad bonds, guaranteed by that State; but when I offered them to the department, Secretary Thompson told me he would take nothing except clear State bonds. I therefore withdrew those bonds, and sold them in New York at my own loss of commission.

Question. Are you able to state at what rate the Florida bonds which were accepted by the department were purchased by you?

Answer. They were purchased, I think, at par. They were purchased, according to my recollection, from the governor and treasurer of the State. We had negotiations and correspondence with the governor of the State on the subject.

I presume your question is asked for the purpose of finding out whether I purchased bonds of the railroads guaranteed by the internal improvement fund of the State for the government. If that be the object, I will state that I never purchased any of those bonds which were received by the department, but that, on the contrary, such bonds were peremptorily refused by Mr. Thompson. He would not touch them. The bonds bought by me, which were received by the department, came direct to me from the State of Florida, in pursuance of correspondence which we had with the governor and treasurer of that State. Some of the checks for the payment of the money were drawn by the treasurer. Some checks were remitted to the governor. They were seven per cent. bonds, purchased at par, issued in payment of Indian hostilities, which they claimed the United States would eventually have to pay. My understanding was, that an appropriation to be made by the United States would be used in payment of the bonds. When applications were made to Mr. Thompson to purchase bonds for the Indian fund, he referred them to me as his broker. He refused to have anything to do with the negotiations for the purchases himself, but referred all applicants to me.

Question. Do I understand you to say that you purchased these Florida bonds of the governor and State treasurer of that State?

Answer. I purchased them, as I understood, direct from the State, accounting to the State treasurer for the money.

Question. Who delivered them to you?

Answer. I could not tell without referring to my books. I think Mr. Austin, the State treasurer, delivered some of them to me, and some were furnished by the governor.

Question. Did the bonds show upon their face that they were issued by the State of Florida in payment of expenses which that State alleged were incurred growing out of Indian hostilities?

Answer. I do not remember. You would have to refer to the bonds themselves for that.

Question. Do you remember what you paid for the other bonds that you purchased.

Answer. I do not. I could ascertain by reference to my books. In this instance I think the governor of Florida told me that he could not or would not sell the bonds below par.

WILLIAM H. RUSSELL appeared before the committee, and requested, before answering definitely the question propounded to him by the committee when he was last before them, he should be allowed the presence of counsel to consult with from time to time as occasion might require. By that means the committee would be able to proceed much more rapidly with his examination. As he had previously stated, he was no lawyer, and did not understand his rights as a witness, having never been before any court or jury as a witness.

The CHAIRMAN said the question propounded to the witness when last before the committee related to but a single point, as to whether the witness desired the evidence given before them by him to become a part of their record or be stricken out, and as to whether he elected that his examination should proceed further. The committee wished the witness to answer that question if he was prepared to do so, and also to state the object for which he desired the presence of counsel.

The WITNESS replied he was willing that his examination should proceed, and that he desired the presence of counsel to advise him from time to time whether questions asked by the committee in the progress of the examination were pertinent and proper. He had prepared a written answer to the question submitted by the committee when he was last before them which he asked to have placed upon record, which answer he then handed to and left with the committee.

The committee then deferred further action as to Mr. Russell.

WEDNESDAY, *January* 30, 1861.

HENRY BEARD recalled.

Examination by the chairman.

Question. I see that in abstract B, furnished to the committee by the Interior Department, embracing the list of missing bonds, that the number is put down at 872. As Russell only received from Bailey 870 bonds, and one was handed to Mr. Fitch, of Indiana, and all the remainder of the bonds are on hand, please explain to the committee how it occurred that 872 bonds were embraced in the abstract?

Answer. In the advertisement 871 bonds were embraced. The Indiana bond, handed to Mr. Fitch, as stated, was not embraced in the list. It occurred in this way: it needed only 143 Tennessee bonds to complete the 870 missing, but our office book or list of bonds, prepared by Mr. Bailey, indicated 144 as missing. The Secretary directed us to include all of the 144 bonds, as at that time some uncertainty was felt as to whether there might not be more than 870 missing. The advertisement was prepared in haste, and before the full investigation by Lammond, Williamson, and myself, was completed. The inaccuracy is in the advertisement and list prepared.

Question. State whether any of the stocks, bonds, or securities held in the Interior Department for the benefit of certain Indian tribes had any marks, designations, or assignments thereon when you delivered them to Bailey; and if so, what ones, and when purchased?

Answer. There was a little over two millions of stock in the chest in 1853, when I took charge of it. It consisted largely of stocks which had been assigned by the Secretary of War to the Secretary of the Interior for the time being—probably as far back as 1849. Another large portion of stocks consisted of certificates, which had been issued to the Secretary of the Interior for the time being, the interest of which was payable by drafts on the State treasurer or other State officers. All the coupon bonds contained in the chest had, upon the backs thereof, the indorsement of the Secretary of War, with the exception of the Virginia coupon stocks. The United States stock fell within the first two classes I have mentioned. A very considerable portion of the Virginia stock was coupon bonds. Some time during that summer a portion of those coupon bonds were indorsed in red ink, with the name of the tribe to which they belonged. I will state that in the summer of 1853 a considerable portion of the United States stock fell due, and $105,000 of Tennessee five per cent. stocks for the Wyandotte Indians was substituted for a large proportion of such stock; and in October $100,000 of Missouri six per cent. coupon bonds were purchased. These together, making $205,000, were coupon stock. I am of the impression that a portion of the Tennessee five per cent. stock was indorsed with the name of the tribe to which they were assigned. The Missouri stock was not indorsed. We could not do it, because it was held in fractional portions by the different tribes. In 1857, when I delivered up the chest, those Tennessee stocks were there, and the Missouri stocks were there. I understand that the $105,000 Tennessee five per cent. stocks to which I have referred have been delivered to the Wyandotte Indians, and receipted for by them; and from an examination made to-day I am fully satisfied that the $100,000 of Missouri six per cent. bonds purchased in 1853 are now in the safe. The result is, referring to my former testimony, that the stocks now in the safe are substantially the same stocks that were there in 1853, except so far as the same have fallen due and been redeemed, or others have been exchanged for other stock of the same State. None of those bonds have been abstracted, but all the abstraction has been confined to bonds lately purchased. The $3,000 of Arkansas bonds have been on hand a long time, and have the assignment of the Secretary of War to the Secretary of the Interior upon the back. All the Maryland stocks are certificates, the interest on which is payable by drafts upon the State treasury, and were issued, I think, to the Secretary of the Interior for the time being. $183,000 of Kentucky five per cent. bonds are all indorsed upon the back by the Secretary of War to the Secretary of the Interior for the time being. The same is true of $70,000 of Indiana stock, and of $250,000 of Tennessee five per cent. certificates. $145,000 of the Tennessee five per cents. were coupon bonds. I think some of these were indorsed with the name of the tribe, but not otherwise. According to my recollection, we indorsed the Wyandotte bonds, and none others. I think they were $150,000. I think they were the bonds delivered to the tribes afterwards. $63,000 of Missouri five per cents. were indorsed by the Secretary of War. All the United States certificates and coupon bonds were indorsed in the same manner. I cannot tell what amount were certificate and what amount were coupons. There were $157,000; a part issued to the Secretary of the Interior for the time being; a part were coupon stock, and all the coupon stocks had the indorsement upon them. The Virginia stocks consisted partly of certificates and partly of coupon bonds. Some of them had no indorsement on whatever, but I am under the impression that part of them had. The certificates, of course, had none. We have them all in the safe now, with the exception that some of the Chesapeake and Ohio canal bonds have been surrendered to the treasurer, who issued certificates for them. I cannot remember about the Michigan stock. There were $64,000 of them, and I think they were indorsed upon the back by the Secretary of War. $100,000 of Missouri six per cent. coupon bonds had no indorsement on whatever. They were purchased in 1853 by Secretary McClelland.

Question. State to the committee more definitely than you have what stocks, certificates, or other securities you find in the safe at this time which were there when you delivered over that safe to Mr. Bailey.

Answer. The result is obtained by subtraction. There were $1,993,741 82, less 105,000 of Wyandotte bonds delivered to the Wyandotte Indians, also less $125,000 of Tennessee five per cent. certificates, which fell due in the meantime, and in some manner had been redeemed—making $230,000—which would leave in the chest $1,763,741 82, which was substantially there at that time.

Question. State more definitely than you have what stocks, bonds, or securities were in the safe at the time you delivered it to Bailey upon which there was no indorsement whatever?

Answer. There were $100,000 of Missouri six per cent. coupon bonds, and at least $40,000 of Tennessee five per cent. coupon bonds, which had no indorsement whatever upon them. There were also $168,000 of Wheeling city bonds, guaranteed by the State of Virginia, which had no indorsement on. A very considerable portion of the Chesapeake and Ohio canal stock was indorsed, but I cannot state here what portion was indorsed and what not. Some of these stocks were purchased by Secretary McClelland, and some by Secretary Stewart, as appears by the books.

MONDAY, *February* 4, 1861.

Hon. J. P. BENJAMIN sworn.

Examination by Mr. Morris.

Question. Have you been employed heretofore, and if so, when, by Duncan, Sherman & Co. as an attorney to ascertain for them whether drafts drawn by Russell, Majors & Waddell on the late Secretary of War, John B. Floyd, and accepted by him, were legal?

Answer. I was written to by an intimate friend, who is their attorney in New York, asking my opinion upon that subject. I was not employed by them directly, nor did I receive any fee for my services.

Question. Did you consult with any of the government officers with reference to those acceptances; and if so, what was said?

Answer. In the letter I received it was stated that those drafts were offered for negotiation on the assurance that they were issued with the approbation of the President and the Attorney General. I called upon the President, therefore, and submitted the inquiry to him. He said he knew nothing about the matter; that they had been issued without any knowledge of his; that he did not know by virtue of what law they were issued; but that I might rely, if Mr. Floyd had issued them, he had done so by virtue of law, and that I had better apply to him to ascertain from him by virtue of what law he was acting; he was confident that Floyd would satisfy me fully. I then called upon Secretary Floyd and inquired of him. He informed me that the matter had not been submitted to the Attorney General, as that letter stated, and that the drafts were issued in virtue of a long established custom of the office, and that he was not aware of any law actually authorizing their issue, but that he would inquire into it. He said the acceptances were issued in favor of those gentlemen only after he had ascertained that the trains for transportation, which they had contracted to send from St. Louis to Utah, had actually started on their way; that the payments were to be made, under the contract, in instalments, as the trains arrived at different points; and that, having received intelligence of the actual departure of the trains, he had accepted in advance of the arrival at the intermediate point, having a certainty that they would arrive; and actuated by a desire to facilitate the operations of gentlemen who had undertaken to perform the contract at a time when it was exceedingly difficult to have the work done, and when the government was not in funds to advance for services it required. I suggested to him that I thought he was acting imprudently; that if any accident should happen to those trains, whether by attacks by Indians or any other cause, and they should fail to arrive, it would be impossible for him to pay the acceptances upon intelligence of that fact; and that that would give good reason for complaints and investigations which would be injurious to him; and I urged upon him that he should discontinue the practice. Two days afterwards I received a note from him informing me that he was obliged for the frank statement I had made to him, and that upon reflection he had determined that he would accept no more. I communicated that to my correspondent.

Question. At what time did you have that conversation with the President and Secretary of War?

Answer. My memory of dates is very bad; it was about a year ago I should think, possibly eighteen months ago.

Question. Fix the time as near as you can.

Answer. It was during the first session of this Congress.

Question. Have you detailed all the conversation you had with the President, Secretary of War, or any other officer, upon the subject of the acceptances to which you have referred?

Answer. I have detailed everything I remember upon the subject.

WEDNESDAY, *February* 6, 1861.

WM. R. DRINKARD recalled.

Examination by Mr. Morris.

Question. What has been the general custom of the War Department in reference to the acceptance of drafts of persons who hold contracts from the War Department?

Answer. I do not know that there is any custom, except that which has prevailed during this administration. I do not know that there was any other outside of that.

Question. Do you know whether any other Secretary of War than Mr. Floyd has ever issued acceptances to persons holding contracts with the War Department?

Answer. I do not.

Question. Then, your answer is, if I understand you correctly, that he was the first Secretary of War who issued acceptances?

Answer. So far as I have any knowledge.

RICHARD B. IRWIN recalled.

Examination by Mr. Morris.

Question. Has any general custom prevailed in the War Department other than that which has prevailed during the present administration in making acceptances for parties who hold contracts from that department?

Answer. I have never known or heard of any such acceptances being given, except by Secretary Floyd.

Question. Please give to the committee such information as you have in your possession pertaining to the amount of outstanding acceptances made by the late Secretary of War, John B. Floyd, for Russell, Majors & Waddell, and also such further information as you possess relating to the amount, dates, and numbers of acceptances which the War Department have been notified are held by corporations and individuals, giving the names of the individuals and corporations holding them.

Answer. I have not the dates, but only the numbers here. A large number of drafts having been accepted with blank months to run, I am, of course, unable to fix the maximum amount; but I have endeavored to fix the minimum amount that can be now outstanding as follows: The drafts shown by the Register to have matured on and after the 28th of September, 1860, when the first drafts of which we have notice of protest fell due, is $510,000. To these add the amount accepted, with blank months to run, since the 1st of January, 1860, the first acceptance of which was on the 12th of June, $795,000, and the total is $1,305,000. Adding the amount of unregistered drafts shown me by the committee, $798,000, makes the grand total of $2,103,000, of which there are held as follows:

By the Department of the Interior		$870,000
By private parties, to wit:		
By Pierce & Bacon, of Boston—		
No. E. J	$20,000	
E. O	20,000	
8	10,000	
33	15,000	
unknown	195,000	
		$260,000
By Hide and Leather Bank of Boston—		
No. unknown		10,000
By Shoe and Leather Bank, New York—		
No. unknown		50,000
By Solon Humphrey, New York—		
No. 61	10,000	
63	10,000	
		20,000
By Western Bank of Missouri—		
No. unknown		10,000
By Merchants' Bank of St. Louis—		
No. unknown		40,000
By Union Bank of Missouri—		
No. 1	10,000	
9	5,000	
		15,000
By Bank of State of Missouri—		
No. E. N	5,000	
E. P	10,000	
unknown	50,000	
E. H	10,000	
E. J	10,000	
		85,000
By Boatman's Saving Bank, St. Louis—		
No. 13	25,000	
17	10,000	
		35,000
By North St. Louis Saving Institution, St. Louis—		
No. 36		15,000
By Branch Bank of Louisville, Paducah, Ky—		
No. 25	10,000	
56	10,000	
		20,000
By South Berwick Bank, North Carolina—		
No. 119		15,000
Making total in hands of private parties		575,000
Adding amount held by Interior Department		870,000
Makes a total of		1,445,000

Question. Do I understand your answer to be, that this $1,445,000 is the amount of outstanding acceptances in the hands of private parties and corporations of which the department has had information?

Answer. It is.

Question. May there not be other outstanding acceptances, of which the department has had no information?

Answer. There may of course be other outstanding acceptances, of the whereabouts of which the department has no information.

Question. Have you in your possession a letter addressed by R. A. Barnes, president of the Bank of the State of Missouri, to the present Secretary of War, Hon. J. Holt, relating to acceptances of Governor Floyd? If so, read it to the committee.

Answer. I have; and it reads as follows:

"BANK OF THE STATE OF MISSOURI,
"*St. Louis, January* 24, 1861.

"DEAR SIR: I embrace the earliest opportunity, after your confirmation as Secretary of War, to notify you that this bank holds the unconditional acceptances of the Hon. John B. Floyd, Secretary of War, to the amount of $85,000, now past due, as per memorandum herewith.

"We commenced taking these bills in May, 1858, at the earnest request of the Secretary of War, contained in his letter of the 5th of May, 1858, as per copy, which I annex; and, in the summer of 1859, requiring further evidence, Colonel Drinkard addressed a letter under date of September 7, 1859, a copy of which we also send, as well as an attested copy of the letter of John B. Floyd, Secretary of War, to J. T. Soutter, esq., president of the Bank of the Republic, New York, of which we also send you a copy.

"The drafts we hold are all drawn against specified contracts; and when the first protest occurred, on the 28th of September last, I went to Washington, had two interviews with Secretary Floyd, in which he told me to make myself perfectly easy on the subject; that not an acceptance had been given except to facilitate the fulfilment of an actual contract; that a memorandum account of every acceptance issued had been kept; that the contracts had been performed, or were in the course of performance; that he kept a large percentage back from Russell, Majors & Waddell, which would always make the government safe; and that while he could not advance the money, if Russell, Majors & Waddell did not make arrangements to take up the paper then under protest, and pay the others as they became due, he would apply their earnings, as fast as they became due, to the payment of the acceptances himself.

"Respectfully,

"R. A. BARNES, *President*.

"Hon. J. HOLT,
"*Secretary of War, Washington City, D. C.*"

Question. Have you in your possession the letter of Colonel Drinkard, chief clerk in the War Department, to which reference has been made by Mr. Barnes in his letter?

Answer. A copy of that letter was enclosed; it has already been communicated to the committee by the department.

Question. You stated in your former testimony that $840,000 of acceptances had been returned to the War Department. Please state more definitely than you have heretofore by whom they were so returned.

Answer. So far as I recollect, they were returned by Mr. Russell himself, with the exception of a few which we received from Samuel & Allen, of St. Louis.

Question. Did any of the acceptances returned by Russell bear any evidence of having been used by him?

Answer. They were drawn payable to the order of Russell, Majors & Waddell; and most, if not all, of them had been indorsed by that firm; and some also by Samuel & Allen in addition.

Question. Have you received letters other than the one from Mr. Barnes pertaining to the acceptances? If so, please state as nearly as you can their substance; and whether you drew up the replies of Secretary Holt to those letters; and if so, the substance of the replies.

Answer. Since the copies of papers in regard to those acceptances were communicated by the department to the committee, we have received letters from several parties containing information of the non-payment of drafts over due. I prepared the replies to those letters; and they stated, in substance, that, so far as the department was informed, no provision had been made to meet the acceptances, and that the amount due to Russell, Majors & Waddell on the first of January was, so far as known to the department, about $8,750, which would be retained until further advised by the Department of the Interior. This matter was stated on the basis of a memorandum from the Quartermaster General's office setting forth the gross amount due as about $23,750; of which, $15,000 was to be withheld to refund a duplicated payment by the assistant quartermaster of this city.

APPENDIX.

EXHIBIT A,

Embracing copies of letters from the Secretary of War, John B. Floyd, and his chief clerk, Mr. Drinkard, recommending Russell, Majors & Waddell to credit, and that acceptances of the Secretary of War be cashed; also letters from bankers and others in regard to acceptances.

WAR DEPARTMENT, *Washington, February* 9, 1858.

SIR: I have received yours of the 5th instant, making certain inquiries in regard to Messrs. Russell, Majors & Waddell, their contract with this department, and the probability of prompt payment under that contract.

In reply, I have to say that these gentlemen have been for some time connected with this department as contractors, and they now have a very large contract for the transportation of army supplies. They have a reputation for integrity, industry, and energy second to none, and no doubt is entertained they will faithfully perform their obligations under the present contract. The times and manner of payment are specified in the instrument itself; and whenever Messrs. Russell & Co. are entitled to a requisition, their direction as to its disposition will be respected by this department.

Very respectfully, your obedient servant,

JOHN B. FLOYD,
Secretary of War.

WM. COX DUSENBERY, *New York City.*

WAR DEPARTMENT, *Washington, March* 4, 1858.

SIR: The entire transportation of supplies for the army of the United States from the borders of Missouri and Iowa to the military posts upon the Great Plains, and to Utah Territory, has been confided to the firm of Russell, Majors & Waddell, who have long been in the service of this department, and have given entire satisfaction. An early movement upon the plains and on the mountains having been resolved upon, a large expenditure of money has become a necessity. As this department will be indebted to Messrs. Russell, Majors & Waddell to a far larger amount, I have accepted two orders, each calling for the sum of one hundred thousand dollars.

These acceptances will be promptly paid, in pursuance of their tenor, when the War Department is provided with funds, which, probably, will be before long, though *possibly* not until towards the close of the present session. The probabilities are, that funds will be appropriated in a deficiency bill, in anticipation of the passage of the regular appropriation bills.

Messrs. Russell, Majors & Waddell desire to get an advance of money upon this paper. If you will accommodate them you will promote the wishes and assist the measures of this department. This firm have been efficient and trusty servants of the government, and were never more essential to it than at the present time. If you will advance the money upon their assignment of the orders to you, I will see that the funds shall be applied to their payment, according to the tenor thereof. This is unusual, but as the wants of the contractors are imperative, as I am informed, and as the department is without funds with which to pay them for services already rendered, and is in no condition to make advances to them, I have thought proper to give you this assurance.

With a hope that it may suit your views to facilitate the wishes of Messrs. Russell, Majors & Waddell, and thus to advance the interests of the government,

I am, sir, with great respect, your most obedient servant,

JOHN B. FLOYD,
Secretary of War.

GEORGE NEWBOLD, Esq.,
President Bank of America, New York City.

WAR DEPARTMENT,
Washington, March 10, 1858.

SIR: The entire transportation of supplies for the army of the United States from the borders of Missouri and Iowa to the military posts upon the Great Plains, and to Utah Territory, has been confided to the firm of Russell, Majors & Waddell, who have long been in the service of this department, and have given entire satisfaction.

An early movement upon the plains and in the mountains having been resolved upon, a large expenditure of money has become a necessity. As this department will be indebted to Messrs. Russell, Majors & Waddell to a far larger amount, I have accepted two orders, each calling for the sum of one hundred thousand dollars.

These acceptances will be promptly paid, in pursuance of their tenor, when the War Department is provided with funds, which, probably, will be before long, though *possibly* not until towards the close of the present session. The probabilities are, that funds will be appropriated in a deficiency bill, in anticipation of the passage of the regular appropriation bills.

Messrs. Russell, Majors & Waddell desire to get an advance of money upon this paper. If you will accommodate them you will promote the wishes and assist the measures of this department. This firm have been efficient and trusty servants of the government, and were never more essential to it than at the present time. If you will advance the money upon their assignment of the orders to you, I will see that the funds shall be applied to their payment, according to the tenor thereof. This is unusual, but as the wants of the contractors are imperative, as I am informed, and as the department is without funds with which to pay them for services already rendered, and is in no condition to make advances to them, I have thought proper to give you this assurance.

With a hope that it may suit your views to facilitate the wishes of Messrs. Russell, Majors & Waddell, and thus to advance the interests of the government,

I am, sir, respectfully, your obedient servant,

JOHN B. FLOYD,
Secretary of War.

August Belmont, Esq., *New York City.*

War Department,
Washington, April 16, 1858.

Sir: I have to acknowledge the receipt of your letter of the 15th instant, with a duplicate of one addressed to me on the 9th, stating that you have cashed the draft of Messrs. Russell, Majors & Waddell on this department for $50,000. Due notice is taken of this statement, and it can only be said, in addition, that all drafts accepted by the department will be duly honored.

I am, sir, very respectfully, your obedient servant,

JOHN B. FLOYD,
Secretary of War.

S. A. Mercer, Esq.,
President Farmers and Mechanics' Bank,
Philadelphia, Pennsylvania.

War Department,
Washington, May 1, 1858.

Gentlemen: The entire transportation of supplies for the army of the United States from the borders of Missouri and Iowa to the military posts upon the Great Plains, and to Utah Territory, has been confided to the firm of Russell, Majors & Waddell, who have long been in the service of this department, and have given it entire satisfaction.

As this department will be indebted to these gentlemen to a far larger amount, I have accepted five orders, two calling for the sum of one hundred thousand dollars each, and three for fifty thousand dollars each, all but two orders of the last named amount having been negotiated.

These acceptances will be promptly paid in pursuance of their tenor. If you will advance the money upon their assignment of the orders to you, I will see that the funds shall be applied to their payment. This is unusual, but as the wants of the contractors are great, as I am informed, and as the department is in no condition to make advances to them, I have thought proper to give you this assurance.

With a hope that it may suit your views to facilitate the wishes of Messrs. Russell, Majors & Waddell, and thus to advance the interests of the government,

I am, gentlemen, very respectfully, your obedient servant,

JOHN B. FLOYD,
Secretary of War.

The PRESIDENT AND DIRECTORS
Of the Bank of the State of Missouri, St. Louis, Missouri.

WAR DEPARTMENT, *Washington, May* 1, 1858.

GENTLEMEN: As this department will be indebted to Messrs. Russell, Majors & Waddell to a large amount, I have accepted five orders, two calling for the sum of one hundred thousand dollars each, and three for fifty thousand dollars each, all but two orders of the last named amount having been negotiated.

These acceptances will be promptly paid, in pursuance of their tenor. If you will advance the money upon their assignment of the orders to you, I will see that the funds shall be applied to their payment.

Very respectfully, your obedient servant,

JOHN B. FLOYD, *Secretary of War.*

The PRESIDENT AND DIRECTORS
Of the Bank of the Republic, New York City.

The same, *mutatis mutandis*, to G. B. Carhart, New York city.

WAR DEPARTMENT, *Washington, May* 5, 1858.

GENTLEMEN: The entire transportation of supplies for the army of the United States from the borders of Missouri and Iowa to the military posts upon the Great Plains and to Utah Territory, has been confided to the firm of Russell, Majors & Waddell, who have long been in the service of this department, and have given it entire satisfaction.

These acceptances will be promptly paid, in pursuance to their tenor. If you will advance the money upon their assignment of the orders to you, I will see that the funds shall be applied to their payment. This is unusual, but as the wants of the contractors are great, as I am informed, and as the department is in no condition to make advances to them, I have thought proper to give you this assurance.

With a hope that it may suit your views to facilitate the wishes of Messrs. Russell, Majors & Waddell, and thus to advance the interests of the government,

I am, gentlemen, very respectfully, your obedient servant,

JOHN B. FLOYD, *Secretary of War.*

The PRESIDENT AND DIRECTORS
Of the Bank of the State of Missouri, St. Louis, Missouri.

WAR DEPARTMENT, *Washington, September* 2, 1858.

SIR: Messrs. Russell, Majors & Waddell, contractors, have commissioned Mr. L. R. Smoot, of the firm of Smoot, Russell & Co., of Leavenworth city, Kansas Territory, to negotiate a loan for them, and have requested the acceptances of this department on account of moneys becoming due and payable to them under their contract with the quartermaster general of the 16th January last. I have, accordingly, accepted the drafts presented for that purpose, and placed them in the hands of Mr. Smoot, as requested.

At the request of Messrs. Russell, Majors & Waddell, I will state that when the stores now in *transitu* are delivered, the department is informed by the officer in charge of that particular business, they will be entitled to receive under their contract not less than two millions of dollars. This, no doubt, is a sufficient guarantee, if any were needed, that the acceptances now offered, like those heretofore issued, will be promptly met at maturity.

As to the necessity for these additional acceptances, it is sufficient to say that it was not created by the act of the contractors, nor will the delay occasioned diminish their ultimate receipts. On the contrary, the department has unabated confidence in their ability and fidelity as contractors, and intends to afford them every reasonable facility in the execution of their contract.

Very respectfully, your obedient servant,

JOHN B. FLOYD, *Secretary of War.*

JAMES T. SOUTTER, Esq.,
President Bank of the Republic, New York.

Same to George Newbold, esq., president of Bank of America, New York.

WAR DEPARTMENT, *Washington, October* 20, 1858.

GENTLEMEN: I received this morning your telegraphic despatch in regard to the payment of a draft for four thousand five hundred and fifty-nine dollars and twenty cents, drawn by Russell, Majors & Waddell in favor of A. M. White.

No such draft has been accepted by the Secretary of War, and it must have been altogether a private transaction between the contractors of this department and a third party, of which the department has no cognizance. Persons who may have contracted with them must look for the fulfilment of their agreements to them, and not to the United States. All amounts due the contractors by this department will be paid as the bills of lading and vouchers are returned; and although I do not doubt that they will meet all their engagements with private parties, this will not become known to, and is in no way the concern of, the Secretary of War.

Very respectfully, your obedient servant,

W. R. DRINKARD,
Acting Secretary of War.

Messrs. RIDGEWAY & Co.,
308 *Walnut street, Philadelphia.*

P. S.—I understand that Suter, Lea & Co., bankers, of this city, are the agents of Russell, Majors & Waddell.

WAR DEPARTMENT, *February* 15, 1859.

SIR: Messrs. Russell, Majors & Waddell, contractors for the transportation of army supplies, desiring to negotiate a loan in advance of payments which they will be entitled to receive from this department, have requested my acceptances on account of moneys becoming due and payable to them under their contract. I have accordingly accepted the drafts they have presented for that purpose.

I am informed that this negotiation would have been unnecessary had a large number of the trains belonging to the firm succeeded in reaching Camp Floyd, Utah, during the past fall; but they were stopped at Camp Scott by a violent snow storm, and detained there all the winter. And as the contractors are not entitled to their freight until they furnish evidence of its delivery at the point of destination, a very large amount now, or soon becoming, due to them cannot be paid for some months to come.

This firm have been efficient and trusty servants to the government, and are entitled to the fullest credit and confidence, and I have only to add that, if you will advance the money they desire upon the assignment of these acceptances to you, I will see that the funds are applied to their payment, according to the tenor thereof.

I have the honor to be, very respectfully, your obedient servant,

JOHN B. FLOYD, *Secretary of War.*

AUGUSTE BELMONT, Esq., *New York City.*

WAR DEPARTMENT, *April* 14, 1859.

SIR: I have to acknowledge the receipt of your letters of the 21st ultimo and 4th instant, containing notice of discount for a draft of Messrs. Russell, Majors & Waddell for five thousand dollars, drawn upon and accepted by this department.

Very respectfully, your obedient servant,

JOHN B. FLOYD, *Secretary of War.*

W. RUSHTON, Jr., Esq.,
Cashier Farmers and Mechanics' Bank, Philadelphia.

[Telegram.]

WAR DEPARTMENT, *June* 17, 1859.

Yours of yesterday was received too late for me to answer by to-day's mail

The appropriations are made to meet the liabilities you refer to, and the drafts will be met at maturity.

JOHN B. FLOYD, *Secretary of War.*

DUNCAN, SHERMAN & CO., *New York City.*

WAR DEPARTMENT, *June* 22, 1859.

GENTLEMEN: I have received your letter of the 21st instant, with the enclosed copy of one addressed to me on the 16th instant, in regard to the payment of certain drafts drawn by Messrs. Russell, Majors & Waddell on this department.

I enclose herewith, in reply, a copy of a telegram despatch to you on receipt of your former communication, advising you that the necessary appropriations had been made, and that the drafts would be honored at maturity.

Very respectfully, your obedient servant,

JOHN B. FLOYD, *Secretary of War.*

Messrs. DUNCAN, SHERMAN & CO., *Bankers, New York.*

WAR DEPARTMENT, *September* 2, 1859.

GENTLEMEN: In reply to the inquires contained in your letter of the 26th ultimo, I have to inform you that the drafts of Messrs. Russell, Majors & Waddell, to which you refer, were drawn on account of moneys becoming due to them under their contract for transporting military supplies to Utah, and were designed to avoid the inconvenience sustained by the contractors in consequence of being compelled to await payment for work actually done during the length of time necessarily involved in the return of their bills of lading from so great a distance. They were accepted as a matter of accommodation, and will, of course, be met at maturity, according to their tenor; although, up to the present time, this department has never been called upon for payment, Messrs. Russell, Majors & Waddell, themselves, having always made timely provision for their discharge.

Very respectfully, your obedient servant,

W. R. DRINKARD,
Acting Secretary of War.

Messrs. POLLARD and RENICK,
St. Louis, Missouri.

WAR DEPARTMENT, *September* 3, 1859.

SIR: In reply to your letter of the 1st instant, received this morning, I have to state that the drafts of Messrs. Russell, Majors & Waddell, to which you refer, are for moneys becoming due to them under their contract for transporting supplies to Utah, and were merely designed to avoid the delay in payment for their work involved in the return of the bills of lading from so great a distance. They were accepted by this department, as a matter of accommodation to the contractors, and will, of course, be met at maturity, according to their tenor; although, up to the present time, this department has never been called upon for payment, timely provision therefor having always been made by Messrs. Russell, Majors & Waddell.

Very respectfully, your obedient servant,

W. R. DRINKARD,
Acting Secretary of War.

W. W. SCARBURGH, Esq.,
President of the Bank of the Ohio Valley, Cincinnati.

WAR DEPARTMENT, *September* 7, 1859.

GENTLEMEN: Messrs. Russell, Majors & Waddell having requested that the terms on which their drafts have been accepted by this department might be communicated to you, I have to acquaint you that these drafts were drawn on account of moneys becoming due to those gentlemen, under their contract for transporting military supplies to Utah, and were merely designed to avoid the inconvenience sustained by the contractors in consequence of the delay in payment for their work, involved in the return of the bills of lading from so great a distance. They were accepted by this department as a matter of accommodation to the contractors, and will, of course, be met at maturity, according to their tenor; although, up to the present time, this department has never been called upon for payment, timely provision therefor having always been made by Messrs. Russell, Majors & Waddell.

Very respectfully, your obedient servant,

W. R. DRINKARD,
Acting Secretary of War.

Messrs. SAMUEL and ALLEN,
132 *North 2d Street, St. Louis, Missouri.*

WAR DEPARTMENT, *December* 22, 1859.

SIR: The drafts of Russell, Majors & Waddell, drawn upon, and accepted by, this department, payable at your bank, are predicated upon their contracts with the commissary general of subsistence of the United States army for supplying the army of Utah with flour and beef, the appropriation for which was made by the last Congress, and payment will be promptly made as they mature, whether held by your bank or other parties.

Very respectfully, your obedient servant,

JOHN B. FLOYD,
Secretary of War.

J. T. SOUTTER, Esq.,
President of the Bank of the Republic, New York.

WAR DEPARTMENT, *December* 30, 1859.

SIR: The drafts of Russell, Majors & Waddell, drawn upon, and accepted by, this department, payable at the Bank of the Republic, New York, are predicated upon their contracts with the commissary general of subsistence for supplying the army of Utah with flour and beef, the appropriation for which was made by the last Congress, and payment will be promptly made as they mature, whether held by you or other parties.

Very respectfully, your obedient servant,

JOHN B. FLOYD,
Secretary of War.

FITZHUGH COYLE, Esq.,
Washington.

WAR DEPARTMENT, *January* 13, 1860.

GENTLEMEN: I did not open your letter of the 12th instant in time to give you an answer by return of mail.

In reply to your inquiry, I have the honor to state that the acceptance you refer to, which is herewith returned, is in due form, and will be promptly paid at maturity; the money to meet it having been already appropriated by Congress.

I will add that all the drafts of Messrs. Russell, Majors & Waddell, which have been accepted by me, are predicated upon contracts, authorizing and making appropriations for the same, and it never has been my intention to accept any others.

Very respectfully, your obedient servant,

JOHN B. FLOYD,
Secretary of War.

Messrs. DUNCAN, SHERMAN & CO., *New York.*

WAR DEPARTMENT, *November* 17, 1860.

GENTLEMEN: I have the honor to acknowledge the receipt of yours of the 10th and 15th instant, notifying me that you are the owners of certain drafts of Russell, Majors & Waddell, accepted by me and not yet due.

But for the press of official engagements your first letter would have been earlier responded to, by the remark that I have no doubt the acceptances referred to will be promptly paid at maturity.

Very respectfully, your obedient servant,

JOHN B. FLOYD,
Secretary of War.

Messrs. DUNCAN, SHERMAN & Co., *New York.*

WAR DEPARTMENT, *December* 24, 1860.

GENTLEMEN: In accordance with the request contained in your letter of the 12th instant, I have filed with the quartermaster general a memorandum of the acceptances therein referred to, which, by arrangement between you and Messrs. Russell, Majors & Waddell, are to be paid out of the first receipts under their contract for transportation.

Very respectfully, your obedient servant,

JOHN B. FLOYD,
Secretary of War.

Messrs. PIERCE & BACON,
Boston, Massachusetts.

WAR DEPARTMENT, *December* 29, 1860.

SIR: I have received your letter of the 26th instant, asking that no advances or payments may be made to Messrs. Russell, Majors & Waddell, contractors for transportation, until advised by your department; and have caused the same to be placed on file in the Quartermaster General's office.

Very respectfully, your obedient servant,

JOHN B. FLOYD,
Secretary of War.

Hon. J. THOMPSON,
Secretary of the Interior.

Letters addressed to the Secretary of War by bankers, relating to acceptances held by them.

BANK OF THE OHIO VALLEY,
Cincinnati, September 1, 1859.

DEAR SIR: Owing to a severe money pressure in St. Louis, drafts on your department, made by Messrs. Russell, Majors & Waddell, for contract of supply of Utah army, and, under your acceptance, have been offered to us for encashment.

Mr. Springer, one of our stockholders, wrote to Messrs. Riggs & Co. upon yesterday in reference to one piece of this paper, of $25,000. To-day these gentlemen propose to negotiate further sums here, and request me to write to you direct.

We shall be glad to aid in their negotiation if we can have implicit dependence upon their punctual payment at Bank of Republic, in New York. Can we depend upon this?

Very respectfully, your obedient servant,

W. W. SCARBOROUGH, *President.*

Hon. John B. Floyd,
Secretary of War, Washington, D. C.

Office of Duncan, Sherman & Co., Bankers,
New York, January 12, 1860.

Dear Sir: We beg to enclose for your examination a bill drawn by Russell, Majors & Waddell, at New York, on the Secretary of War, dated November 19, 1859, for $20,000, begging you to inform us if the same is in due order, and if such provision has been made by law as will insure its payment at maturity.

With your advice, have the goodness to return it to us in due course, and oblige,

Your most obedient servants,

DUNCAN, SHERMAN & CO.

John B. Floyd, Esq.,
Secretary of War, Washington.

Russell, Majors & Waddell:

On the Secretary of War, for $20,000, dated New York, November 19, 1859, payable five months after date at Bank of the Republic.

Office of Duncan, Sherman & Co., Bankers,
New York, January 16, 1860.

Dear Sir: We are in receipt of your favor of the 13th instant, with enclosure as advised, and note your remarks, for which we beg to thank you, and have the honor to remain,

Your most obedient servants,

DUNCAN, SHERMAN & CO.

Hon. John B. Floyd,
Secretary of War, Washington.

Franklin Savings Association,
St. Louis, October 4, 1860.

Dear Sir: This association having become responsible to a considerable amount by indorsing drafts drawn by Messrs. Russell, Majors

& Waddell on the Secretary of War, and by him accepted, it is important for us to know whether said drafts will be promptly paid at maturity, and I take the liberty to request you to inform me whether I can rely on it.

I remain, respectfully, sir, your obedient servant,

F. RINGELING, *Cashier*.

Hon. JOHN B. FLOYD,
Secretary of War, Washington City.

BOATMAN'S SAVING INSTITUTION,
St. Louis, October 4, 1860.

SIR: This institution holds your acceptance, No. 13, of Russell, Majors & Waddell's draft for twenty-five thousand dollars, protested for non-payment, in the city of New York, on the 28th ultimo.

Respectfully, yours,

C. HODGMAN, *Cashier*.

Hon. JOHN B. FLOYD,
Secretary of War, Washington City.

BOATMAN'S SAVING INSTITUTION,
St. Louis, October 5, 1860.

SIR: This institution holds your acceptance, No. 17, of Russell, Major & Waddell's draft for ten thousand dollars, protested for non-payment in the city of New York, on the 1st instant.

Respectfully, yours,

C. HODGMAN, *Cashier*.

Hon. JOHN B. FLOYD,
Secretary of War, Washington City.

THE MERCHANTS' BANK OF ST. LOUIS,
St. Louis, October 8, 1860.

SIR: This bank is the owner and holder of your three acceptances of Russell, Majors & Waddell's drafts, amounting to forty thousand dollars, twenty-five thousand of which has been protested in New York for non-payment.

We have a lengthy communication from Mr. Russell, now in New York, in which he enumerates the causes which have prevented their being able to provide as usual for the prompt payment of their drafts; the main cause being the late period at which the freight was given them for transportation—being some months later than usual. We understand that some two hundred thousand dollars will be earned and due them for this transportation in the course of a short time. I desire to know whether the amount will be first applied upon your acceptances, and for what amount you have given your name; also, in view of their failure, to what extent are you secured; and, in *any contingency*, how may we regard the paper.

An early reply will oblige—

Yours, very respectfully,

J. J. BROWNLEE,
President.

Hon. J. B. FLOYD,
Secretary of War, Washington, D. C.

HIDE AND LEATHER BANK,
Boston, October 10, 1860.

DEAR SIR: Your acceptance of Russell, Majors & Waddell's draft for ten thousand dollars went to protest in New York yesterday.

Will you have the kindness to inform us when the department will be in funds for this, and if similar bills, yet to mature, will be met when due?

Yours, very respectfully,

JOHN S. MARCH, *Cashier.*

Hon. J. B. FLOYD,
Secretary of War, Washington.

WESTERN BANK OF MISSOURI,
St. Joseph, October 17, 1860.

DEAR SIR: A bill accepted by you as Secretary of War, drawn by Russell, Majors & Waddell, indorsed by same, dated June 12, 1860, due January 12 and 15, 1861, for $10,000, and payable at the Bank of the Republic, New York, was discounted by this bank, and is left for collection at the Bank of the Republic, (New York,) when due, in the hands of our agents, the American Exchange Bank, of the same city.

By order.

Yours, respectfully,

B. M. HUGHES, *Cashier.*

Hon. JOHN B. FLOYD,
Secretary of War.

SHOE AND LEATHER BANK,
New York, October 18, 1860.

DEAR SIR: This bank owns drafts of Russell, Majors & Waddell, accepted by yourself, amounting to $50,000.

I enclose a copy of each acceptance so held.

Please put them on file and notify us when they will be paid.

Respectfully, yours, &c.,

W. A. KISSAM, *Cashier.*

Hon. JOHN B. FLOYD,
Secretary of War.

BRANCH BANK OF LOUISVILLE,
Paducah, Kentucky, October 22, 1860.

DEAR SIR: This bank is the holder of two bills of $10,000 each with your acceptance. The one due October 7–10, has gone to protest in New York, at Bank of the Republic, where due. We wish to learn from you why it went to protest. The bill is drawn by Russell, Majors & Waddell, and dated Washington, June 7, 1860. We would be pleased to know what course you desire to be pursued on these bills.

Very respectfully,

J. CAMPBELL, *President.*

Hon. JOHN B. FLOYD,
Washington, D. C.

SHOE AND LEATHER BANK,
New York, October 22, 1860.

DEAR SIR: I have received your letter of the 20th instant, and in reply would state that two of your acceptances of Russell, Majors & Waddell's drafts, past due, have not been provided for by the drawers, viz: one due 16th instant, for $15,000, and the other due 18th, for $10,000. The former we have agreed to extend thirty days from maturity of the acceptance.

Respectfully,

W. A. KISSAM, *Cashier.*

Hon. J. B. FLOYD,
Secretary of War.

SHOE AND LEATHER BANK,
New York, November 21, 1860.

DEAR SIR: We now hold your acceptances of drafts drawn by Russell, Majors & Waddell, as stated below. We have given them additional time to provide for the payment of the same, viz:

$25,000, due October 28; $15,000, due October 18.

Respectfully, yours, &c.,

W. A. KISSAM, *Cashier.*

Hon. J B. FLOYD,
Secretary of War.

SHOE AND LEATHER BANK,
New York, November 22, 1860.

DEAR SIR: On the 21st I advised you of $40,000 of your acceptances with us. I should have stated $35,000—one of $25,000, due October 28, and one of $10,000, due October 18.

Respectfully, &c.,

W. A. KISSAM, *Cashier.*

Hon. J. B. FLOYD,
Secretary of War.

WASHINGTON, D. C., *December* 12, 1860.

SIR: Below we hand you memoranda of your acceptances of Russell, Majors & Waddell's drafts held by us, and for which you have promised to place an order on file for their payment, as they mature, from the earnings of the contract upon which these acceptances were issued, viz:

Your acceptance of Russell, Majors & Waddell's drafts due—

September 26–29, 1860, for	$20,000
October 1–4, 1860, for	10,000
October 1–4, 1860, for	5,000
October 8–11, 1860, for	10,000
October 21–24, 1860, for	20,000
November 8–11, 1860, for	10,000
December 14–17, 1860, for	15,000
January 10–13, 1861, for	10,000
January 11–14, 1861, for	10,000
January 11–14, 1861, for	10,000
January 12–15, 1861, for	15,000
January 13–16, 1861, for	15,000
January 18–21, 1861, for	10,000
January 20–23, 1861, for	10,000
January 23–26, 1861, for	10,000
February 11–14, 1861, for	10,000
February 13–16, 1861, for	10,000
February 16–19, 1861, for	10,000
February 17–20, 1861, for	15,000
March 12–15, 1861, for	10,000
March 15–18, 1861, for	5,000
March 17–20, 1861, for	10,000
March 20–23, 1861, for	10,000
	260,000

Now over due	$75,000	
Due in December, 1860	15,000	
Due in January, 1861	90,000	
Due in February, 1861	45,000	
Due in March, 1861	35,000	
		260,000

Awaiting advices of appropriations for payments of the above, and where to present the same for payment,

We are your very obedient servants,

PIERCE & BACON, *of Boston*.

Hon. J. B. FLOYD,
Secretary of War.

EXHIBIT B.

Referred to by Mr. Atkinson, Third Auditor, in his testimony, and containing particulars of payments to Russell, Majors & Waddell.

No. 1.

Abstract of payments to Messrs. Majors & Russell, on account of transportation, by Captain Stewart Van Vleit, assistant quartermaster United States army, at Fort Leavenworth, Kansas Territory, during the year 1858.

April 19, 1858	$2,277 42
May 27, 1858	12,250 90
June 28, 1858	116 06
Total	14,644 38

No. 1½

Abstract of payments to Messrs. Russell, Majors & Waddell, on account of transportation, by Captain Stewart Van Vliet, assistant quartermaster United States army at Fort Leavenworth, Kansas Territory, during the year 1858.

Date.	Amount.	Date.	Amount.
May 27, 1858	$50,592 95	August 14, 1858	$12,792 70
Do	15,638 96	August 20, 1858	25,389 49
Do	12,639 74	Do	11,344 83
June 4, 1858	26,322 12	Do	27,968 62
June 28, 1858	35,832 95	September 6, 1858	53,330 12
Do	15,958 28	Do	62,958 52
Do	14,760 49	Do	2,575 88
Do	14,365 07	Do	9,596 80
June 30, 1858	48,698 58	Do	68,827 01
July 26, 1858	20,664 70	Do	10,672 48
Do	31,634 03	Do	17,821 25
Do	19,397 02	September 20, 1858	39,445 22
Do	28,984 89	Do	40,282 42
Do	19,025 88	Do	11,947 25
Do	6,138 33	Do	14,016 38
July 31, 1858	14,458 22	Do	18,001 12
Do	7,576 34	Do	8,794 17
Do	12,515 12	September 21, 1858	4,597 14
August 2, 1858	25,586 51	September 22, 1858	10,678 96
Do	14,475 06	Do	14,613 52
Do	18,981 22	September 23, 1858	4,044 46
Do	1,166 20	Do	7,447 86
August 6, 1858	10,001 87	Do	10,839 95
Do	18,135 32	Do	16,778 98
Do	22,697 47	Do	28,063 53
Do	6,093 71	Do	16,061 06
August 10, 1858	364 04	Do	8,955 53
Do	1,408 49	Do	6,676 37
August 13, 1858	36,090 48	Do	8,684 58
Do	12,487 82	September 30, 1858	17,018 82

No. 1½—Continued.

Date.	Amount.	Date.	Amount.
September 30, 1858	$20,199 94	November 2, 1858	$11,627 17
Do	8,706 35	Do	15,015 66
Do	17,429 17	Do	14,715 20
Do	9,914 81	Do	4,623 62
Do	10,471 19	November 4, 1858	11,954 05
Do	8,935 25	Do	928 00
Do	8,454 51	November 15, 1858	1,008 93
Do	34,104 60	November 22, 1858	726 51
October 4, 1858	18,026 41	November 26, 1858	15,008 26
Do	3,963 07	Do	12,594 25
Do	4,330 47	Do	11,870 22
Do	13,578 40	Do	11,484 42
October 10, 1858	9,189 36	Do	12,092 43
Do	3,634 70	Do	8,586 31
October 14, 1858	28,887 11	Do	15,739 84
Do	13,374 96	Do	1,441 16
Do	13,786 38	Do	3,282 70
Do	12,592 74	November 30, 1858	15,812 35
Do	14,332 55	Do	14,923 54
Do	9,889 54	Do	16,624 34
Do	14,250 11	Do	17,678 92
Do	9,984 72	Do	12,601 50
Do	14,152 69	Do	11,540 51
Do	14,138 38	Do	11,606 22
Do	14,112 21	December 7, 1858	13,979 88
Do	13,537 76	Do	13,689 40
Do	9,154 69	Do	4,730 83
Do	26,784 19	Do	13,540 55
Do	3,782 96	Do	362 63
Do	10,960 26	Do	527 94
October 15, 1858	1,439 49	Do	1,266 64
Do	2,706 55	December 11, 1858	11,139 56
October 23, 1858	28,295 87	Do	13,043 17
Do	14,540 56	Do	10,915 08
Do	12,597 39	Do	12,017 50
Do	13,368 82	Do	14,985 45
Do	12,891 45	Do	16,522 87
Do	13,312 88	Do	17,126 79
Do	10,417 98	Do	16,723 27
Do	639 22	Do	11,090 82
Do	627 88	Do	8,406 58
October 26, 1858	13,390 51	Do	13,930 38
Do	13,485 70	Do	16,683 43
Do	13,377 75	Do	10,392 77
Do	13,170 40	December 20, 1858	11,717 08
Do	13,658 52	Do	19,101 92
Do	9,353 03	Do	13,231 88
Do	6,534 24	Do	9,661 84
Do	38,961 95	Do	18,524 20
Do	32,191 08	Do	9,928 41
Do	2,084 21	Do	2,385 61
Do	8,064 35	December 30, 1858	13,769 43
November 2, 1858	12,564 40	Do	2,455 38
Do	13,442 19	Do	1,238 17
		Total	2,425,378 35

No. 2.

Statement of payments made by Captain M. S. Miller, assistant quartermaster at Washington, D. C., to Messrs. Majors & Russell, and Messrs. Russell, Majors & Waddell, during the year 1858.

Date.		Number of voucher.	On what account.	Amount paid.	To whom paid.	Disallowed.
1858.		1st quarter.				
Jan.	25	23	Transportation	$37,017 83	Majors & Russell	
	30	29	do	17,326 88	do	
		2d quarter.				
May	13	37	do	29,019 76	do	
		38	do	15,925 96	do	
		39	do	1,919 58	do	
		41	do	1,889 93	do	
		42	do	80 40	do	
		43	do	15,171 34	do	
	14	44	Demurrage	55,437 50	do	
		45	Transportation	4,781 54	do	
June	29	82	do	30,533 88	do	
		83	do	6,420 05	Russell, Majors & Waddell	
		84	do	59,164 06	do	
		85	do	13,365 89	do	
		86	do	6,683 88	do	
		87	do	3,292 31	do	
		88	do	8,675 83	do	
		89	do	11,439 73	do	
	30	106	do	15,884 44	do	
		107	do	36,369 97	do	
		108	do	5,842 21	do	
		3d quarter.				
July	28	14	do	38,641 00	do	
	29	15	do	7,868 89	do	
		16	do	74,545 32	do	

No. 2—Continued.

Date.	Number of voucher.	On what account.	Amount paid.	To whom paid.	Disallowed.
1858.	3d quarter.				
Aug. 19	36	Transportation	$50,479 66	Russell, Majors & Waddell	
25	39	do	27,734 23	do	
	40	do	19,010 28	do	
	41	do	10,214 66	do	
	42	do	12,872 25	do	
	43	do	8,314 14	do	
30	45	do	3,909 93	do	
	46	do	14,567 28	do	
	47	do	4,983 88	do	
	48	do	4,548 70	do	
	49	do	8,433 18	do	
31	60	do	55,448 78	do	
Sept. 25	86	do	41,248 71	do	
	4th quarter.				
Nov. 29	74	do	13,912 27	do	
	75	do	16,769 85	do	
	76	do	5,734 72	do	
	77	do	1,990 69	do	
	78	do	7,861 70	do	
	79	do	12,720 35	do	
	80	do	6,789 53	do	
	81	do	3,804 88	do	
	82	do	6,861 63	do	
	83	do	5,471 93	do	
	84	do	11,055 52	do	
Dec. 24	111	Feeding oxen and mules	31,575 00	do	
30	116	Transportation	37,706 32	do	
			921,318 25		

No. 3.

Abstract of payments to Messrs. Russell, Majors & Waddell, on account of transportation, by Captain Stewart Van Vliet, assistant quartermaster United States army, at Fort Leavenworth, Kansas Territory, during the year 1859.

Date of payments.	What transported.	Amount.
1859.		
Feb. 12	Sundries	$44 05
	do	10,423 56
	do	508 51
	do	160 80
May 3	do	1,444 69
24	do	4,061 95
28	do	1,087 55
	do	109 00
June 8	do	8,776 42
9	do	8,465 91
15	do	1,108 54
17	do	1,470 70
	do	8,912 63
	do	91 16
22	do	4,484 54
25	do	10,726 73
	do	7,709 17
30	do	4,878 04
	do	1,965 73
	do	2,505 87
July 6	do	4,143 10
	do	52 40
7	do	12,477 69
9	do	5,962 04
14	do	1,370 91
16	do	2,402 55
23	do	15,907 34
	do	15,465 08
	do	11,188 99
	do	10,063 80
	do	13,226 65
	do	6,383 55
	do	1,743 50
	do	19,370 78
	do	14,915 69
	do	95 17
25	do	5,083 42
	do	28,868 67
	do	25,739 75
	do	27,110 58
Aug. 2	do	2,970 78
	do	49,143 57
3	do	9,347 76
8	do	10,197 97
	do	15,878 49
	do	14,597 93
	do	12,414 44
9	do	6,213 07
	do	3,689 29
1859.		
Aug. 2	Sundries	$3,848 91
	do	4,143 09
	do	4,817 33
	do	6,006 40
	do	18,953 00
11	do	978 76
12	do	919 94
13	do	8,106 68
	do	15,848 34
	do	6,831 16
16	do	3,070 47
18	do	3,421 42
	do	7,846 70
19	do	13,605 13
20	do	4,126 27
	do	11,425 03
	do	20,517 13
	do	9,393 70
22	do	37,765 10
29	do	6,804 97
	do	10,968 96
30	do	1,626 01
Sept. 3	do	2,435 38
	do	9,821 40
	do	475 30
6	do	3,984 84
7	do	8,242 36
12	do	31,918 64
	do	15,937 36
	do	9,508 62
16	do	6,207 66
17	do	10,229 19
	do	1,086 74
	do	14,335 42
19	do	8,682 97
	do	1,979 16
	do	3,676 14
24	do	5,729 15
	do	10,143 80
	do	8,382 14
	do	8,518 39
	do	9,607 08
29	do	7,940 40
30	do	10,520 82
	do	6,960 85
	do	9,646 26
	do	9,712 17
	do	8,479 40
Oct. 6	do	10,500 46

No. 3—Continued.

Date of payments.		What transported.	Amount.	Date of payments.		What transported.	Amount.
1859.				1859.			
Oct.	6	Sundries	$974 97	Oct.	29	Sundries	$8,544 82
		....do	2,187 69			....do	8,352 39
	10	....do	9,578 14			....do	9,532 82
		....do	9,977 99			....do	9,487 64
	13	....do	520 67			....do	13,601 98
	22	....do	2,770 83	Nov.	5	....do	5,619 52
		....do	13,201 39		15	....do	2,012 60
		....do	728 95		26	....do	3,374 67
		....do	9,659 90	Dec.	7	....do	767 18
		....do	9,528 89		9	....do	10,152 14
		....do	9,840 50				
	29	....do	9,669 05				1,010,731 84

Of the above, $742 32 was stopped in settlements of 1st, 2d, and 3d quarters. The 4th quarter's account is unsettled.

No. 4.

Statement exhibiting payments made by Captain M. S. Miller, assistant quartermaster, at Washington, D. C., to Messrs. Majors & Russell; to Messrs. Russell, Majors & Waddell; to Messrs. Brown, Russell & Co.; to Brown & Russell; and to Jones & Russell, during the year 1859; *and also the disallowances made thereon.*

Date.		Number of voucher.	On what account.	Amount.	To whom paid.	Amount disallowed.
1859.		1st quarter.				
Feb.	11	37	Transportation	$18,585 14	Majors & Russell	
Mar.	18	71	do	6,759 43	do	
		2d quarter.				
April	6	6	Transportation, excess of stores, &c	35,333 50	Russell, Majors & Waddell	$265 28
		7	do do	17,390 69	do	840 82
	15	15	Forage	8,729 90	do	
	19	18	Transportation	11,334 27	do	849 81
	29	24	do	13,462 49	do	891 07
May	4	39	Transportation of damaged stores	12,873 14	do	2,712 90
	5	40	Transportation, deductions, &c	11,426 60	Majors & Russell	3,907 07
		3d quarter.				
July	15	11	Transportation	10,074 92	Brown, Russell & Co.; Brown & Russell; Jones & Russell; and Majors & Russell	
Sept.	5	65	do	6,628 80	Russell, Majors & Waddell	
		4th quarter.				
Nov.	15	23	do	7,687 05	do	
Dec.	6	100	Deficiencies and damages improperly charged.	2,339 15	do	159 49
	23	131	Short payments	10 51	do	
	31	142	Demurrage	11,110 00	do	
				173,745 59		9,626 44

No. 5.

Abstract of payments to Messrs. Russell, Majors & Waddell, on account of transportation, by Captain Stewart Van Vliet, assistant quartermaster United States army, at Fort Leavenworth, Kansas Territory, during the 1st, 2d, and 3d quarters of 1860.

Date	Amount
January 9, 1860	$1,856 49
Do	147 04
Do	93 56
March 2, 1860	23 00
June 1, 1860	11,106 49
June 15, 1860	1,944 86
Do	13,138 12
June 29, 1860	10,946 32
July 19, 1860	20,911 19
July 28, 1860	16,831 00
July 31, 1860	5,514 20
Do	28,226 10
August 18, 1860	13,023 29
Do	4,747 69
Do	43 22
August 20, 1860	3,831 69
August 31, 1860	11,193 42
Do	50 00
September 3, 1860	7,300 02
September 12, 1860	2,180 29
September 20, 1860	24,316 69
September 26, 1860	75,257 23
Total	252,681 91

No. 6.

Statement exhibiting the payments made by Captain M. S. Miller, assistant quartermaster, at Washington, D. C., to Messrs. Russell, Majors & Waddell, and to Messrs. Majors & Russell, during the 1st, 2d, and 3d quarters of 1860; and also the amounts noted for disallowances on the respective vouchers thereof.

Date.	Number of voucher.	On what account.	Amount of payment.	To whom paid.	Noted for disallowance.
1860.	1st quarter				
Feb. 6	83	Transportation from Nebraska to Utah	$9,509 30	Russell, Majors & Waddell	$7,018 94
	84	Transportation of damaged stores, &c	2,175 61	do	2,106 71
	85	Transportation	7,831 16	Majors & Russell	7,831 16
	86	do	6,810 38	do	6,810 38
	87	do	1,480 99	do	------
	88	do	3,623 61	do	3,623 61
	2d quarter.				
May 22	127	Property turned over to Captain Turnley at Camp Floyd	54,250 00	Russell, Majors & Waddell	Not acted on.
	3d quarter.				
July 21	17	Additional transportation	69,656 09	Majors & Russell	Not acted on.
			155,337 14		

EXHIBIT C,

Being letters from the Chairman, Secretary Holt, General Johnston, and Colonel Taylor.

No. 1.

WASHINGTON, *January* 28, 1861.

SIR: Will you be kind enough to furnish the committee appointed to investigate the fraud recently perpetrated upon the Interior Department by the abstraction of certain Indian trust bonds specific information on the following points:

1st. The amount now due Russell, Majors & Waddell upon their contracts with the War Department.

2d. The amount of extra allowances claimed by them, and the date when such claims were made, and for what services.

3d. The amount of extra allowances made to them, the date of said allowances, and for what services rendered.

Your early reply will oblige the committee, as they are anxious to bring their labors to a close.

Very respectfully,

I. N. MORRIS, *Chairman.*

Hon. JOSEPH HOLT,
Secretary of War.

No. 2.

WAR DEPARTMENT, *January* 29, 1861.

SIR: In answer to the inquiries contained in your letter of yesterday's date, I have the honor to enclose to you reports of the Quartermaster General and Acting Commissary General, communicating the information desired by your committee touching the amount now due Messrs. Russell, Majors & Waddell, and of all extra allowances claimed by or allowed to them.

Very respectfully, your obedient servant,

J. HOLT,
Secretary of War.

Hon. I. N. MORRIS,
Chairman of the Select Committee, &c.,
House of Representatives.

No. 3.

QUARTERMASTER GENERAL'S OFFICE,
Washington, D. C., January 29, 1861.

SIR: I have the honor to acknowledge your reference to this office of the letter of the Hon. I. N. Morris to you, dated the 28th instant.

In reply to the first question, I respectfully report that, on the 4th instant, Captain Van Vliet stated the amount known to be due to Messrs. Russell, Majors & Waddell to be $23,750 49. Services not yet reported may have been rendered by them in New Mexico. There are suspended accounts in the Third Auditor's office amounting to $27,390 80, of which at least $9,125 62 must be "disallowed," which "disallowance" the late Secretary of War directed to be charged to the contractors. That sum is to be deducted from the amount stated by Captain Van Vliet.

In reply to the second and third questions, I respectfully report that I can find no accounts of extra allowances paid to or claimed by them. All payments have been for services performed under contracts.

I was informed, verbally, several months ago, by Mr. Russell, that he had large claims before Congress for services performed under the contracts, but do not remember the amount.

I remain, sir, very respectfully, your obedient servant,

J. E. JOHNSTON,
Quartermaster General.

Hon. J. HOLT,
Secretary of War, Washington City.

No. 4.

OFFICE COMMISSARY GENERAL OF SUBSISTENCE,
Washington, January 29, 1861.

SIR: In compliance with your instructions to report upon the communication of the Hon. I. N. Morris, chairman of the select committee on the Indian bond robbery, dated the 28th instant, I have the honor to state that, at this date, there is nothing due Russell, Majors & Waddell by the Subsistence department of the army.

No extra allowance has been claimed by Russell, Majors & Waddell from the Subsistence department of the army, nor has any extra allowance been made them through this office.

The letter of the Hon. I. N. Morris is herewith returned.

Very respectfully, your obedient servant,

J. P. TAYLOR,
Acting Com. Gen. of Subsistence.

Hon. JOSEPH HOLT,
Secretary of War.

EXHIBIT D,

Containing a copy of Mr. Bailey's appointment, a copy of his bond, and a letter from Mr. Kelly.

No. 1.

DEPARTMENT OF THE INTERIOR,
Washington, January 25, 1861.

SIR: As requested in your letter of the 24th instant, I have the honor to enclose herewith a copy of the appointment of Godard Bailey as a disbursing clerk in this department; also a copy of his official bond as disbursing clerk, furnished from the office of the First Comptroller of the Treasury.

Very respectfully, your obedient servant,

MOSES KELLY, *Acting Secretary.*

Hon. I. N. MORRIS,
Chairman Committee of Investigation,
U. S. House of Representatives.

No. 2.

DEPARTMENT OF THE INTERIOR,
City of Washington, July 1, 1857.

SIR: You are hereby appointed a disbursing clerk in this department, under the act of March 3, 1853, at a salary of two hundred dollars in addition to what you now receive, thus making your compensation two thousand dollars per annum.

Under this appointment I desire, particularly, that you should take charge of the stocks held in trust by the head of the department for the benefit of the Indians, collect the interest thereon as it may become due, and see that the same is properly paid into the public treasury.

The law requires a bond from each disbursing clerk, and you will be pleased to furnish the same as early as convenient, in the form herewith furnished.

Very respectfully, your obedient servant,

J. THOMPSON, *Secretary.*

G. BAILEY, Esq., *Present.*

No. 3.

DISTRICT OF COLUMBIA, *County of Washington:*

Know all men by these presents that we, Godard Bailey, of the city of Mobile, in the State of Alabama, as principal, and Benjamin McCullough, of Galveston, in the State of Texas, and William C. Corrie, of

Charleston, in the State of South Carolina, as sureties, are held and firmly bound unto the United States of America in the full and just sum of five thousand dollars, lawful money, to be paid to the said United States; for which payment well and truly to be made, we, jointly and severally, bind ourselves, our heirs, executors, and administrators, and each of them, firmly by these presents. Signed with our hands, and sealed with our seals, and dated this first day of August, in the year of our Lord one thousand eight hundred and fifty-seven.

The condition of the foregoing obligation is such, that, whereas the Secretary of the Interior hath, pursuant to law, constituted and appointed the said Godard Bailey a disbursing clerk for the Interior department: Now, therefore, if the said Godard Bailey shall truly and faithfully execute and discharge all the duties of said office of disbursing clerk for the Interior Department according to the laws of the United States, and shall, moreover, truly and faithfully keep safely, and disburse and pay out, all sums of public money placed or coming into his hands from time to time, without loaning, using, depositing in banks, or exchanging for other funds than as allowed by law, and shall do and perform all other duties as disbursing clerk which may be imposed on him by any act of Congress, or by any regulation of the Interior or Treasury Departments made in conformity to law, then this obligation to be void and of none effect; otherwise it shall abide and remain in full force and virtue.

GODARD BAILEY. [L. S.]
BEN. McCULLOUGH. [L. S.]
WM. C. CORRIE. [L. S.]

Signed, sealed, and delivered in presence of—
W. W. Lester.
W. L. Stricklin.

Personally appeared before me, Moses Kelly, a justice of the peace in and for the District of Columbia, W. W. Lester, who, being duly sworn, declares that he saw the above-named Godard Bailey, Benjamin McCullough, and Wm. C. Corrie, sign, seal, and, as their own act and deed, deliver the above instrument of writing, and that he, with W. L. Stricklin, witnessed the execution of the same.

Witness my hand and seal of office, at Washington, this eighth day of September, in the year of our Lord eighteen hundred and fifty-seven.

[L. S.]

MOSES KELLY, *J. P.*

W. W. Lester.

I certify that the sureties to this bond are good and sufficient for the penalty thereof.

PHIL. BARTON KEY,
U. S. Attorney.

Approved October 1, 1857.

J. THOMPSON.

EXHIBIT E.

No. 1.

HOUSE OF REPRESENTATIVES, *December* 27, 1860.

DEAR SIR : I am directed by the select committee appointed under the resolution of the House of Representatives of the 24th instant to investigate alleged frauds in the Department of the Interior, to request that you will meet said committee at committee room No. 6, (House of Representatives,) this afternoon, at two o'clock, with such papers and documents in relation to said fraud as you may have in your possession.

Respectfully yours,

I. N. MORRIS, *Chairman.*

Hon. JACOB THOMPSON,
Secretary of the Interior.

No. 2.

HOUSE OF REPRESENTATIVES, *December* 28, 1860.

SIR: I am directed by the select committee appointed under the resolution of the House of Representatives of the 24th instant to inquire into the alleged frauds in the Department of the Interior, to respectfully request your attendance before said committee at their room, No. 6, (House of Representatives,) on Saturday, the 29th instant, at 11 o'clock a. m.

Yours respectfully,

ISAAC N. MORRIS, *Chairman.*
Per T. F. ANDREWS, *Clerk.*

Hon. JOHN B. FLOYD,
Secretary of War.

No. 3.

WAR DEPARTMENT, *December* 29, 1860.

SIR: I have the honor to acknowledge the receipt this morning of your letter of the 28th instant, requesting me to attend before your committee at 11 a. m. to-day.

I regret to say that, in consequence of the late hour at which this notification reached me, and of intervening official engagements of a pressing character, I shall be unable to comply with the request of the committee to-day, but will be happy to appear before them at any time hereafter that may be named.

Very respectfully, your obedient servant,

JOHN B. FLOYD,
Secretary of War.

HON. ISAAC N. MORRIS,
Chairman Select Committee on alleged frauds in the Interior Department, House of Reps.

No. 3½.

WASHINGTON, D. C., *January* 17, 1861.

SIR: I am directed by the select committee appointed by the House of Representatives to investigate the late abstraction of bonds from the Interior Department to request that you will attend at their committee room to-morrow at half-past ten o'clock a. m., or as soon thereafter as may suit your convenience.

By inadvertence the subpœna of the Sergeant-at-arms was directed to be served on you.

I am, very respectfully, your obedient servant,

I. N. MORRIS, *Chairman.*

I certify that the foregoing is, in substance, a copy of a letter sent to Hon. H. M. Rice on the 17th of January, 1861.

FRANCIS H. SMITH,
Clerk of Select Committee.

No. 4.

SENATE CHAMBER, *January* 17, 1861.

SIR: In reply to your note of this day, I have to say that any questions addressed to me in writing touching the subject named will receive full and prompt answers.

Very respectfully, your obedient servant,

HENRY M. RICE.

Hon. I. N. MORRIS,
Chairman, &c.

No. 5.

WASHINGTON, D. C., *January* 1, 1861.

SIR: I am directed by the select committee appointed by the House of Representatives to investigate the late frauds alleged to have been made upon the Interior Department to request that you will furnish them at your earliest convenience with a copy of all contracts heretofore made by the War Department with Russell, Majors & Waddell. Also with a copy of any acceptances given by Hon. John B. Floyd, late Secretary of War, during his term of office, and of memoranda concerning the same on file in your department.

I am, very respectfully, your obedient servant,

I. N. MORRIS,
Chairman.

Hon. JOSEPH HOLT,
Secretary of War.

No 6.

WASHINGTON, D. C., *January* 5, 1861.

The condition of the business of the select committee to investigate the alleged frauds in the Interior Department is such as to render it highly desirable to have, by the return of the messenger, if possible, copies of the papers heretofore requested by the committee on file in the War Department.

Respectfully, your obedient servant,

I. N. MORRIS, *Chairman.*

Hon. JOSEPH HOLT, *Secretary of War.*

No. 7.

WAR DEPARTMENT, *January* 7, 1861.

SIR: I have received your letter of the 4th instant, enclosing a copy of a communication addressed to me on the 1st, but which failed to come to hand.

Several of the papers called for in your letter were sent up to the committee on Saturday; the others I have the honor to enclose herewith.

Very respectfully, your obedient servant,

J. HOLT,
Secretary of War ad interim.

Hon. I. N. MORRIS,
Chairman Select Committee, &c., House of Representatives.

EXHIBIT F,

Containing statement of Mr. Russell, as also his letters.

No. 1.

WASHINGTON CITY, *January* 16, 1861.

SIR: I find that I cannot get my statement completed as early as I had expected; a friend whom I obtained to make me a perfect copy made several omissions, which make it necessary to recopy; I will try and have it at your room prior to 5 p. m.

Very respectfully,

W. H. RUSSELL.

Hon. I. N. MORRIS, *Chairman, &c.*

No. 2.

Statement of William H. Russell.

WASHINGTON CITY, D. C.,
Wednesday, January 16, 1861.

GENTLEMEN: My responses to the questions put to me on Monday, the 14th instant, by you in regard to the bonds received by me from Mr. Godard Bailey, were accurate as far as they went, but not sufficiently explanatory of the transaction for a perfect understanding of it. Having no wish to conceal any fact necessary to convey such understanding to the committee, I then expressed a desire to make a fuller and more satisfactory statement in writing, further responsive to the questions put to me, which I now present, and respectfully ask that it may be received and recorded.

In January, 1858, the firm of Russell, Majors & Waddell contracted with the quartermaster's department of the United States army for the transportation of all the military stores or supplies which were required to be sent from Fort Leavenworth and Fort Riley, in Kansas; from Fort Union, in New Mexico; from Kansas city, in Missouri; from Fort Laramie, in Nebraska; and from any other depot that might be established on the west bank of the Missouri river, north of Fort Leavenworth, and south of latitude forty-two; and the delivery of them at any or all military posts or depots which then were or might be established in Kansas and New Mexico, including El Paso del Norte, and posts in that vicinity in the territory known as the Gadsden Purchase, in the Territory of Utah, south of latitude forty; at any depot or depots which then were or might be established in Nebraska, south of latitude forty-four; in the Territory of Oregon, south of latitude forty-four; in the Territory of Utah, north of latitude forty, and as far west as longitude one hundred and thirteen.

At the time of making this contract the government owed the contractors several hundred thousand dollars for services under a similar contract in 1857, which was not paid for the want of an appropriation by Congress.

The performance of this contract on the part of said firm necessarily involved a very heavy expenditure of money, as during its existence they were required to transport all the supplies necessary for the army in New Mexico, Arizona, and Utah. During that year alone the transportation exceeded eighteen millions of pounds.

In executing this contract, and transporting these large supplies, it became necessary to raise large amounts of money in advance, and, in order to do so, to obtain from the Secretary of War his acceptances in advance of the earnings under the contract, so that money could be raised upon them in order to enable the firm with which I was connected to perform the contract faithfully. Without these facilities we must have failed to procure the necessary means of transportation, and not only have subjected the government to great inconvenience and loss, but portions of the army to almost certain starvation. The Secretary of War, in view of this necessity, gave to said firm his acceptances, which from time to time, including those paid and unpaid, have reached an aggregate of several millions of dollars; the precise amount I do not know, and have no present means of ascertaining.

In July last upwards of two hundred thousand dollars of these acceptances, upon which our firm had raised money, were about to mature, and I became apprehensive that they would be protested for non-payment, which, from declarations made to me by Governor Floyd, I then feared and believed would bring discredit upon the War Department, resulting in his necessary retirement from the cabinet. At that time the government was indebted to the contracting firms of which I was a member to an amount largely exceeding these acceptances, and independent of the transportation then on the route. We were at the same time compelled to keep up our immense trains in order to transport the supplies then necessary; and, having exhausted all our means and credit, the government still withholding the large sums of money due us, we found it absolutely impossible to make sufficient negotiations to carry forward our contract, and at the same time protect the acceptances of the government.

While engaged in making efforts in New York to raise money to execute this contract, and to meet these acceptances of the Secretary of War, I casually heard that a man by the name of Baylor, residing in Washington, had been in New York on several occasions negotiating the sale of Florida bonds in connexion with the Fernandina railroad, and other stocks and securities, and that he was a dealer in stocks. Finding that I could not raise the money to meet these acceptances in New York, and they maturing in a few days, I came to Washington, in order to get from the government a sufficient amount of the money due the contractors to protect them from protest, desiring that the credit of the government should not be injured on my account. On the train from New York to Washington I met Colonel Luke Lea, with whom I had been long acquainted, and who was and is a partner of mine in the banking business in Leavenworth City, Kansas. I conversed with him freely about my embarrassed condition, and fully revealed to him all the facts in relation to it, and desired to know of him if he could aid me in procuring a sum necessary to relieve me, and sufficient to take up the acceptances of the Secretary of War. He replied that he was unable to do so, but would if he had the ability. I then asked him if he knew anybody in Washington from whom I could borrow either money or securities, and he told me that he did not think the amount could be obtained there. I then called his attention to the report I had heard in New York about a man by the name of Baylor, as I supposed, and he said that he knew no such man. He afterwards remarked that he knew a man by the name of Bailey in Washington who had dealt in Florida bonds, but thought that he was unable to aid me, except by influence with others; that he was a distant relative of Governor Floyd's, a man of high legal attainments, and possibly could serve me in getting the claims of the contractors allowed and paid by the departments. I then requested him to see Bailey as soon as he could after arriving in Washington, and make known to him the condition of my claim against the government, and of the acceptances of the Secretary of War, and the danger of their going to protest, and ask him if he could aid me in any way. The next or the following day after I arrived in Washington, and while at the War Department pressing the payment of money due, I was informed that Mr. Bailey was there and desired to be introduced to me. I had never seen him before. This was on or about the 13th day of July. I was then introduced to him by Colonel Drinkard, the chief clerk, whereupon he inquired of me if the facts he had learned from Colonel Lea and Colonel Drinkard, about the probability of the acceptances of the Secretary of War being protested, were true, and whether it was my opinion that, if the acceptances were protested, the Secretary would be likely to be disgraced, and have to retire from the cabinet. I stated to him that the facts were true, and that I feared that would be the result upon the Secretary. He asked me what amount would be necessary to protect the acceptances, and when I could return it. My reply was that $150,000 would relieve me, and I could return it in ninety days. To this he replied that his mind was made up; that he had some State securities, which I could hypothecate, that were at my service, and that he would meet me at my room at two o'clock with them. At the time appointed he brought me the State bonds, amounting at par value to $150,000, and required that if I took them I should only hypothecate them and return the identical bonds. I did take them upon those terms, having no knowledge whatever that he was a government officer, or that the bonds belonged to the government. I supposed that he had a perfect right to control them, and no questions were asked by me and nothing said by him in regard to the ownership of them. These bonds were hypothecated by myself and my agent, and with the proceeds thereof the maturing acceptances were protected.

Before the time had arrived when these bonds were to have been returned, stocks declined, and the parties with whom they were hypothecated required an additional deposit to secure the payment of the money raised upon them, or otherwise they would sell them. Finding our business in this condition, and our facilities for procuring money from the west being cut off by derangement and depression in the money market, and being still embarrassed in consequence of the government having failed to pay what was clearly due us, I came to Washington, and reported to Bailey my inability to protect the stocks from sale, and desired additional assistance. He then informed me, for the first time, that the State bonds he had given me were held in trust by the government for certain Indian tribes. I was astounded at this disclosure. Difficulties surrounded me on every side. I had no time to weigh the responsibility of wrecking my firm, discrediting the government, and losing the bonds already pledged; and on the other hand, that of making myself a party, in any way, to a breach of trust. I conversed freely with Bailey about the amount that was due us by the government, and he said, substantially, that his letting me have the bonds was only the use of the means of one department to protect the credit of another; that it was not a criminal act, but a mere breach of trust, on his part; and that on mine, it was certainly not criminal. Driven by the necessity of protecting the bonds already given me, and extricating ourselves from the embarrassments surrounding us, and having other acceptances of the Secretary of War, exceeding $300,000, then about to mature; relying confidently upon the government and my own resources for the means to protect all the bonds I might receive; and being persuaded that the act on my part was not criminal, although I did not then, and do not now, think it was fully justifiable; and being also desirous to protect Mr. Bailey in what he had done, and the credit of the War Department; and knowing that if I failed to protect these bonds and acceptances, the credit of our firm would be entirely destroyed, our transportation thereby defeated, and the supplies of the army cut off, I did accept from Bailey additional bonds, to the amount of about $387,000 at par, upon the same terms and conditions upon which I had received the former ones. These bonds were hypothecated in the east, and the money obtained upon them was applied to make good the margin of the first lot, and the payment of the other acceptances of the Secretary of War.

When I received the first lot of bonds, I gave Bailey the note of Russell, Majors & Waddell for the full amount of the face of the bonds; and when I received the second lot I took up that note, and gave him another covering the whole $537,000.

By the month of December the monetary crisis, owing to the agitation of the country, became such as to cause increased embarrassment all over the country, and to render it almost impossible to raise money upon any kind of stocks or securities. All stocks were running down so rapidly that I became apprehensive that the holders of the bonds I had hypothecated would sell them at a great sacrifice, and thus put it out of my power to save them to the government; whereupon I again visited Washington about the 12th or 13th of December last, and laid the whole matter before Bailey, and after a full and free conversation as to the best mode of protecting him and the government, I told him that it would require an additional amount of about $350,000 to protect additional acceptances of the Secretary of War then maturing, and the credit of our firm, so that we could execute our contracts, and thus be enabled to restore the bonds. He suggested to me that if I would procure acceptances of the Secretary of War, drawn against our transportation contract, for the amount of bonds that I had already received, and such additional amount as I might require to protect additional acceptances of the Secretary of War and the credit of our firm, he would furnish me with the additional amount of bonds necessary for the purposes aforesaid. I did procure from the Secretary of War his acceptances, drawn upon our transportation contract, which, with others then on hand, made the aggregate amount of $870,000. I then gave him a receipt in the name of our firm for the 870 bonds. I received these at a time when all stocks were rapidly declining, and with the distinct understanding that I should take advantage of the market and dispose of them so that, with other means to be raised by me from other sources, I could repurchase and restore, at the lowest market price, bonds equivalent to those I had thus received. It was further distinctly understood between us, that I should have until June next to replace these bonds, or their equivalents, up to which time he, Bailey, said he would hold me harmless.

Having thus made a full statement of these transactions, I beg leave to add a word more.

I submit that as our firm was, at the time of this transaction, and is now, entirely responsible and able to execute our contract with the government, and as our pay therefor will largely exceed the acceptances deposited with Bailey in lieu of the bonds received from him, there could have been no criminal intent on my part, nor was there any purpose to defraud the government, but, on the contrary, an actual deposit of the best possible guarantee against such a contingency.

There is no other transaction in the course of a long business life, in which I have had very large operations with a great variety of persons, upon which I cannot look with entire satisfaction, and there is nothing in my life which has given me such mortification and regret as this. I cannot impress upon the committee the great necessity which then pressed upon me, and I forbear to enlarge upon it. But it was a necessity brought on entirely by the failure of the government to fulfil its engagements, and if I have thus, without any criminal intent, used a portion of the stocks held by the government to protect myself and the government from the most disastrous consequences, I have the satisfaction to know that they were indebted to me in an amount far exceeding the sum thus used. And, besides, it is important to add that, in any event, we have property and means with which we can ultimately protect the government from loss; and as fast as our just claims are allowed by them, and our earnings under our present contract, which runs through 1861, shall be passed to our credit, they shall be withheld by the government until we produce bonds to an equal amount to replace those which have been thus employed.

It is due to justice and fair dealing that I should say further, that Mr. Bailey has in this matter assisted me, as I have stated, without any advantage, pecuniary or otherwise, direct or indirect, received or promised to him, so far as I know or believe, and that so far as I am able to judge by his words and acts he has been prompted therein by a sincere desire to protect the Secretary of War and the public interest, however much he may have been mistaken.

I wish it to be understood that in this statement of conversations with different persons I do not profess to give the exact words used by either, but only the substance and results.

Very respectfully,

WM. H. RUSSELL.

The COMMITTEE OF INVESTIGATION, &c.,
House of Representatives, Washington.

No. 3.

WASHINGTON CITY, *January* 24, 1861.

GENTLEMEN: I have had a very limited consultation with my counsel in relation to the suggestions made and the questions put to me on yesterday by your committee, and have not had time to mature my reply. I therefore beg the indulgence of the committee until to-morrow morning.

Very respectfully,

WM. H. RUSSELL.

Hon. I. N. MORRIS,
Chairman, &c., Investigating Committee, &c.

No. 4.

WASHINGTON CITY, *January* 25, 1861.

GENTLEMEN: In reply to your proposition to expunge from the record of your proceedings all of my testimony, and to discharge me from further examination, or if I declined to withdraw, to go forward and answer such further questions as you may put to me, I have to say, that I appeared before the committee in obedience to a subpœna issued by the Speaker of the House of Representatives, and gave my former answers to your inquiries, first, because they were "pertinent to the matter of inquiry in consideration" by you; and, second, because I was not permitted by law "to refuse to testify to any fact" within the scope of your inquiries.

I would respectfully state to the committee that, having been thus required to testify to the extent to which my testimony has already gone, I am still ready to obey said subpœna, and to answer any additional questions which the committee may put to me, touching the Indian trust bonds referred to in the preamble and resolution appointing the committee, and my connexion with them.

I beg leave further to state that the testimony already given by me having been recorded as a part of the proceedings of the committee, no consent of mine can authorize the committee to expunge it.

Very respectfully,

WM. H. RUSSELL.

The INVESTIGATING COMMITTEE,
House of Representatives.

EXHIBIT G.

Being correspondence between J. Thompson, Dr. Fitch, and G. Bailey.

No. 1.

WASHINGTON, *December* 28, 1860.

SIR: During the session of 1857–'58, application was made to Congress for an appropriation for the arrears of interest due on five per cent. stocks of the State of Indiana, held in trust for the Pottawatomie and other Indians. One of the bonds was, with your consent, delivered to the Hon. G. N. Fitch, to be used as a memorandum before the Senate Committee on Indian Affairs, of which he was a member. Dr. Fitch mislaid the bond, and it has never been returned to the department. I enclose a letter from Dr. Fitch, explaining the transaction, and request that it may be filed with this communication.

Very respectfully, your obedient servant,

G. BAILEY.

Hon. J. THOMPSON,
Secretary of the Interior.

No. 2.

LOGANSPORT, INDIANA, *August* 8, 1859.

DEAR SIR: Yours of the 2d instant is received. I have received a previous letter from you on the same subject, and owe you an apology for not having answered it. It was laid aside for a search for the bond, and, amid a multiplicity of engagements, forgotten.

I received the bond of you for the purpose of copying a description, (this State having issued bonds for more than one fund,) with the view of writing to the governor upon the subject of some arrangement for their payment. It has become misplaced. I have, after a search to-day, failed to find it, but intend soon moving my library and papers into a new room preparing for the purpose, and will then overhaul every package, and can scarce fail to find it. If successful in my search, it will be immediately forwarded to you.

Respectfully, yours,

G. N. FITCH.

G. BAILEY, Esq.

No. 3.

DEPARTMENT OF THE INTERIOR, *December* 26, 1861.

SIR: It is ascertained that a certain bond of Indiana State stocks, of the issue of 1835, is missing from the number now in the custody of this department; it has been represented to me by Mr. Bailey that he enclosed said bond to you for the purpose of receiving information as to whether the unpaid interest on the class to which it belonged would eventually be paid. I should be pleased to receive at an early day any information you may have on the subject.

Very respectfully,

J. THOMPSON.

Hon. G. N. FITCH, *United States Senate.*

No. 4.

WASHINGTON, D. C., *December* 27, 1860.

SIR: Yours of yesterday is before me. You say: "It is ascertained that a certain bond of Indiana State stocks of the issue of 1835 is missing from the number now in the custody of the department. It has been represented to me by Mr. Bailey that he enclosed said bond to you for the purpose of receiving information as to whether the unpaid interest on the class to which it belonged would eventually be paid." And you add: "I should be pleased to receive at an early day any information you may have on the subject."

I remember the bond to which you doubtless allude; and the purpose for and circumstances under which my attention was called to it are, to the best of my recollection, as follows: Two or three years since, a clerk in your department (Mr. Bailey) handed or enclosed me an Indiana State bond, which he informed me was one of a class belonging to the Indian trust fund in charge of your department, upon which bonds that State had neglected or refused to pay interest, and asked my advice or opinion as one of the senators from Indiana, and a member of the Committee on Indian Affairs, relative to an application, which he stated you would make, or had made, to Congress, to appropriate for the benefit of the Indians a sum equal to the amount of the arrears of interest on the bonds, and direct suit to be brought on them against the State. Unwilling to believe that Indiana had repudiated any just bonds, and unwilling there should be any congressional action, or any suit relative to the matter, if it could be amicably arranged otherwise, I stated a wish that such application for action or suit should be delayed, and that I would correspond relative to the matter with Governor Willard. Accordingly, I described or enclosed (I do not remember which) the bond to Governor Willard, asking, in effect, an explanation of the non-payment of interest, and if some arrangement could not be made for its payment. His answer was, in substance, that the bond was of a class which the State had retired, by what is known in Indiana as the "Butler bill," by which the Wabash and Erie canal was exchanged for the bonds; that due notice had been given by the State to the holders to surrender them, according to the provisions of that bill, and that the State, therefore, acknowledged no further liability upon the bonds. Discovering from the governor's answer that no arrangement would be made by the State for payment, and that consequently the bond was valueless, I did not use that care I otherwise should have done to see that it was returned to the department. Some months afterwards the same clerk wrote me in relation to it, at a time, as I stated in my answer, (which answer must be on file in the department,) when my library and papers were soon to be moved, after which a search would be made for it. Since that time the little importance I attached to it has prevented that search I then expected to make, and which will be made at the earliest opportunity.

Very respectfully, yours,

G. N. FITCH.

Hon. JACOB THOMPSON,
Secretary of the Interior.

EXHIBIT H.

Statement of acceptances, by the Secretary of War, of Russell, Majors & Waddell's drafts, on account of their contracts for transportation.

Number.	Accepted.	Dated.	Time.	Amount.	Total.
	March 25, 1858	March 25, 1858	August 1	$50,000 00	
			July 1	100,000 00	
		Do	September 1	50,000 00	
			July 1	100,000 00	
					$300,000 00
	April 25, 1858	April 23, 1858	May, BL	9,000 00	
	May 1, 1858	May 1, 1858	October 1	50,000 00	
	May 3, 1858	do	May, BL	4,500 00	
					63,500 00
	May 4, 1858	May 3, 1858	August 1	5,000 00	
		May 1, 1858	do	15,000 00	
		May 3, 1858	September 1	5,000 00	
					25,000 00
	May 5, 1858	May 4, 1858	October 1	25,000 00	
		Do	September 1	25,000 00	
		Do	do	25,000 00	
		Do	October 1	25,000 00	
					100,000 00
	May 13, 1858	March 8, 1858	September 1	3,050 00	
	May 31, 1858	May 19, 1858	May, BL	12,000 00	
					15,050 00
	June 29, 1858	June 21, 1858	Two months	10,000 00	
		Do	do	10,000 00	
		Do	August 15	25,000 00	
		Do	August 10	25,000 00	
					70,000 00
	July 9, 1858	June 28, 1858	May, BL	16,107 00	
		Do	June, BL	16,107 00	
					32,214 00
	August 25, 1858	August 17, 1858	October 1	25,000 00	

		Do	November 1	25,000 00	
		Do	December 1	25,000 00	
		Do	do	25,000 00	
			January 1	25,000 00	125,000 00
28	September 2, 1858	August 21, 1858	November 1	25,000 00	
29			October 1	25,000 00	
30			December 1	25,000 00	
31			do	25,000 00	
32			January 1	25,000 00	125,000 00
33	October 23, 1858	October 21, 1858	Three months	25,000 00	
34		do	Four months	25,000 00	
35		do	do	25,000 00	
36		do	do	25,000 00	100,000 00
37	December 10, 1858	December 10, 1858	do	25,000 00	
38		do	Three months	25,000 00	50,000 00
39	December 16, 1858	December 16, (?) 1858	Four months	10,000 00	
40		do	Five months	15,000 00	
41		do	Six months	25,000 00	
42		do	Seven months	25,000 00	75,000 00
43	December 18, 1858	December 18, (?) 1858	Six months	5,000 00	
44		do	Nine months	5,000 00	10,000 00
45	January 4, 1859	January 4, (?) 1859	Six months		12,000 00
46	January 8, 1859	January 8, 1859	Four months	25,000 00	
47		do	do	10,000 00	
48		do	do	15,000 00	
49		do	Five months	25,000 00	
50		do	Six months	25,000 00	
51		do	do	25,000 00	125,000 00
52	February 10, 1859	February 10, (?) 1859	Three months		17,363 50
53	February 15, 1859	February 15, 1859	Five months	80,000 00	
54		do	Six months	50,000 00	130,000 00

EXHIBIT H—Continued.

Number.	Accepted.	Dated.	Time.	Amount.	Total.
55	February 28, 1859	February 28, (?) 1859	Four months	$25,000 00	
56		do	do	25,000 00	
57		do	Five months	25,000 00	
58		do	do	25,000 00	$100,000 00
59	March 18, 1859	March 18, (?) 1859	Four months	25,000 00	
60		do	Five months	25,000 00	50,000 00
61	March 25, 1859	March 10, 1859	do	10,000 00	
C. 62		March 12, 1859	do	10,000 00	
63		do	Six months	10,000 00	
64		March 20, 1859	Four months	10,000 00	
65		March 25, 1859	do	25,000 00	
66		do	do	10,000 00	
67		do	Five months	25,000 00	
68		do	Six months	25,000 00	
69		do	do	15,000 00	140,000 00
C. 70	March 31, 1859	March 27, 1859	Five months	15,000 00	
C. 71	do	March 28, 1859	do	25,000 00	
72		March 29, 1859	Six months	10,000 00	
73		March 31, 1859	Four months	25,000 00	
C. 74		do	Five months	25,000 00	
75		do	Six months	25,000 00	125,000 00
76	April 1, (?) 1859	April 1, 1859	Five months	25,000 00	
77	April 2, (?) 1859	April 2, 1859	do	10,000 00	35,000 00
78	April 26, 1859	April 26, (?) 1859	Four months		21,000 00
79	May 3, 1859	May 3, 1859	Two months	10,000 00	
80		do	do	15,000 00	
81		do	do	25,000 00	

82		do	Three months	15,000 00	
83		do	do	20,000 00	
C. 84		do	do	25,000 00	
C. 85		do	Four months	15,000 00	
C. 86		do	do	25,000 00	150,000 00
87	May 7, 1859	May 7, 1859	Two months	7,000 00	
88		do	do	8,000 00	15,000 00
89	May 11, 1859	May —, 1859	Three months	10,000 00	
90		do	do	10,000 00	
91		do	do	10,000 00	
92		do	do	15,000 00	
C. 93		do	do	15,000 00	
94		do	do	15,000 00	
C. 95		do	Four months	25,000 00	100,000 00
C. 89²–95²	June 8, 1859	June —, 1859			110,000 00
C. 96–103	June 9, 1859				90,000 00
C. 104–115	June 11, 1859				300,000 00
A–I	do		Blank		200,000 00
J	June 13, 1859	June 10, 1859	do		25,000 00
K–N	June 18, 1859		do		50,000 00
O–X	June 21, 1859	June —, 1859	do		175,000 00
Y–AD	June 29, 1859	do	do		100,000 00
AE–AF	June 30, 1859	June 30, 1859	Four months	5,000 each	10,000 00
AG–AK	July 2, 1859		Blank		50,000 00
AL–AU	August 26, 1859	August 12–23, 1859	do		150,000 00
C. in part*	do	do	do		150,000 00
AV–BF	September 17, 1859	September 1–13, 1859	do		150,000 00
C. 1	April 26, 1860	April 26, 1860	Four months	10,000 00	
C. 2	do	do	Five months	10,000 00	20,000 00
C.†	do	do			20,000 00
1	(Not noted)	May 4, 1860	Five months	10,000 00	
2		May 10, 1860	Four months	20,000 00	
3		May 6, 1860	Five months	10,000 00	

* AL to AU duplicated numbers.

† Duplicated, numbers 1 and 2.

EXHIBIT H—Continued.

Number.	Accepted.	Dated.	Time.	Amount.	Total.
4		May 8, 1860	Four months	$10,000 00	
5		May 1, 1860	Six months	15,000 00	
6		May 4, 1860	Five months	10,000 00	
7		May 9, 1860	130 days	10,000 00	
8		May 8, 1860	6 months	10,000 00	
9		May 9, 1860	Five months	5,000 00	
					$100,000 00
10	May 28, 1860	May 18, 1860	Five months	15,000 00	
11		May 19, 1860	Four months	15,000 00	
12		May 23, 1860	do	15,000 00	
13		May 25, 1860	do	25,000 00	
14		do	Five months	25,000 00	
15		May 26, 1860	do	15,000 00	
16		do	do	10,000 00	
17		May 28, 1860	Four months	10,000 00	
18		do	Five months	10,000 00	
19		do	Six months	10,000 00	
					150,000 00
20–28	June 12, 1860	June 1–11, 1860	Blank		100,000 00
29	June 15, 1860	June 12, 1860	Five months	20,000 00	
30		June 13, 1860	Four months	10,000 00	
31		do	do	15,000 00	
32		June 14, 1860	Five months	10,000 00	
33		do	Six months	15,000 00	
34		June 15, 1860	Four months	10,000 00	
35		do	Six months	20,000 00	
					100,000 00
36–46	June 19, 1860	June 2–19, 1860	Blank		150,000 00
47–54	July 16, 1860	July 10–16, 1860	do		95,000 00
55–71	August 15–22, 1860	August 15–22, 1860	do		175,000 00
72–77	September 10, 1860	August 25, 1860	do		60,000 00
78–89	September 18–22, 1860	September 18–22, 1860	do		125,000 00

C. in part, 90–105	October 10, 1860	October 1–10, 1860	do		150,000 00
106	October 13, 1860	October 11, 1860	Eight months	7,000 00	
107		do	do	8,000 00	
108		do	Nine months	7,000 00	
109		do	do	8,000 00	
110		do	Ten months	7,000 00	
111		do	do	8,000 00	
112		October 12, 1860	Eight months	5,000 00	
113		do	do	10,000 00	
114	October 13, 1860	do	Nine months	10,000 00	
115		do	Ten months	5,000 00	
116		do	do	10,000 00	
117		October 13, 1860	Eight months	10,000 00	
118		do	Nine months	5,000 00	
119		do	do	10,000 00	
120		do	Ten months	10,000 00	
					120,000 00
					5,036,127 50
62 cancelled				10,000 00	
70 do				15,000 00	
71 do				25,000 00	
74 do				25,000 00	
84–86 do				65,000 00	
93 do				15,000 00	
95 do				25,000 00	
89²–95² do				110,000 00	
96–103 do				90,000 00	
104–115 do				300,000 00	
AL–AS* do				100,000 00	
1 & 2 do				20,000 00	
1 & 2* do				20,000 00	
104 do				10,000 00	
105 do				10,000 00	
					840,000 00
Total on account	transportation contracts				4,196,127 50

* Second issue.

NOTE.—Drafts cancelled are marked "C" in the margin.

On account of supplies for the army in Utah.

[NOTE.—B signifies drafts on beef contract; F on flour contract; and S on contracts for supplies.]

BG–BK	B	October 13, 1859	October 4 to 8, 1859	Blank		$25,000 00
BL–BN	F	October 10, 1859	October 10 to 12, 1859	do		30,000 00
BO–BQ	F	October 14, 1859	October 3 to 5, 1859	do		60,000 00
BR–BS	B	do	October 6 and 7, 1859	do		35,000 00
BT	B & F	November 8, 1859		do		73,267 50
BU–CG	B & F	November 19, 1859	November 14 to 19, 1859	do		150,000 00
CH–CU	B & F	December 19, 1859	December 12 to 19, 1859	do		200,000 00
CV	F	December 23, 1859	December 20, 1859	Four months	$25,000 00	
CW	F		December 21, 1859	do	25,000 00	
CX	B		December 22, 1859	do	25,000 00	
CY	B		December 23, 1859	do	25,000 00	
						100,000 00
CZ	F	December 30, 1859	November 21, 1859	Five months	10,000 00	
DA	F		November 24, 1859	do	10,000 00	
DB	F		November 26, 1859	do	10,000 00	
DC	B		November 27, 1859	do	10,000 00	
DD	B		November 30, 1859	do	10,000 00	
						50,000 00
DE	B	November 30, 1859	November 28, 1859	Seven months	20,000 00	
DF	B		November 30, 1859	do	20,000 00	
						40,000 00
DG	B	December 5, 1859	December 2, 1859	Eight months	20,000 00	
DH	B		December 3, 1859	Seven months	15,000 00	
DI	B		do	Eight months	15,000 00	
DJ	B		December 4, 1859	Seven months	10,000 00	
DK	F		December 5, 1859	Six months	10,000 00	
DL	F		do	do	10,000 00	
						80,000 00
DM	F	December 12, 1859	December 6, 1859	Seven months	10,000 00	
DN	F		December 7, 1859	do	10,000 00	
DO	B		December 8, 1859	Six months	5,000 00	
DP	B		December 12, 1859	do	10,000 00	
DQ	F		do	Eight months	10,000 00	
						45,000 00

DR	B	December 30, 1859	December 23, 1859	Seven months	15,000 00	
DS	B		do	Six months	5,000 00	
DT	B		December 27, 1859	do	5,000 00	
DU	B		December 29, 1859	Five months	5,000 00	
DV	B		December 30, 1859	do	5,000 00	
						35,000 00
DW	S	November 19, 1859	November 19, 1859	Eight months	5,000 00	
DX	S		do	do	15,000 00	
DY	S		do	Nine months	10,000 00	
DZ	S		do	do	10,000 00	
EA	S		do	do	5,000 00	
EB	S	December 9, 1859	December 9, 1859	Eight months	15,000 00	
EC	S	December 17, 1859	December 17, 1859	do	20,000 00	
ED	S	December 20, 1859	December 20, 1859	do	10,000 00	
EE	S	December 24, 1859	December 24, 1859	do	10,000 00	
						100,000 00
EF	S	November 26, 1859	November 26, 1859	Nine months	10,000 00	
EG	S	do	do	Ten months	10,000 00	
						20,000 00
EH	S	November 25, 1859	November 25, 1859	do	10,000 00	
EI	S	do	do	do	10,000 00	
EJ	S	November 26, 1859	November 26, 1859	do	20,000 00	
EK	S	November 28, 1859	November 28, 1859	do	5,000 00	
EL	S	do	do	do	5,000 00	
EM	S	December 17, 1859	December 17, 1859	do	5,000 00	
EN	S	December 20, 1859	December 20, 1859	do	5,000 00	
EO	S	December 21, 1859	December 21, 1859	do	20,000 00	
EP	S	December 24, 1859	December 24, 1859	do	10,000 00	
EQ	S	December 27, 1859	December 27, 1859	do	10,000 00	
						100,000 00
Total on account contracts for supplies						1,143,267 50
Total on account contracts for transportation						4,196,127 50
Aggregate						5,339,395 00

RICH'D B. IRWIN, *Corresponding Clerk.*

WAR DEPARTMENT, *December* 26, 1860.

Letter from the Secretary of War in relation to the policy of the War Department in granting acceptances to the contractors for transportation across the plains, &c.

WAR DEPARTMENT, *December* 27, 1860.

SIR: So much has been said, very recently, about the policy of this department in granting acceptances to the contractors for transportation across the plains, that I deem it due alike to Congress, to the public, and to myself, to make a short, plain statement of the facts connected with the subject.

At one time, in the year 1858, it became absolutely necessary to start large trains of transportation across the plains to Utah, when there was no available means to put those trains in motion. Acceptances were given to the contractors then to enable them to start, and they did so. The practice, thus begun, was continued for a good while from necessity, and was afterwards followed to afford accommodation to the contractors in their very large and extensive work. Their purport is to give preference to the holder, when filed in the department, out of any moneys due the contractors. These acceptances have, until the past autumn, been regularly paid to large amounts; nor has any complaint whatever, until then, been heard that means were not provided to meet and redeem them. There has never been the least concealment or mystery about this business. It was perfectly known to all who have any interest in knowing anything about it.

They have been given only when there was a subsisting contract out of which the means to meet them would certainly arise, and for the execution of which there was an existing appropriation. They are prohibited by no law.

The issue of these acceptances within this month rested upon the following considerations: Those given for the last season's work, and which were held as collateral security in different places, the contractors were anxious to postpone until the next season. They represented that this could be done with acceptances, which on their face represented that they would be paid when the money they called for was earned by the contractors for the next season's work. The strongest assurances were given that this paper was only to go, and certainly to go, by agreement already made, into the hands alone of those banks and firms who then held unpaid acceptances, and for which they were to be substituted and held as collateral security to their own obligations.

The pay accruing under their contract next season will be more than enough to cover the amount of the acceptances predicated on it.

To insure this stipulation, I consented to issue the paper only in large amounts, and in a form which would be acceptable, if at all, to those who knew perfectly the solvency of the contractors, and who had already money engagements with them to a large amount, and who had, as I was informed, and as I believed, already consented to and desired the arrangement. If these promises and faithful engagements had been performed, no difficulty could ever have resulted from the transaction. It could not and would not have misled or deceived any one; no expectation based upon it could by any possibility have been disappointed. But the promises made me were not kept; they were broken. This paper was, it seems, placed in the hands of a clerk of the Department of the Interior, who had abstracted a large amount of the securities belonging to the Indian trust fund. Finding this to be the case, I have not hesitated to give an order to cancel and annul all those acceptances. The perversion rendered them void and of no effect.

I am gratified to assert the confident belief that no one connected in any way, directly or remotely, in any shape or form, with the duties of the War Department, had any, the least, connexion with or knowledge of this embezzlement in its inception or its progress.

The issue of this paper resolves itself into a question of administrative consideration alone, I think; and so regarding it, I will be pardoned for adverting very briefly to this aspect of the subject.

These contractors have, by a long series of years of faithful, honest, and most efficient service, won the confidence and good feeling of all persons having any connexion with the transportation of the army in the country lying beyond our western settlements. They had never failed in any of their engagements, and had executed many of them under circumstances of peculiar embarrassments. They were men of very large wealth and most extensive means, and possessed fully the confidence of all who knew them. It has become latterly pretty evident that but small profits, if any, were likely to be realized from their operations; and this was put into great danger from recent reverses in money affairs.

The revulsions which have recently swept over the country have arisen from no causes which business men could be fairly called upon to take the risk of; they have been from political causes, and not from any violated law of commercial or monetary action. Under this evident fact, I was not unwilling to afford these employés of the government any assistance likely to save them from serious injury growing out of political disturbances, if that could be done without running any risk of loss to the government. I think such a course can derogate nothing from a sound administrative discretion, although the sequel has shown that such a confidence has been misplaced.

But there is another and higher public consideration connected with the subject of contracts for transportation, and one which cannot be overlooked with any just appreciation of good administration. Good and thoroughly responsible contractors for transportation across our immense plains are extremely important persons to our little army, and difficult to obtain. There is no other service like it known in the world. Nowhere else on the globe would the idea be entertained of subsisting an army by transporting its supplies over land a distance of a thousand or twelve hundred miles through an uninhabited wilderness; and yet a very large part of our army is furnished and subsisted by this means.

If the present contractors, who have so long and so faithfully performed their work, should fail, or become so embarrassed as to be unable to do their work and supply the army, it would result in a loss to the United States of a vast sum of money—probably a million of dollars. But the pecuniary loss would be small in comparison with the risk and damage which such a failure would subject our troops to who are stationed in the deserts of New Mexico and Arizona. Should any accident befall these men, or any serious inconvenience result to them from a failure of a regular and certain transmission of supplies, it would be difficult to estimate the just indignation which would be heaped upon the head of the ignorant or delinquent officer whose inefficiency had allowed it.

The trains necessary for the transportation to be performed by Russell, Majors & Waddell could not have cost much short of a million of dollars, and would require months of industry and activity to prepare.

It must be very clear to any one that a wise forecast demanded of the government to sustain these contractors by all fair and legitimate means.

I have now nearly brought my administration of the War Department to a close, and I will be excused for adverting to it briefly. There is not one branch of the military service that is not in perfect order, as far as any means are afforded of knowing—and they are very complete. Some have been particularly encouraged, I think improved. The discipline is excellent, and the accountability to superior authority in every department could scarcely be excelled. A strict economy is enforced, and a perfect responsibility in all money expenditures is and has been successfully carried into effect.

Within the four years since I have presided over this department, not a dollar, I believe, has been lost to the government by embezzlement or theft, and within that time sixty millions of dollars have been disbursed. No system of administration, no line of policy, I think, could reach better results. No system of accountability could be more perfect.

These facts I confidently assert, and the department is everywhere full of the proofs of them.

I invite any investigation which the House may think proper to institute into any or all of my official acts.

Very respectfully, your obedient servant,

JOHN B. FLOYD,
Secretary of War.

Hon. WILLIAM PENNINGTON,
Speaker of the House of Representatives.

ABSTRACTED INDIAN TRUST BONDS.

MARCH 2, 1861.—Ordered to be printed.

Mr. I. N. MORRIS, from the select committee, made the following supplemental

REPORT.

The select committee, appointed by the House to ascertain the facts in relation to the fraudulent abstraction of certain bonds from the Interior Department, submit a supplemental report, embracing the testimony of the Hon. Henry M. Rice, of the Senate, Thomas W. Pierce, of Boston, Massachusetts, and Hon. Thomas P. Akers:

In the first report submitted by your committee Mr. Rice was referred to as not appearing before them in a manner which somewhat reflected upon him. Not the slightest suspicion, however, was entertained that he was in any way implicated in the fraudulent abstraction of the bonds. Your committee are also gratified in being able to state further, that, at a subsequent interview between them and Mr. Rice, the impression that he intended to treat them and the House with discourtesy, by proposing to submit his testimony in the form of answers to written interrogatories, was wholly removed, and his position left honorable and free from just criticism. Any seeming reflection that may appear to have been cast upon him was entirely the result of misapprehension. When the facts came to be known, your committee were satisfied that Mr. Rice labored with energy and zeal to aid the government, and is entitled to the thanks of the House and the country for it.

The evidence of Mr. Pierce will be read with interest, as it sheds much light upon Governor Floyd's assurances in regard to the payment of the acceptances, and the state of alleged facts under which he was in the habit of making them.

The testimony, however, which is the most important is that of Hon. Thomas P. Akers, one of the counsel of William H. Russell. Mr. Akers is a gentleman of the highest character and integrity, and none regrets more than himself that Mr. Russell failed to appear before your committee and testify under the resolution adopted by the House on the 27th of February, which authorized them to examine witnesses "touching the matter as to whether William H. Russell, or any person or persons for him, ever, directly or indirectly, paid any money or other valuable consideration to any officer of the United States, or any other person or persons, for assisting him, or any firm with which he has been heretofore or is now connected, in obtaining contracts or allowances from any of the departments of the government, or assisting him or them in the transaction of business with the same.'' After the passage of the resolution Mr. Russell was at once telegraphed to at New York, where he evidently was and is, by your chairman, and Mr. Akers, and his attendance requested. No doubt was at the time entertained, nor was there up to Friday afternoon, (the 1st instant,) but that he would comply. The character of the despatches then indicated otherwise; copies of three of which are given, and will be sufficient to disclose the whole matter in connexion with Mr. Akers's testimony.

"NEW YORK, *February* 28, 1861.

"Your despatch to Mr. Russell received to-day. Have not yet seen him. He has not yet been at the office. Will try to reach him.

"A. LOCKWOOD, *Pony Express.*

"Hon. I. N. MORRIS, *Chairman.*"

The committee do not know who Mr. Lockwood is, but suppose he is Mr. Russell's agent in New York.

"NEW YORK, *March* 1, 1861.

"Did not receive your telegraph until half-past six. Will bring or send him (Russell) by the early morning train, if I can find him. If I do not, shall I bring him in the evening train? If he starts in the morning I will telegraph. Let me know if to-morrow evening will do if I cannot find him this evening.

"ISAIAH RYNDERS.

"Hon. I. N. MORRIS."

Mr. Rynders, who is the United States marshal, was, in reply to the above, directed by the chairman to bring Mr. Russell to Washington as soon as he could be found. The following is his answer:

"NEW YORK, *March* 2, 1861.

"I have been looking for him all last night and to-day. I cannot get any trail of him. It is said he is in Philadelphia, but I think he is here hid away. I shall try to get him before to-morrow evening, and bring him on.

"I. RYNDERS.

"Hon. I. N. MORRIS,
"*Chairman of Committee.*"

The despatches would seem to indicate that Mr. Russell has kept out of the way to avoid an appearance before your committee, notwithstanding his declared willingness to appear previous to the passage of the resolution herein referred to. When it is remembered that he was not only willing, but anxious, to make a clean breast of it, and tell the whole story, if he could be relieved from the penalty of the act of 1853, it is only necessary to say that the public and the

House will conjecture the reason. Many will conclude that he has been operated on by other parties. The act of 1853 is as follows:

"SEC. 6. *And be it further enacted*, That if any person or persons shall, directly or indirectly, promise, offer, or give, or cause or procure to be promised, offered, or given, any money, goods, right in action, bribe, present, or reward, or any promise, contract, undertaking, obligation, or security for the payment or delivery of any money, goods, right in action, bribe, present, or reward, or any other valuable thing whatever, to any member of the Senate or House of Representatives of the United States, after his election as such member, and either before or after he shall have qualified and taken his seat, or to any officer of the United States, or person holding any place of trust or profit, or discharging any official function under or in connexion with any department of the government of the United States, after the passage of this act, with intent to influence his vote or decision in any question, matter, cause, or proceeding which may then be pending, or may by law, or under the Constitution of the United States, be brought before him in his official capacity, or in his place of trust or profit, and shall be thereof convicted, such person or persons so offering, promising, or giving, or causing or procuring to be promised, offered, or given, any such money, goods, right in action, bribe, present, or reward, or any promise, contract, undertaking, obligation, or security for the payment or delivery of any money, goods, right in action, bribe, present, or reward, or other valuable thing whatever, and the member, officer, or person who shall in anywise accept or receive the same, or any part thereof, shall be liable to indictment as for a high crime and misdemeanor in any court of the United States having jurisdiction for the trial of crimes and misdemeanors, and shall, upon conviction thereof, be fined not exceeding three times the amount so offered, promised, or given, and imprisoned in a penitentiary not exceeding three years; and the person convicted of so accepting or receiving the same, or any part thereof, if an officer or person holding any such place of trust or profit as aforesaid, shall forfeit his office or place; and any person so convicted under this section shall forever be disqualified to hold any office of honor, trust, or profit under the "United States.—(Stat. at Large, vol. 10, p. 171.) Act approved February 26, 1853.

The following despatch was sent to Governor Floyd, to which no reply has been received by your committee:

"WASHINGTON CITY, *February* 27, 1861.

"SIR: The committee appointed to investigate the facts in regard to the abstraction of bonds from the Interior Department, under a resolution of the House, will on to-morrow commence the examination of witnesses as to whether any money or other valuable consideration has been paid, directly or indirectly, to any officer of the government or other person by William H. Russell, or any one for him, for aiding him or his firm in obtaining contracts from or assisting in his or their business with the government. If you should be implicated, you will be allowed to be present.

"Respectfully,

"I. N. MORRIS.

"Hon. JOHN B. FLOYD, *Abingdon, Va.*"

Your committee will only add that Mr. Akers believed it to be his duty, as an honorable man, to detail the facts embraced in his evidence after the non-appearance of Mr. Russell.

All of which is respectfully submitted.

I. N. MORRIS, *Chairman.*

MONDAY, *March* 4, 1861.

WEDNESDAY, *February* 20, 1861.

Upon consultation, it was concluded by this committee that a personal interview with the Hon. H. M. Rice would be the most satisfactory, as it was difficult to frame in writing all the questions which they might desire to propound to him. This conclusion of the committee was communicated to Mr. Rice; whereupon he readily consented to appear, and the following was the result:

By Mr. THOMAS:

Question. You will please state what you know in reference to the disclosure made by Mr. Bailey concerning the bonds that have been abstracted from the Indian trust fund, and give a history of your knowledge upon that subject.

Answer. Had I, in the first place, understood the wish of the committee, as I now understand it, I should have appeared at the earliest moment consistent with my duties.

Some time in the month of December last Mr. Bailey called upon me and made inquiries in regard to matters pending in Congress touching the interests of Russell, Majors & Waddell. After speaking of those, he told me that he was in trouble. He stated that he had been told some time last summer that Governor Floyd's acceptances were about going to protest; that Governor Floyd had been a friend of his, and he was anxious to aid him. He was told that if those acceptances did go to protest Governor Floyd would resign; that he at once went up to the War Department to see Governor Floyd; that he was engaged with General Scott; that he waited some time, and finding it would be late before he could have an interview, he asked Colonel Drinkard, chief clerk, if the information he had received in regard to Governor Floyd resigning was correct; that Colonel Drinkard told him that if Governor Floyd's acceptances were protested he would resign; that in order to protect Governor Floyd he gave to Mr. Russell Indian trust bonds to a certain amount, I think it was $150,000; that those bonds were to be returned at some time specified—I do not recollect what time—and he wanted to know of me what he should do. I told him he had better communicate the facts at once to the Secretary of the Interior. He said he was aware that he had committed a great wrong, but that in doing what he had he had not done it out of any selfish or pecuniary motives. Mr. Bailey stated that Mr. Thompson had confided in him fully, and that he had betrayed his trust, and that he would sooner sacrifice himself than have Mr. Thompson censured for his acts, and that he should communicate all the facts to him, Mr. Thompson. He stated that, owing to the difficulty in monetary affairs, Russell, Majors & Waddell were unable to return the bonds, or prevent them from being sold—they having been given to Russell with the express understanding that they should not be sold, but only hypothecated, and that the identical bonds should be returned; that he was informed that they had got to be sold unless further aid was given, and that he had gone on and had advanced more bonds. I told him that the matter should be promptly communicated to Mr. Thomson and the Secretary of War. He informed me that he would make out a statement in writing of all the facts, and would communicate it to Mr. Thompson, and, I think, to the Secretary of War; that he should not attempt to escape; that he would remain here and take the consequences, as he alone was to blame. He informed me soon after that he had communicated the statement of facts to the Secretary of War, and that he would to Mr. Thompson at the earliest moment —Mr. Thompson then being in North Carolina. On Saturday evening following I returned home between 4 and 5 o'clock from attendance upon the committee of conference of thirteen; I found a package in my house addressed to Jacob Thompson, Secretary of the Interior. I also found a note from Mr. Bailey requesting me to deliver that package to Mr. Thompson the moment he returned. I took it and went at once to see Mr. Bailey, and told him that Mr. Thompson was not here, and that it was not proper for me to keep that package until he returned. He told me he had written out a full confession of all the facts and placed it in the hands of a friend who would deliver it to Mr. Thompson. I told him I knew not what was in the package which he left at my house, but that I did not desire to keep it, and I wanted his permission to deliver it at once to the President of the United States, if it had any connexion with that matter. He said it had connexion with the matter, and he gave me permission to deliver it at once to the President. I went immediately and called upon the President, gave him the package, and told him that he was authorized to open it by the person who had written it. He opened the package and it contained the acceptances of the Secretary of War to the amount of $870,000; also a receipt of Russell, Majors & Waddell for the bonds for the same amount.

During the conversation the Secretary of State, Mr. Black, and the Attorney General, Mr. Stanton, came in. While conversing upon the subject Mr. Thompson, who had returned from North Carolina sooner than expected, came in. A discussion arose then inregard to the proper course to pursue; Mr. Thompson remarked that he had left in the safe some two or three millions more of bonds, and it was important to ascertain whether they had been disposed of or not, and at his urgent solicitation I returned to Mr. Bailey's room and asked him for the keys of the safe. Mr. Bailey handed them to me at once. In the room was General Wagner, who stated that he had just returned from Mr. Thompson's house; that his object in going was to deliver a sealed package from Mr. Bailey, if he had returned. I think Mr. Bailey suggested that General Wagner should give me the package, as I was about to return to the Executive mansion. I took the package and keys, returned to the President's, and there delivered them to Mr. Thompson. Mr. Thompson then requested that the Secretary of State and the Attorney General should go down to the Interior Department, and it was decided that he and myself should call upon Mr. Bailey and request him to go there also. We returned to Mr. Bailey's house; Mr. Thompson got out of the carriage and went in. In a few moments returned with Mr. Bailey and General Wagner. They got into the carriage and we went up to the Interior Department. The chief clerk was sent for. Prior to the arrival of any others, Mr. Bailey stated to Mr. Thompson and myself the motives which induced him to do as he had, which were, in fact, such as he had communicated to me. The safe was opened, and Mr. Bailey took out the remaining bonds, spread them out there upon the table, and assisted in counting them to ascertain if all were left which he said were undisposed of. I remained there, and soon after Mr. Black and Mr Stanton came in.

We had, during the evening, several conversations in regard to the proper method of proceeding to trace the matter up, and ascertain who were implicated and who were not. I remained until two o'clock in the morning. I then asked if I could be of further service, and they replying that I could not, I went home.

The next morning Mr. Thompson sent General Wagner with a special request that I should try to ascertain who was the person who first mentioned the subject of bonds to Mr. Bailey. I saw Mr. Bailey, and he stated that he had rather suffer himself than to violate a breach of confidence, but authorized me to call upon Colonel Luke Lea. I went down to see Mr. Lea and explained to him my business. Mr. Lea said that most of the trouble brought upon him had been by trying to aid others; that he had delivered a message to Mr. Bailey from Mr. Russell, and that Mr. Bailey said that he had nothing but trust bonds in his hands. Lea said, "Of course you cannot use those;" he said that when he, Mr. Lea, mentioned Governor Floyd's name, and that unless his acceptances were met that Governor Floyd would resign, that Mr. Bailey did not stop to hear any further explanation from him upon the subject; that he seemed distressed at the idea that Governor Floyd was in the condition that he was, and that he, Bailey, left him; I told Mr. Lea that the Secretary of the Interior was the person to whom it would be proper to state all the facts. He got into the carriage with me, and rode up to Secretary Thompson's; he was, I think, at dinner; I sent up for him, and he came into the parlor; about the time he came down Secretary Black came into the parlor also. I told Mr. Thompson that Mr. Lea had come up to give him such information as I believed he desired; I left the three mentioned together.

In conclusion, I will state that I communicated to the President and the three aforementioned cabinet officers, all the information that came to my knowledge, and that the foregoing is, in substance, if not in detail, all the facts that were in my possession; that until Mr. Bailey, in December, mentioned the subject to me, I had never heard of the acceptances of Governor Floyd, or of the Indian trust bonds, and that the parties who received them were entire strangers to me.

THURSDAY, *February* 28, 1861.

THOMAS W. PIERCE sworn and examined.

By the CHAIRMAN:

Question. Where do you reside?

Answer. In Boston, Massachusetts.

Question. What is the business in which you are engaged?

Answer. The firm I represent is Pierce & Bacon, of Boston; our business is a general commission financial business, buying paper, accepting on property of all kinds, selling on commission, &c. We have also several ships which we manage.

Question. Has the house with which you are connected ever at any time bought any acceptances drawn by Russell, Majors & Waddell upon the Secretary of War, and accepted by John B. Floyd as such Secretary?

Answer. Yes, sir.

Question. Have you any of those acceptances now on hand?

Answer. Yes, sir.

Question. To what amount do you now hold those acceptances?

Answer. $260,000; we hold these acceptances not wholly for ourselves; the most of them have been negotiated through us, upon information which we communicated; we represent that amount $260,000, about $150,000 of which is our own.

Question. Of whom did you purchase those acceptances?

Answer. I reckon that the most of those we now hold we bought of Russell, or of his agent in New York, Mr. Simpson; he bought a great many through Mr. Suter, President of the Bank of the Republic; and that is where we first made inquiry in regard to them.

Question. Did you ever have any conversation with John B. Floyd in reference to these acceptances?

Answer. Yes, sir; I did.

Question. What was that conversation? please detail it.

Answer. In January, 1860, I came to Washington to inquire specifically about this paper. It had had a currency in the north for some time before. I was introduced to Mr. Floyd by a letter from Mr. Toucey, Secretary of the Navy. I told Governor Floyd that the object of my visit to Washington was to see him and ask him in relation to these acceptances, if such had been issued by his department; and if they had been issued, then was there authority for their issue, had there been consideration for them, and would they be paid at maturity. To all of which questions he answered in the affirmative. He then went into an explanation of the exigencies of his department, which called for something of that sort. He explained that matter at full length, but I cannot give his words; I might give the substance of them.

Question. Go on and state the substance of what he said.

Answer. The idea was substantially this: that there was an exigency in the affairs of the department growing out of the Utah war. In the first place, I think he said to me that there was some little difference of opinion between him and General Scott. He considered it his duty to maintain the army there; that it was a bad season when the war began, and that as the contracts were very large they required a very large outlay; that there were no contractors with the government who had money sufficient to make the necessary outlay and perform the service as promptly as it should be done; that these gentlemen, Russell, Majors & Waddell, were large contractors, and had been for years; that they were prompt and reliable; but their outlay was so managed that the government had to give them some aid. I said to him, "while your treasury is full of money, why not give them the money?" He responded that there was an express law against that, but there was authority for securities of this character. In reply to the question if there was any authority for giving these acceptances, he said that it had been the custom of the department, in certain contingencies, since the organization of the government. After he had got through with his relation, I said to him—"Governor, these are very good papers, I should judge, from your relation. I am now a holder of about $70,000 worth of United States stock, at five per cent., and I can dispose of that stock now at a premium, and invest in these securities if they are safe." The governor said that he regarded these acceptances as the best securities extant of the government, because they did not depend upon any action of Congress, for the appropriations were all made and the money already in the treasury to pay them as they became due. I therefore thought I better sell my United States stock, as it was bearing a low rate of interest, and I could dispose of it at a premium, and invest it in these acceptances, which I could get at 9 or 10 per cent., that being the best rates for commercial paper. Then it was that he remarked to me that he regarded these acceptances as the best obligations extant of the government. I accordingly concluded, after that interview, to go home and sell out my United States stock, which I did.

Question. Investing your money in these acceptances?

Answer. Yes, sir. Of the $70,000, $40,000 was my own and $30,000 belonged to our firm. We always had stocks of that kind to meet any exigency in the money market. They matured in 1865, and bore a premium, and I sold them at a premium and invested the proceeds in this paper. And since this interview with Governor Floyd, whenever we have had any surplus money we have given this paper the preference. We thought that thirty-one millions of people were better security than any one or half a dozen individuals could be. We supposed the government was bound legally by this paper.

Question. Did Governor Floyd state to you to what amount he was in the habit of accepting? That is, did he state whether he accepted for moneys due or to become due to the parties?

Answer. The interpretation I put upon his language was this: that he made no acceptances until the trains were ready to start, when the contractor had nothing to do but to perform his service, having incurred all his expenses. When the trains were ready to start he gave these acceptances for about 50 per cent—"40 or 50 per cent.," I think was his language—upon the amount which would be due when the full service had been performed.

Question. And for no more?

Answer. That was the impression I got from his language. That was not in answer to any particular inquiry of mine, but as part of his explanation of the whole matter, as I regarded it, showing me the prudence with which he was managing the affairs of his department. That is the way I regarded it.

Question. Have any of the acceptances which you purchased been protested for non-payment?

Answer. Yes, sir. I have some of them here. Mine are nearly all protested. The last one, I think, was protested on the day before yesterday.

Question. Since your conversation, in January, 1860, with Governor Floyd, late Secretary of War, and since the first of these acceptances purchased by you were protested, have you had any conversation with him in relation to these acceptances? If so, please state what was said in that conversation.

Answer. I have had a conversation with him at his house. I talked with him about these matters, and asked him why they were protested. He said there was no money in the treasury at that time. The conversation was a very short one, because he agreed to meet me at the War Department the next morning; but he did not do so. He said he could not say much until he could see Mr. Russell. I asked Governor Floyd how many of these acceptances were out. He said that he could not tell without referring to the War Department. I then told him that Mr. Russell had told me, on my way through New York, that there was but $85,000 worth out, besides what I had. Then we made an appointment to meet at the War Department the next morning; but I have not seen him since.

Question. Governor Floyd did not meet you there, according to appointment?

Answer. No, sir. I went there and waited a couple of hours; but the excuse was, that there was a cabinet meeting that day. I did not see him, and that night I left for New Orleans.

Question. Have you seen him and conversed with him since that time?

Answer. No, sir. I have but just returned from Texas.

Question. When did this last conversation occur that you had with Governor Floyd?

Answer. It was early in the month of December last.

Question. Can you fix the particular day of the month?

Answer. It was on the night of Friday, the 7th of December, I think.

Question. How long previous to that was the conversation with Mr. Russell to which you have referred, in which he stated to you that there were only $85,000 of these acceptances out, besides those which you held?

Answer. That must have been on Wednesday, the 5th of December last, I think.

SATURDAY, *March* 2, 1861.

JOSEPH A. MONHEIMER sworn and examined.

By the CHAIRMAN:

Question. Do you know where William H. Russell now is?

Answer. No, sir; I know that he is in New York; I do not know where at particularly.

Question. Have you heard from him since he went there?

Answer. Yes, sir.

Question. When?

Answer. I heard from him this morning.

Question. Do you know whether he is coming here?

Answer. I do not.

Question. How did you hear from him this morning?

Answer. By a letter sent to me by my brother, who lives in New York.

Question. Whereabouts did he say Mr. Russell was then?

Answer. He did not say; he just enclosed a note to me from Mr. Russell in a letter from himself.

Question. Do you know what took Mr. Russell to New York?

Answer. I do not, indeed.

Question. Do you know when he expected to return when he left?

Answer. I do not; he told me he would be back in a few days; he did not state any particular time.

SATURDAY, *March* 2, 1861.

THOMAS P. AKERS sworn and examined.

By the CHAIRMAN:

Question. Please state to the committee what you stated to the chairman in reference to Mr. Russell's willingness to appear before them and respond to interrogatories as to when and to whom he paid money for assisting him in procuring contracts from, and in the transactions of his business with, the War Department.

Answer. In reply to your question, I will state that on or about the 20th of February, 1861, I had a conversation with the chairman of the committee, in the course of which I had occasion to refer to the report of the committee submitted to the House of Representatives. I spoke particularly of that feature of the report which represented Mr. Russell as declining to answer the question in relation to his having paid officers of the government money with the view of influencing them in obtaining contracts and allowances. I then informed the chairman of the committee that Mr. Russell had no desire to withhold the answer to that or any other question. On the contrary, when the question was propounded to him, he had asked permission to confer with his counsel, which was granted; the result of which conference was a determination on his part to so respond to the question as to indicate to the committee a willingness on his part to reply, if they should obtain power from the House of Representatives to examine him on that point. I also stated to the chairman of the committee that it was the opinion of Mr. Russell's counsel that the committee had no power to examine witnesses touching that point; and that in framing Mr. Russell's answer they had intimated so much by quoting a portion of the statute of 1857, marked as quoted, and emphasized by being underlined, substantially as follows: "The question propounded to me by you on the 18th, and upon which you adjourned, '*is not pertinent to the subject under investigation before the committee.*'" I further informed the chairman of your committee that Mr. Russell was perfectly willing and anxious to make a clean breast of it in regard to the matter; and his counsel supposed that the form of his written reply, to which I have before referred, would point the committee to the fact that additional power to examine him was necessary.

Question. Did you suggest to the chairman of the committee that they had better get additional power from the House?

Answer. Yes, sir, I did. And I also suggested, at the same time, that it was the opinion of Mr. Russell's counsel that the committee would ask for additional power as soon as the written answer of Mr. Russell, that I have referred to above, was presented to them.

Question. Did the chairman of the committee state to you that, in pursuance of the suggestion of Mr. Russell that he was not only willing but anxious to make a clean breast of it, and disclose all the facts as to whether he had paid money to public officers and other persons for assisting him in the transaction of his business with the War Department, he would offer a resolution to the House and ask for the additional power?

Answer. I do not think the chairman at first agreed to it. He was several days determining in his own mind, I think, whether he would offer the resolution. I remember distinctly that on one occasion he remarked to me that the committee was unwilling to assume any position in regard to this matter different from what they had assumed in the examination in regard to the Indian bonds, by which I understood the chairman to mean that the committee was unwilling to take the attitude of compelling Mr. Russell to testify. But afterwards, and the day after Mr. Russell went to New York, which was Tuesday, the chairman of the committee informed me that he had determined to offer the resolution. Whereupon I stated to him that if he did so, and it was passed, to inform me so, that I might telegraph Mr. Russell, as he had gone to New York for papers, and would be gone a few days.

I think it proper to state, in this connexion, that in a subsequent conversation between me and the chairman of the committee, I held that this examination, touching the payment of money to public officers or other persons, was altogether a different affair from the examination relating to the abstraction of the Indian bonds. Whereupon the chairman replied that in that view the committee were willing to assume the attitude of compelling Mr. Russell to answer touching the former subject.

Question. Please state to the committee what led to the conversation between you and the chairman in reference to the matter you have detailed here.

Answer. As I before remarked, I was talking to the chairman concerning the report of the committee. I remarked to him that the report represented Mr. Russell as declining to answer the question in relation to the payment of money to officers of the government or other persons ; whereas the truth was he had requested the committee, when the question was propounded to him, to give him an opportunity to confer with his counsel, which they accordingly did. He did confer with his counsel, and the result of that conference was the preparation of the written response to which I have before referred. When he returned, with the expectation of delivering his written answer to the committee, as I learned from him, the committee made to him substantially this proposition : that they would return to him the written statement which he had placed in their hands concerning his connexion with the Indian bond transaction, and expunge from the record all of his testimony ; or if he declined that, he might come forward and answer such additional questions as might be asked him. Upon this suggestion being made to him, Mr. Russell requested permission to confer still further with his counsel, which was also granted. When he again returned, and the committee called up the subject, he commenced reading his response to that proposition, upon which, as I learned from him, the chairman of the committee informed him if that was his answer he could leave it to be recorded. He then retired, at the suggestion of the chairman, from the committee room, with the expectation of being called before the committtee again at some future time, to answer the other question in relation to the payment of money to officers of the government, but was not afterwards called before the committee. I stated these facts to the chairman of the committee, and then added that Mr. Russell was then willing, and had always been willing, to answer any question that they had the power to ask him.

It was in this connexion that I made the suggestion above referred to, that the committee apply to the House of Representatives for further power, if they desired Mr. Russell to appear before them again. And I have no doubt that the application for additional power which was made to the House of Representatives by the chairman of the committee was in consequence of what I had then stated to him.

Question. At the time that this conversation occurred, were you acting as counsel for Mr. Russell, and are you so acting at the present time?

Answer. Yes, sir.

Question. Have you made exertions, since the passage of the resolution granting the committee additional power, to procure the attendance of Mr. Russell before the committee?

Answer. I have made all that I could make, and I am unable to state the reason why he has not appeared.

www.ingramcontent.com/pod-product-compliance
Lightning Source LLC
LaVergne TN
LVHW010142110826
845151LV00002B/403

* 9 7 8 1 4 2 5 5 3 8 6 7 5 *